Just Joan

Just Joan: A Joan Crawford Appreciation
© 2010 Donna Marie Nowak. All Rights Reserved.
Epilogue © 2010 James Sibal.

No part of this book may be reproduced in any form or by any means, electronic, mechanical, digital, photocopying or recording, except for the inclusion in a review, without permission in writing from the publisher.

Published in the USA by:
BearManor Media
PO Box 1129
Duncan, Oklahoma 73534-1129
www.bearmanormedia.com

ISBN 978-1-59393-542-9

Printed in the United States of America.
Book design by Brian Pearce | Red Jacket Press

Just Joan

A Joan Crawford Appreciation

DONNA MARIE NOWAK

Table of Contents

Acknowledgments 15
Introduction 17

The Essays

A Portrait of Joan...21
Joan Crawford: My Feminist Hero...27
The Gay Connection to Joan..55
Joan and Diana: Two Great Dames..59
Joan and Agatha: Two Great Artists...63
Joan Crawford's Home Movies…In Color!...69

The Films

Master List of Films with Selected Stats...79

Films of the Twenties

Films Unavailable for Review 87
Lady of the Night (1925)..88
Pretty Ladies (1925)..90
Tramp, Tramp, Tramp (1926)...92
The Boob (1926)..95
Winners of the Wilderness (1927)...97
The Unknown (1927)..102
Twelve Miles Out (1927)...104
Spring Fever (1927)...106
West Point (1927)..109
Across to Singapore (1928)..112
Our Dancing Daughters (1928)..116

Hollywood Revue of 1929 (1929) 120
Our Modern Maidens (1929) 122
Untamed (1929) 127

Films of the Thirties

Montana Moon (1930) 133
Our Blushing Brides (1930) 136
Paid (1930) 139
Dance, Fools, Dance (1931) 142
Laughing Sinners (1931) 145
This Modern Age (1931) 148
Possessed (1931) 150
Grand Hotel (1932) 154
Letty Lynton (1932) 158
Rain (1932) 163
Today We Live (1933) 165
Dancing Lady (1933) 167
Sadie McKee (1934) 172
Chained (1934) 176
Forsaking All Others (1934) 178
No More Ladies (1935) 181
I Live My Life (1935) 185
The Gorgeous Hussy (1936) 189
Love on the Run (1936) 193
The Last of Mrs. Cheyney (1937) 195
The Bride Wore Red (1937) 199
Mannequin (1938) 205
The Shining Hour (1938) 210
Ice Follies of 1939 (1939) 213
The Women (1939) 216

Films of the Forties

Strange Cargo (1940) 221
Susan and God (1940) 223
A Woman's Face (1941) 228
When Ladies Meet (1941) 232

They All Kissed the Bride (1942) 236
Reunion in France (1942) 239
Above Suspicion (1943) 242
Hollywood Canteen (1944) 244
Mildred Pierce (1945) 246
Humoresque (1946) 249
Possessed (1947) 252
Daisy Kenyon (1947) 255
Flamingo Road (1949) 259
It's a Great Feeling (1949) 263

Films of the Fifties

The Damned Don't Cry (1950) 269
Harriet Craig (1950) 272
Goodbye My Fancy (1951) 276
This Woman is Dangerous (1952) 279
Sudden Fear (1952) 282
Torch Song (1953) 285
Johnny Guitar (1954) 290
Female on the Beach (1955) 293
Queen Bee (1955) 297
Autumn Leaves (1956) 300
The Story of Esther Costello (1957) 303
The Best of Everything (1959) 306

Films of the Sixties

Whatever Happened to Baby Jane (1962) 311
The Caretakers (1963) 315
Strait-Jacket (1964) 318
I Saw What You Did (1965) 320
Berserk (1968) 323

Films of the Seventies

Trog (1970) 327

Television

1950s

The Revlon Mirror Theater: Because I Love Him *(1953)* 333
The General Electric Theater: The Road to Edinburgh *(1954)* 334
The General Electric Theater: Strange Witness *(1958)* 336
The General Electric Theater: And One Was Loyal *(1959)* 338
Zane Grey Theatre: Rebel Ranger *(1959)* 339

1960s

Zane Grey Theatre: One Must Die *(1961)* 340
Route 66: Same Picture, Different Frame *(1963)* 342
Della a.k.a. *Fatal Confinement (1964)* 342
The Man From U.N.C.L.E.: The Five Daughters Affair *(1967)* 343
Journey to the Unknown (1969) 344
Night Gallery: Eyes *(1969)* 345

1970s

The Virginian: Nightmare (1970) 347
The Sixth Sense: Dear Joan,
    We're Going to Scare You to Death *(1972)* 349

Book Reviews

Fiction Made Into Film

Above Suspicion by Helen MacInnes 353
All the Brothers Were Valiant by Ben Ames Williams
   (Across to Singapore) 354
The Best of Everything by Rona Jaffe...356
The Caretakers by Dariel Telfer...359
Claustrophobia by Abbie Carter Goodloe *(I Live My Life)* 362
Daisy Kenyon by Elizabeth Janeway...364
Dancing Lady by James Warner Bellah..367
Flamingo Road by Robert Wilder 369
Grand Hotel by Vicki Baum 371
Humoresque by Fannie Hurst 374
Johnny Guitar by Roy Chanslor..375
Letty Lynton by Marie Belloc Lowndes 378
Love on the Run by Alan Green and Julian Brodie..382
Marry for Money by Katharine Brush *(Mannequin)* 386
Mildred Pierce by James M. Cain 388
Not Too Narrow…Not Too Deep by Richard Sale *(Strange Cargo)*........391
One Man's Secret by Rita Weiman *(Possessed '47)* 393
Our Dancing Daughters (Novelized) by Winifred Van Duzer 396
Out of the Dark by Ursula Curtiss *(I Saw What You Did)*.......................399
Possessed (Fictionalized) by Jean Francis Webb...401
Pretty Sadie McKee by Vina Delmar..403
Queen Bee by Edna Lee..409
Rain by W. Somerset Maugham..413
The Story of Esther Costello by Nicholas Monsarrat....................................414
Sudden Fear by Edna Sherry 420
Turn About by William Faulkner *(Today We Live)*....................................421
Whatever Happened to Baby Jane by Henry Farrell 424
Why Should I Cry? by I.A.R. Wylie *(Torch Song)*......................................427
Within the Law by Marvin Dana *(Paid)*..429

Plays Made Into Film

The Besieged Heart by Robert Hill *(Female on the Beach)* 433
Craig's Wife by George Kelly *(Harriet Craig)* 436
Forsaking All Others by Edward Roberts
 and Frank Morgan Cavett 441
Goodbye, My Fancy by Fay Kanin 444
The Last of Mrs. Cheyney by Frederick Lonsdale 448
The Shining Hour by Keith Winter 450
Susan and God by Rachel Crothers 453
Torch Song by Kenyon Nicholson *(Laughing Sinners)* 457
When Ladies Meet by Rachel Crothers 460
The Women (1936) by Clare Boothe Luce 465

Non-Fiction

Bette and Joan: The Divine Feud by Shaun Considine 471
The Complete Films of Joan Crawford by Lawrence Quirk 475
Conversations with Joan Crawford by Roy Newquist 478
Crawford: The Last Years by Carl Johnes 481
Crawford's Men by Jane Ellen Wayne 484
Jazz Baby by David Houston 488
Joan Crawford, A Biography by Bob Thomas 491
Joan Crawford (A Pyramid Illustrated History of the Movies)
 by Stephen Harvey 494
Joan Crawford: Her Life in Letters by Michelle Vogel 495
Joan Crawford: The Enduring Star by Peter Cowie 498
Joan Crawford: The Essential Biography by Quirk & Schoell 502
Joan Crawford: The Last Word by Fred Lawrence Guiles 505
Joan Crawford: The Raging Star by Charles Castle 508
Joan Crawford: The Ultimate Star by Alexander Walker 513
Legends: Joan Crawford by John Kobal 517
My Way of Life by Joan Crawford 520
Not the Girl Next Door: Joan Crawford by Charlotte Chandler 522
A Portrait of Joan by Joan Crawford 528

Fun With Joan Puzzles

Crawfordgram I 536
Crawfordgram II 537
Joan Logic Problem 539
Fun With Joan Trivia 542
Bring back the Fine Art of Lounging! 544

Miscellaneous

Joan Crawford Paper Dolls by Marilyn Henry 547
Joan Crawford Paper Dolls in Full Color by Tom Tierney 550

Answers

Crawfordgram I 554
Crawfordgram II 555
Joan Logic Problem 556
Answers to Trivia 558

Epilogue

Crawford Second Hand by Jim Sibal 565

About The Author 577

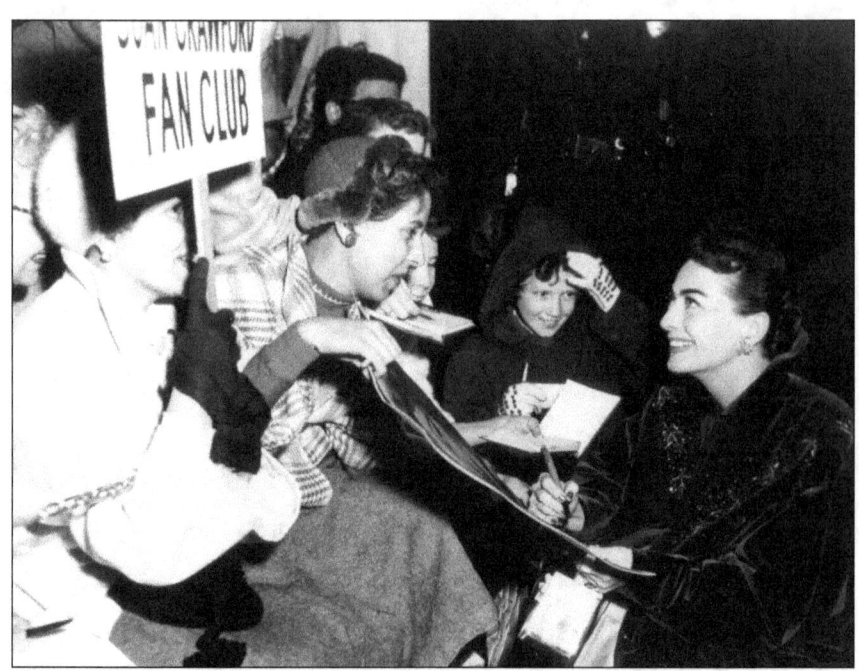

So very, very grateful! PHOTO COURTESY OF NEIL MACIEJEWSKI

*To My Beloved Parents
Barbara and Leonard Nowak
and to the Fans*

Acknowledgments

My thanks and gratitude to:

My publisher Ben Ohmart for making a dream come true; the superb Brian Pearce of Red Jacket Press; the many avid fans from across the world who have supported my website "The Films of Joan Crawford" *(www.filmsofcrawford.com)*; The New York Public Library for its phenomenal film and theater archives where I obtained original scripts and plays made into Crawford films; the inimitable Charles Busch who brilliantly channels these Great Ladies of the Cinema in his work and kindly endorsed this book; Shaun Considine, whose *Bette and Joan: The Divine Feud* gave me hours of laughter and joy and who kindly endorsed this book and lent moral support; Jim Sibal who kindly wrote the afterword for this book and passed on to me some treasured Joan memorabilia given to Carl Johnes, Joan's beloved friend in her last years; Neil Maciejewski (webmaster of "Legendary Joan Crawford"), Theo Pouros, Jerry Murbach and Jim Mahoney for their generous assistance with photos; Michael Kupperman and Peter Joseph Swanson for their awesome "Joan" cartoons which appear in this book; Movie Star News; David Cerda of Hell in a Handbag Productions (with his own Crawford-inspired rock group "The Joans") for his support and for giving Joan a mosh pit; Adam, Tom Clark, and Sid Bloomberg for enabling me to buy rare Crawford films, television appearances and silent films; Jared Case of Eastman Kodak House for his efforts in trying to track down elusive silent films; those venues (particularly Turner Classic Movies) that screen Crawford films, introducing her to ongoing generations; and Bette Davis for not installing a Coca-Cola machine in my book which would annoy the B-Jesus out of Joan.

BLESS YOU ALL!

Introduction

Just Joan, based on my website, *The Films of Joan Crawford (www.filmsofcrawford.com)*, is dedicated to my favorite actress, Joan Crawford. Crawford is one of the most fascinating stars of the golden age of Hollywood and has few peers. No actress projected as much raw emotion and gave so much of herself to every role, her charisma such that she was a force whether playing sinner or saint. With a career spanning fifty years from the silents onwards, she had many personas and looks from endearing flapper to sleek sophisticate to mink-clad career woman to garish accused axe murderess, evolving with the times. She was alluring and glamorous, yet strong and assertive, an underdog and woman in a man's world fighting for her chance to make good (which was her real story). Her toughness (which was actually only apparent in a small percentage of her latter-day films) was offset by vulnerability, charm and élan. Her face was both angular and delicately sculptured, her eyes wide and dreamy and expressive. She carried herself with unparalleled panache, a star from head to toe. Having succeeded with lots of hard work and determination, she remained eternally grateful to and generous with her fans. Crawford was truly one of the greats, complex and fierce, fragile and shy. She embodied what I love most about classic films and continues to inspire me.

Here you will find film reviews, essays, book reviews and more dedicated to a great actress and the ultimate star. Viva the diva! Viva Joan! Thank you, Joan, for the wonderful legacy of work you've left and for your enduring bold spirit.

Donna Marie Nowak

The Essays

PHOTO COURTESY OF NEIL MACIEJEWSKI

A Portrait of Joan

"If you want
the girl next door,
go next door."
Joan Crawford

Of all the stars in Hollywood, Joan Crawford is by far my favorite. No star past or present has ever fascinated or pleased me quite as much, and having seen and read just about everything possible on the lady, I can say she does not disappoint as she never disappointed her fans in life. Called the "ultimate star" and honed in the heyday of the studio star system with a career that spanned an incredible fifty years, Crawford's position as a legend and screen icon didn't become fully comprehensible to me until I saw *They All Kissed the Bride*, in which she played a role originally intended for Carole Lombard. Her charm, romantic lightness, beauty and jaw-dropping glamour were astonishing. It revealed a beguiling Crawford devoid of any of the steeliness that she had come to be associated with and made me realize there was a whole other side to this woman's career and personality that I didn't know, that too few knew or remembered, apart from the bitch-goddess and latter-day roles she made memorable. Curious, I sought to fill in the blanks. My admiration and gratitude has only grown for a woman whose work and persona indeed captures everything I've ever loved about the golden age of Hollywood and whose strong, complex and rich image still resonates, entertains and inspires.

Born Lucille Fay LeSueur, on March 23 in 1904, 1905, 1906 or 1908, whichever you prefer, in San Antonio, Texas, Crawford suffered a Dickensian childhood of abuse, neglect, overwork and — most seriously — lacking in love. Her birth father, French-Canadian Thomas LeSueur, left before she was born and she and older brother Hal relocated to Lawton, Oklahoma, with their mother Anna and "stepfather" Henry "Billy" Cassin who ran a vaudeville house and whom little Lucille adored (taking on the name Billie Cassin), although some biographical accounts indicate that he molested her. When Cassin abandoned the family, who moved onto Kansas City, the children were forced into grunt work in a laundry and suffered aborted educations. In exchange for classes, Crawford worked as a drudge, first at St. Agnes Academy and then from dawn to dusk at Rockingham where she scrubbed floors on hands and knees (leading to a lifelong obsession with cleanliness), washed dishes and tended smaller children (her favorite part of a miserable lot) while being ostracized by the other girls, maltreated and occasionally beaten senseless by a cruel school mistress. The young girl sought solace and escape in dancing, often sneaking out to dances even if she risked punishment. Although essentially shy, she had boundless energy, good looks, tenacity and charisma and was immensely popular with boys. She initially found revue work which led to being cast in the Broadway chorus of *Innocent Eyes* and eventually caught the eye of MGM exec Harry Rapf who brought her to Hollywood. Adela Rogers St. John recalls the early Crawford as "a generous, kindhearted, hard-working kid with nobody to back her." Making friends among the film technicians and forming a strong alliance with gay leading man William Haines, a friendship that would last for life, Lucille LeSueur (rechristened Joan Crawford in a contest) rose from the ashes like a phoenix as she would again and again through numerous setbacks in her career.

Beginning in the silent age as an extra, Crawford shot to stardom playing her own freewheeling "jazz baby" personality in *Our Dancing Daughters*. In those silent and early sound films, she was winsome and childlike with doll-like features and sensual, dreamy eyes — bubbling with vivacity, ever-dancing and smiling and coquettish in a way that explained her popularity at the Coconut Grove where her Charleston and black bottom dancing netted numerous trophies. Yet even when the centerpiece of a youthful gang in the "beach party" films of her day, she was refreshingly spunky, outspoken and liberated. In *Dancing Daughters*, she says, "I want to hold out my hands and catch [all of life] — like the sunlight" and in *Montana Moon*, she snaps at new hubby, "You can't treat me like you treat your cattle." By the early '30s, shedding her baby fat and garbed in ever more haughty and fabulous creations by designer Adrian, she had evolved into a more glamorous and elegant beauty with a marked growth in her acting. Her silent screen experience enabled her to use her extraordinary eyes to express emotions eloquently, the camera often lingering on the sculptured Garboesque planes of her face. Her own Cinderella story appeared in various incarnations throughout her career and she played the mistress, prostitute and "other woman" with sympathy and without apology. "In my fallen-women roles — and God knows there were a lot of 'em," she said, "nobody saw me do the actual falling. Sometimes I wonder if I ever played a character the audience could regard as a virgin. I don't think so."

Today, outside of Turner Classic Movies, most audiences only know Crawford's early work, if at all, from *Grand Hotel*, in which her image seems an anomaly. Yet, in actuality, she resembled the flirtatious, vivacious creature in *Grand Hotel* in the greater canon of her work than she did either the hard-shell (yet still beautiful) dame of *Mildred Pierce* or the steelier, harshly-lipsticked gunslinger of *Johnny Guitar*. Indeed, knowing her work as intimately and thoroughly as I now do, I've come to reevaluate that harsher image. By the 1950s, Crawford was a mature woman in an industry unkind to mature women and wanted to hold onto her hard-won leading lady status. She seemed to be a fundamentally decent person — generous and loyal and a good friend to many, somewhat idealistic and romantic — who had tragically been damaged. She approached her job in movies with, for the most part, a professional attitude and sense of commitment, although her alcoholism later in life and the traumas of failed marriages and a studio that was willing to cast her out after she made millions for it understandably led to less desirable behavior during some periods of her life. (In the early '40s, frustrated by sub-standard scripts, Crawford made the bold and difficult move of leaving her home at MGM and immediately was invited to join Warner Brothers. Thus began a golden period with the new studio where she finally enjoyed choice scripts and established her iconic look, although she would continue to regard her days at MGM as her happiest.)

Crawford was a star and temperamental. She also seemed very eager to please and be liked, whole-heartedly devoted and grateful to her fans, indeed corresponding avidly and signing autographs to the point of exhaustion. She had four husbands, countless love and sexual relationships, and adopted five children, one of whom was traumatically taken back by his birth mother. Whatever difficulties she might have had with her older children, she seemed to have achieved a close relationship with her two younger daughters. Even after adopting a more severe look with exaggerated lip line and brows in the mid-1950s, her characters are rarely forbidding and never entirely without sympathy. Crawford, wanting audience approval, wouldn't allow for it. In good or bad films, she gave her 200% and one believed every tear (and I believe she did, too). She continued to embody the woman and underdog maneuvering in a man's world and surmounting the odds through drive, ambition, sass and sex appeal.

In a Crawford film, one can find all the schmaltzy, elegant, classy artistry cinema's golden age embodied. Bejeweled gowns on beautiful people, sumptuous apartments, tony enunciations, sassy dialogue, colorful character actors, stunning lighting and musical scores, huge MGM casts storming the Bastille in song, unabashed and shameless romanticism. Even her entrances are notable. Think of her being led to the courtroom in *A Woman's Face*, her back to the audience, face veiled by a Fedora. Think of her in the distance in her white glittering gown (fitting her trim dancer's body like a glove) in *Humoresque* and then the close-up when all the men bend to light this glamorous creature's cigarette. Think of the shoes with ankle straps and the mink with linebacker shoulder pads on the rain-slicked docks in *Mildred Pierce*. It isn't until suspenseful moments later that you actually see her face since her back is to the camera and she in shadows.

In Crawford's universe, utility never comes at the expense of glamour and smoking isn't bad for your health. Her smoking techniques are as creative and diverse as her hats and shoes. Rare are the times when Crawford isn't dressed to the nines. She moves through her celluloid world, strong and bold and sexy, with the authority of a queen. She stands up to and often eclipses the most formidable of men, but remains a lady. She is at once earthy Proletarian and haughty film goddess. "I dropped out of school when I was 14," she told friend Carl Johnes, "and everything I've learned was from scripts I've read and listening to everybody older and wiser."

I embrace the struggle, the glamour, the beauty, the chutzpah, the courage, the charm, and resilience embodied in Joan Crawford, immortalized in glorious black and white (and in rare cases, Technicolor), this brazen broad who encourages and inspires me as she doubtless emboldened and comforted her largely female audiences throughout her career, this star who remains surprisingly vital, natural and contemporary in the creakiest of her films. Professor Drew Caspar said, "Even now, years later, decades later, you can't take your eyes off of her on the screen."

I echo the construction workers who, according to a *New York Times* piece, looked her up and down after she shook hands all around and greeted them before entering her building, "They don't make 'em like you anymore, baby!"

They sure don't.

PHOTO COURTESY OF NEIL MACIEJEWSKI

My Feminist Hero

PHOTO COURTESY OF JERRY MURBACH

Dividing the Pie on Her Own Terms

Filmmaker and writer Mark Toscani wrote a wonderful essay about Joan Crawford called "Reflections on Joan" while fan Jonathan Denson, on a small poignant website created in teen years, explains why she is his hero. As I delve deeper and deeper into the life of the actress and her prodigious body of work, I not only marvel at her achievements and influence, but also connect deeply with the sort of grassroots feminist she embodied in life and on film (perhaps out of necessity since she had to fight and work to survive after a turbulent childhood and aborted formal education) while keeping every long eyelash, manicured nail, ankle-strapped heel, broad "a" and blessedly unpolitically-correct-fur in place. Some call her a glamorous feminist. I call her my feminist hero. There aren't piss-and-vinegar, sexy dames like *that* around anymore and we will perhaps never see her like again. She was a complex, enigmatic, contradictory product of her era and difficult life, but just as she devoted herself whole-heartedly to her fans (giving back where she felt she received), she doubtless inspired myriad women in the audience to want more out of life and go the mile to get it. She relied on men as her conduit in a man's world, and was often required to suffer for her ambition, but she was living in an age when she was actually allowed and expected to carry and dominate a film, and she was more than up to the task. Joan Crawford was a powerhouse.

Amazingly, Crawford was sassy from the get-go, even though she was also tender and waiflike and sweet in a way that many have forgotten, if they ever knew. She was extremely vivacious and cute in her early, flapper films, a mere girl. But even in the silents, her presence was virile and charismatic. You couldn't look away from her, despite occasional bad hairstyles and grating rawness. Her energy and charm was undeniable. Unlike a number of other actresses who came to Hollywood, Crawford did not have a strong, loving family behind her, however, so in her eagerness to keep the job that kept her off the streets, she worked diligently, even while ill. Soon, when she made good, she was supporting her hardscrabble mother who many seem to fault for neglecting her daughter and favoring son Hal. But, frankly, mother Anna was as hapless and vulnerable as her children, horribly poor and having to scramble and work to keep body and soul together. Anna made an effort to send Joan to school, although the girl was apparently badly abused, overworked and maltreated at these establishments, particularly by a sadistic school mistress at Rockingham Academy, and victimized by snobbery on top of it. A victim herself, Anna

With mother Anna and brother Hal.

was undereducated, promiscuous and dependent on shiftless men. The arguments Crawford heard at night between mother and men which frightened her draw comparison to sounds of violence chilling Christina in her bed way past the hour a generation later. Crawford also was supporting Hal, who she described as "chronically mean," and did not enjoy a close relationship with. He once allegedly locked her in a dark closet. Predictably, the good-for-nothing family came in for the kill when Crawford reached success, but then why wouldn't they? I'd grab the life raft, too, wouldn't you?

In a 1947 interview on *The Louella Parsons Show* before the release of *Daisy Kenyon* and prior to what she bills as her "next Warner Brothers picture," *Until Proven Guilty* (uh — guess she — and we — missed that one!), Crawford cuts to the chase about a "subject she feels deeply about." Parsons laughs and counters Joan feels deeply about everything. Crawford sounds very cute and bubbly, much like her flapper-girl personality, admitting that's true, but adding, "Louella, honestly I do want to answer the one question that so many girls write me about. [T]hey write me about the whole big subject about whether or not to become career women. Those poor little kids just starting out — oh, golly — I can't exaggerate how mixed up they are about it!" When asked by Parsons what mixes them up, she wryly responds, "What mixes up a woman on anything except men. I think it's a crying shame that so many girls let themselves be scared out of self-improvement and success by the same, old, sly masculine lies." Parsons wants to know which particular ones. "Oh, that threat of theirs that if you become a successful career woman, you lose your femininity and, therefore, they won't like you. Oh, what a lie that is." Using Louella as an example, she adds, "Nobody can be more feminine than you are and that same thing goes for any big career woman you can think of in any line like Mrs. Roosevelt or Clare Boothe Luce or Helen Hayes or Ingrid Bergman." Louella laughs and tells her to calm down. "Okay, kid me," Crawford responds sassily. "I warned you how I felt on this subject, but I do want to assure the girls that there's so much less danger in going ahead and proving themselves than there is in lingering behind while your dream boy goes ahead somewhere else to — uh — somebody else." After Parsons objects that not everyone can become a "glamour girl" like Joan, Crawford savvily responds, "Oh, yes, they can," adding that if she came from nothing and became the "assembly job" that "tags glamour," anyone can do it, it being a matter of discipline and applied art. She says "to the girls just starting out" that "if you have the capacity to be a career woman, you can be a careerist and a woman, too… That way your life will be always exciting."

Clearly and happily, Crawford did care about encouraging her female fans, letting them know, too, that she was *listening* and responding to their concerns. Evidently, given her slavish devotion to her audience, it was no pose. As one listens to her live interviews, right from the horse's mouth, it becomes apparent how much she mirrored the life-hungry, life-affirming, gutsy and ambitious women she played onscreen. She was effective in these roles, because she lived them, lived every emotion and, according to co-star James Stewart, did it spontaneously in one take. ("My first impression of [her] was of glamour," he says in Charles Castle's *The Raging Star*. "Glamour had nothing to do with aloofness or temperament, it had to do with friendliness, tremendous vitality and hard work, ambition and constant desire to improve her work, and to get knowledgeable about things that were important to her work…We have both been referred to as perfectionists, but I don't know what that word means. If it means trying to keep things going by learning your craft so that you can get it done to the best of your ability and not have the acting show, then I suppose that's what it is. If it means standing up against this tremendous technical thing which you have to cope with in the movies all the time, doing things with credibility and being believable when you're surrounded by machines and cameras and technical men with lights and everything else to surmount…This is part of a craft that takes learning, and if you get so that it doesn't bug you, then you can understand why Joan Crawford was so good at her job.")

Crawford could do six impossible things before breakfast — at least, you believe she'd try — and was evidently telling her audience, *women*, they could do it, too. She whole-heartedly befriended her fans in a way that no star ever had (to my knowledge) or certainly would (or even could, given stalkers) today. Whether her motive was a desire for love, sense of professionalism or wanting to give back for their support, her commitment and certainly generosity was there. How many fans must have blossomed with her example, inspiration and the attention she gave to their *importance?* How many letters must have brightened an anonymous life? What a unique devotion and collaboration with the public. It was a mighty big thank you.

In 1975 when Crawford was in her "later years," Barbara Ribakove of *Photoplay* reported: "[Crawford] gets blazingly angry at professionals who do not take their work seriously as she feels they should. 'When you stop being grateful, forget it. You might just as well leave the screen, because that camera picks up everything inside you. You cannot hide your attitude towards work.' Another pause. Then, all the way up from the gut: 'And when you consider those of us that cannot get a job because nobody writes for women anymore…and we are *dying* to work! *Dying!*' "

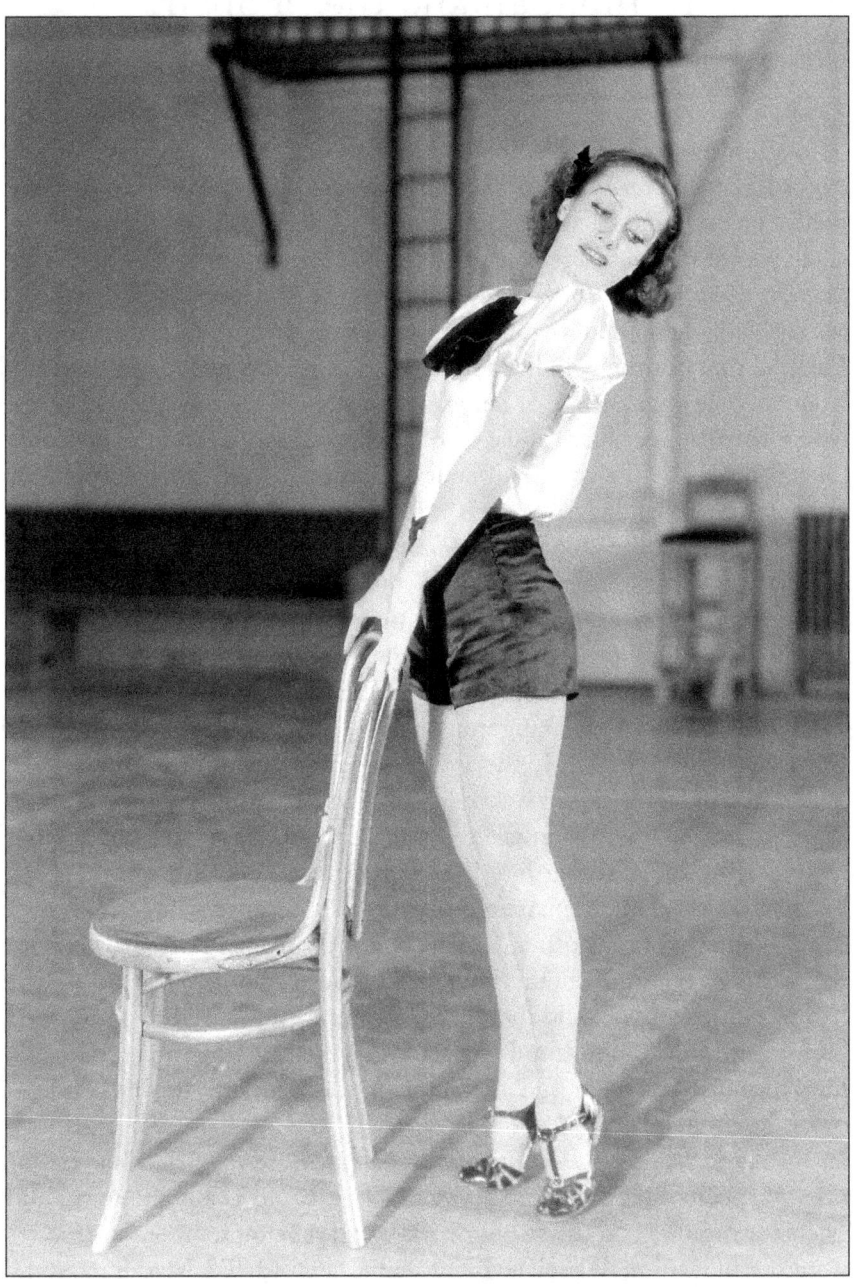

A cute and leggy ingénue. PHOTO COURTESY OF JERRY MURBACH

Young Joan and the Shopgirl Who Made Good

Beginning in the 1920s, Joan had an enormous following of women. According to *Popcorn Venus* by Marjorie Rosen, in a group of studies made by the Payne Fund between 1929 and 1933, she was cited repeatedly as a behavioral model by teenage girls. "When I go to see a modern picture like *Our Dancing Daughters*," one high-school sixteen-year-old wrote, "I am thrilled. These modern pictures give me a feeling to imitate their ways. I believe that nothing will happen to the carefree girl like Joan Crawford." Many people are unaware of her impact on youth, clearly commensurate with a Britney Spears or Lindsay Lohan or, even more, Annette Funicello (like Annette, with a coterie of energetic, romantically canoodling "kids" as backup "pals" in Jazz Age days). She was a rabble rouser, but a rabble rouser who was sensible in *Our Dancing Daughters* and *Our Blushing Brides*. She was the role model for "young moderns." Interestingly, the girls in her trio of "Our" films, beginning with *Dancing Daughters*, all taste the wild life: drinking champagne, tooling in fast cars with boys, and black bottoming the night away in clingy fringed dresses. "See you at dawn!" Crawford as "Dangerous Diana" calls to her liberal parents in *Our Dancing Daughters*. By the 1930s, she morphed into a working girl who toiled in factories, but wanted more. How devastating she is in *Mannequin* with the line, "Women are weak and men are strong. My mother wasted a lifetime of strength trying to prove that." In *Possessed*, where she became Clark Gable's mistress and rebukes a disapproving crowd with dignity, she tells her mother, "If I were a man…you'd think it was right for me to go out and get anything I could out of life and use anything I had to get it. Why should men be so different? All they've got are their brains and they're not afraid to use them. Well, neither am I!" (In that film, they also show her on a merry-go-round with, yes, the brass ring — metaphor, metaphor!)

In Maria Buszek's *Pin Up Grrrls: Feminism, Sexuality, Popular Culture*, she posits that Crawford revamped her image as a homemaker and "bachelor mom" when the strong working girl she represented in the '30s went out of fashion. It's self-evident that Crawford, like Madonna, was a master marketer, continually reinventing herself to move with the times, but the inference that she was a mere image-maker is inaccurate. It's not surprising that women like Madonna and Crawford who knew struggle learned to be hucksters and play top brass at their own game, but the housewife image had weight for Crawford. Even in the '20s, she was knitting and baking and doing some of her own housework; in the '40s she became a complete homemaker (yes, in the days of Rosie the Riveter) and clearly taught her children to be self-sufficient domestically, as Christina's roommate attested in Fred Lawrence Guiles' *Joan Crawford:*

Getting off the merry-go-round of poverty.

The Last Word. To the end, she was known to scrub her own floors, believing in "hands and knees" elbow grease which is why her maid Mamacita (a German woman) got the job. She'd grown up doing drudge work. In 1975 *Photoplay*, Barbara Ribakove said, "Joan is a scrubber of kitchen counters, a picker-up of microscopic bits of lint. Everything is immaculate. To Joan, a clean home is the outward and visible form of an inner and spiritual discipline. Her daily chores around the house are things Joan has done since her childhood, things that give her satisfaction." In later years, this was to manifest itself in obsessive-compulsive disorder. Despite Crawford's efforts and amazingly resilient spirit, repercussions from a harsh and love-deficient childhood were inevitable. There were enormous hurdles to surmount and she did it with discipline and order, maintaining schedules (which some ridicule, but frankly they strike me as reasonably sane) to keep all on track, and industrious effort.

As Jeanine Basinger reveals in *The Star Machine*, MGM, for one, demanded nothing less from its stable of stars. Crawford's second husband Franchot Tone describes her grueling schedule (although one suspects he wouldn't complain too loudly if such "demands" were on him, it being well-documented that he resented his wife's career eclipsing his own). Still, a star could hardly be asleep at the wheel even on few hours of sleep: "She must get her homework done, her lines learned every day. She has continuous meetings with the producer or the director or somebody else equally important each evening. She has to get up at four or four-thirty in the morning in order to get to the hairdresser and onto the set. She needs a massage at night before she can sleep for a few hours. She has to eat sparingly and exercise constantly. This goes on and on…and when Saturday night comes…other duties, other priorities arise. Conferences about the next script…she's a star." Other stars had it no easier, although it evidently reaped incalculable rewards, too, and Crawford thrived on it — on industry, usefulness and challenge. She was grateful to the hand that fed her.

Although she did her share of cheesecake (and sports-oriented) publicity photos with other young starlets at MGM and was featured frequently in her underwear in films, Crawford was serious about being more than decorative. She hung around soundstages, absorbing sponge-like, and became extremely knowledgeable about all aspects of filmmaking. From the get-go, she endeavored to ingratiate herself with the technicians, too — remembering uncannily and diplomatically small details about their families and lives, and treating them generously financially. She anonymously set up a wing at Hollywood Presbyterian Hospital so that newspapermen, extras, aging stars, gaffers and grips could get operations and treatment they otherwise couldn't afford and paid the bills for years. "She has an amazing effect upon people — an almost hypnotic power over them," Helen Louise Walker of 1934's *Silver Screen* observed. "Yet, Joan cares more than anyone I have ever known about what people think of her. She reads every word that is written about her and usually cries bitterly over it…She wants approval and admiration and friendship so desperately…I should hate to try to live with Joan, try to cope with her moods and her intensity. Yet, that very vitality, that electric something, that abandonment of herself to emotion, is what makes her so interesting, so personally powerful." Elsa McKenzie, a dancer at MGM during those early years, recalls how hard Crawford worked, adding, "[A]nd once in a while, when she relaxed, you could see something in her eyes that was like — well, like fright and loneliness mixed together."

Much is made of Crawford's "easy" or voracious sexuality, her sexual aggression, some of it perhaps natural, some possibly resulting from childhood sexual abuse (at age eleven) by stepfather Henry Cassin ("the center of my child's world"), the latter abuse confessed to friend Lawrence Quirk in later years and which she felt completely responsible for. Like her mother, she was wildly promiscuous. But she was also prey to

Sweet-faced and lovely at the time of *Dream of Love*.

exploitation, particularly in those early years, as so many girls in Hollywood were. She was one of the girls MGM provided for visiting execs, the men often not kind. In her memoirs, *Being and Becoming*, Myrna Loy details meeting Crawford when they were both extras/chorus girls in the film, *Pretty Ladies*. "One day Joan came into the dressing room looking very unhappy," Loy recalled. "She fell into my lap — we were snowflakes covered with marabou that kept getting into our mouths — and she began to cry. Joan always worried terribly. I did, too, but never showed it. Apparently, Harry Rapf, the producer who discovered her, had chased her around the desk the night before. She was having a terrible time. She had such a beautiful body that they were all after her. I didn't have quite that much trouble — my sort of snooty attitude put them off a bit…Joan and I became friends and stayed friends, which is the most that came out of my first MGM experience."

Shoulder Pads and Power Suits

Crawford took necessary risks in her career and fought for challenging roles, not wanting to stagnate. When her career reached a stalemate in the late 1930s, she lobbied for an unsympathetic but meaty role in *The Women*, then opted out of her contract altogether at MGM when she was being pushed out by a younger crop of stars. "It was a strange period, however you judge it," she later told author Roy Newquist in *Conversations with Crawford*. "They might just as well have sent all the women 'of a certain age' to Alaska and pensioned us off." She staged an amazing coupe at Warners with her Oscar for *Mildred Pierce*, but this was after she actually went off salary until a worthy part came her way. She had to close up part of her house, worked in her victory garden and ostensibly became a housewife. *Mildred Pierce*, my favorite Crawford film, is shown in Women's Studies classes since it's about a female entrepreneur who is "punished" (allegedly) with hardship for leaving the family, a take I don't buy (see my review of the James M. Cain novel).

In *Mildred Pierce*, Crawford is at her most iconic — linebacker shoulder pads, glamorous furs, expressive eyes, ankle-strap shoes, suffering and allure, outrageous rolled '40s hairstyles, stylized smoking, determination. An ordinary housewife takes the bull by the horns, jilting the philandering husband. She learns to succeed in a man's world with a combination of feminine wiles and smarts, on men's terms in some ways — learning to fight dirty (yet remaining human). Mildred had many parallels to Crawford: she was the breadwinner ultimately betrayed, publicly and privately; desire for love remained tragically unfulfilled in spite of phenomenal success; and both had a daughter who used their money and influence liberally and then betrayed them. Crawford ate crow and although an established star, submitted to an audition to win the part and went to bat for Ann Blyth for the role of Veda, the two stars becoming friends for life.

Classic '40s look. PHOTO COURTESY OF NEIL MACIEJEWSKI

PHOTO COURTESY OF JERRY MURBACH

Her face, although lovely, shows signs of strain in *Mildred*, indicative of the Hollywood saw mill that continually taxed Crawford, a ravished look that befit the character. (In the late '30s and early '40s with career and marriage disintegrating, she suffered from bouts of depression and pneumonia, according to MGM files.) One of my favorite moments is when Mildred returns from Mexico in her dynamic, impeccably cut suit and strappy heels. Her hair is swept fetchingly up. Smoking and crossing sleek legs, she removes a fleck of tobacco from her tongue and tells friend Ida (Eve Arden) that she learned to drink from men. The same was true of Crawford in real life, who avoided alcohol in early years because of the alcoholic scenes she'd witnessed as a child (funny how history repeats itself), yet eventually was introduced to cocktails with third husband Phil Terry and began relying increasingly on alcohol to "jack myself up to meet people," as she puts it in *Conversations*. ("I'm not a public person, at all…Vodka relaxed me, chased away the butterflies, put a certain safe distance between me and everybody else…a type of fright worse than stage fright.") For me, Mildred Pierce, the role for which she won an Oscar after Hollywood assumed she was through, sums up Joan Crawford more than any other.

Ann Blyth (Veda of *Mildred Pierce*) on Crawford: *"I never saw her edgy or nervous. She was very kind. Very beautiful. Always exquisitely dressed. Her professionalism was stunning."*

In the 1940s, Crawford shed most of her former girlishness, although it was still discernible even in later years. Mindful of critics and wanting to please her public, she was evidently criticized in neophyte days for nervous tics like hand wringing and lip biting, so she rehearsed with her hands tied. She rarely played an actual shopgirl, but onscreen and off, she was often a sexual outlaw, combating social disfavor with dignity. Many believe feminism is about equal wages. To my mind, feminism is about sex, about the idea that a woman's body is sinful and primarily for the control and gratification of men. It's about the use of words like "whore," "tramp," "ho," "bitch," and the like used to describe women who are sexually active in the way men traditionally have been. Crawford's characters frequently "don't stand on ceremony," as Joan's cub reporter Bonnie Jordan puts it in *Dance, Fools, Dance*. In real life, Joan didn't either.

In spite of being fairly small and petite (yet occasionally creating a statuesque illusion), Crawford could hold her own against any man onscreen (and in some ways, off). As director Steven Spielberg put it after directing her in *Night Gallery* (his neophyte debut), "In a two shot with anyone, even Gable, your eyes fix on her." In *A Portrait of Joan*, her "autobiography" of sorts (written "with" Jane Kesner Ardmore), she talks about an unnamed deep love of hers (identified as Charles McCabe elsewhere) from New York, who "taught me to hunt and fish, we used to go on these expeditions with a whole group of men. The first time, I'm sure, their reaction was, oh, no, not a dame tagging along! I carried my own gun and my own camera, waded through streams in the vanguard; and at noon when we'd camp, I'd help fix lunch and surprise them with all sorts of snacks packed away in my knapsack just in case they didn't catch any fish. This friend introduced me to politics, to banking, big business and public affairs." Just as she learned to drink from men, she learned to play them at their own game in business and sex. She was nonetheless reduced to tears easily and often went to directors in tears about difficulties she was having with a part. She would have inconsolable crying spells, according to first husband Douglas Fairbanks, Jr., but emerge refreshed.

Ladies man/attorney Greg Bautzer, with whom Crawford had a celebrated tempestuous relationship for a number of years, in a taped interview said, "I had been in several fights with men during my lifetime. I've won some and I've lost some but no man ever put a scar on my face. I've got about four scars on my face that she put on. She should've been on a New York Yankees pitching staff. She could take a cocktail glass across a room and hit you right in the face two out of three times." (Go, Joan!) "When she was in love," adds friend Radie Harris, "she was over-in-love and very predatory, very possessive about her men." Of course, Bautzer, although he admits he was "stuck on her," doesn't mention the black eye he gave her or that he climbed a rose trellis after she locked him out of the house to be with her (leading to what she termed "the most exciting sexual experience" of her life), their fights and reconciliations dramatic, disturbing (especially since men and women are not of equal size or body weight) and legion. These occasionally volatile relationships with men were a sad sign of cracks in the foundation of order and, as always with Crawford, not the whole story. Fairbanks said the only arguments they had were very civil and she admitted to being a different person with each husband. She enjoyed a number of enduring platonic male friendships including Cesar Romero, Van Johnson and William Haines. In Jane Ellen Wayne's *Crawford's Men,* an anonymously identified former real estate broker who had a one night stand with Crawford is interviewed. "She was lovely, and the night we met, I admired her gown, jewelry, and furs because she knew how to wear them." Crawford asked him to drive her home and in the car asked all about him. "By the time we got to her house we were laughing, and she asked me to have a brandy with her," he continued. "She teased and flirted but was very sophisticated…I don't know many men who would turn down an opportunity with a woman, but even fewer who were almost hypnotized." He described her as being in complete command. "I had never been with any woman like Crawford. I forgot about the dinner party, who I was, who she was, and where I was…From what I understand she always found out about the men she chose." In *The Ultimate Star* documentary, a biography of her life, friend Herbert Kenwith mentions going to lunch with her and finding all three of her ex-husbands (Steele, of course, died, leaving her a widow) at her table! "She could go to a sales meeting and all the boys would clamor around her and she would shake their hands," he added, referring to her days promoting Pepsi Cola for fourth husband Al Steele, Pepsi honcho.

Even while amusing herself with one night stands, however, Crawford remained at heart a romantic. Director Vincent Sherman felt she was looking for the knight in shining armor. She often slept with her directors, allegedly feeling more secure if they loved her and presumably were invested in her, therefore. She was also very loyal, ensuring that crew members from early days and friends found employment. "You know, Louella, I believe a career woman has earned the right to be an idealist in love," she tells Louella Parsons in 1947. For excerpts of her early love letters, see my review of Michelle Vogel's *Joan Crawford: Her Life in Letters*. A poem written between marriages in the early '40s begins, "Where are you? My heart cries out in agony, In my extended hands, I give my heart with, All its cries — its songs –its love." With typical distortion, she is now often portrayed as a calculator, marrying for advancement. It strikes me as odd that women, in general, would be vilified as "gold diggers" when given such scant economic clout, but clearly the situation is inaccurate with Crawford. From all accounts, she seemed genuinely interested in finding a partner who would be an equal, weighing marriage carefully after the first one failed. Furthermore, she was already an established star with all of her marriages and frequently her husbands had more or at least as much to gain in the alliance as she did; in the case of her three actor-husbands, she easily eclipsed them in terms of power. Brentwood was Crawford's house and her husbands who lived there were living in her home, not the other way around. She was very involved with corporate sponsorship after marrying Pepsi exec Steele, campaigning internationally for the product and becoming a forerunner in product placement. The "Joan Crawford" name helped Pepsi tremendously and gave Crawford a renewed sense of worth and activity when she no longer found it in Hollywood. She was the breadwinner for husbands, studio, and children.

The Damned Don't Cry and the 1950s Films — Vinegar and Spice and Not Everything Nice

The Damned Don't Cry is perhaps my favorite Joan Crawford film of the 1950s. It's a superb film noir and crime drama, vastly underrated. Because it has so many Crawford screen personas rolled into one and because she is such a brassy dame in it, some view it as camp. But it's actually hard-hitting, fast-paced and brilliantly cast, acted and shot. The black-and-white cinematography alone is stunning. It's got everything and it's got Joan. For once, Crawford has supporting actors, even if they're known essentially as B-actors, who are as strong as she is, each a perfect fit for his character. Crawford as Ethel Whitehead/Lorna Hansen Forbes — sleeping her way to the top of a crime syndicate for sheer survival — is an aggressive, ballsy, sassy woman. She doesn't let herself get pushed to the sidelines; she strides through a room as if she owns it, sleek as a racehorse. She plays hard ball with the boys — gangsters, no less — and tangles with men several times her size, unafraid to speak her mind, unafraid to trick the tricksters, irritated to be left out of their secret "men's club," and savvy, whatever her limitations are. She's tough, but vulnerable and sensitive. "You might invite me into the library," she tells gangster George Castleman (David Brian), to which he responds, "There's one thing I never do in the presence of women — discuss business." "That should leave you room for plenty of other interests," Ethel retorts icily. Ethel Whitehead wants her piece of the pie and she's gonna get it. She's not content with mere survival; her ambition is to constantly improve herself. She is pure Joan Crawford.

The interesting thing about Crawford, as embodied in roles like Ethel Whitehead/Lorna Hansen Forbes (Ethel's manufactured persona), is that she had a masculine energy and assertiveness without being at all masculine. People joke about her eyebrows, which were not yet overstated in *The Damned Don't Cry*, but she was actually an extremely feminine woman, as most who knew her mentioned. Men held open doors for her and lit her cigarettes on film and in life. Rare were the times she was not sleekly dressed with fetching high heels ("f-me shoes," as they were called) and furs, never eschewing ruffles and elaborate hats, opera gloves and ankle bracelets. There is that fascinating duality about her face. In her early years, she was like a soft doe with baleful yet sultry eyes, and, although the shape of her face was perfect and could be photographed well from any angle, her jaw line became more hollowed or sunken as she aged (like her birth father Thomas LeSueur), giving an arguably harsher look. The harsh look wasn't the whole story, either; it softened from moment to moment and film to film, depending on the role, but it reflected, for me, the grit and determination Crawford felt as she was bucking a system that was fighting her. What would have happened if women like Joan Crawford and Bette Davis hadn't challenged that system? Both fought to hang onto the careers they had hard-earned when studios would have buried them at age 35. They were ambitious in an age when ambition in women was reviled (as if it still isn't). In order to swim upstream, Joan Crawford played with the boys, as she had in childhood. In a taped interview, director Vincent Sherman said Joan felt men were the enemy, although clearly she loved and desired them, too. Funny, that made me like her even more. Given the status of women worldwide, how could any woman believe otherwise?

Female on the Beach: Swimming Against the Tide

In the 1950s, Crawford had a steelier edge because she played characters who were velvet bitches or who were supposed to be perceived as such. (I found them smart and on the money, devious by necessity in hostile surroundings.) Roles offered at this time leaned heavily toward older woman being "punished." (In *Queen Bee*, she is actually murdered by alcoholic hubby in a fiery car crash for the crime of adultery and general uppity-ness, something which still leaves me chilled and inflamed — no pun intended.) In *Autumn Leaves*, it's pronounced to a twisted extreme, although she gives a superb, nuanced performance as typist Millicent Weatherby in a May/December romance. Degrading ads for the film, advancing masochism and abuse toward women, include one reading: "I never know what's coming next...a kiss or a slap. Yet I can't let them take him...the one man who needed me...the way I need him..." (That kind of need you can bypass, sister. Ask the battered wives in the morgue.) Millie is subjected to horrific abuse, including black eyes and having a typewriter thrown at her hand. But Crawford prevails, as she always does — uneasily in that film, its "happy" ending leaving me queasy and distrustful, not happy. In *Female on the Beach*, a guilty (or not-so-guilty) pleasure, she gets romantically entangled with a younger beach bum (Jeff Chandler), but — another glitch -she's not sure if he plans murder for the honeymoon. Still, Crawford is victorious in that one after being chased up and down the beach in strappy heels and cocktail dresses; she's an unparalleled hoot. The mature Crawford's ballsiness has a new connotation, an unmasked cynicism that is refreshingly on the money. Even her disgust with youth — the look she flashes her genuinely annoying "niece" in *Queen Bee* — is priceless. She could say a lot with a look or an intonation. And I'm sure her post-forty female fans understood.

Harriet Craig, directed by Vincent Sherman, is satirically alleged to be a role tailor-made for Crawford, meant to vilify a beautiful, yet "controlling" woman who worships her orderly home at the expense of her marriage. To my mind, Harriet is wholly sympathetic, clearly far more capable of running things than hubby Walter (Wendell Corey), her power covert and manipulative by necessity. How laughable it is that she should be condemned for objecting to Walter's all-night poker games, his natural slovenly tendencies or a job that would send him and one of his buddies to Japan for *three months without her*. Crawford is sexy, regal and magnificent in the role, giving it a full range of shading and authority. Interestingly, Dorothy Arzner, who directed Crawford in *The Bride Wore Red*, adapted George Kelly's misogynistic original play for the film version *Craig's Wife* with Rosalind Russell. (See my review of the play.) As Julia Lesage noted in *The Hegemonic Female Fantasy*, Arzner infuriated author Kelly by suggesting Walter was dominated by his mother (as he appears to be) and fell in love with a woman stronger than he. Arzner recalled, "Kelly rose to his six-foot height and said, '*That is not my play*. Walter Craig was a sweet guy and Mrs. Craig was an SOB.' He left. That was the only contact I had with Kelly." Therefore, the condemnation of Crawford in this "signature" role has many layers, her own "icy" capability or authority faulted in a way that a man of authority never would be. The irony also is that women are thrown brickbats for succeeding in the very narrow domain they are forced to occupy.

Some biographers posit that during the mid-'50s, Billie Cassin began to assert herself beneath the façade of Joan Crawford. In *Conversations*, when speaking of the way she and Clark Gable gave each other courage, Crawford explained, "We had become people and images foreign to ourselves, and we were trying to really live the new parts." And in a 1955 interview: "When I'm tired, Billie's child voice, Southern accent and all, rises again in my throat." Certainly in the '50s films, once again facing a cross-roads in her career, she often shows signs of strain and exhaustion.

Regal and beautiful in *Harriet Craig*. PHOTO COURTESY OF NEIL MACIEJEWSKI

Anna Raeburn noted in *Legends*, "[F]or the first time, there were reports of her being unpleasant to her colleagues on the set. It is easy to see how, as she knew she had peaked in terms of how she looked and what she could accomplish, so she began to increase her demands that she should be noticed, have attention paid to her, be acceded to..." Some claim she was "threatened" by younger actresses (another old sawhorse used to diminish women); however, she was more of a pro than that, championing up-and-coming co-stars like Geraldine Brooks, Ann Blyth, and Diane Baker but frustrated (and showing it) by those who weren't measuring up like Lucy Marlow.

In a 1952 interview with the uber-annoying Mary Margaret McBride (she frequently prattles on about herself, is unwittingly insulting and addresses Crawford as "Joan Crawford"), Crawford's grit leaks out beneath grandstanding befitting the Miss America pageant ("I just love people!"). Our gal, ever the marketer, even makes a plug for Lux soap, which she probably genuinely used, and reveals how she is misinterpreted by press. This is, of course, after McBride embarrasses her by saying she doesn't like Crawford's interviews on paper and wonders why they come out so poorly. "I know several women interviewers particularly have an idea of Joan Crawford," Crawford explains, her voice lapsing into heavy Southern twang. "They say it's a clothes horse idea, a show off idea and they never give me any idea for thinking or constructive thinking. As a matter of fact, they never even talk to me about anything but clothes." (McBride would talk to her primarily about children.) Her Southern drawl surfacing repeatedly, Crawford later breaks from the long discourse on motherhood (are famous men ever questioned so obsessively on fatherhood?) to plug *Sudden Fear*, her upcoming film. She doesn't read a lot when working on a picture, she explains, because "I'm concentrating on dialogue or rewriting it, preparing it, and studying it and rehearsing it for the next scenes. I don't like to be distracted from my one character when I'm working...I can't go out and play. I can with my children, but I mean I can't go out and do radio shows and get into characters. If I started to read *Gone with the Wind* in the middle of a picture, I'd come back the next morning and say, 'I could let it go until tomorrow.' I'd take on the character."

After marrying Al Steele in 1955, Crawford became deeply involved with Pepsi-Cola as an Ambassadress of the product, pioneering (as mentioned earlier) product placement in her films, traveling internationally on its behalf, thrilled to be involved with business and surrounded by crowds again at bottling plants. She was the first woman to be elected to the Board of Pepsi-Cola, a fact that gets sadly overlooked today. When Steele died of a heart attack, leaving her in debt, she remained on the Board for some time although she clashed with Donald Kendall who became president. He always resented her high-profile presence in the company, calling her "a goddamn actress" and she nicknamed him "Fang," borrowing the idea from Phyllis Diller's nickname for her husband. Ultimately, Pepsi retired Crawford from the Board, which left her aggrieved that they had dismissed her contributions on the product's behalf.

In financial and personal ruin after the death of Steele, Crawford was given a small role in *The Best of Everything* as compensation, her role later cruelly cut. But she gave it her 200 percent (as always) and delivered one of the most memorable and hilarious lines with venom, "Now you and your rabbit-faced wife can go to hell!"

George Cukor, according to Shaun Considine's *The Divine Feud*, remembered it as a period of "sheer terror for Joan." "One night she would call and say she was so happy to be out of the business…[t]wo nights later she would call again, begging me to reassure her that she would work again. She needed what we all needed — another job, another movie — the chance to create, to keep busy, to stop thinking of ourselves and what we had in the past."

Author Alexander Walker makes illusions to Crawford feeling that others were ungrateful to her, but given the evidence, it appears she was accurate. In *Ultimate Star*, Walker, in fact, describes her leaving MGM, the studio for which she made millions — clearing out her dressing room, washing and cleaning everything, then driving through the rear gate alone "without a backward glance." She was booted out of Pepsi after she had tirelessly campaigned on its behalf. She deferred to her husbands, but was mistreated by a few of them. It was indeed a continual uphill battle. Christina, who had the audacity to refashion her mother's early life (Joan's relationship with her mother and brother which was painful) as being her mother's fault ("I've often thought they paid a terrible price for the early years they shared with my mother" — say what??), also rejected the idea of being grateful for anything her mother did for her. "I was still supposed to feel unending love and deepest gratitude for the benevolence of my long suffering, hardworking mother," she says in *Mommie Dearest*. When her mother explains her allowance will be late because she is having financial difficulties (this was the period when she was getting little work), Christina is incensed. Joan Crawford indeed tragically did not find the love she so desired, but it certainly wasn't for lack of trying.

Various Crawford friends and biographers detail the anguish she faced in an industry that was casting her out and humiliating her (in some respects) onscreen because she was no longer young. In *The Million Dollar Mermaid*, Esther Williams gives an eyewitness account during the filming of *Torch Song*:

> Once she'd made her grand departure, I got myself together to go home, but as I was leaving I heard some noises coming from Stage 4. It sounded like yelling, so I walked over to take a look. Stage 4 was where they did all the show business pictures, because it was set up like a theater. The house was dark; no one was in the audience. There was nothing on but the work light in the center of the stage; in the far corner a janitor was sweeping up. Downstage under the middle of the proscenium arch was Joan, still in her bird outfit, talking to the empty seats.
>
> I stood there and listened in the darkness as she cried out, "Why have you left me? Why don't you come to my movies? What did I do? What did I say? Don't turn your back on me!" Joan had been star since the 1920s, with an Oscar and a fine body of work behind her, but here she was, almost fifty, reduced to begging an imaginary audience not to forget her. Tears were streaming down her face, streaking her copper makeup. Suddenly she looked old and pathetic. I slipped away without her noticing.

When asked by Newquist if her career might have been easier if Women's Lib had been established during her acting years, Joan Crawford said, "I don't think things would have been different for me. I was a very headstrong woman, and I learned to turn off the sensitivity button when I felt pushed…I don't think strong characters like me or Kate or Roz Russell were ever intimidated simply because we were women. (God knows Bette Davis wasn't; look at the great battle she put up with Jack Warner.) We all knew 101 ways to say, 'Go f--- yourself!' without ever, or almost ever, being vulgar…I don't think Women's Lib came on very attractively…I wasn't exactly what you'd call a housewife, but I wonder how many housewives wanted to be told they were leading useless lives and working as unpaid slaves. Later on they toned down a bit and issues like — oh, equal pay for equal work began to mean something. But at first — well, the wrong people led the parade." [My note: Thank God *someone* was leading the parade, Joan!] "As far as the film industry is concerned, Women's Lib is a laugh. The strong parts are still being written for men…I'm not anti-feminist, but I'm inclined to agree with Adela Rogers St. John, when she said that Women's Lib is a lot of hogwash, that women have always had their rights, but they were too dumb to use them. She says that any woman with intelligence and ambition has always been able to make it in the so-called man's world. I think she's right."

Berserk — She Runs a Business and Has a Love Muffin

Crawford in her golden years was minus none of her valiant chutzpah, even when visibly ailing. In *Berserk*, she not only wears tights and fishnets at sixty, sporting damn good legs (let's face it), but she also has taken a young stud for a lover. Oh, where's my own blue stationery? I'll send this woman a thank you note! (And had she been alive, she would have returned one of her own.) Over a candlelit dinner, beefcake Ty Hardin simpers, "I'm crazy about you, Monica," to which she (as Monica Rivers, circus owner) responds, "I'm fond of you, Frank." "No more?" he asks. Then he later adds, "I'm interested in the future — our future," to which she responds, with a cutting laugh (this is why we love Joan!), "Not so fast, Frank. I like you but I don't want this to mushroom." And (delicious cheesy dialogue): "Let's enjoy what we have…it makes this crazy circus life more bearable." The scripts gave her good lines, but Crawford said them as if she wrote them. Detractors complain she played roles written for younger women, but why wouldn't she when leading lady roles weren't available for mature women? She made these parts riveting and certainly no younger actress or younger self could have brought the commanding vitality to, for instance, Ethel Whitehead/Lorna Hansen Forbes in *The Damned Don't Cry*. In her later years when offered dreck (and she knew it was dreck), she still gave her pro best, the reason *Berserk* and *The Best of Everything* and especially *Strait-Jacket* have cult followings today.

In *The Last Years*, Carl Johnes, who became Crawford's friend in her later life, recalls her enthusiastic plans for returning to school with a private tutor. They went so far as to make arrangements, but sadly, it was not to take place. One night when she was in a "racy" mood and joking with him, it struck him that she had "never really lost all traces of that 'hotcha' vamp she had been in the 1920s." "I smiled at her and said, 'You know, when you're like this, I get an uncontrollable urge to pinch your ass!'" To her credit, she responded, "But just before you did, you'd think twice about it, right?" He also notes the alarm experienced when sensing she was not well, down ultimately to eighty-five pounds, although with her indomitable spirit, she didn't seek out help or sympathy, refusing with selfishness or pride to worry friends and family. "She'd lost more weight, and there was a faint expression, a grim etching of pain across her face." His last visit with her was haunting. She didn't answer the house phone for several minutes, seemed to take even longer to open the door to her apartment, and appeared "terribly tired." Johnes offered to leave,

Still the same saucepot at approximately sixty as she was...

but waving away protestations, she "went to the freezer compartment of her refrigerator, knelt down and proceeded to chop away at some congealed ice cubes." She was making him a drink, even though she could barely straighten up to walk. Answering her own door at her insistence, she received a delivery of groceries in several heavy shopping bags. She then began to struggle with them, "painfully inching them across the floor into the kitchen." Johnes tried to help, but she brushed him aside, "almost spitting" at him, "Just get out of my way. It's done." He was alarmed and frightened by how frail she appeared, but then she changed into a housedress and tied her hair back, relieving him slightly.

"The last thing I would let myself imagine," Johnes said, "was that she was seriously ill because Joan Crawford was indestructible."

Biographer Bob Thomas recalled the final tribute to Joan Crawford at Samuel Goldwyn Theater following her memorial service at All Souls Unitarian Church, which fifteen hundred attended. Lines formed around the block. At the end of the evening, a series of Crawford portraits flashed on the Academy screen and he observed that "even if she had appeared in no movies, the photographs would have made her famous...Most of

...at approximately twenty.

all, the eyes. Those huge, luminous, omniscient eyes that had known so much agony, not all of it self-inflicted, and the endless, unrealized pursuit of love."

As a child, Crawford — then Lucille LeSueur or Billie Cassin, as she called herself — dreamed of being a dancer but severely injured her foot on a broken bottle. The doctor said she would walk with a limp and should not exercise, but she refused to accept this grim diagnosis. According to David Houston's *Jazz Baby*, Crawford — her trials rivaling Scarlett O'Hara — had to walk thirty-two blocks on her bum foot since the family was too poor to afford streetcar fare, but amazingly, she actually achieved her dream and went on to dance on Broadway in the chorus of *Innocent Eyes* and eventually found a career with one of the most celebrated and powerful studios in film history. Crawford represented proletarian struggle and *lived* it. She never wavered in her commitment to her public. Not surprisingly, she enjoys a huge following in the gay community, although not all of her fans are gay. The sign "WWJD," which stands for "What Would Jesus Do," is also an in-joke among Crawford fans, refashioned as "What Would Joan Do?" The sign "WWJD" hangs above a photo of Joan Crawford reading a book in St. Mark's Bookstore in New York City.

Ironically, adopted daughter Christina, via her malevolent tome, *Mommie Dearest*, successfully co-opted her mother's image, manipulating things to paint herself, not her mother, as the survivor and focal point — the "star," if you will. Yet, it was Joan Crawford who swam against the tide with courage. To the end, she gave life, audience and work her all. In a 1955 radio broadcast, she says, "Speaking for myself, I feel a deep sense of responsibility. It matters greatly to me what people think of me on the screen. And I'm sincerely grateful when they like what I do. I've spent my lifetime trying to measure up to what the movie-goer expects of me. The most important reward is something more than merely success. What I *truly* appreciate is the approval of the audience. If I have that...I'm happy because motion pictures *are* my life...and a *good* life, too." And to *Screenland* in 1964: "I'm not interested in taking anybody else's place. Sometimes it seems that you have to keep proving your right to your own place in the sun every minute. I want only the place I've earned."

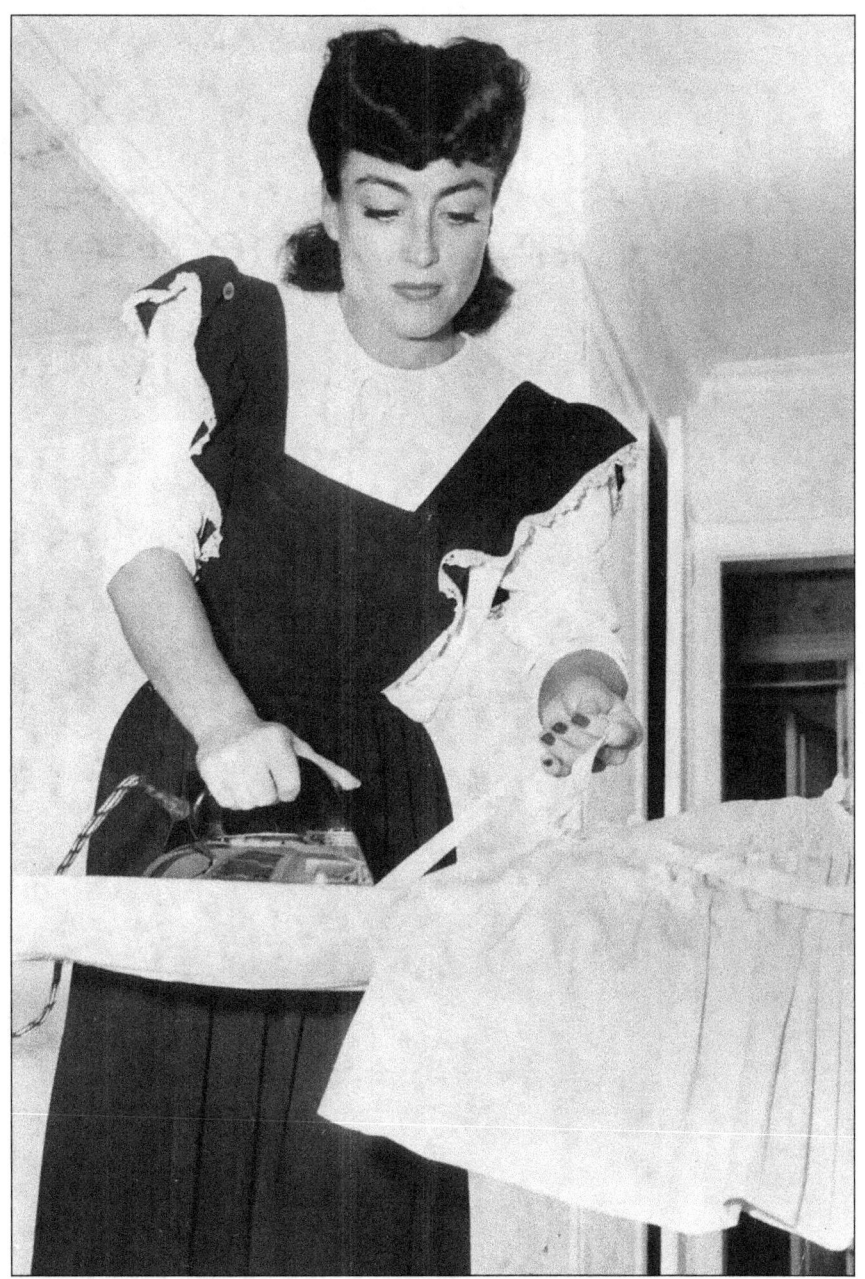

Crawford irons one of Christina's little frocks in the early forties. CREDIT: ARCHIVES OF DETROIT DAILY NEWS

The Gay Connection to Joan

PHOTO COURTESY OF JERRY MURBACH

Let me start with a disclaimer. All opinions expressed here are mine. As the Red Queen in *Alice's Adventures in Wonderland & Through the Looking-Glass* says, "I don't know what you mean by *your* way. All ways about here belong to *me!*" So the theories expressed here are mine and they may be subject to change, as the mood and life takes me, and maybe yours differ. So be it. That's the beauty of creating. As a writer, I've always felt like actor, director, set designer, costume designer — in control of a whole world! If only we could air-brush and manipulate real life so beautifully! But even when constructing a fictional reality, characters start going in their own seemingly independent directions (all Red Queens of the mind) or words take on a momentum beyond control, due to racing thoughts, like running down a hill in San Francisco, steep and on an incline. I don't know if they really mean anything or capture my intent. Writing is a frustrating business even if one knows the ins and outs of it. I may say one thing, but the exact opposite may be true and I might mean it as well. So with this nonfiction piece, perhaps I will speak a truth (my truth) or perhaps I won't, but it's my attempt to conceptualize what is at heart abstract and a personal perspective — the gay connection to Joan as I see it.

If I must admit it, most of the Joan Crawford fans I've encountered predominately are gay, just as, by and large, the gay *male* population is what keeps the lights of these great classic films burning bright (for which we can all be grateful).

Why is it that so many gay people respond to Joan Crawford especially?

My own theory is that it's because Joan was an underdog and a powerful, beautiful, creative force — an underdog who embraced good taste, glamour, fantasy — and who continually addressed and defied her oppressors and the whole parochial, class-conscious, patriarchal, snobby system that sought to marginalize and deprive her. Through all her trials she kept her head held high. In her films, as in her life, she demanded to be counted in — as a woman, as an outsider, and once she was on the inside, no one let her forget the precariousness of her position. Her struggle is every woman's struggle, every marginalized person's struggle, but especially resonant to gays. She was ridiculed for her excesses and yet the emotion is raw and real and she often underplayed. Beneath the toughness was the frightened little girl and one sees it often in her eyes. Gays recognize and love that vulnerability. Beneath the flamboyance was shyness. As the Melancholy Eskimo (who is not gay, however) put it, "She is a tigress and a lost lamb. She is a predator, only because she is so irresistible as a prey." Her promiscuity was another mirror of gay male sexuality, in general. Most gays can appreciate why Joan would hide her insecurities and grim past behind an armor of Hollywood perfection and love that she did it for her public, to whom she was eternally grateful. It didn't really protect her, did it? One of her directors (and lovers) Vincent Sherman said her personal life was terrible and that it took hours to bring her down from crying scenes. Yet in her own book, she brims with girlish enthusiasm and Carl Johnes, who knew her in her later years, while recognizing her loneliness, called her "my youngest friend."

Although we're all outsiders, gay people are marginalized and have often found identification through idealist or outrageous films and alternate realities (as perhaps many non-gays do) even when, yes, still living very much real lives in the real world. But, biologically, men and women are designed to mate together — at least for procreation. So it makes gays always "deviants" from the blueprint as Joan was never (and still is never) quite accepted even when at the pinnacle of stardom. It makes homosexuality eternally controversial, as Joan was. I believe the stories of Joan going to Hollywood parties and leaving in tears when she no longer felt she belonged in later years, when she was made to feel ridiculous for "playing the star." Her bad behavior seemed to usually stem from fear, although she was most often a consummate professional on the set. Hers was a search for love and belonging and she never quite found it. But also there was the grand lady and bitchy strong side of Joan — like the gay community's defiant bitchiness and good taste.

Have I said anything new? Perhaps not. I'm not sure I even expressed what it is I see. Joan was a glamorous feminist icon and very human, a diva and survivor who never forgot her fans, who exuded anguish and hope onscreen, the complex contradictions of her own life. This humanity, this flawed being beneath a stunning glamour and power and largeness, makes her belong and resonate with us as she's always wanted to belong.

Crawford had panache like no one's business. Even a tree limb becomes a fabulous prop!

Joan & Diana: Two Great Dames

PHOTO COURTESY OF NEIL MACIEJEWSKI

Before Joan Crawford eclipsed one and all as my favorite star of all time, Diana Rigg had left an indelible impression on my being. I'd grown up watching reruns of *The Avengers* and, frankly, Diana Rigg as Mrs. Emma Peel was the Alpha and Omega to me at age eleven. Emma Peel was the first strong female role model television ever offered and on that scale, has never been bested. She could match men in brains and combat without sacrificing her cool or femininity. She was mod and sophisticated and alluring in a leather or lycra cat suit, plus arch and — well, at the time, my ideal. There was that aristocratic nose, the '60s eyeliner, the high cheekbones and creamy skin, the auburn hair and lithe, almost boyish body that nevertheless wore clothes like a model. She was haughtily dignified and yet had a touch of kinkiness in her black leather catsuits or "Emma-peelers" with holes and ropes and chains, plus she was good at everything from nuclear physics to sewing to jujitsu. Loved when she got mad and snarled at a man, her vocalizations strong, since Rigg was primarily a Shakespearean stage actress. Her allure was as intoxicating and subtle as a fine wine, her repartee and relationship with debonair partner John Steed understated and delectable like Nick and Nora Charles in *The Thin Man* — only better. Unfortunately, as much as I admire Rigg, she never equaled her role as Mrs. Emma Peel and her choices in film work strike me as curiously disappointing. A theatre animal, she returned to her roots to great acclaim. When I got into

Diana.

Joan Crawford, Rigg was supplanted on the throne, because Crawford is fascinating and supplied glamour, mystique and a strong female role model that quite blows everyone else out of the water. The more I delve into her, the more she grows in estimate.

But to compare my two divine feminist icons…

Originally, I appreciated Crawford in the mindless way I did Bette Davis without putting either actress on my list of favorites — they were both compellingly enjoyable firecrackers. Primarily I knew their latter-day work (which is the work most frequently broadcast). Of course, when *Mommie Dearest* came out and caused a scandal, I did page through it. Joan Crawford was the only one I felt sorry for, a sentiment I still hold strongly today, striking me as an incredibly vulnerable person who had been battered badly by life yet was trying hard to find love. The abuse she suffered shocked me. In any case, *They All Kissed the Bride* is the film that shed new light on her, because she was so beautiful in it with a glamour that knocked my socks off and a persona quite unlike her steelier stereotype (which I've come to reevaluate). Although I'd seen her as a young beauty in films like *Grand Hotel* and *Rain*, it had been so long ago that I'd forgotten. Curious, I sought out more of her work and shortly fell head-over-heels in love. Then I read every single book on her I could find. The woman simply does not disappoint me, as I've underscored in my other essays. With all the odds stacked against her — a childhood of immense abuse and overwork and neglect, she succeeded — going at it alone and rising like a phoenix from the ashes again and again. Even on film her vitality is stunning. Without having much education, she proved smart and savvy. She exudes an interesting mix of things including a fey, wistful, sad yet romantic spirit. Seeing her in the full glory of beauty, charm and vivacity in her youth made me recognize those qualities in the older woman when she had moved into hard-boiled roles. I understand and empathize with her struggle. Amazingly, she is the first star whose entire canon of work is watchable, even the bad films, because her presence redeems them. I think of her as a great artist whose likes we will never see again.

What do these great dames have in common? 1. Great bone structure — sculptured, almost aristocratic faces. 2. The ability to wear clothes like a model with Joan having the shapelier body; she was a dancer and more curvaceous than Diana, but both look sensational in clothes. 3. Working-class backgrounds — Joan's being an unloving, ultra-abusive one; Diana's being simply difficult. 4. An angularity about their faces (although also delicacy) and broad, though feminine, shoulders. 5. They are strong women who are often the equal of men without sacrificing their femininity. 6. Neither is huge-breasted with Joan having more than Diana, but they're no less sexy for it. 7. They exude sophistication in spite of their "peasant" backgrounds. 8. Distinctive deep voices. Actually, Crawford's voice in her youth was more high, chirpy and girlish, although she kept it in the husky lower register as she moved into film noir; that pleasant deep voice assured her transition to sound film. 8. Both smoke. 9. Rigg is tall, Crawford is small, yet both move with confidence and grace. 10. Both have a powerful presence onscreen and a crackling vitality. Their strength is inspiring.

Crawford is hard to touch, the more I get to know her. Watching her move, the way she holds her body, even the way she puts on her shoes is a treat. She embodied the Hollywood glamour fantasy through and through like no other. Sadly, stars are extinct, but even when Hollywood manufactured them, no one came close to her. Rigg is definitely a child of the sixties with a swinging sixties attitude, yet with a fascinating womanly maturity even in her youth. Both women embody my idea of the Perfect Woman and hit all my spots in a very good way.

Joan & Agatha: Two Great Artists

I'll take Joan any day. PHOTO COURTESY OF NEIL MACIEJEWSKI

Perhaps it seems that Agatha Christie and Joan Crawford have little in common besides a last name beginning with the initial "C." But, in truth, they were two of the world's most remarkable women, leaving behind a prodigious body of work spanning the 1920s through the '70s. They are the only artists whose entire body of work I enjoy, whose tenacity and distinctive mark I admire tremendously, who thrill me in fact as women/strong female role models. Both gave voice (to use that chestnut) to outsiders with Crawford's "shop-girls" slogging it out in a man's world, usually triumphing over a tide of social disfavor (like the real actress), and Christie's Hercule Poirot and Miss Marple — one a foreigner, the other elderly — dismaying detractors by proving much more than their humble exteriors convey. In the Crawford and Christie universe, there is a leveling of gender, class, and morality even while all inequities remain firmly in place. Crawford's women, like Crawford, were often self-motivated, ambitious, stylish, and savvy, using sexual allure as collateral of sorts yet retaining a certain unexpected power and virility equal to any man. They crossed respectable lines and could be tough but they were also vulnerable and human (sometimes their fatal flaw, as in *The Damned Don't Cry* and *Sudden Fear*, where both Ethel and Myra get in over their heads yet try to pull out when it's too late). Christie's underclass, her butlers and maids and chauffeurs, had as many layers, motives, desires and resentments as their "betters" and whether male or female, privileged or servant, they were interchangeable as murderers or victims,

I'll take Agatha's career any day.

their creator as indifferent as God. Because Christie and Crawford could appeal to the working-class, their work is often underrated, but remains far more sophisticated and complex than some credit. Wrongly derided as limited at times, their gifts were innate, imbued with each woman's curiosity, boldness and voracious passion. They exceeded any artist's wildest expectations in terms of success, productivity, and enduring relevance.

This book bears testament to why Crawford is queen for me, eclipsing any artist I've ever fancied and never disappointing in the least. She was most definitely a woman ahead of her time (and yet intrinsically part of her time), a continual dichotomy. Her detractors shoot themselves in the foot, because shallow stereotypes of actress and woman don't hold up under analysis. She is called phony, for instance, yet she was also real and tirelessly accessible to her public, believing she owed them all and she was nurtured in a studio system that sold fantasy. The fact that she bothered to present herself as glamorous to please that public strikes me as an asset, not a negative. She is criticized for harshness and even insipidly called a gorgon (perhaps based on Faye Dunaway's over-the-top caricature), but she was known for generosity, kindness, and softness, too, maintaining many lifelong friendships and doing much charity work without fanfare, her image continually and savvily changing to fit roles and demands of the times. Coming from an impoverished and essentially loveless family, she had to negotiate solo to survive in Hollywood. She was the moneymaker for studio, husbands and children. She was as vivacious as allegedly glacial, domestic (cooking, knitting, scrubbing her own floors often) and feminine, yet competed as well as any man. Formally under-educated yet voraciously self-educated and disciplined, she embraced people from all walks of life, as friend Carl Johnes attested. Like Christie, Crawford had all the raw material to dazzle in her craft. Fan Kellye Walker Baptiste put it beautifully: "Joan was an Aries (The First Sign of Fire) to the core. She demonstrated fierce creativity, constant passion, and she always moved forward in her life from point A to point B without distraction. She truly represented the heat, intensity and light of fire." Both Crawford and Christie continued producing into old age, their "fire" never abating.

Christie, like Crawford, belied stereotype and simplistic analysis. She created mysteries that were ambiguities upon ambiguities in a way that has never been paralleled; she, in fact, exceeded the writers who inspired her (with perhaps the exception of Sir Arthur Conan Doyle who is an equal). Her best detectives, Hercule Poirot and Miss Marple, were unassuming and underestimated, defying stereotype. In a Christie mystery, of course, nothing is ever as it appears to be, beginning with the detectives. Miss

Young Joan with the great Lon Chaney — old enough to be her dad here.

Marple is dithery and resides in a quiet English village, often knitting or observing birds (and crimes) with binoculars ("so useful!"). She can slip in anywhere and be overlooked like gas, yet she has a mind like a meat cleaver. Without agility, youth or other advantages, she succeeds where agile and youthful crime professionals fail. In one of my favorite Miss Marple mysteries, *At Bertram's Hotel*, reminiscent of *Grand Hotel*, she returns to a beloved traditional hotel, left standing "unscathed" since the war, a relic of a vanished world. Outwardly all appears unchanged and above board, yet beneath the surface it has been irrevocably corrupted. It could be a microcosm for Europe itself, for the tragedy of its ravaged glory, grandeur and achievements, for its physical and spiritual post-war scars. It also represents Miss Marple facing age, change and loss. Christie achieves this world of implication flawlessly. Miss Marple, like the older Joan Crawford, turns the expectation of age on its ear. She is one thing and the exact opposite.

People spit out the word "fifty" as if it's tuberculosis, so witness the reaction to Crawford portraying herself as sexy and desirable (gasp!) at "a certain age." It flips the wig of many that she doesn't know her age-appropriate place which apparently — for older women — is in the dustbin. Actually, the most absurd comment from one reviewer — incensed that Crawford was playing a carnival dancer in *Flamingo Road* at age forty-five (actually possibly forty-three, depending on when you believe she was born) — was that romantic partner Zachary Scott "appears about half her age" — this after said reviewer also complained Crawford was referred to as a "girl" *"at least a dozen times."* Half her age? Actually, he was thirty-five, making him eight to ten years her junior, a fact I never even noticed. Meanwhile, in *The Unknown*, a barely-out-of-her-teens Crawford is lusted after by Lon Chaney who is *seventeen years* her senior (and looks more than that), yet no one ever brings up the clear age difference. It's a non-issue. In her earlier career, in fact, Crawford's romantic leads were often notably older than her, a detail never referenced by any. Yet it causes a firestorm, apparently, when men are shown physically admiring a "middle-aged" Crawford in *any* film; it becomes pure camp. Women aren't "distinguished grays," they're "harpies." And what about the ribald contempt Crawford gets for showing shapely gams in tights and fishnets at age *sixty* (or thereabouts) in *Berserk and* pairing herself with a young stud? What's more, she has the brass balls to portray the *woman* as holding the cards, telling her eager stud she doesn't want to get involved. Snap! Snap! In *Johnny Guitar*, she completely role reverses. All the women own businesses, they even have a showdown, and Johnny Guitar (in pink) asks her plaintively if she loves him. Isn't sexual degradation fun, guys?

Miscast? Hooray for miscasting! Like Miss Marple, Crawford steps out of the expected social realm, smashing stereotypes even while playing to them. She shows women as having desire and ambition at all ages, a lust for life, as unworldly Miss Marple experiences the entire world through her village. Both women and their characters did not allow limitation of any kind to hold them back.

In *Cat Among the Pigeons*, my favorite Poirot, a few males are introduced into an all-female school. There is also Middle Eastern intrigue involving missing jewels and royalty. What I love especially is the suggestiveness of it all — men penetrating the female fortress to corrupt, the gardener distracting the school mistress as she deliberates on a worthy successor upon her retirement (a speculation cut short when one of the candidates is found dead). There is always this rocking-to-the-core of venerable British institutions, the crack in the sidewalk or stiff upper lip. Detractors claim that Christie's characters lacked depth, which I decry, but no mystery author (and I've read many of the most celebrated) crafted plots as cleverly or as enjoyably. Not only did she keep myriad histories, clues, connections and plotlines boiling, but she never dropped the ball. I tried to find loopholes, as so many of her readers did, always without success. Christie was one ahead of us. Poirot also was an eccentric — dandified, fond of growing vegetable marrows, meticulous about home and appearance as our gal Joan. Yet this little egg-shaped man with his mincing walk and waxed moustache, like Miss Marple, missed nothing and could trump the most devious criminal. In his denouements "where all was revealed," he not only told the murderer how he did it, but constructed ways and means and motives for *all* suspects to have accomplished the crime. Christie used mirrors, glass, twins, and every trick under the sun so ingeniously that she could throw her readers like a master magician.

How grateful I am to both great artists for leaving behind a legacy of supremely entertaining work — suggesting the dark vagaries of human nature without ever being blatantly crude. Both exhibited sophistication, wit and strength, both championed the underdog. Although Agatha Christie and Joan Crawford would not necessarily classify themselves as feminists, neither allowed social conventions to stand in the way of their progress and success. They broke rules and molds, defied convention even while pandering to it, and participated fully in the world, realizing their own ambitions to a degree perhaps beyond their wildest dreams. And we're all immeasurably enriched by their grand contributions. They are with few parallels. They remain, each in her own way, enigmatic.

Joan Crawford's Home Movies ...In Color!

On December 5, 2008, UCLA ran as part of its tribute to Joan Crawford a selection of her predominately *full-color*—yes, *color*—home movies that grandson Casey LaLonda unearthed in his mother's home (his mother was Cathy, one of Crawford's twins). They were tantalizing, unedited excerpts which ran about a half hour from approximately four hours of footage. One can imagine that some of that footage was scenery and doting images of Christina or other children (and naturally we fans long to see every minute). Their date range was 1939-1942 approximately. This was my best Joan Crawford experience ever, exceeding my wildest expectations. In these candid moments we see another Joan Crawford — a surprisingly natural, buoyant, sweet, playful one who was evidently happily in love and a happy new mother. She was unpretentious, warm and incredibly beautiful — moreso than the professional camera has ever captured; neither has the professional camera ever captured this side of her (how could it?). She is unguarded and free in the presence of people she obviously trusts. One such person is the mystery man named Charles McCabe whom we finally see. He is the unnamed deep love she references in her autobiography of sorts, *A Portrait of Joan*. ([He] "taught me to hunt and fish, we used to go on these expeditions with a whole group of men…I carried my own gun and my own camera, waded through streams in the vanguard; and at noon when we'd camp, I'd help fix lunch and surprise them with all sorts of snacks packed away in my knapsack just in case they didn't catch any fish. This friend introduced me to politics, to banking, big business and public affairs.") Christina also mentions him in *Mommie Dearest*, saying her mother would tear up whenever she talked about him. These clips speak volumes and help explain and fill in a few biographical mysteries.

Most special to me is that this window into Crawford actually coincides with the image I've always secretly maintained or cherished of her. We've always heard she was a star 24/7. This shows her as "a person" off-camera. It reveals the BS of the publicity machine, the BS of biographies written by people who don't know her and only rehash the BS handed down to them. She is shown having fun, *happy* times — yes, happiness and fun, not just angst and drama, as biographies paint it. There is something unguarded and innocent about her and more in keeping with the fun-loving Crawford one glimpses in her early films (a side to her that I always believed never disappeared and this confirms it). At one point, she is even walking through the woods, swinging her arms like a child (not walking at all elegantly or self-consciously). She carries a gun in one shot (the hunting trips she referred to). She's in a canoe in another scene, waving at Charles. She is walking through a beautiful forest and even peeking out at him from behind a tree and waving again. The surprising thing, too, is that he is not handsome — actually not attractive-looking at all, although she is clearly happy with him. (More on this later.) She, on the other hand — at last in *full color* — is *ravishing*. It was understandable why so many men fell in love with her. It's quite apparent he is *very* in love with her and as mesmerized as we are. She is speaking with him in some scenes, addressing the camera, her eyes very warm. At one point she is lying in the grass. It was amazing to me how truly beautiful she was — no key lights, no makeup men and yet far more beautiful than any photograph I've seen. He shot her giggling with her hands over her face, doubling over with laughter. In one shot, she throws a scarf over her head, then peers out at him with beautiful eyes. I saw an enormous natural warmth and genuine shyness (so not in keeping with the image that is continually projected of Joan Crawford). She was enchanting — yes, surprisingly so.

My favorite thing was when her hair is dyed dark for perhaps *When Ladies Meet*. (In some scenes, her hair is red.) Then she recalls some of her most goddessy photographs without effort; that look sent me to the moon! Relaxed and natural, you see her exquisite profile. You see that her eyes are deep blue and velvety, really gorgeous. He zeroes in on her face in one shot that is amazing because she's looking full at the camera and her eyes are so naked and well, sweet. She's both little girl and beautiful woman (more on my theories about this, too). At one point they decide to display a flower he obviously bought for her that she is wearing on her shoulder. His camera passes over her face in extreme close-up en route to this flower. Oh my God, forget the flower. You see the little cleft in her chin (rarely noticeable onscreen except in her very early films), all her freckles (which I love) — and skin like alabaster. She also makes a mock "professional pose," then breaks up. There are scenes of her camping and eating, completely non-glamorous and seeming not to give a damn.

For a time, I puzzled at the dichotomy between this young woman who had the beauty of a goddess (truly natural splendor), who appeared

Although this shot by Bert Six is not taken from the home movies, it is the approximate period of these films. Here, Joan relaxes in the California sunshine in her garden in Brentwood with her dachshund Pupschen. PHOTO CREDIT: BERT SIX

very unaffected, and this man who was — well, no Clark Gable and older than her. I thought, "That lucky stiff! He must've felt like he died and went to heaven to land *that* babe — a famous movie star and beautiful young woman!" Then I got it. Of course! Joan Crawford's own birth father abandoned her. She had a stepfather Cassin she called "the center of my child's world" whom she adored who also left her. She went pounding the pavements all around town to find Cassin, looking for his shoes in the crowd, and finally did locate him. He took her for an ice cream, but she never saw him again. Cassin was also alleged to have molested her at age eleven (which I have no reason to doubt). In any case, it makes sense that this Charles was perhaps a "daddy" figure, a man who was taking her fishing and canoeing and hunting. It explained why in his presence, she radiated such the little girl. It explained why the breakup of their relationship (he was married and wouldn't leave his wife for her, one assumes) devastated her so much and why she married Phil Terry — an exceedingly handsome man, ironically — on the rebound and perhaps even why she could never love Terry. It was also clear she wanted this man to love Christina as much as her. She has Christina with him in quite a few of the shots.

The scenes of her with Christina and with the first Christopher are very impressive and contrary to what is popularly depicted. Clearly Crawford really loved Christina and did channel so much of that love to her, whatever mistakes she may have made. There is footage of Christina falling asleep in her high chair, close-ups of this baby face. Footage of Christina dancing on the rooftop. Joan is also dancing around with her, laughing. We see Christina beautifully dressed at one of her elaborate birthday parties, Christina shrieking with laughter (looking very well taken care of). This is footage not for the public, but Joan's personal recording of the event. Black and white kids are at the birthday table and Joan films each one of them. Some of this was rather wrenching when we see the care Joan took to make sure everything was perfect for her little girl. Each child has a scoop of ice cream shaped like a different animal. Some kids are standing on Joan's tables. Joan and two women friends wear lookalike dresses which Joan points to and laughs at — so much for Joan not having a sense of humor. Clearly she didn't take the lookalike outfits all that seriously and realized they were campy! Never hear that in the bios, do you? In one part, Joan carries Christina into the pool and sets her carefully on the step, then brings one of her little friends and places her next to Christina. Another child is apparently eager to come in, too, so Joan puts a life vest on her and takes her into the pool, holding her the whole time. She is completely unpretentious. Christina starts to get up from the step and Joan runs over, making sure she stays on the step where she is safe and doesn't venture further into the pool. This particularly touched me, since Christina gives her mother credit for nothing — least of all for all the care that she gave. These films show that, yes, she loved this child.

Also rare is the footage of the "first" Christopher, mentioned above, a child Crawford adopted and whose mother came and claimed six months later. Crawford was devastated by this. It evidently had a deep effect on her for the rest of her life and she continued to mention "five children" even in latter day interviews. We see her feeding Christopher who is black-haired. She looks as she does in *When Ladies Meet* — that hairstyle, and again, she is beautiful, so beautiful in full color. *(Joan Crawford in color in the 1930s and 1940s!* Can you beat it?) She is feeding him a bottle and attempting to burp him, getting frustrated and shaking her head to someone off-camera as if to say that it's not going to happen. She is also kissing him. Sad.

Some impressions: I would concur with Jeanine Basinger who said she never believed Crawford had any trouble knowing the difference between her screen image and real life. All that crap about Crawford playing the star 24/7 and going to the bathroom even as a star is just that - crap. My own theory is that Crawford dressed for her fans as part of her job and had definite shyness (which she herself admitted), evident here. She was not always herself for the press; in taped interviews I have, there is a marked difference between how she talks to interviewers who are friends and those who are not. She obviously presented glamour, whenever possible, and was somewhat trapped by her efforts to live up to this image, not wanting to go out much except to Club 21 in later years (when it was all on the wane — a difficult time). But, in private life among people she trusted, these films copiously display a very unpretentious, natural side that found its release, too.

It was rewarding to me to see Crawford so happy. It made me realize how, in spite of all the suffering she went through, she definitely had times of joy. I could now imagine the good times she had with Franchot Tone in Canada, when he read Shakespeare to her and took her on the lake just as Charles did. It made me recognize a more fully-rounded portrait of Crawford. It is a rare opportunity for we fans to see her as a human being, quite apart from the movie star — living her own life.

Joan simply does not disappoint.

And the upshot is that if I was in love with Joan Crawford before, I'm a thousand fold more in love with her now! She was warm, sweet, unpretentious, charming, full of life and fun, at a positive point and time in her life — and a knockout! (Oh — there is a sunbathing scene where one sees her lying face down on a towel on the roof and, yes, she is nude — but it is tasteful. Charles, who was filming evidently, never zeroes in on anything and she keeps a towel modestly around her top and bottom when she is sitting up. You only see the back of her and her backside as she lies there. Her body is beautiful — like marble and not an ounce of fat.)

Thank you, UCLA! Thank you, Casey! Thank you, Joan gods — and anyone else who made this happen! It was deeply thrilling and memorable. If Joan Crawford had never been a star, she would still completely enthrall, based on these movies. Her allure and magnetism was manifold. It's why, with all the deck stacked against her, she shot up to the pinnacle of stardom.

The Films

"Joan Crawford was one one of the people that made Hollywood the place that touched the imagination of the world."
George Cukor

PHOTO COURTESY OF JERRY MURBACH

Master List of Films with Selected Stats

MGM

Lady of the Night (1925)
Pretty Ladies (1925)
Old Clothes (1925)
The Only Thing (1925)
Sally, Irene and Mary (1925)
Paris (1926)
The Boob (1926)
Winners of the Wilderness (1927)
The Taxi Dancer (1927)
The Understanding Heart (1927)
The Unknown (1927)
Twelve Miles Out (1927)
Spring Fever (1927)
West Point (1928)
The Law of the Range (1928)
Rose-Marie (1928)
Across to Singapore (1928)
Four Walls (1928)
Our Dancing Daughters (1928)
Dream of Love (1928)
The Duke Steps Out (1929)
Hollywood Revue of 1929 (1929)
Our Modern Maidens (1929)
Untamed (1929)
Montana Moon (1930)
Our Blushing Brides (1930)
Paid (1930)
Dance, Fools Dance (1930)

Laughing Sinners (1931)
This Modern Age (1931)
Possessed (1931)
Grand Hotel (1932)
Letty Lynton (1932)
Today We Live (1933)
Dancing Lady (1933)
Sadie McKee (1934)
Chained (1934)
Forsaking All Others (1934)
No More Ladies (1935)
I Live My Life (1935)
The Gorgeous Hussy (1936)
Love on the Run (1936)
The Last of Mrs. Cheyney (1937)
The Bride Wore Red (1937)
Mannequin (1938)
The Shining Hour (1938)
Ice Follies of 1939 (1939)
The Women (1939)
Strange Cargo (1940)
Susan and God (1940)
A Woman's Face (1941)
When Ladies Meet (1941)
Reunion in France (1942)
Above Suspicion (1943)
Torch Song (1953)

Costumes/Wardrobe: All of the MGM films featured costumes by Adrian with the following exceptions: Andre-ani *(The Taxi Dancer; The Understanding Heart)*, Gilbert Clark *(West Point)*, Lucia Coulter *(Winners of the Wilderness; The Unknown; The Law of the Range)*, David Cox *(Spring Fever; Rose-Marie; Across to Singapore; Four Walls; Our Dancing Daughters; The Duke Steps Out; Hollywood Revue of 1929)*, Erte *(Sally, Irene and Mary; Paris; Hollywood Revue of 1929)*, Irene *(Reunion in France)*, Rene Hubert *(Twelve Miles Out)*, David Mir *(The Only Thing)*, Helen Rose *(Torch Song)*, Gile Steele *(Above Suspicion)*, Unspecified *(Lady of the Night; Pretty Ladies; Old Clothes; The Boob)*.

Filming *Grand Hotel*.

Directors: Dorothy Arzner *(The Bride Wore Red)*, Harry Beaumont *(Hollywood Review of 1929; Dance Fools Dance; Laughing Sinners; Our Blushing Brides; Our Dancing Daughters)*, Monta Bell *(Lady of the Night; Pretty Ladies)*, Richard Boleslawski *(The Last of Mrs. Cheyney)*, Frank Borzage *(Mannequin; Shining Hour; Strange Cargo)*, Clarence Brown *(Chained; The Gorgeous Hussy; Letty Lynton; Possessed; Sadie McKee)*, Tod Browning *(The Unknown)*, Eddie Cline *(Old Clothes)*, Jack Conway *(The Only Thing; Our Modern Maidens; Twelve Miles Out; Understanding Heart; Untamed)*, James Cruze *(The Duke Steps Out)*, George Cukor *(No More*

Ladies; Susan and God; A Woman's Face; The Women), Jules Dassin *(Reunion in France)*, Edmund Goulding *(Grand Hotel; Paris; Sally, Irene and Mary)*, Edward H. Griffith *(No More Ladies)*, Nicholas Grinde *(This Modern Age)*, Howard Hawks *(Today We Live)*, Lucien Hubbard *(Rose-Marie)*, Robert Z. Leonard and Orville O. Dull *(When Ladies Meet)*, Harry Millarde *(The Taxi Dancer)*, Fred Niblo *(Dream of Love)*, William Nigh *(Across to Singapore; Four Walls; Law of the Range)*, Charles Reisner *(Hollywood Revue of 1929)*, Reinhold Schunzel *(Ice Follies of 1939)*, Edward Sedgwick *(Spring Fever; West Point)*, Malcolm St. Clair *(Montana Moon)*, Richard Thorpe *(Above Suspicion)*, W.S. Van Dyke *(Forsaking All Others; I Live My Life; Love on the Run; Winners of the Wilderness)*, Charles Walters *(Torch Song)*, William A. Wellman *(The Boob)*, Sam Wood *(Paid)*.

Producers: Harry Beaumont *(Our Blushing Brides)*, Henry Berman *(Torch Song)*, Paul Bern *(Grand Hotel)*, Frank Borzage *(Mannequin; The Shining Hour; Strange Cargo)*, Clarence Brown *(Chained; The Gorgeous Hussy; Possessed)*, Jack Conway *(Our Modern Maidens)*, Jackie Coogan Sr. *(Old Clothes)*, William Cowan *(Law of the Range)*, James Cruze *(The Duke Steps Out)*, Orville O. Dull *(When Ladies Meet)*, Sidney Franklin, Jr. *(Torch Song)*, Leon Gordon *(Above Suspicion)*, Edward Griffith *(No More Ladies)*, Howard Hawks *(Today We Live)*, Bernard H. Hyman *(Forsaking All Others; I Live My Life)*, Robert Z. Leonard *(When Ladies Meet)*, Joseph Mankiewicz *(The Bride Wore Red; The Gorgeous Hussy; Love on the Run; Mannequin; Reunion in France; The Shining Hour; Strange Cargo)*, William Nigh *(Across to Singapore)*, Harry Rapf *(Ice Follies of 1939; Possessed)*, Malcolm St. Clair *(Montana Moon)*, Victor Saville *(Above Suspicion; A Woman's Face)*, David O. Selznick *(Dancing Lady)*, Hunt Stromberg *(Chained; Letty Lynton; Our Dancing Daughters; Our Modern Maidens; Susan and God; The Women)*, Irving Thalberg *(Grand Hotel; Hollywood Revue of 1929; Letty Lynton; No More Ladies; Possessed; Twelve Miles Out)*, W.S. Van Dyke *(Love on the Run)*. Lawrence Weingarten *(The Last of Mrs. Cheyney; Sadie McKee)*, Sam Wood *(Paid)*.

First National

Tramp, Tramp, Tramp (1926)

Director: Harry Edwards
Producer: Harry Langdon

United Artists

Rain (1932)
The Caretakers (1963)

Costumes/Wardrobe: Moss Mabry *(The Caretakers)*, Unspecified *(Rain)*.
Director and Producer: Hall Bartlett *(The Caretakers)*, Lewis Milestone *(Rain)*.
Producer: Joseph M. Schenck *(Rain)*.

On the set of *Esther Costello*. PHOTO COURTESY OF THEO POUROS

Columbia

They All Kissed the Bride (1942)
Harriet Craig (1950)
Queen Bee (1955)
Autumn Leaves (1956)
The Story of Esther Costello (1957)
Strait-Jacket (1964)
Berserk (1968)

Costumes/Wardrobe: Irene *(They All Kissed the Bride; Berserk)*, Jean Louis *(Queen Bee; Autumn Leaves; The Story of Esther Costello)*; Sheila O'Brien *(Harriet Craig)*, Jay Hutchinson Scott *(Berserk)*, Unspecified *(Strait-Jacket)*.

Director: Robert Aldrich *(Autumn Leaves)*, William Castle *(Strait-Jacket)*, Alexander Hall *(They All Kissed the Bride)*, Ranald MacDougall *(Queen Bee)*, David Miller *(The Story of Esther Costello)*, Jim O'Connolly *(Berserk)*, Vincent Sherman *(Harriet Craig)*.

Producer: William Castle *(Strait-Jacket)*, Herman Cohen *(Berserk)*, William Dozier *(Harriet Craig)*, William Goetz *(Autumn Leaves)*, Edward Kaufman *(They All Kissed the Bride)*, David Miller *(The Story of Esther Costello)*, Jerry Wald *(Queen Bee)*.

Warner Brothers

Hollywood Canteen (1944)
Mildred Pierce (1945)
Humoresque (1946)
Possessed (1947)
Flamingo Road (1949)
It's a Great Feeling (1949)
The Damned Don't Cry (1950)
Goodbye, My Fancy (1951)
This Woman is Dangerous (1952)
Whatever Happened to Baby Jane (1962)
Trog (1970)

Costumes/Wardrobe: Adrian *(Humoresque; Possessed)*, Milo Anderson *(Hollywood Canteen; Mildred Pierce)*, Norma Koch *(Whatever Happened to Baby Jane)*, Sheila O'Brien *(Flamingo Road; The Damned Don't Cry; Goodbye, My Fancy; This Woman is Dangerous)*, Unspecified *(Trog)*.

Director: Robert Aldrich *(Whatever Happened to Baby Jane)*, David Butler *(It's a Great Feeling)*, Michael Curtiz *(Flamingo Road; Mildred Pierce)*, Delmer Daves *(Hollywood Canteen)*, Felix Feist *(This Woman is Dangerous)*, Freddie Francis *(Trog)*, Curtis Bernhardt *(Possessed)*, Jean Negulesco *(Humoresque)*, Vincent Sherman *(The Damned Don't Cry; Goodbye, My Fancy)*.

Producer: Robert Aldrich *(Whatever Happened to Baby Jane)*, Henry Blanke *(Goodbye My Fancy)*, Herman Cohen *(Trog)*, Alex Gottlieb *(Hollywood Canteen, It's a Great Feeling)*, Robert Sisk *(This Woman is Dangerous)*, Jerry Wald *(The Damned Don't Cry; Flamingo Road; Humoresque; Mildred Pierce, Possessed)*, Jack Warner *(Hollywood Canteen)*.

20th Century-Fox

Daisy Kenyon (1947)

Costumes/Wardrobe: Charles LeMaire
Director and Producer: Otto Preminger

The Best of Everything (1959)

Costumes/Wardrobe: Adele Palmer
Director: Jean Negulesco
Producer: Jerry Wald

RKO

Sudden Fear (1952)

Costumes/Wardrobe: Sheila O'Brien (Howard Greer, lingerie)
Director: David Miller
Producer: Joseph Kaufman

Republic

Johnny Guitar (1954)

Costumes/Wardrobe: Sheila O'Brien
Director: Nicholas Ray
Producer: Herbert J. Yates

Universal-International

Female on the Beach (1955)

Costumes/Wardrobe: Sheila O'Brien
Director: Joseph Pevney
Producer: Albert Zugsmith

Universal

I Saw What You Did (1965)

Director and Producer: William Castle

Films of the Twenties

Films Unavailable For Review

Old Clothes (1925)
The Circle (1925)*
Sally, Irene and Mary (1925)
Proud Flesh (1925)
A Slave of Fashion (1925)
The Merry Widow (1925)
The Midshipman (1925)
The Only Thing (1925)
Paris (1926)

The Taxi Dancer (1927)
The Understanding Heart (1927)
The Law of the Range (1928)
Rose-Marie (1928)
Four Walls (1928)
Dream of Love (1928)
The Duke Steps Out (1929)
Tide of Empire (1929)
Great Day (1930)**

* Not available at time of press. ** Never completed.

A beauteous, young Crawford with John Gilbert in *Four Walls*. PHOTO COURTESY OF NEIL MACIEJEWSKI

***Lady of the Night* (1925)** ★★★★

In *Lady of the Night,* Norma Shearer, the darling of Irving Thalberg at MGM, was given the opportunity for a tour de force, playing two women from dramatically different worlds who fall in love with the same man. The theme might be pedestrian (and is anything really new?), but this is a remarkable silent film for a number of reasons. One is that it has been gorgeously restored with a shockingly nearly pristine print, beautiful piano accompaniment by Jon Mirsalis, and scenes wonderfully colored either pink, blue, or sepia/orange-toned. For another, this is the "debut" of Joan Crawford, but unfortunately, she only plays the "back" of Shearer in scenes in which both women appear on camera at the same time, a fact which apparently and understandably rankled her. There are a few instances in which a split screen was used and Shearer does play alongside herself in those scenes, but, otherwise, back shots later in the film are of Crawford and, in one scene in which the two women share a cab, Crawford's face in profile is clearly seen for some moments.

Beyond all that, there is Shearer, who is remarkable in her dual role and clearly favored by Thalberg who gave her this loving showcase when another actress might've easily played one of the parts, identical appearance not intrinsic to the plot. Having seen little of Shearer's work, I was deeply impressed. She is very young and quite lovely here, resembling Sarah Jessica Parker or Glenn Close, but with her own unique look. She is most interesting as the woman from the wrong side of the tracks, Molly Helmer, surprisingly contemporary in appearance and with a fabulous Bohemian sense of style, occasionally recalling Madonna with her dramatic eye makeup and beauty marks. The fashions were outstanding from the beautiful dresses of Shearer's wealthy half, Florence Banning (motherless daughter of a judge), to the detailed outfits worn by Molly and friends, including their snazzy shoes, one scene showing in close-up Molly's knickers and stockings as she kicks a fresh guy in the shins. The sets by Cedric Gibbons, in fact, are gorgeous and so are the street scenes where horse and buggy carriages still traversed dirt roads, this period in history being not far removed from the 1800s. Remarkable shots include the opening sequence showing Molly as a baby visited by her convict father where her tiny baby's hand rests between his large handcuffed ones and "18 years later" Molly admiring her reflection in a horse-drawn hearse.

Molly is the longtime girlfriend of the goofy "Chunky" Dunn (George

Note: all of the film reviews in this section are in a range of five stars.

K. Arthur), Prince of Fashion. When she meets handsome Dave Page (Malcolm McGregor) in a dance hall, she quickly falls in love and soon has him over for dinner. Dave, as it turns out, is an inventor (yes, that feeling of burgeoning industry that permeated many silents as America blossomed industrially) and has a brainstorm that he shares with her, hoping he might use it in the world of crime. But Molly, who, for all her gum-chewing and eccentric attire, is a decent, heartfelt girl, convinces him to take his idea to bankers, not hoods, which he does. Unsurprisingly, he impresses Judge Banning, the father of Florence, with his invention, and meets the fair daughter by chance. As "Chunky" cynically predicts, Dave will give Molly "the gate" when he has the judge's daughter as a prospect. And Dave does fall for Florence without much thought at all for Molly's feelings, soon seeing his new sweetheart incessantly. The two women later cross paths, meeting at Dave's apartment, and Florence, observing Molly, says after she leaves, "She loves you, David. I could see it in her face." He pooh-poohs it, claiming to have never loved Molly, unaware that she is listening, crushed, on the other side of the door. That same night the rivals share a cab (Crawford's moment to appear onscreen and a great irony, since Shearer would become her own rival at MGM) and Molly heroically gives up Dave to Florence, resigning herself to a life with longtime beau Chunky whom she clearly doesn't love passionately.

Once again, I'm reminded that silent films could be a superb and unique art form, parallel to great ballets and opera. The depth of emotion and expression is incredible and rarely seen onscreen today. Shearer is luminous, far more interesting and multi-dimensional as Molly, yet unfortunately would be typecast in the "saintly" good woman roles that Florence represents throughout her career. She makes Molly's heartbreak palpable and one can appreciate how actors learned to convey so much through body language, lessons Crawford absorbed, dedicated and quick study that she was. Shearer walks with defeat in this film the way Crawford would several years later in *The Unknown*. Also interesting and odd in this film are the "product placements," ostensibly not intended as such, but no less fascinating, such as when Molly opens up a cupboard in Dave's apartment and one sees Kellogg's toasted cornflakes! Another interesting segment is when Chunky looks at an ad for the best-dressed man in the world, who is the Prince of Wales, and he bears a striking resemblance to the current prince, Princess Diana's son William. There are also some fun lines such as when Molly's friend says, "Well, ta ta, dearie, we're entertaining some shy sheiks from Cheyenne."

Thrilling restoration of *Lady of the Night*, a film that still looks shockingly modern and contains an eloquent illustration of Shearer's talent.

Pretty Ladies (1925) ★★★★

Pretty Ladies is surprisingly pleasant viewing, full of eye candy, with a simple plotline based on Adela Rogers St. Johns' story "Maggie Quinanne." It's a silent film and the bootleg print I acquired was completely devoid of even a score, so it was truly a silent film experience. It involves a female comic, Maggie Keenan (ZaSu Pitts, her rueful clown reminiscent of Giulietta Masina), who works in the Follies, along with an entire chorus line of showgirls. Among these girls are a very young Joan Crawford (still Lucille LeSueur) and Myrna Loy. Crawford, at least, is prominent in many scenes and even has some subtitled lines and a few close-ups. A malicious "pretty lady" Selmar Larson (Lilyan Tashman) is upset with Maggie, whose comedy is crabbing her applause, and vows to get even. She finds her chance when desperately lonely Maggie — always left out of the gay revelry and lovemaking the other girls enjoy after the show — finally meets a prospect by falling into the orchestra pit and smashing his drum. The opening scene, in fact, shows the musicians playing cards backstage at the Follies until a light signals them it's time to go on. Aloysius "Al" Cassidy (Tom Moore), the drummer, is shown banging out what appears to be a jazzy tune. When Maggie buys Al a new drum and he in turn writes "The House Fly Blues" for her, a number that brings Maggie to everyone's attention, man killer Selmar wastes no time in seducing him. The archetypes are none too subtle, but it doesn't matter, because it almost works like a ballet — all sets, operatic emotions and striking visuals, including a winter production with snow. (Crawford and Loy as "snowflakes" were covered with marabou, according to Loy, which kept getting in their mouths.)

Although obviously film was still in its infancy, the lushness of the sets, costumes and the imaginative shots are extremely impressive. The dance numbers are delightful chorus line extravaganzas with nifty, little steps and kicking legs, plus those coy touches that were so popular in the '20s and '30s — in one instance, the girls point at the audience simultaneously. Striking shots include the shadows of the girls running up the spiral staircase reflected on a wall and on the face of a watching man. I couldn't help thinking how much fun it would've been to be in that chorus at that age. Crawford, only nineteen years old, however, was evidently having a less happy experience, according to Myrna Loy in her autobiography, *Being and Becoming*, due to all the lecherous men who were chasing the shapely chorine around their desks. As the chattering girls sit at their dressing tables (another great shot), one can see Crawford (Lucille) clearly for the first time (but certainly not the last). She is fresh-faced and beautiful, already a vibrant presence, and in a later scene, it's apparent how much heavier she was at this age. For those who say she became more beautiful as her star ascended (which it did quite rapidly), I'd contest that she was actually lovely (and so much more natural) from the start. Also amusing are the little touches of character, such as the showgirl with the baby at

A young Joan Crawford's big scene with ZaSu Pitts. This wig seems to have resurfaced on Crawford in *Winners of the Wilderness.*

her feet (and the shots of showgirl legs under the dressing tables), the girls "breaking character" off-stage.

The messages can cause a groan, hinting as they do that masochism is an inherent part of female sexuality (that dangerous load of hay) with Maggie singing, "I want a man, anyone at all — To kiss me, and miss me, To beat me and cheat me…" Is it better to be beaten or to take anyone rather than be alone? (Imagine lyrics sung by a man, professing that he wants a girlfriend who beats him!) Later, Crawford, in her white wig and Minuet costume, flounces down on a chair in Maggie's dressing room to complain about man trouble. She keeps her eyes downward through so much of the scene that, at one point, I thought she was sleeping! Maggie goes home to a loveless house at that point, but apparently lives in luxury with servants, an incredible balcony overlooking a New York City skyline that looks more like a Bavarian fairytale, and sumptuous living room. She fantasizes that her ideal man joins her for dinner since even her servants are canoodling in her absence (is love everywhere?). This "ideal" fantasy man must be bodily moved when Al takes his place at her table.

Some of the corny, but fun humor includes lines like "What do you think of that? He beat it!" to which the response is, "Sure, he's a drummer." And my favorite (straight out of vaudeville): "Just a lot of applesauce, dearie!" The most hilarious part comes when Maggie performs "The House Fly Blues," a really fun number where the dancers are "miniaturized" on a giant set and Maggie is dressed as a house fly, replete with fuzzy and awkward fly legs, two of them sticking out at front and impeding her arms. A man in the wings (no pun intended) remarks on what a "wonder" she is (I'll say!) and his pretty wife (why do they always stick these pretty, young things with forbidding old geysers?) remarks, "Why didn't you marry her instead of me?" "It never occurred to me," he responds, which sends his sexy, young wife into a snit. Meanwhile, the camera cuts to the object of his fascination — Maggie, stuck in this unwieldy fly suit, doing an inane and obviously impromptu dance. Even better is when you see poor Maggie/ZaSu — the human fly — trying to navigate the spiral staircase.

Pretty Ladies is a winner — visually a treat and quite enjoyable. It gives a small window into several vanished worlds like "old New York" (in a painfully obvious backdrop of its streets, still looking distinctly 1800s, during a "street car" scene and a shot of a virtually unrecognizable Times Square) and vaudeville (the grand theater where "The Follies" perform.) Maggie marries Al and has a tyke of her own (again living in a sumptuous apartment with fireplace and sky-high ceilings), but hubby cheats with the seductive Selmar. Sadly, at the end, Maggie (still suffering from poor self-esteem) looks upon her sleeping husband and baby and prays he won't do it again — a happy ending of sorts, if pathetic. This heavy-handed sentiment only becomes part of the film's charm, however. It's a fairytale, basically splendid with a few morals thrown in.

Tramp, Tramp, Tramp (1926) ★★★

Tramp, Tramp, Tramp starring Harry Langdon is a silent film and really looks like one with chalky made-up actors of both sexes and speeded-up movements a la "The Keystone Kops." Some of the sepia-tone frames recall Dorothea Lange's affecting portraits of Dust Bowl America depicting salt-of-the-earth people, clapboard houses and dirt streets. There's a feeling of burgeoning industry in it. It's amazing how much progress studios like MGM made in only a few short years with motion pictures, their beautiful cinematography, chic costumes and tony worlds a great contrast to these more primitive yet evocative pantomimes. Steven J. Ross in *Working-Class Hollywood: Silent Film and the Shaping of Class in America* describes how a working-class film movement tuned to proletarian concerns rose in the silent era and gave way under pressure to lavish fantasy films that appealed to people's dreams of luxury and upward mobility. Interestingly, *Tramp, Tramp, Tramp* and Langdon's doleful "little man" character seems geared to both "have-nots" and advancement with the child-like underdog winning his dream girl (a shoe tycoon's daughter, Betty Burton, played by Joan Crawford) plus the necessary money for his boot maker father's rent.

Langdon is sometimes referred to as the "fourth clown" with the heralded top three being Charlie Chaplin, Harold Lloyd and Buster Keaton and also is reminiscent of British comedian Mr. Bean (Rowan Atkinson), who relies much on pantomime, and Stan Laurel of Oliver and Hardy. They all follow in the lines of traditional clowning. Langdon's makeup could be defined as "hobo/tramp" with solid skin base and simply-accented eyes and mouth, a modified version of the Auguste clown. Historian Kevin Brownlow said, "Langdon's character stared at the world like a startled white mouse." This "fourth clown" had a short-lived career, spiraling downwards after he dismissed director Frank Capra and went out on his own. Not having seen much of Langdon's work, any judgment I make might be premature. But, based only on this film, I wouldn't rank him as quite in the league of the other three heavyweights. He is undeniably talented and a first-class mime, but to my mind, an acquired taste without Chaplin's charm and subtlety, Keaton's brilliant acrobatics and psychological insight, and Lloyd's daring. Or maybe I just don't like virtually sexless and dim-wittedness, preferring wilier approaches. But he definitely might have been a contender.

The plot concerns Harry Logan (Langdon) entering into a cross-country walking race, hoping to win the $25,000 prize money to help his crippled, elderly boot maker father (Alec B. Francis) pay the rent, as mentioned above. Harry is also obsessed with Betty (Crawford), the daughter of the shoe tycoon sponsoring the contest whose face adorns billboards enigmatically. It is Burton Shoes, in fact, that is the cause of his father's financial problems, since the small business man cannot compete with the big manufacturers whose sales are bolstered by advertisements such as the one Betty graces. Harry, vowing to get his father the money "in three months if it takes me a year," will be up against Nick Kargas (Tom Murry), their landlord and the "champion walker of the world." He tells Nick, "I'm so crazy about that girl, I'm crazy" and Nick responds, "If you show me that billboard again, I'll break it over your head!" At the barbecue sponsored by Burton Shoes, for which the entire town turns out in support of the walkers, Betty lays eyes on Harry for the first time as he is mistakenly introduced as the world-class walker. She comes upon him moments later eyeing her billboard longingly and the pantomime Langdon does when he sees her in the flesh is quite funny. (According to Frank Capra, Crawford couldn't film her scenes with Langdon without collapsing into laughter, so their big scene together had to be shot with her back to the camera.) The pretty maid convinces him to walk in the race and now he has extra motivation to join.

During the race, numerous obstacles come up for the little clown, including a late start, a herd of sheep that he becomes caught up in (a similar and much more hilarious scene exists in Evelyn Waugh's *Scoop* where the hero is besieged by lowing cows), a steep precipice that he sleds down, and sentencing to a chain gang for stealing food. The gags steadily escalate, capping in a spectacular whirlwind finale where a cyclone blows into town and Langdon must rescue his damsel-in-distress dream girl as buildings collapse around them. (Crawford is very cute in that scene, her hair blowing back as she calls Harry from the second-floor window.) He manages to get through it all and claim his two prizes — the money and the hand of the fair Betty.

As one absurd thing happens after the next, it's hard not to laugh out loud at times, but some gags go on far too long and, rather than building momentum as many of them do, tend to lose steam. Still, there are a few wonderful bits. My favorite is when Harry tries to escape with the chain gang on a train. As the train is moving and all the other prisoners have hopped onto it, he throws his ball into a car and then tries to jump on, but the car unhooks from the one in front of it and he's left hopping along on one foot in mad pursuit as his chain is drug by the train. The entire sequence is hilarious.

Crawford in this early role is adorable, and a worthy object of any admirer's devotion. She has a wonderfully expressive face and love her page boy, cloche hat and white Mary Jane heels. She makes the most of a relatively small role and her presence pervades the film as it does Harry's consciousness even when she's not onscreen via news reel, billboards and photos. As silents go, this was a great experience for her, giving her a chance to do something close to a Keystone comedy and play against a well-regarded clown. One can see her laughing occasionally (such as when Harry carries her through a cyclone) which is very charming. Another interesting note is that Langdon does a bit as "baby Harry" that Crawford would do four years later in a drunk scene of *Montana Moon* — perhaps coincidence, perhaps imitation as the sincerest form of flattery.

Overall, *Tramp, Tramp, Tramp* is a fairly witty showcase for Langdon with a good, though small role for ingénue Joan, but not one of the best silents or comedies I have seen. Since a movement is afoot to rescue Langdon from obscurity and gain recognition for his work, it is a definite must for his fans — and Crawford completists.

The Boob (1926) ★★½

The Boob isn't a great film and the chances I'd be watching it if Joan Crawford weren't in it are slim, yet it has its own eccentric charm just the same with an oddball cast of characters and even a few nifty (for the time) special effects. If not for the appearance of Crawford, one of the only members of the cast who became a major film star after talkies got underway, this silent film might have lapsed into complete obscurity, never to be aired on Turner Classic Movies even, or worse, it might have suffered the fate of all too many silent films and been lost or destroyed, turned to dust. Luckily, it survived and may strike more than a few viewers as a pleasant surprise.

The basic premise is simple. Peter Good (George K. Arthur) is a farm hand in love with Amy (the pretty Gertrude Olmstead) who has taken up with an oily city slicker, Harry (Antonio D'Alay of the beautiful eyes). He watches them kissing on a swing and fears that he doesn't have what it takes to win back his childhood sweetheart who is planning to marry Harry. When his attempt to impress as a cowboy fails, Peter decides to become a prohibition agent and discover whether Harry is a private detective or a bootlegger. He is given the idea by Cactus Jim (Charles Murray), an annoying, overblown comic wearing Texas Ranger get-up and a handlebar moustache. The comedy here is broad and the characters even broader, yet that very peculiarity grows on you as the film goes on. Harry plans to take Amy to the Booklovers Club which might be a roadhouse and front for the bootlegging operation.

In one of the best scenes, Amy (with fetching curls in an upsweep) is having dinner with Harry at the Booklovers Club and notices that all the spines of the books bear the names of liquor. She says, "I've never been to a place like this before." Sure enough, the books are actually flasks in disguise and people choose books and pour liquor from them

Secret agent girl.

into glasses. On hand among the revelers is rotund comedienne Babe London (who once played Oliver Hardy's wife). The roadhouse actually provides imaginative fun. Dancing girls are stripped to their long, frilly underwear when a man manipulates a coat rack. Later a very enjoyable tango is performed, although it depicts a violent love affair with the woman being treated roughly as part of the dance, requiring incredibly fast footwork. Amy is delighted by it all and claps gleefully. Joan Crawford is introduced as "Jane, one of Uncle Sam's crack revenue agents" who is "getting the lowdown on the Fount of Knowledge." She is seated at a table, looking suitably mysterious and definitely projecting a certain charisma. Although quite unrecognizable from the Joan Crawford most know, her face is startlingly beautiful, her profile stunning and, with the smaller lips of the '20s, one notices what a pretty chin she had. She looks great with the thinner eyebrows and has a more voluptuous body, this being before she slimmed down considerably. One thing that always strikes me about her early films is the way she moves. Throughout her career she always carried herself with elegance and panache, but in these early films, there was a certain drama and quickness and sensuality about the way she carried herself and moved. Her strides are feminine and dramatic and she appears tall and stately, amazing when she was actually small.

In any case, Jane wonders if Peter is an agent on the case like her as they are both after the same quarry (Harry), but for different reasons. A chase scene ensues with Peter's friend, a little black boy named Ham Bunn, in pursuit on a mule with dog Benzine, plus Cactus Jim, and the nefarious Harry and his bootlegging cronies in a fast roadster with the fair Amy. There's also a wonderful, touching scene at a Home for Impoverished Women, dream sequences and a picture that comes to life.

Not a great film and, again, I would probably not seek it out if not for Crawford's appearance, but it has its quirky charms. One of my favorite lines is when Cactus Jim says of Harry, "Oughta make him drink his own likker!"

Winners of the Wilderness (1927) ★ ★ ½ *(ten stars for Joan's beauty)*

Winners of the Wilderness, a silent, allegedly tells the story of the French and Indian wars, namely General Edward Braddock's failed attempt to capture the French Fort Duquesne in the summer of 1755. Although creaky and only available in snowy bootleg print, it's a tragedy that more of these obscure films can't be restored and preserved, since they truly are gems and a unique art form. In this case, the Indians are played by real

Cherokees (although I would have no problem if they had been played by whites, as they sometimes were at that juncture; that's why they call it acting — people pretend to be what they are not and having pioneered the film business, whites originally dominated it). There's something fascinating about seeing the battles reconstructed and certain shots — such as when the camera pans a line of Indians with rifles raised — are

The young beauty with William McCoy. PHOTO COURTESY OF NEIL MACIEJEWSKI

very effective. William McCoy plays Colonel O'Hara, the hero who romances General Contrecoeur's daughter Rene (a young and beautiful Joan Crawford). McCoy apparently worked on a Wyoming ranch, became an expert horseman and roper, and developed a keen knowledge of the ways and language of Indian tribes in his area. He brought real Indians to work as extras in his Westerns, as is the case here.

Disguised as a bandit, O'Hara breaks into Rene's bedroom as she is being attended on by her maid Mimi (Louise Lorraine) and appreciatively watches her before he is noticed. A very erotic flirtation begins between them. It's an amazing scene (and one rues it isn't restored to full clarity), since Crawford is in a white wig and looks absolutely stunning. She is also in a shockingly low cut dress and gives O'Hara a provocative eye, lifting her chin, before drawing her shawl around her. When O'Hara pulls out a gun and tells her to say she is alone as her father bangs on the door, she defies him and announces O'Hara's presence. He laughs and says it would be an honor to die for such a courageous and beautiful woman. (Ironic that Crawford is called a "woman" in these films when she is clearly still a girl and no one squawks yet when referred to as a "girl" in films when she is clearly mature, people have conniptions). O'Hara manages an escape

With her masked paramour (Tim McCoy). She is possibly wearing same wig from *Pretty Ladies*.

and later tussles with and spares an Indian's life, asking that the "red man" not forget.

The costumes and period details are good. Minuets are featured with everyone in white wigs. The battle is fairly visually impressive and one title card has General Braddock's "exact words": "The Indians may constitute a menace to his raw Colonials, but they can avail nothing against the King's Regulars." Unfortunately, the military riding on horses into battle are actually going to their doom, because this would be known as "Braddock's Defeat," a massacre. Braddock is felled on the field. O'Hara dons the uniform of one French man (making the switcheroo behind a bush, that old chestnut) and is able to escape in their ranks. He manages to find Rene on the balcony of the Fort Duquesne ball and by his ring, she recognizes that he is the bandit. Crawford is, again, amazingly beautiful, her eyes almost velvety. She is clearly very young and perhaps at her most exquisite. She gives everything a palpable sexual undercurrent and yet is sweet and dainty. When soldiers come onto the balcony to enquire if O'Hara has been there, she denies his presence, although he is near her in an alcove, kissing her wrist. He wonders why she spared him, which might be considered treason, and believes she loves him.

As always, Crawford is a male magnet and my own sentiments are echoed by one soldier who rhapsodizes, "His daughter is exquisite" when his mind is supposed to be on the general. Unfortunately, she is paired with McCoy who is fifteen years her senior and looks even more than that, which makes the coupling incongruous. (What would this girl see in him?) McCoy is given the chance to do a lot of swashbuckling and derring-do as he escapes his pursuers (the French and Indians both) while Crawford is a perfect "fair damsel" who is spirited yet actually swoons in a dead faint in one scene. Can you get any more feminine than that? Lawrence Quirk's *The Films of Joan Crawford* mentions a plot contrivance of Rene being captured by Indians and rescued, but no footage of that kind existed in the version I saw, if it ever did.

Ultimately O'Hara is captured and put to the firing squad in front of Indians, but "red man never forgets" and his life is spared by Potomac (Chief John Big Tree). (There is a moving scene when the white man shakes hands with the red man; it actually brought a lump to my throat.) Prior to his alleged execution, however, O'Hara is given a few moments alone with Rene after she begs her father to spare him and a true highlight is their close-up. Again Crawford is almost ethereally beautiful. Her eyes are so dreamy and lush, they almost don't look real and her face so delicately sculpted. Yes, they had faces then. The kiss between her and O'Hara is far more erotic than if it had been spelled out as in a contemporary film. Here the focus is on the ardor of their expressions as their lips are about to meet, the close-up prolonged and incredible.

Needless to say, the hero and heroine ride off to happiness, making an eccentric escape with a lot of acrobatics on O'Hara's part (or is it a stand-in?), and prepare to marry. Even Rene's maid finds her old flame whom she believed felled in the massacre. "You can't marry this woman," O'Hara is told, "she's an enemy." With a British father and French mother, the couple is asked what the children would be and the response is "American!" Crawford wrinkles her nose very fetchingly at the finale as the couple prepare for "happily ever after."

Winners of the Wilderness would definitely not be to all tastes, perhaps more suited to devotees of silents or Crawford completists, but it does have its fascination and some historical interest. It also is worthwhile to get a gander at a Crawford barely out of her teens and a total fox.

One of the *Winners* publicity photos which sadly displays the way Crawford was exploited in cheesecake photos at this early juncture in her career. She also had a more voluptuous body prior to the ongoing stringent diets the studio encouraged in starlets to achieve "picture weight."

The Unknown (1927) ★★★★

The Unknown is a very intriguing, mesmerizing film set in a gypsy circus with great dreamlike music and bizarre images. It's from the director of "Freaks," Todd Browning, a former sideshow performer who had a penchant for the macabre, twisted romance and carney life. Set up like

A young, lithe Crawford with Chaney. PHOTO COURTESY OF JERRY MURBACH

a folk tale, it opens with a glittering shot of a circus tent reminiscent of Coney Island's Dreamland and involves an armless knife thrower, Alonzo's (Lon Chaney, Sr.) ill-fated obsession for the circus owner's daughter, Nanon (a very young Joan Crawford), a story from Old Madrid, as the title cards explain, "they say is true." Apparently, Browning and Chaney formed a successful collaboration while both under contract at MGM and this was considered one of their best efforts.

Chaney, known as The Man of a Thousand Faces because of his chameleon-like ability to transform himself into odd and far-ranging characters, was adept at making viewers both repelled and empathetic through his arrestingly expressive face, a skilled makeup artist whose success in that vein, in his own words, "relied more on the placements of highlights and shadows, some not in the most obvious areas of the face." Raised by deaf parents, he learned early on to communicate and express without words.

In *The Unknown,* he performs with arms tightly strait-jacketed in order to appear armless just as he had simulated a double-amputee in "The Penalty" by devising a leather harness with stumps that allowed him to strap his legs behind him and walk on his knees. His Alonzo has sinister motivations, however, merely pretending to be armless to hide a deformity in his hand that would identify him as a killer to the police. Meanwhile,

Lecherous Alonzo gives his beloved Nanon a skirt. Beware of gypsies bearing gifts! PHOTO COURTESY OF JERRY MURBACH

the comely Nanon fears the touch of men's hands, trusting Alonzo as a non-threatening friend and not suspecting the depths he feels or will go to in order to possess her.

When Malabar the Mighty (Norman Kerry), the strong man, expresses romantic interest in the alluring and sweet-faced Nanon, Alonzo is ultimately compelled to commit a rash act: he has his own arms surgically removed. As a reviewer amusingly put it — a farewell to arms! But fate pulls another fast one on Alonzo, leading to a sequence by Chaney that Burt Lancaster called "one of the most compelling and emotionally exhausting scenes I have ever seen an actor do."

Chaney is incredible, his concentration apparently impressing the young Crawford greatly, as she considered him one of her most influential teachers. Not only is this film beautiful to look at with many of Crawford's scenes being filmed behind a scrim for softening effect (the silent film era a ripe time for experimentation and creativity), but the dialogue is poetically beautiful. "Then if you do care for me," Malabar tells Nanon, "why won't you ever let me hold you in my arms?" or "Eyes that adore you...hands that long to caress you...and strength to protect you." Crawford, clearly not much out of her teens, is a natural beauty with incredibly soulful, tender eyes and a sleek, voluptuous body as taut as a

Malabar, the Mighty (Norman Kerry) and gypsy girl Nanon (Joan Crawford) comfort the peculiarly stricken Alonzo (Lon Chaney).

cheetah, able to show both innocence and fire. She moves with balletic grace and exhibits much presence and charisma, her face as striking and expressive as her role model Chaney. The documentary *Joan Crawford: The Ultimate Star* noted that she learned to channel resources from an abused childhood into her more difficult scenes. It's not surprising she became a major star. A great silent film; I wouldn't be surprised if some of the Italian giallos were influenced by this one.

Twelve Miles Out (1927) ★★★★

Before Clark Gable became the ultimate man's man and woman's man with his rakish screen charisma, John Gilbert was setting hearts on fire with his equally raffish and buccaneerish charm, the successor to

Rudolf Valentino as the screen's Great Lover and offscreen paramour of the enigmatic Greta Garbo. With *Twelve Miles Out*, Gilbert's gifts as a silent artist become astonishingly clear, making the fact that he drank himself to death at age thirty-eight because of his failure to catch on in "talkies" all the more tragic.

Since the version of *Twelve Miles Out* currently in bootleg distribution

Our gal with dashing John Gilbert and a much-too-old fiancé (Edward Earle). Willing captor?

appears to be missing footage, according to the synopsis in Lawrence Quirk's book *The Films of Joan Crawford*, I can only judge the core that is left which is quick-moving, dramatic and lean. As in opera and classical ballet, crescendos of music, action, and pantomime create emotional torrents without words. The story concerns a bootlegger Jerry Fay (Gilbert) who seizes the coastal home of Jane (Joan Crawford) and her fiancé, John Burton (Edward Earle — tiresomely old enough to be Crawford's father) to store his cargoes. When Jane threatens to get the police with a foolhardy valor reminiscent of Nancy Drew, Jerry kidnaps the couple, holding them as prisoners on his rum boat. Naturally, bad boy Gilbert is much more sexually attractive than the noble, but ineffectual (and too old) fiancé and tensions between female prisoner and captor take on a potent and believable undercurrent. With his insolent playboy edge and intensely hypnotic eyes like Lon Chaney, Gilbert manages to be both dynamically sexy and surprisingly emotionally nuanced. A very young Crawford is just beginning as an actor, yet her face is so exquisite with its large, eloquent eyes and sculptural luminosity that it makes her an affecting innocent for Gilbert. Their sexual chemistry together is tremendous. Ernest Torrence, whom Crawford referred to as the "lamb of the world," shows up as rum runner Red McCue and Jerry's competitor, making an attempt not only to seize the boat but Jane. However, Jerry who has come to care for Jane as much as she evidently has fallen for him, determines to protect her as the Coast Guard closes in.

Sadly, since only grainy prints exist of most silents, as is the case here (although the quality is only slightly grainy and therefore, respectable), most people dismiss them as badly dated relics. Furthermore, prints are hard to come by which adds to their obscurity and neglect. This is unfortunate, because silent films are a unique art form — and many gems and masterpieces lie forgotten. *Twelve Miles Out*, even in its abridged form, is one of those gems. Not only are the actors exceptional with Gilbert outstanding in particular and Crawford unbelievably stunning and expressive (yes, they did have faces then, as Gloria Swanson pointed out in *Sunset Boulevard*), but the visuals are at times arresting. A scene depicting heavy gusts and Crawford's billowing dress on deck is an example. At the opposite extreme, a shot of a sailboat — clearly a toy — jarringly breaks the illusion so effectively wrought elsewhere. In any case, a fascinating silent that warrants distribution and preservation.

Pet line (spoken by the besieged Edward Earle to Gilbert): "As an American citizen, I demand to know what time it is."

Spring Fever (1927) ★★½ *(five stars for young Joan Crawford and Billy Haines)*

Well, someone at MGM had the bright idea of making a golf movie with the naturally athletic and charismatic William Haines, but in spite of a rather boring premise and setting, *Spring Fever* (based on the Vincent Lawrence play) remains a wonderful showcase for its two bright young stars, William Haines and Joan Crawford. This is their second film together and first romantic pairing. Both were incredibly good looking, plus natural and fresh as performers, their charisma immense; in a cast of dated silent film stars, they look contemporary and brim with youthful vitality and beauty. It is understandable how these two fun-loving, talented individuals became best friends, this closeness lifelong. (Crawford, in fact, stuck by Haines when he was ousted by Hollywood for being a homosexual and helped jump start his career as a successful interior decorator.) At the time, Haines was an established star and Crawford acknowledged being only "window dressing" in his films, according to author Lawrence Quirk. In *Spring Fever*, Haines is Jack Kelly, a wise acre (what else?) shipping clerk (allowing him to do some superb schtick) who

PHOTO COURTESY OF JIM MAHONEY

gains a two week membership to the posh "Oakmont Country Club" for helping his boss with his golf swing. There he encounters the beauteous Allie Monte (Crawford), whose name he discovers when she signs into the hotel, and attempts to meet her with the old "don't-I-know-you" routine, "Well, if it isn't Miss Monte!" The saucer-eyed lass plays along a bit and then gives him the brush-off, but now Jack is hooked — and not just on golf.

Haines, as usual, gets too full of himself, so must be brought down to earth before he can earn the girl he loves. In this case, when his two weeks are up during which he rated as a champion golfer, he is determined not to leave, boasting to his father (the marvelously expressive Bert Woodruff) that he will "marry for money." He then heads straight for Allie as his father and boss Mr. Waters (George Fawcett) look on in disgust. The sweet Allie has a revelation of her own, however, confessing to Jack that her father lost all his money, and when it seems Jack is now not willing to propose to her, she accepts a proposal of marriage from another admirer, Harry Johnson (Edward Earle), although clearly unhappy. Jack, meanwhile, resolves to return to the shipping room, but one look at Allie when he goes to say good bye to her and he is proposing

PHOTO COURTESY OF JIM MAHONEY

marriage, boasting to her desperately that he is wealthy and comes from a long line of peers. The pair run off together. Will Allie still love Jack when she finds out the truth?

Crawford and Haines make a stunning and very appealing team. It is understandable why these Jazz Age hotties were so popular. Crawford has an unaffected charm and lithe grace. Without all the makeup to overpower her features and here, in its innocent glory, her face is like a work of art — delicate, sculptural, and porcelain-like. Haines is charming and adorable, full of fun, but registers well in the tender moments, too.

Although the script isn't remarkable, the acting sometimes elevates it considerably. A piece between Jack and his father when Jack calls his golf club (or "spoon") the best friend he ever had, then counters, "I didn't mean that, Pa. You know who's my best pal" is effecting and touching. Actually Haines is so engaging and "real" that he lends what might have been "nothing" scenes an emotional trueness, a talent Crawford shared. It is a tragedy that this fine star is not better known today, although his association with Crawford is possibly changing that as, through her continuing popularity, her co-stars (especially frequent ones like Haines) are re-discovered. There are also lovely Art Deco sets at the country club by Cedric Gibbons (who else?).

One of the most charming scenes — practically worth the whole film — is the honeymoon night for the newly-married Kellys. Suddenly shy, they nervously eye the bed and turn out the lights to undress. Their conversation continues in the blackness with eager casualness, her titles on the left and his on the right. It's endearing and witty and the pair plays the whole scenario beautifully. They also achieve a real sensuality together.

In sum, *Spring Fever* is a nice showcase for William Haines and Joan Crawford at the height of their Jazz Age popularity. TCM recently restored the print to amazing clarity with only occasional snowiness, a pity that all silents aren't as fortunate. It's not a great script nor is the music notable, but there are occasional deft or witty touches such as the above "wedding night" scene and some amusing title cards ("Eustace Tewksbury was born in London and had been in a fog ever since"). It also provides a fun record of hip '20s fashions with cloche hats and checkered caps, but its main draw remains the opportunity to see Joan Crawford and William Haines together.

West Point (1928) ★ ★ ★ ★ ★

West Point is a surprisingly moving story of a brash and wise acre West Point cadet, Brice Wayne (William Haines), who learns lessons in humility, ethics and character ("the spirit of the corps") when he enters the academy. Filmed with the cooperation of the U.S. Military Academy, it was shot on location with real cadets functioning as extras and great live action footage of actual training and daily routines giving a genuine feeling for the real deal.

Haines is terrific in the lead and completely believable, owing to the superb script and his solid, engaging characterization. It's clear why he was a star and one can only rue that so many silent stars of his ability are now largely forgotten. He certainly warrants rediscovery. Not only is he good-looking and boyishly charming, but he is a natural at both drama and comedy, his vitality, charisma and sex appeal qualities he had in common with co-star Joan Crawford. While still on the ferry en route to West Point, Brice is already pulling practical jokes, having the other future cadets line up and inspecting their teeth, clearly not about to take anything or anyone seriously. His eye is quickly caught by pert, pretty Betty Channing (Crawford), and he says to the men he's just tricked,

Crawford with William Haines. PHOTO COURTESY OF NEIL MACIEJEWSKI

"Pardon me, gentlemen…I feel my weak moment coming on." He then pretends to be blind in order to engage Betty's sympathy and, although she is offended and gives him the brush off when she finds out he has duped her, she is simultaneously amused and drawn to him. Still, she gets a chance to give him a taste of his own medicine by pulling a fast one on him as they depart, leaving him in the dust.

As it turns out, Betty's mother owns the West Point Hotel where Brice once again encounters the pretty miss. This time she is with a smitten suitor, Cadet Bob Sperry (Neil Neely) who is on furlough especially to see her. In his characteristic fashion, Brice plays the clown, serenading the couple on his banjo and singing the sort of sassy jazz tunes that were frequently a part of Max Fleischer's Betty Boop and Koko the Klown cartoons. The witty lyrics recall vaudeville entertainment:

I'm canned heat to the Mommas
No matter where I rove
Once I made an Eskimo
Throw away her stove

And, of course, there is the refrain, "Mammy!" Crawford and Haines are cute together and it is in these early films that one gains a fuller sense of the personality of the real actress — her lively, fun-loving, girlish side that attracted friends and was loyal in return. She and Haines clearly genuinely like one another and are having fun. Unfortunately, Brice, although kind at heart, also has an arrogant, quick-tempered side and socks a guy who interferes with his flirtation with Betty. But later, upon learning of the cadet's financial hardships, he secretly pays the cadet's fees.

Haines proves himself to be a delightful comedian in the film's first half, pulling off some great physical gags as he defies the straight-laced expectations of West Point. In one sequence, he discovers that he is rooming with delicate and small Tex McNeil (William Bakewell) and, obviously impressive to the shyer cadet, Brice boasts as a senior officer orders them about, "Hereafter we'll take our time doing things. Let him squawk!" Then when the officer yells at them to come out of their rooms, Brice jumps a mile and goes sliding down the stairs on his behind. The story takes Brice through the paces, showing the tough fitness routines and demands of life in the Academy, Brice approaching each new hurdle with devil-may-care buffoonery. The sight of the long line of cadets in formations is nothing short of awe-inspiring, however, and it's impossible not to be moved at the sight of young boys being turned into soldiers, boys being ushered into manhood.

Ultimately Brice proves to be a stellar football player (football all the rage in the 1920s) and is scoring well for the Army until he gives an arrogant newspaper interview that threatens his future career. He is shocked to learn that West Point will not sacrifice its integrity even for a star player. ("If ever a player means more than the Corps' honor…we'll abolish football.")

West Point is an fine film combining poignant drama and uproarious slapstick with excellent characters and story. It is a strong tale of ethics, friendship and character that is extremely moving. It offers a wonderful showcase for the talents of William Haines and an intimate and believable look at life in West Point. Crawford, although in a small role, still makes an impression. She has great chemistry with her dear friend and, quite simply, she was a real dish in these tender years — very natural, demure yet strong. William Bakewell also does wonderful work as Tex, touching and genuinely noble.

Across to Singapore (1928) ★ ★ ¾ *(five for Joan's beauty)*

I immensely enjoyed the pairing of dashing, adorable Ramon Novarro with a beauteous and sweet Joan Crawford in *Across to Singapore*. Their contemporary beauty and liveliness are the chief fun of this silent film, since the script is the stuff of yellow prose: illogical, heavy-handed melodrama replete with a swashbuckling thrill or two. Joel Shore (Novarro) and Priscilla Crowninshield (Crawford) are childhood playmates in seafaring New England who are now grown. In the opening scene, the pair enacts mutiny at sea, then fall giggling onto the sand, the fresh-faced and fair Priscilla in a very provocative dress. The youngsters then go to meet Joel's brother Mark's ship, the Nathan Ross, which has returned from a two year journey. Trouble ensues when it is clear that Mark (Ernest Torrence) is smitten with the fully-blossomed, coquettish Priscilla and a close-up of the girl's eloquent, lovely face makes it understandable why he would be. When Mr. Shore invites the returning sailors to his home for dinner, Priscilla finds herself the solo female (hey — it's Joan!), all of the men eagerly offering her their arms for escort into the dining room. The two brothers, Mark and Joel, horse around in believable fashion at the table and, although Crawford is given little to do beyond giggling into her handkerchief, she makes her character wholly alive. She is very young and beautiful in an extremely natural way — no iconic exaggerated lips or brows — just youthful freshness and prettiness. She gives Mark those eyes in a moment by the staircase and this seals her doom, because unbeknownst to her (the first red flag in the script), the men observing them decide she is going to be betrothed to Mark — and cruelly don't plan to let her in on it.

As Priscilla and Joel frolic impishly upstairs, actually sitting together

Dolllike and adorable in *Across to Singapore*. PHOTO COURTESY OF NEIL MACIEJEWSKI

on his bed (however innocently), downstairs Mark is asking Mr. Crowninshield for Priscilla's hand in marriage and the deal is sealed. ("We'll have it announced in church tomorrow and surprise everybody...even Priscilla.") I'll say. Upstairs, as Priscilla plots the next trick Joel can play on Mark, they have a close moment and she impulsively kisses him. His dreamy smile afterwards shows that he is equally besotted with her.

In true sea faring fashion, Mark's "sudden burst of love" inspires a drinking and carousing night on the town (must be fun to be married to him, eh?) and Joel shows up at the bar in Mark's best jacket, looking like a kid who got into his father's clothes closet. There is lots of singing and showing of tattoos before all hell breaks loose — yep, men are still the same (too much testosterone and it doesn't mix well with alcohol). Inadvertently youngster Joel gets credit for licking "Dog-nose Danny," a tough sailor, which entitles him, according to sailor logic, to sail for Singapore with his brother Mark, his dream come true. Oh, the way men must prove their might and merit!

As is typical among the pious, after the Saturday night shenanigans, everyone is in church next morning on Sunday, bruised or not. More hell breaks loose, albeit quietly — the betrothal of Mark and Priscilla is announced. Shock and unhappiness show on the faces of Priscilla and Joel yet the die has been cast and Priscilla appears to glumly accept her fate, leaving the church with Mark. As the brothers are about to set sail the next day, she comes to see the ship off. Like a true damsel-in-distress, her doll-like face peeping from beneath a bonnet, she is repelled by Mark's advances and refuses his kisses. Yet when she tries to let Joel know her true heart's desire in a fabulous pantomime scene (one of my favorite scenes in the entire film) and that she is not in love with Mark, he scorns her inexplicably, telling her she is betrothed. It seems not to matter that the whole dang marriage was arranged without her consent, might as well have been sold into slavery. One wonders why Joel would do this to her and to himself.

At sea, Mark has obsessive visions of Priscilla, haunted by her rejection (and the vision of loveliness scorns him in his dreams, too), and these "storms of the heart," as he puts it, occupy him more than the storms at sea. The scenes at sea are fun with backdrops of huge waves that would've swamped the boat hours ago and lots of water splashing the principals. Again, Joel inexplicably reassures his brother about Priscilla's love, even though Mark believes she loves someone else (and Joel must know who that is.) Brother Noah is shortly swept to sea and the two surviving brothers reach Singapore where a lively set has been provided to lend exotic flavor including lots of extras in costume. An uncredited and beautiful Anna May Wong takes up immediately (and inexplicably) with the homely Mark, much to the fury of her sailor-man. Like Crawford, Wong is very young, cute as can be, and fuller-faced here. She's an exotic beauty — dainty and alluring, and the fact that the sailors help themselves to the women as if they're commodities pretty much tells us that East is as bad for women as West. Joel again is intent on keeping Priscilla and Mark true to each other and, in typical male fashion, Mark blames Priscilla for his troubles as if she had any say in anything.

Attacked for stealing the Oriental beauty from the original sailor-beau (oh, these poor girls), Mark is taken for dead and the Nathan Ross comes home with flags flying at half mast. Joel is brought back in irons for deserting his brother, trumped charges by shipmate Finch (Jim Mason).

Although Novarro is a heartthrob of the first order, reminiscent of that cutest boy in any high school and charms in the "light" scenes, he isn't terribly convincing dramatically. Given that I've only seen him in one film, I can't comment on his abilities as a whole, but here his idea of conveying serious emotion is letting his face go slack. Consequently, when confronted about the charges of cowardice and given a chance to explain, he assumes a limp look. Then, kicking into life unexpectedly, he tries to throttle Finch for lying, which only makes him look worse. Later he seeks out Priscilla (who has no cause to champion him after his shameless lack of support for her plight) to ask if she believes in his innocence, hinting that he is still attracted to her. But Priscilla's hopes for being with her true love are quickly sabotaged when Joel brings up the "M" word and insists that he is still alive and waiting for her. Worse, he forces the poor girl to go to Singapore with him to get back this man she doesn't love, outrageously saying, "You made him love you and now you're not goin' to quit him when he needs you." He actually carries the sobbing and protesting damsel away bodily, shameless cad. However, as the ship sets sail with Priscilla "trapped" on board, helplessly watching the gangway drawn up, a sexy little expression crosses her face to indicate she isn't completely unhappy with the arrangement. Meanwhile, Mark has become a "gibbering derelict," as the title cards reveal, with even his Asian love muffin and her sympathetic mother cringing from him, and just as Priscilla is working her charms on Joel deep at sea, a bedraggled and grotesque Mark comes crawling over the side of the boat like anyone's worst nightmare and Joel is ready to fling his beloved back into his brother's seaweed-draped arms.

Who will win the fair lady's hand in the end? Will the ship survive mutiny at sea? Or will Crawford, as in *Twelve Miles Out* and *Strange Cargo*, find herself the "booty prize" for a pack of predatory seafaring wolves, the sassy wench mutinous sailors lust after?

In spite of a script that falls to pieces as it goes along, the leads are quite good. It's an interesting study in gender roles with rough housing, horsing around and even brutality supposedly making men men and demureness, helplessness and true-heartedness defining the woman although Crawford shows spirit beneath the sweet, wistful beauty and fragility. And once again, it is her face that blows me away, extraordinary faces like hers making silents a powerful art form. The tenderness and expressiveness of her eyes alone is astonishing. To appreciate the older actress fully, it is essential to see her in her early career. Her silent screen heritage was rich training that made her such an effective, emotional and facially communicative actress and her artistry was that she gave her all.

Our Dancing Daughters (1928) ★★★★★

Critic Leonard Maltin called *Our Dancing Daughters* one of the best Jazz-Age silents. In it Joan Crawford was catapulted to stardom, her presence moving F. Scott Fitzgerald to say, "[She] is doubtless the best

Gorgeous photo of Crawford with Dorothy Sebastian. PHOTO COURTESY OF JERRY MURBACH

example of the flapper, the girl you see in smart night clubs, gowned to the apex of sophistication, toying iced glasses with a remote, faintly bitter expression, dancing deliciously, laughing a great deal with wide, hurt eyes. Young things with a talent for living." The reasons for its impact are justified. From the fabulous opening shot of an Art Deco statue that dissolves into the dancing feet of Crawford — who pulls on undies and dresses, all the while doing the Charleston and without ever seeming the least tawdry — to the last frame, this film is so vibrantly alive, brimming with gay visuals and flaming youth, that lack of spoken words is never

That glittering, Art Deco jazz age!

felt. Backstory adds that Crawford was finally allowed to express her real self before the camera, her room at home filled with Charleston trophies from long nights at the Coconut Grove where beaus vied for her attention. In *Our Dancing Daughters*, the first of a trio of youthful "Our" films directed by Harry Beaumont, she is "Diana the Dangerous" Medford, a young exuberant thing who wants "to hold out my hands and catch [all

Two of the dancing daughters. PHOTO COURTESY OF JERRY MURBACH

of life] like the sunlight." She wraps herself in a flamboyant, fur-lined coat and flirts with her beautiful mother ("If I do say so, I picked myself some snappy parents!"), and then cries, "I'm going to the Yacht Club. See you at dawn!"

As Diana meets her gang of young male friends and sips champagne from each of their glasses, it's clear she is a coquette and belle of the ball, as was the real Joan. Her friend Beatrice (Dorothy Sebastian) is warned by her mother as she joins the gang not to smell of cigarettes or her allowance will be cut and both parents are wary of "wild" Diana. Meanwhile, "Bea" has a boyfriend Norman (Nils Asther with the thin Continental moustache) who wants to marry her, but she fears her past might stand in the way. We meet the third of the "dancing daughters" in the fabulous Anita Page as Ann. As with Crawford, her introduction comes via her legs as she rolls her stockings and tears them impatiently (a great touch). Although baby-faced Ann looks like an angel, she pooh poohs her mother's formula of "beauty and purity" and shrugs off the card her mother finds in a bouquet that reads "Hurrah for giraffes and other long neckers." Ann is no angel, but Page is so delightful, she makes her a hoot all the same. Rivalry — and the essential meat of the story — ensues between Dangerous Diana (who is actually quite sweet and sincere) and the sweet-looking but insincere and devious Ann when Diana meets handsome Ben Blaine (Johnny Mack Brown) of Birmingham who, as friend Freddie (the delicious Edward Nugent) puts it, has lots of "dough-rey-mi!" Jazz babies, start your engines!

The writing has a snap and rhythm that matches the equally snappy music, fabulous '20s costumes and Cedric Gibbons Deco sets. ("Lil hot baby want a cool lil sip?") The visuals are gilt-edged, festive and spectacular as scores of balloons are released to the ceiling above the heads of young revelers and rooms resemble the paintings of Erte and Charles Barbier with lavish Art Nouveau staircases and archways. The attempts of both girls to gain Ben's attention provide impish fun, such as when Diana skids on her bottom across the floor into him, laughing all the way.

Crawford is sensational in the lead. She has a kinetic energy, yet an innocent sensuality and wistfulness. It's not hard to see why she made a stunning impact on teen girls of the day. Her eyes can be all tenderness or playful and flirtatious. There's a gorgeous shot of her in profile, standing by a window through which a seascape glitters; she's simply exquisite with finely molded face, delicate chin, and long neck. No surprise either that photographers like Hurrell and artists made her their subject. Anita Page, playing the "villainess," is too cute for words. Although we're meant to applaud any comeuppance she is dealt, I can't help feeling sorry for her when even the washerwomen are judging her "loose morals." It seems natural that these fun-loving girls should want to play with their frivolous but harmless "good time Charley" friends yet their men frown on it. (Hey — they're young; why shouldn't they act it?) The three ingénues sport shingled mops, wide eyes and beaded dresses.

The odd thing about the sets, however fabulous, is that all the girls appear to live in the same building, sometimes sharing the same room, with the "Yacht Club" right downstairs! What kind of a joint is this? And who are those fabulous dancers on the yacht? Oh, it gives one a sense of "living in history," as was once said of F. Scott Fitzgerald's work — a scintillating, divine party! To Black Bottom the night away in a fringed, beaded dress!

Hollywood Revue of 1929 (1929) ★★★★

Hollywood Revue of 1929 was the first of the all-star, no-plot, talkie variety entertainments from MGM and certainly they pulled out the stops to make it an extravaganza. Cedric Gibbons and Erte had a hand in the set decoration and, as in vaudeville, which it strongly resembles unsurprisingly, the acts range from comedy and music to acrobatics and drama, a mixed bag, with the addition of amazingly inventive camerawork and visuals, including two-strip Technicolor and Busby Berkeley style configurations. As a historical record of the period, it's incredible. Many of the faces in this cast were doomed by sound, so one can only imagine the trepidation of these stars, although they perform with spirit. Few of them survive in memory today, Joan Crawford among the exceptions. Crawford, in fact, expressed her fear in a letter to fan Dan Mahoney, listing all the stresses facing her including family unexpectedly arriving and having to find them places to live, law suits, reporters, etc., adding: "And worst of all, talking pictures!" Yet she made the transition smoothly and remains one of the highlights here. The fabulously fun, playful choreography of some numbers; an enchanting Anita Page; and a nail-biting acrobatic "adagio" with one girl and three guys are also high points in this impressive array of entertainment. Basically, though, it was sink or swim with the MGM cast being thrown to the lions, pun intended!

A young Jack Benny with the delivery and mannerisms that would be his hallmark (and eye makeup common to stage/silent film) serves as the Master of Ceremonies, as it were, and the opening is fantastic with a line of dancers in wonderful, symmetrical patterns and flashy lighting techniques. I'm only sorry I couldn't have been one of those chorus girls. The continual experimentation and ingenuity found in these early films is fascinating with influences of modern art, jazz, Art Deco, cantoring, and the like in evidence. Although Greta Garbo and Lon Chaney are among those conspicuously absent from the cast, the MGM pool is certainly well represented.

Our gal Joan Crawford makes her appearance fairly early on, introduced by co-host Conrad Nagel as the "personification of youth and beauty, joy and happiness," which she certainly indeed was. She is fresh and beautiful with eyes that could melt steel. What she lacks in pipes in her rendition of "Got a Feeling for You," she makes up in charm and delivery. She does a Charleston typical of the period — a bit ungainly, yet cute with good freestyle hoofing. Other solo dancers in the show employ a similar style, clunky as it might look today. Crawford's vivacity here is enchanting and she has that special something, be it sex appeal, charisma, or a combination of a whole lot of things that ensured her stardom. None of the latter day hardness she is continually and tiresomely criticized for is in evidence.

Anita Page also stands out among the cute and delectable young actresses (like Crawford). Page is probably the cutest blonde ever, a precursor to Jean Harlow, the prototype for all cute blondes to follow, and she was equally talented. Another cutie making a brief appearance is Ann Dvorak who slaps Benny in one scene. Special effects include miniaturized

Two-strip Technicolor sequence of "Singing in the Rain" was featured in this, MGM's first all-star, no-plot, talkie variety entertainment which doomed the careers of many silent stars — but not our Joan!

actors like Charlie King and Bessie Love, a wavering camera to suggest underwater in a "King Neptune" piece with Buster Keaton (and an amazingly provocative dance from a woman who emerges from an oyster shell), and the clever and appealing use of black and white. Crawford's friend Billy Haines proves to be another gem in his brief comedy stint where he eats Benny's buttons. He does the bit expertly, adept at both comedy and drama, his career sadly derailed because of his homosexuality, although, with Crawford's help, he became a successful interior decorator. Marion Davies performs an awful song and a dance routine on a par with Crawford's and Love does an enjoyable circus-style act. Norma Shearer and John Gilbert perform the balcony scene from "Romeo and Juliet" in a color sequence that has become famous for derailing Gilbert's career, due to his high-pitched voice.

Admittedly, this is not going to be for all tastes, since it is a mixed bag (as was vaudeville) and some unfortunately eschew anything smacking of the past, but its grand variety tradition and jazz age/period flavor is exactly what makes it so delightful. It's a period I adore, unique, artistic and lively. I prefer the dance and acrobatic numbers to the comedy bits, which were often interminable (including the one with Laurel and Hardy, surprisingly). The "adagio," as mentioned earlier, set in Turkey was one of the most outstanding pieces requiring astonishing skill as a girl is swung around by three men, her head skimming the floor. A ballet in color is also particularly gorgeous, full of configurations and reflections. And the whole extravaganza is capped with a phenomenal color sequence of "Singing in the Rain" featuring the entire cast. How can you go wrong?

In short, it's clearly apparent why this film made a great splash in its day. It remains a spectacular record of the period, astonishing in its array of influences and innovation, an invaluable historical record of early cinema and its brightest stars. And Joan Crawford is as adorable as she's ever going to be, a real ray of sunshine. Who could ask for anything more?

Our Modern Maidens (1929) ★ ★ ★

Our Modern Maidens is a semi-talkie about Jazz Age babies, part of a trilogy that began with *Our Dancing Daughters* (the film that launched Joan Crawford to stardom) and penned by the same author as *Daughters*, Josephine Lovett. Joan Crawford (as Billie Brown; interestingly, using her "real" first name or the one she used after being born Lucille LeSueur) and Douglas Fairbanks, Jr. (as Gil Jordan) had just announced their engagement off-screen. This film capitalized on the media frenzy by pairing them in what would be their one and only film together and Crawford's last silent. And I have to say, as a duo, they have tremendous chemistry. They are young, fun-loving and adorable and clearly besotted with one another. Music and occasional sound effects accompany the visuals (the best being the assembled girls yelling what they are preoccupied with: "Men! Men! Men!" which appears on soundtrack and in titles both), but aside from that exception, title cards are used throughout for the dialogue. With the young female stars dressed by Adrian and glittering Art Deco sets by Cedric Gibbons, it is visually bright and striking and, for the most part, moves along at a clip that almost matches the dancing and the opening sequence of college kids in fast cars.

Crawford with poodle mop hairdo known as a "shingle" in twenties. PHOTO COURTESY OF NEIL MACIEJEWSKI

The plot, such as it is, is thin and a tad moralistic (if also risqué), involving the usual mix-up of romantic duos and scandals. As flapper Billie, Crawford is an enthusiastic exhibitionist for the assembled jazz babies, wide-eyed and smiling and fetchingly flirtatious. The only child of B. Bickering Brown who owns a radio company, Billie is secretly engaged to childhood sweetheart Gil. When wealthy Glenn Abbott (Rod LaRocque) makes a pass at her on the Seven Eleven train and she reads of his position in the society pages, she decides to seduce him (however innocently) so that he'll give fiancé Gil a break and, meanwhile, Kentucky (the adorable Anita Page) has her eyes on Gil. This is where modern maidens learn the folly of their ways. Crawford is still raw in the acting department with broad and exaggerated reactions and expressions, for the most part, lots of lip-biting and eye-rolling and manic activity, but her charisma is undeniable. As always, the girls (in fact, the entire cast) seem(s) to live in the huge, Art Deco Cedric Gibbons house (or set) with its sweeping staircases and geometric designs. It is a great setting for a party and showcase for Crawford's high spirits and dancing. A whirling dervish, seemingly on speed, she spins across the dance floor in a swirl of fabric and then lapses into a melodramatic pantomime. How fun that must have been for audiences of that time, ostensibly mimicking popular entertainment, as when Douglas Fairbanks, Jr. does a host of impersonations, including his own father.

The two couples that cross-pollinate and return to their intended (as by the script) mates are Crawford and Fairbanks, Jr. and Page and LaRocque. Gil sees that Billie is making a "play" for Glenn (on his behalf) and immediately Kentucky moves in, gazing adoringly at him so that one thing leads to another. Following the party and splendid fireworks (metaphor, metaphor), the "kids" board gondolas hung with Chinese lanterns. Billie is preoccupied with Glenn so Gil shares the romantic boat ride with Kentucky and then kisses her in a forest. Billie assures Glenn that Gil is just a boy and friend, so he agrees to give Gil his start for her sake, however initially reluctantly. Afterwards he reads of her official engagement to Gil and he is brooding and angry. As storm clouds gather (metaphor, metaphor), he drives Billie in his roadster to his little cottage. The car gets stuck in the mud, causing the pair to be drenched. Crawford looks especially young and endearing in the scenes that follow, trying to use charm to disarm him as she senses his anger and bitterness at her dishonesty. Disturbingly, as Billie changes into a robe out of her wet clothes, Glenn enters the room, becoming villainous. His intention appears to be rape or forcing his attentions on her and he yanks her head back by the

An endearing Joan Crawford with her at-the-time real-life hubby, Douglas Fairbanks, Jr. in the wedding scene. *Our Modern Maidens* is the only film the couple made together.

hair to kiss her. She begins sobbing pitifully. With those big, woeful eyes filled with genuine tears, Crawford/Billie looks so young and fragile and helpless, it seems monstrous that anyone could or would harm this girl! What a disturbing message to young girls of the time as well. Glenn does take pity, however, but when Billie tells him she knew he was decent as he releases her, he only laughs scornfully and says he doesn't want her.

Crawford and co-stars clowning and playing cards on the set.

Meanwhile, the wedding of Gil and Billie occurs, but another wrench gets thrown into the mix as Billie learns of Kentucky's secret heartache and pregnancy (quite the soap opera!). Realizing that she hasn't achieved the "brass band," Billie goes on a groom-less honeymoon, facing the crowds with brave smiles as Crawford would repeatedly stand strong in the face of defeat throughout her film career. Edward Nugent and Josephine Dunn (as Ginger), as always, lend delicious support as Billie's fresh (and avant garde) friends. And Crawford has her usual glimmer of sass. When Ginger asks as Billie announces her modern invention of a groom-less honeymoon, "Is this a modern moral or just another immoral modern?," Billie replies, "Do you think you'd know the difference, darling?" In the final frame, love outs, but I hardly feel the ultimate matches are suitable.

Anyway, it's not a great film, but still a wonderful window into the period and a pleasant look at the young stars. Page practically steals the film, adorable beyond the pale, and the moments between the two women are great. She is also a terrific actress, adept at being both naughty and angel. But Crawford holds her own and then some. Vivacious, sweet, and brimming with hey-hey joie de vivre, she shows clearly why she shot to stardom and influenced her jazz age generation.

Untamed (1929) ★★★½

Untamed is Joan Crawford's first sound film and presents a creaky bridge between silents and talkies, although the young Crawford is, as always, vivacious and natural even when speaking like "Lady Vere DeVere" (as neighbor/critic George Oppenheimer once put it). Not a great film, its rawness and that of its largely youthful cast nonetheless lend it abundant charm. There are occasional issues with sound, such as when background music almost drowns out the dialogue, and title cards are used, if sparingly. The plot concerns a wild child named Alice "Bingo" Dowling (Crawford) who lives in the jungles of South America with her prospecting father (Lloyd Ingraham). The film opens with the deeply-tanned Bingo in sexy, little dress and bare legs doing Crawford's standard hoochie-koochie dance (lots of legs, limbs and flapping) for the natives and singing "Chant of the Jungle." It's hilarious when she flashes a swarthy (and who isn't?) lecher a big, white, saucy smile after he asks her to repeat her dance for he who hasn't seen a woman for many months and says, "Sure! Signor has been so kind. Sure, I'll dance again!" When Daddy Dowling is on his death bed, felled by a bad heart and the bad lecher with designs on Bingo, he makes his friends, Ben Murchison (Ernest Torrence) and Howard Presley (Holmes Herbert) promise to look after his little girl (in a hilariously protracted death scene) and reveals the whereabouts of a deed that essentially makes her an oil heiress. Shortly, "Uncle Ben," as Bingo refers to him, is taking his ward via ship to New York and finding her a handful, but "worth it." As Murchison remarks when looking on their prettily sleeping charge, "Sometimes the sweetest flowers grow in the mud."

On board, Bingo literally stumbles into handsome Andy McAllister (a young Robert Montgomery) and quickly falls for him, expressing her interest quite openly, "untamed" girl that she is. He is equally taken and amused by her. Her rough edges are still in evidence as she tries to punch those she dislikes in the nose, runs around barefoot, and keeps a mischievous monkey on ship (which hilariously — and evidently unexpectedly — squirts the actors as they try to corner it in the cabin). But she is firm about her love for Andy, even though Uncle Ben is against the union because they are both "children" and Andy has no money to compete with Bingo's millions. ("You know a lot about oil, Uncle Ben, but you don't know anything about girls!" she wails.) Crawford looks pretty like the proverbial picture, blue eyes like big flowers, a dainty bow

Crawford with Ernest Torrence whom she later called "the lamb of the world." PHOTO COURTESY OF NEIL MACIEJEWSKI

around her hair, heart-shaped face fresh and dewy. For whatever reason, however, she has notable sweat stains under her arms (okay, it's hot in that thar jungle!). Andy does not want to live off Bingo's money, however, and takes up with big, blonde Marge (Gwen Lee).

In the second half, Bingo, now in New York, has quickly transformed into a beautifully-garbed young sophisticate with polished drawing room accent, and a whole coterie of young friends (the ubiquitous kids who appear in many of Crawford's early films) and still has eyes only for Andy (and what eyes!). The truant suitor attends her youth-filled soiree. She gives him those big soulful orbs often on the dance floor (who could resist?) and a huge highlight of the entire film comes when the star-crossed pair break out suddenly into impassioned, off-key song while dancing cheek-to-cheek! Oh, such shameless, endearing fun! Naturally the flame still burns in Andy for his "sweet" Bingo and during the party he's willing to prove his mettle with a fight (revealing Montgomery's underdeveloped physique). The deck is stacked against the kids, however, with even Uncle Ben conspiring against them, due to Andy's lack of funds.

Celebrating a birthday on the set. PHOTO COURTESY OF NEIL MACIEJEWSKI

Bingo doesn't take things lying down, though, and soon she has a revolver behind her chiffon-draped back! (Hey, it's Joan!)

One mildly prurient aspect of a number of Crawford's early films is the way the script often had her kissing her co-stars — male or female — on the lips, including much older men or "uncles," and finding excuses to display her in her underwear. Well, she did have adorable legs, but still! In this case, there is a scene in which she flips up the skirt of her dress to prove to her uncle she is indeed wearing her "thingamabobs."

Oh, it's all nonsense and awkward as adolescence and that's its appeal. Crawford is still very much a girl, winsome, beautiful and irresistible. Her buoyancy has not yet given way to the chic sophistication she would embody in *Possessed* only two years later. Even in grown-up Adrian gowns of chiffon and silk, she is all eyes, spirit and spunky cuteness. Montgomery also surprises and charms. Rather than being stiff as he often is, he is refreshingly lively, almost as vivacious as his co-star, and so very boyish. His droll line readings are a stitch, most notably to Mrs. Mason (Gertrude Astor): "No man would ever let you be lonely" and "I love your eyes!" (rolling his own) — and one of my favorites, to Crawford: "Sweet girl, I love your spirit!" The plot may be dopey, but who cares? *Untamed* and its young cast are hard to resist.

Films of the Thirties

PHOTO COURTESY OF JERRY MURBACH

Montana Moon (1930) ★ ★ ¾

Montana Moon is redeemed from being merely a creaky, God-awful, early sound film by the bright and charming presence of a very young Joan Crawford. It also features some fascinating historical film prototypes. It is part MGM musical, the first "singing cowboys" western, and part early "beach party" film with Crawford at the center of a cast of harmless, misunderstood "kids" just wanting to dance and cut loose — the Annette Funicello of the jazz age. The plot, ridiculous as it is, concerns a vivacious flapper named Joan "Montana" Prescott (Crawford) who is taking a train with her father, sister Lizzie (Dorothy Sebastian) and party-happy friends to the family ranch in Montana. Embarrassed by the fact that Jeff Pelham (Ricardo Cortez), Lizzie's boyfriend, keeps coming on to her, she packs her suitcase and gets off at a stop before the family's intended destination. There she flirts with a ticket seller and crosses the railroad tracks (Joan's on the right side of the tracks, this time) where she encounters an aw-shucks cowboy, Larry Kerrigan (Johnny Mack Brown) and spends the night at his fireside campsite. As it turns out, he's working the Bar L Ranch that belongs to her father and has no idea she is one of Prescott's "high-falutin," as he puts it, daughters, both of whom he's never met. Staying incognito, she allows him to call her "Montana." Understandably he falls for the sweetly seductive (though presumably chaste!) lass, so that in the very next scene of singing cowboys, the couple has married! Crawford sings a few solos, including "The Moon is Low" and "Let Me Give You Love" (with a chorus of cowboys) and sounds quite good. After a "honeymoon" night under the stars in sleeping bags beneath the prying eyes of Larry's eclectic cowboy friends, the couple travel to the Prescott ranch house. Joan has an amusing moment there as, clad in jodhpurs and cap, hands on hips, she makes an entrance in the main room where her friends are gathered and says, "Hey! Hey!," her tiny personage the center of attention. Announcing the marriage to her father proves to be only the beginning of the difficulties for the new couple.

As Larry is ready for bed, Joan's revving up to paint the town red. She does a shuffle into the bathroom, singing, "It'll be a hot time in the old town tonight" and emerges in an exquisite Adrian dress! The kids, meanwhile, have a big party planned for the newlyweds, but nose-to-the-grindstone Larry wants no part of it. Although vivacious Joan is ready to stay home and stand by her man, her disappointment is clear as she flashes Larry some baleful eyes (and what eyes!) until he relents, urging her to go without him. My favorite line is when, bubbling with glee, she tells

Home on the range with Johnny Mack Brown.

Larry, "I promise to make it a short session, really I do." The kids, meanwhile, are piling into their roadsters and squealing like the Munchkins and Joan eagerly squeezes in with them. She arrives the next morning as Larry is about to go to work, tipsy (and awfully adorable), full of life and singing. But she apologizes and covers his faces with kisses so he leaves her with a smile. The next night is another big bash where Joan is eager and proud to show off her man to the gang. They arrive, arm-in-arm, but Larry is as uncomfortable with the revelers as he is in his tuxedo and his efforts to "subdue" his young wife — who is in her element, flitting around flirtatiously and happily, and sitting atop a piano as her friends sing — backfires miserably. Will they ride off into the sunset together?

The many delights here are all due to the leading lady. Unfortunately, there are a few cogs in the wheels, not the least of which is Johnny Mack Brown with his dreadful, slow-witted acting and accent ("Excuse me,

Sexy Joan does an impromptu tango to enrage cowpoke hubby. PHOTO COURTESY OF NEIL MACIEJEWSKI

ma'am," he says, pronouncing "ma'am" "mon" as if he is Jamaican, sputtering and blinking and twisting his hat) and the very non-humorous and incongruous shtick of two Yiddish vaudevillians (Cliff Edwards and Benny Rubin) who belong in the West as much as Brown does — i.e., not at all. But Crawford is so alive, she smooths over the dead wood floating around her. From the minute she arrives on the scene, she is bursting with energy and charm. It's great fun to hear her squeal, "Oh, sure!" like the atypical chorine, wide-eyed in her cloche hat. Full of sweet smiles, she fusses over new husband (so dreadfully wrong for her and doomed not to make it in sound pictures either apparently) and meets his sullenness with humor and beguile, my favorite moment being when she says to him, "Come out from behind that veil, Reginald Pemberton!" Whether looking soulfully at Larry and making us believe she is charmed by him or dancing a tango and batting her eyes at other understandably besotted men, Crawford is nothing less than magical. And for her and her alone, the film has some redeeming value.

Our Blushing Brides (1930) ★★★★

This is one of my favorite early Joan Crawford pictures. While most creak at the seams, having been made in the early days of sound, the datedness in this film is part of its charm. In fact, one of my favorite lines is when Crawford as Gerry March says of her roommate's boyfriend, "Just what you'd expect. 1910 motor. 1930 chassis." The paper-thin plot concerns the romantic lives of three young women sharing a coldwater flat in the Bronx, practical Gerry; dreamy Connie Blair (the always-adorable Anita Page); and Franky Daniels (Dorothy Sebastian) who all also happen to work in the same department store (for $22.50 a week!) where they are apparently required to perform some prurient showroom lingerie-modeling for customers on the side. Amusingly, the opening reminds me of Robert Altman or the film *Coma* where supposedly "real life" conversations are filmed as our three female protagonists move through the locker rooms of the store and converge with dozens of other women at the mirrors. The conversations between various "extras" sound stagy and unconvincing here as they do in "Coma" with my favorite being a gum-chewing (what else?) broad saying to her girlfriend like something out of Dashiell Hammett, "And he says to me, 'Yeah?' and I says to him, 'Yeah.'" The crowded female locker room resembles a sweat shop.

In any case, the store owner's son, Tony Jardine (Robert Montgomery) makes clear his interest in Gerry as she poses in lingerie (all doe-eyed and softness) before him and a female client. She tells her roommates later, as they prepare to go out on the town and poor Gerry remains at home, that all men run pretty "true to form," particularly in a taxi cab, but that Tony Jardine seemed different. Given that he eyes her and makes leading comments about her "form" in the showroom and later boldly enters her dressing room when she is in the middle of changing and sits down

Prurient lingerie modeling (Crawford last one on right — closest to camera, of course!) PHOTO COURTESY OF NEIL MACIEJEWSKI

to watch, I can't see how she figures that. For some unknown reason, Montgomery was paired frequently with Crawford, although they have zero chemistry together and he is at all times stiff however suave. (Only in *Letty Lynton* does his artificiality work).

Meanwhile, Connie is involved with Tony's brother David (Raymond Hackett), a rake. Gerry cottons onto Davey's insincerity before Connie does when she spies him with another girl in a movie theater, which puts her in the awful dilemma of keeping mum over Connie's misguided happiness or trying to let her friend down gently.

A fanciful Art Deco ballet/modeling sequence is a highlight in which Crawford in becoming platinum wig dances a ballet with a chorus line of identically dressed platinum blondes, showcasing her high kicks. She is very alluring, girlish and coquettish in this sequence and when Tony invites her to walk with him, she says, coyly, "I really shouldn't in this gown." Then the pair go to a lavish Art Deco tree house where the whole set looks like a painting and Crawford seated on the edge of a divan like part of its design. Tony makes the expected moves on our demure Gerry, but she sets him straight with some strange dialogue. (Pushing him away

Life in the tenements. PHOTO COURTESY OF NEIL MACIEJEWSKI

as he attempts another kiss, she says, "Why is it when men get emotional, they all use ridiculous rubber stamp lines?" to which he replies, "That's clever, but you're being clever at the wrong time. Let's have a cigarette!" What else?) All in all, not an auspicious courtship. He doesn't seem much less a rake than his brother. But he is given the opportunity to prove his mettle later on.

Crawford as the center of the piece delivers, her charisma potent, and in spite of some nervous tics and feminine swooning, she registers solidly in the more demanding dramatic sequences. In a cross between her flapper/dancer and shopgirl persona, her sensible girl on her own is a charming counterpoint to the two flightier but equally charming roommates. The camera also has a love affair with her at times, lingering over her perfectly sculpted face in show room sequences. Page, as usual, impresses as a perhaps underappreciated talent, revealing a fine dramatic potential and range.

In all, it's hard not to like these girls. With their big, soft eyes; trim and feminine forms; vulnerability; and wistful voices, hiding mess behind sofa cushions for guests and rinsing out stockings in the sink, these "blushing brides" are immensely appealing.

Paid (1930) ★★★

Paid is a creaky, but interesting early talkie starring Joan Crawford as Mary Turner, a young woman wrongfully convicted of theft who, upon her release, seeks revenge upon the man responsible for her imprisonment, Edward Gilder (Purnell Pratt). Having achieved major stardom only two years earlier as a flapper in *Our Dancing Daughters* and not yet typecast into the "shopgirl-makes-good" formula that would become her milieu in the '30s, Crawford is uncharacteristically non-glamorous for a substantial part of her screen time and has a fascinating, almost feral look at times with shadowy eyes, reflecting her tribulations in prison. Life in the pen, in fact, is depicted with surprising grittiness with scenes of communal showers, mug shots, bad food, tough prison wardens, and hair-shearing. It's not pretty.

The interesting thing about Crawford in these early films is that, even when playing tough and strong characters (which she inevitably did, her own "fiber strong" because it had to be, as Rosalind Russell put it in Charles Castle's Crawford biography, *Raging Star*), she is fragile and beautiful, projecting an affecting, vulnerable, waif-like quality with huge eyes and soulful expressions. She wrings her hands and bites her lips periodically. One noticed how beautifully shaped her face was, and even dressed down, she has an arresting, natural glamour with high cheekbones and chiseled features, the fine profile. As much as she projected somewhat of an "alligator hide" in later years, she was quite the soft damsel in her youth, this quality discernible to the trained eye in later roles. When she prepares for the seduction of Gilder's son as part of her revenge, she sports a vamp look with dark lipstick, heavier eye makeup, spit curls and slinky, satiny gowns with lots of décolleté.

As the script has it, the newly-released Mary hooks up with also recently-released prison pal, Aggie (Marie Prevost) who seems to be "in the dough" and through Aggie, meets Joe Garson (Robert Armstrong), a racketeer. Returning with him to his apartment, Garson expects to look after Mary in return for sex, but upon attempting to kiss her, recognizes her inexperience and, taking pity on the poor kid, tells her to leave. As she is about to go, he decides he might be able to work with a "dame" and through her association with Joe, Mary becomes involved in his "gang." However, he also is respectful of her, giving her money for a cab and hoping that she might be ready for him one day. Having studied law while in prison, the savvy Mary first uses her knowledge to win a

PHOTO COURTESY OF JERRY MURBACH

$20,000 breach of promise suit against a wealthy man for Aggie and later, dressed to the nines in sleek gown, makes her move on Bob Guilder (Douglass Montgomery), Edward's son. Rejecting his initial moves on her, she succeeds in impressing him, her desired aim. When the elder Guilder (Purnell Pratt) meets Mary at a hotel and is informed by Bob that Mary is his wife, the outraged Edward arranges a police sting operation in which

Crawford with Douglass Montgomery. PHOTO COURTESY OF NEIL MACIEJEWSKI

the gang will steal the Mona Lisa painting from the Guilder house and, thus, he can send Mary back to the pen. Things do not quite work as planned, however, and a shooting gets thrown into the mix.

This crime drama is distinguished by the smart, feisty female protagonist, although it does suffer somewhat from datedness and minor sound issues. Amusingly, the floozies in this period always wear the same sort of negligees with lots of feathers, the "gauche" uniform, their voices squeaky and "common," as the gangsters "talk tough." Crawford smokes and has a take-charge, brassy attitude, and still gets in some wisecracks. When Bob says, "Aw cut it, Mary, you're making me feel like a fool," she gives him the big eyes over her shoulder and, without skipping a beat, responds, "And is it such a novel sensation?" Although it was a good opportunity for Crawford to showcase her dramatic range, there is a slightly amateurish feeling about this film, the acting occasionally broad and hokey. Montgomery is sweet and appealing and quite engaging paired with Crawford. He seems to be wearing eyeliner, as was customary in silent films.

One shot that jumps out for me is the close-up of Mary smoking as she spots the elder Guilder in the hotel lobby and recognizes him. One isn't used to seeing this harder look on Crawford's face at this point in her career when she was for the most part softer, nobler and more girlishly vivacious than she would be in her later career. In spite of moments of silent screen grimacing and over-emoting, her technique yet evolving, she ably carries the film.

Dance, Fools, Dance (1931) ★★★★

Dance Fools Dance is one of my favorite early Crawford films. Directed by Harry Beaumont, it is a gently risqué and fast-moving pre-code film circa 1931. Joan Crawford, in her early twenties here, is particularly adorable, vivacious and sexy with gently waved hair, spit-curl, and big,

Crawford becomes a cub reporter after the stock market crash. PHOTO COURTESY OF NEIL MACIEJEWSKI

Crawford (with becoming spit curl) at the approximate period she appeared in *Dance, Fools, Dance*.

long-lashed eyes. As Bonnie Jordan, she's a spoiled rich girl who becomes a cub reporter after the stock market crash leaves her family penniless (yes, the girl down on her luck who makes good, her staple role at this stage in her career). Her assignment is to infiltrate the gang who murdered fellow reporter and friend, Scranton (Cliff Edwards), by posing as a dancer in the nightclub of gang leader Jake Luavo (Clark Gable). "Use any weapon you've got," her editor tells her. We all know what that means!

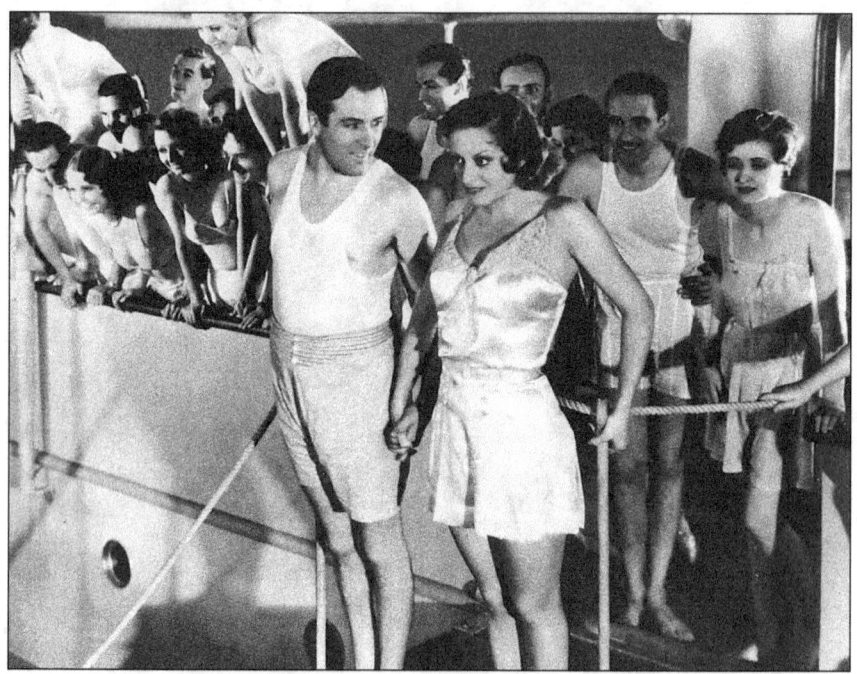

Lester Vail and Joan Crawford. The pre-code kids take a swim in their underwear — satin for our gal (what else?)!

Gosh, if not the flirtatious and exhilarating tap dance number Crawford does as the new act, the sight of her walking confidently across the room towards Gable in a gold lame gown is worth the price of admission alone. When she meets the King, the sexual sparks fly like no one's business, their real attraction palpable. Gable is appropriately rugged and ruthless and gives a very effective, hard-edged performance. Unbeknownst to our heroine, it is her own brother Rodney (William Bakewell) who unwittingly got caught up with the Mob and was forced to perform the contract hit on the reporter he'd earlier confided in (touching since brother and sister are both likeable good kids). Crawford plays the spunky, independent woman she is so good at, mirroring her own ambitions and tenacity.

The pre-code moments are delicious such as when beautiful Bonnie is blow drying her hair after jumping from the deck of a yacht in her underwear (modest underwear, folks) and her boyfriend Bob (Lester Vail) enters the room. They are both in their pajamas, Bonnie in a glamorous satin jumpsuit. Before a seductive kiss, she assures him that she isn't old-fashioned and believes in trying out love on approval.

There are several interesting aspects of this film. For one, it's based on real events of the day, the St. Valentine Day's Massacre, so it's a good window into the period. There aren't simplistic happy endings; the gangsters, however charming they may appear, are presented ultimately as sociopaths. For another, there's the absolutely combustible and electric chemistry of Gable and Crawford in their first pairing. Crawford is a free-spirited, yet practical heroine with courage and moxie — that '30s staple, the girl reporter. It's clear why she was a reigning star of MGM and why she and Gable were paired together in seven more films.

Laughing Sinners (1931) ★★★

This initially struck me as one of the weakest of the Crawford-Gable pairings, but its charms grew on me in repeat viewings. Based on a Broadway play *Torch Song* by Kenyon Nicholson, *Laughing Sinners* stars Joan Crawford as Ivy "Bunny" Stevens, a vivacious chorus girl working in a two-bit hotel and having a heavy romance with Howard Palmer (Neil Hamilton), a "heel" who plans — unbeknownst to Ivy — to drop her and marry the boss' daughter. When Howard leaves "Bunny" a goodbye note after she sings a "torch song" to him ("What Can I Do — I Love That Man") and does a spirited dance, she is crestfallen and tries to commit suicide by jumping off a bridge (shades of *Mildred Pierce*). But Clark Gable, woefully miscast yet appealing as a pious Salvation Army preacher named Carl Loomis, comes to the rescue and gets her to don the cloak and take to a life of good deeds for the misfortunate. He urges her to meet him in the park on Sunday for a picnic and ultimately she decides to take up his offer, appearing like a beauteous blonde angel (and she is very young and beautiful here) as he plays ball with the kids (among them Mary Ann Jackson of *Little Rascals* fame who always seems more a midget than child). The moment Carl catches sight of Ivy on the edge of the park is nothing short of magnetic. She is a vision and the two have chemistry that burns the screen.

Crawford is a blonde babe in *Laughing Sinners*.

Oh, it's creaky, but the simple messages of hope and redemption are rather touching. There is also an interesting pre-code sauciness such as the frank scenes of bawdy boarding house life and Crawford undressing in silhouette as she converses with fellow chorus girl and friend Ruby (a delightfully salty Marjorie Rambeau who later played her mother in the unrelated film *Torch Song*). It's worthwhile just to see the very young

Crawford as Bunny Stevens before singing a torch song for the man who jilts her. PHOTO COURTESY OF NEIL MACIEJEWSKI

Gable sans facial hair (delivering some terribly sincere dialogue) and Crawford — a mere girl and oh so cuddly and vibrant. As in *Dance, Fools Dance*, she has shades of her flapper persona, dancing with the cheeky abandon and boundless energy that made her so eye catching in nightclubs in real life. A highlight is when sincere Ivy runs across old flame Howard who convinces her to have a one night stand. The poor kid is so ashamed afterwards of her transgression with this man she once loved that she takes a few nips and dances on top of a table for a room full of men, shaking her tambourine. Best of all, Carl comes to the rescue, willing to fight for Ivy's virtue. Rather than judging, he assures her that her one mistake is no reason to shed the cloak and happiness is restored! Ivy realizes that her former lover is a selfish cad and that she has more self esteem, enough to put him behind her forever. Arm in arm, she walks to the horizon with Carl in a lovely fadeout, both of them in Salvation Army garb once again.

To see Crawford, a blonde babe, laughing recklessly in the table scene, and Gable, slightly uncomfortable in his role but persuasively attractive enough to make Ivy's conversion palatable — well, it's priceless and endearing. That's what makes these old movies such treasures! That and

Bunny Stevens (Joan Crawford) in a cuddly kitchen scene with Carl Loomis (Clark Gable — who else?), her "salvation." PHOTO COURTESY OF NEIL MACIEJEWSKI

the cheap, but somehow sincere sentiment. Pet moment: Crawford and Hamilton in a clinch of passionate theatrical angst. Johnny Mack Brown played the Carl Loomis role but was wisely replaced midstream with Clark Gable.

This Modern Age (1931) ★★¾

Nothing was spared in way of chic wardrobe or sleek Art Deco sets and props for *This Modern Age*, making it visually sumptuous as "our dancing daughter" rallies against stiff-necked respectability and kicks up her heels in Jazz Age Paris. There's a look of silver and cream in the black and white cinematography because of all the chrome, and mother and daughter heroines are the height of 1920s elegance. A buoyant, blonde, youthful Joan Crawford stars as Valentine Winters, the 19-year-old daughter of Diane ("Dee-ahn") Winters (the effusive, deliciously melodramatic Pauline Frederick). Valentine shows up unexpectedly at Diane's swank home in Paris (Diane is a kept woman) upon the death of her father and

A beauteous blonde Crawford with Pauline Frederick, an actress she was said to resemble in her youth.

although initially unsettled, Diane takes one look at the classy beauty who is her long-lost offspring and embraces her. The admiration is mutual and mother and daughter quickly pick up their aborted relationship (aborted because Pauline's father had been granted custody and Pauline was denied visiting rights). Soon Valentine is living the high life with other young people in sexy, svelte gowns; smoking cigarettes; and tooling in big cars with beaus, her motto being "make virtue of vice, never take anything seriously and always be amusing." An accident allows Valentine to meet Harvard football man, Bob Blake, Jr. (Neil Hamilton) and quickly the two bright young things fall in love and become engaged. But when Blake's parents come to meet Valentine's mother, they quickly disapprove of the freewheeling lifestyle they observe there — and naturally the whole carousing cast of kids piles in as Val and future in-laws are playing bridge, some of them imitating Rudolf Valentino, asking Val to find them the Scotch. Worse, Bob learns Diane's secret of being a kept woman and nobly or ignobly, confronts Valentine, wanting to take her away from the "atmosphere" that she is "too good for." Val, furious, gives him the boot, but later learns from Diane that his "monstrous" claims were true! Diane agrees to end that lifestyle for Valentine's sake, however, and the two hole up in a homespun hovel together, Val still heart-broken over Bob. Quicker than Valentine can tack another picture to the wall with heel of her shoe, Diane has taken up with her former lover again and a distraught Valentine turns to old boyfriend Tony Girard (Monroe Owsley) and champagne in despair. Will love out?

This Modern Age is slight and not the best of Crawford's canon, but still easy to swallow due to the swank visuals and uncanny pairing of Frederick and Crawford. Evidently Frederick was the actress that the young Crawford was most compared to, and the two formed an affection for one another that transmits delightfully. They bear a pleasing resemblance to one another in looks, personality, enthusiasm and flair. Both are also given to ebullient melodrama with Frederick tossing her head and making theatrical gestures, and Crawford mincing and mugging occasionally with "dancing daughter" "hey-hey-girl" enthusiasm. It's hard to tell which one is hammier at times or if the younger actress is indeed imitating her elder on occasion, but they are nonetheless charming. Crawford is also beautiful and sexy, wearing one of my favorite dresses — a tiered chiffon, floor-length creation with lots of décolleté. She rallies tearfully against smug upper crust disapproval, something that would become her milieu; has enough brass, sass and sweetness for the youth crowd; and indeed makes virtue of vice. My favorite line: when Tony flirts with her, Val says, "In Spain they call that baloney."

Possessed (1931) ★★★★

Possessed is the quintessential example of Joan Crawford's "shop girl makes good" screen persona of the 1930s and it is also the peak of the Crawford/Clark Gable love affair. Crawford plays Marian Martin, a young woman working in a small town paper box factory (can it get any more pathetic than that?) who has higher ambitions for herself (understandably). Reluctant to marry her bombastic hometown suitor Al Manning (Wallace Ford), she watches an array of people, some obviously wealthy, through the windows of a passing train and decides to seek her fortunes

Crawford at the height of her love affair with Gable and gardenias. PHOTO COURTESY OF JIM MAHONEY

in New York City. Interesting shots are interspersed through *Possessed*, such as the scene of Marian and Al walking home through grimy, squalid surroundings with Al arguing with Marian about marriage while in the background an older woman squabbles with a drunken man. Crawford is also given the opportunity for some surprising pre-feminist speeches, this admirable defiance and sass something that distinguishes all her films, for the most. "You don't own me," she tells Al. "Nobody does. My life belongs to me" and to her mother, "If I were a man…you'd think it was right for me to go out and get anything I could out of life and use anything I had to get it. Why should men be so different? All they've got are their brains and they're not afraid to use them. Well, neither am I!"

In New York Marian meets lawyer Mark Whitney (Clark Gable) and becomes his mistress, telling him with complete lack of guile that she is after him for his money, which amuses him. Shortly she is living in the lap of luxury on Park Avenue attired in stunning Adrian gowns and one offensive (to my mind) scene shows an increasing array of glittering bracelets on her wrists as her hand tears the pages from a calendar to denote the passing years. Mark and Marian entertain (and as in the case of the real life star, Marian has learned how to "be a lady" and choose the proper forks and wines), but Mark is reluctant to marry his lover, forcing her instead to adopt the guise of "Mrs. Mallard" to lend her position more respectability, because he had been burned (what else?) in the past by his first wife. Pre-code moments show the two drop-dead gorgeous and glamorous figures (both attired in black evening wear) canoodling in front of a mirror and kissing as Marian's fur drops to the ground, then arriving late at a party. Crawford also has a touching scene where she sings in several languages, notably in English "How Long Will This Last?," looking with abject love and sweetness at Gable the whole time. Their off-screen love is palpable. But it isn't easy being a mistress, her position making her vulnerable to insults and when Mark decides to run for governor, his colleagues urge him to dump "Mrs. Mallard."

Although dated, the beauty and sizzling chemistry of Crawford and Gable and a few of the situations give it a real distinction. Crawford shows a remarkable growth in her acting with this film, particularly in a tour de force scene in the library where she secretly listens to Mark's colleagues advising him to end his relationship and shifting emotions cross her face. She is completely heartfelt, using her lips and eyebrows (thin here) to express emotion as so many from that period did. In the typical woman-sacrificing-all-for-her-man-and-suffering-torment mode, she nobly decides to make it easier for Mark to leave her and thereby not jeopardize his career by telling him she was only using him and that she intends to marry Al. She tells him she is "common, smelling of sweat and glue" and that she likes it. She intends to return to the "level that I came from," at which point Mark slaps her face and our poor suffering girl leaves the room in tears. For me, this brought Mark down a few pegs

Marian is confronted in the library with the indignities of being a mistress.
PHOTO COURTESY OF NEIL MACIEJEWSKI

in my estimate, since Marian's suffering beneath the pretense was quite transparent and how could he believe this story after being involved with her for three years? Cruelly he adds, "You might have given me two weeks' notice. My cook does that." Ouch.

Then *(Spoilers!)* in a finale both intriguing and ridiculous, Marian (in a great Adrian dress and hat at a rakish angle, what else?) secretly attends Mark's election rally. Seeing that a campaign is afoot to ruin Mark when confetti is scattered through the crowd with notes saying, "Who is Mrs. Mallard?," Marian bravely faces the crowd. She identifies herself without apology, telling them that her love with Mark Whitney was real and not a crime. As a mistress and "sexual outlaw," the dignity with which Crawford presents herself through the film truly elevates it from the mawkish mores that were typical in this era. As applause rips through the auditorium, Marian runs away, sobbing, into the rain, no less (first the paper box factory, now the rain — does our girl have no reprieve?). Mark follows her, however, and tells her that she is more important to him than winning or losing the election and they embrace sweetly under the elevated train.

This is the young, enchanting 1930s Crawford that so few get to see, unfortunately. Characteristically she mirrors and upbraids the social hypocrisies of the time. She is absolutely fetching and appealing with expressive, limpid, huge eyes; the swanlike shoulders of the 1930s, prior to what would become her signature look of linebacker shoulder pads; very vivacious yet strong; very affecting. This film captures one of my favorite screen couples at their height of passion and sweetness and is an interesting window into how women were treated.

According to the biography *Crawford's Men*, a technician on the set of Possessed said: "Crawford and Gable were attracted to each other instantly. He had what she wanted and she had what he wanted. Call it chemistry, call it love at first sight or physical attraction. The electricity between them sparked on the screen, too. It wasn't just acting. They mean every kiss and embrace." Since both Gable and Crawford were married (albeit unhappily) at the time, supposedly Louis B. Mayer, head of MGM, put the kibosh on their relationship, which they carried on covertly. Crawford said she cried every morning on her drive to the studio and wept all the way home. According to *Crawford's Men*, she couldn't sleep but dreaded her thoughts when awake and feared for her future, her marriage, and her passionate love for Gable. "I no longer enjoyed parties and small talk," she said. Occasionally she met Gable on the beach and he'd listen. Needless to say, they never did marry, but, according to Crawford, carried on their relationship, on and off, for thirty years, remaining great friends. Crawford confessed, according to several bios, that Gable was the only man she ever loved (and I believe it!). Gable, meanwhile, ultimately found the "love of his life" in Carole Lombard, although Crawford evidently meant a great deal to him.

Grand Hotel (1932) ★★★★★

I adore *Grand Hotel*. I think Pauline Kael summed it up best when citing the sheer star power of the cast and the ultra glamour as the enduring magic of this film. The plot basically involves a cast of characters whose lives intertwine when they come to stay at the opulent Grand

Hotel in 1930s Berlin, then the cultural hub of the world and magnet to the elite and notorious in all walks of life. What a cast to do justice to this premise — yes, star wattage at operatic levels with John Barrymore as a thieving Baron; Lionel Barrymore as the dying Kringelein attempting to live out his last days in splendor; Greta Garbo as an aging ballerina; Joan Crawford as the lovely stenographer Flaemmschen; and Wallace Beery as Preysing, the industrial magnate who hires Flaemmschen and

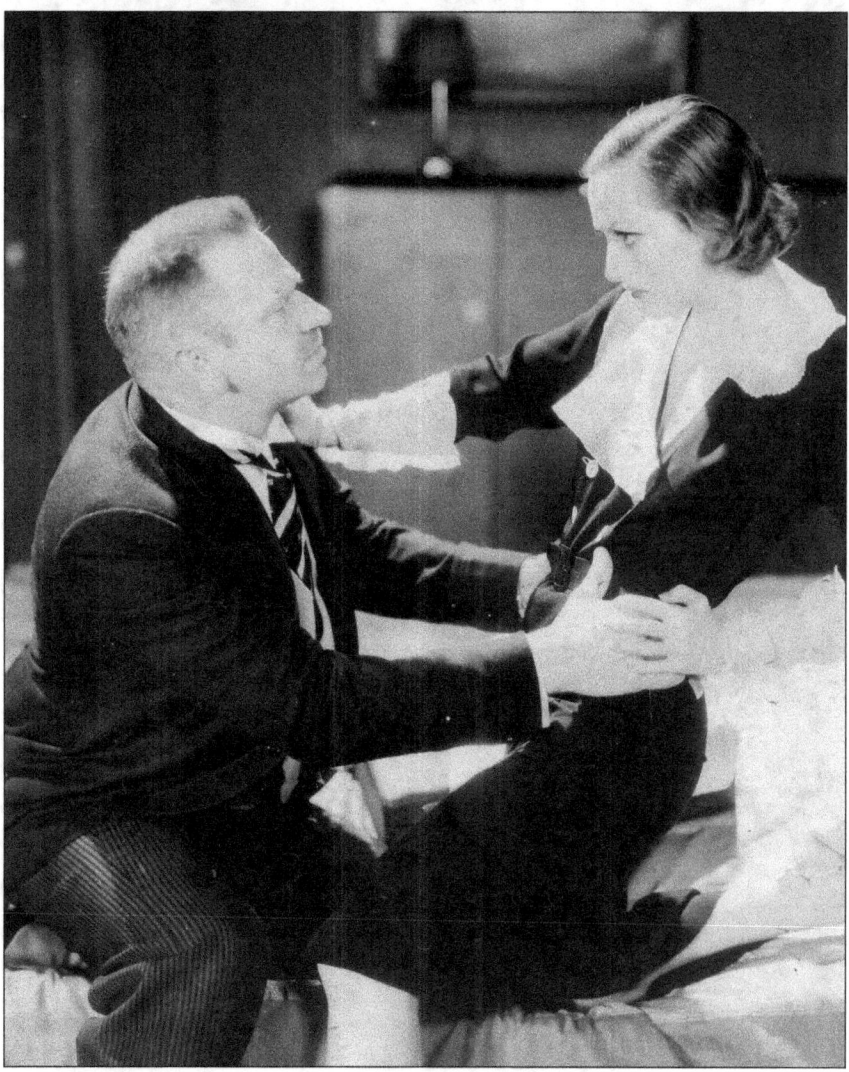

Beautiful Flaemmschen (Joan Crawford) with her lecherous employer Preysing (Wallace Beery) at the Grand Hotel. PHOTO COURTESY OF NEIL MACIEJEWSKI

You can never have enough beautiful profile shots of Joan!

hopes to possess her. The hotel after the war teems with desperation and corruption beneath the surface of elegance and wealth.

Based on the book by Vicki Baum, *Menschen Im Hotel*, which became a stage play, Irving Thalberg pulled out all the stops by having nearly all the studio's major stars in one film in an ensemble style. This film won the first Academy Award deservedly and captures a grand old Europe and way of life now gone. Crawford is young, elegant, and enchanting here as Flaemmschen, her fresh, earthy and cheeky wit a great contrast to the melodramatic Garbo. She is also warm and sympathetic. TV Guide summed it

With John Barrymore. PHOTO COURTESY OF NEIL MACIEJEWSKI

up accurately when saying of Crawford, "Even though her face looks like a deco statue's, — perhaps the most beautiful eyes and nose ever photographed — she's brimming like a livewire of ambitious current." They also note how modern she looks with her casual hair and little black dress, which she does; her attitude and demeanor is refreshingly contemporary. To my opinion and evidently that of many critics, she steals the show. But Garbo

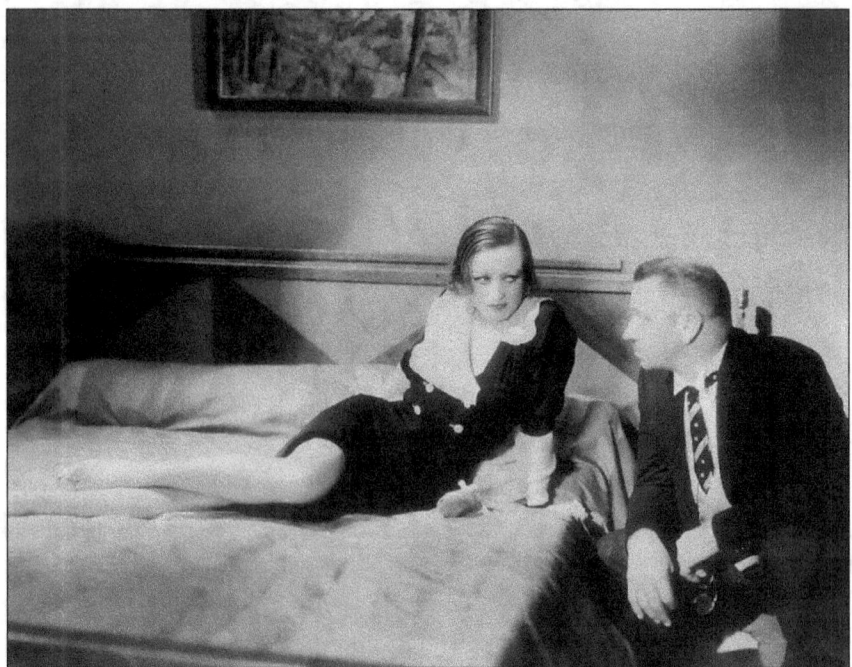

Stenographer and siren — what secretary can afford to buy her own threads? PHOTO COURTESY OF JERRY MURBACH

is still luminous, her exaggerated style almost a pantomime left over from the silents yet fascinating; when she walks down the hall in her minks, she is thrillingly enigmatic. John Barrymore is touching as Baron Felix von Geigern, a hotel thief with a soul (and a dachshund) and fundamental decency. And Lionel is unforgettable as the man clinging to the final chance.

Absinthe, anyone?

Letty Lynton (1932) ★★★★★

Letty Lynton is the ultimate Joan Crawford film and a cinematic treasure that tragically is not available for sale or broadcast, due to a legal entanglement of decades in which it was said to infringe upon the play

Dishonored Lady. This needs to be rectified so that this fascinating and important film can be restored to pristine condition and seen in all its glory. Not only is it sublimely glamorous with Crawford attired in some of Adrian's most stunning creations, leading designer Edith Head to call it "the single most important influence on fashion in film history," but it is one of the most intriguing of the pre-Code films I've seen with

With the nefarious Nils.

Joan Crawford as Letty Lynton in the white organdy dress that allegedly sold by the millions in knock-off copies storewide.

an amazing performance from Crawford. Its lack of distribution is an immense loss to film history and film lovers.

Crawford plays the title role, a wealthy heiress who has been living the "high life" in Montevideo, the capital of Uruguay, with oily South American playboy Emile Renaul (Nils Asher). He is smitten with Letty, but she is bored and announces that she's "had enough." This is a familiar

Crawford was at her gayest (err — not that kind) and most enchanting here. PHOTO COURTESY OF NEIL MACIEJEWSKI

game for him, since apparently Letty runs away and then sends him impassioned love letters, but she insists that this time their affair is finished. While fleeing with her loyal maid Miranda (Louise Closser Hale) on board a ship bound for New York, Letty meets genial, debonair Jerry Darrow (Robert Montgomery) who has the cabin across the hall from hers. Both parties secretly arrange to be seated at the same table where Letty exchanges witty banter with Jerry and together they take a brisk and playful walk around the deck. Their affection grows and after their weeks spent together on board, they become engaged. To Letty's dismay, Renaul is waiting when their boat docks and makes clear to her that he is not going to let her go, using her letters as blackmail. With all chances of her happiness threatened, Letty confronts him in his room which leads to murder.

Along with giving a superb performance in a challenging role, Crawford is at her most stunning with that exquisite beauty and girlish vivacity that was so enchanting in the 1930s, a personality that is now most familiar to viewers through *Grand Hotel*. This alluring and youthful quality and her gay laugh would pretty much disappear after the '30s. In later films, she indeed still exudes charm and sex appeal, but the girlish, softer Crawford would give way to a hard-boiled image that would become increasingly steelier as her screen and perhaps private persona toughened. What makes *Letty Lynton* so astonishing is that because the tone of the film in the shipboard romance between Letty and Jerry is so light and even humorous, the murder scene and the viperish, feral Crawford that emerges there is shocking and intense. Her silent screen experience really comes into play to make expression, eyes and body language transfixing and chilling, followed by very real terror. "Yes, I did it! Yes, I did it!" she hisses as Renaul drinks the poison that she had intended for herself. "I'm glad I did it, you dirty, filthy, greedy mongrel." Never have I seen Crawford quite this way, comparable only perhaps to her turn in *A Woman's Face* and one wonders why, having shown her abilities, she wasn't given meatier roles as opposed to the endless frothy concoctions she was served at this juncture in her career. When she emerges from behind the doorway of the bedroom to confront Renaul, it is riveting like something out of *Nostrafu*.

Crawford also has a genuinely touching scene when she is crying on the ship as "Silent Night" plays because there are no messages for her for Christmas, her relationship with her mother strained and unloving (her image in the moonlight in white dress against a background of sea and night sky is visually sumptuous and breathtaking). Montgomery is pleasant, although his pairings with Crawford in this and other films are devoid of the sexual chemistry she had with Clark Gable and even Franchot Tone. Asher is appropriately sinister and villainous, his dark looks aiding the authenticity of the characterization, and Robson and Hale are wonderful in the supporting roles.

(Spoilers!) Equally shocking and unusual for 1932 is the ending when Letty is brought in for Renaul's murder where not only does she lie, but is aided and abetted in the lie by both Montgomery and her mother (May Robson). In the final frame, Miranda whistles the wedding march as Letty and Jerry happily depart. Thus, as in *Rain*, the essentially good "bad" girl is not punished, but actually triumphs.

An absolute cinematic treasure that one hopes will be restored to the pristine print and release it sorely deserves.

Rain (1932) ★★★★★

Rain is one of my favorite films of all times. With the rhythm of the steadily falling rain and South Seas island drumbeats as backdrop, it tells the story of a spirited, "fallen woman," Sadie Thompson (Joan Crawford) whose sauciness, vivacity and sexual vitality entrance the men

"Here's the shy Kentucky refugee!" Sadie Thompson (Joan Crawford) with the boys (what else?). PHOTO COURTESY OF NEIL MACIEJEWSKI

at a Pago Pago hotel but put her at the mercy of a puritanical preacher, Alfred Davidson (Walter Huston) who demands her repentance and conversion. Based on Somerset Maugham's short story, this story of hypocrisy and human frailty has at its heart a magnetic performance by Crawford. Clad in a slinky dress that reveals her lovely, lithe figure; the cigarette dripping from heavily-reddened lips; a fur hanging from her shoulder; and that halo of outrageous curls, she is exciting, ripe, and very alive — even in the worst prints, she lights the screen the minute she makes her appearance (and what a memorable entrance). One first sees each heavily braceleted wrist and then her ankles in shoddy pumps (with bows!) emerge from a doorway. Huston, by contrast, is indeed more wooden, but effectively conveys the rigidity (and later torment) of Davidson.

The storyline is potent and moving and certainly ahead of its time; I remember being deeply affected by this film as a child seeing it on television. Director Lewis Milestone's adventurous visual style adds to the impact. Love the double entendres such as when Crawford asks for a corkscrew and Guy Kibbee supplies it so insinuatingly, his hand with the corkscrew appearing from around the door. Shots of fisherman bringing up nets of fish counterbalance with later shots of the net bringing a more sinister catch. Some have complained about the lack of "explicitness" in this film, but I beg to disagree strongly. Do we need to see everything blow-by-blow to "get the picture," pun intended? Isn't the creak of the door and the struggle on the preacher's face far more effective? And Crawford's large eyes like lamps and that slinky dress say it all. Love the shots of the preacher towering over her on the stairs and she forced to look up at him, the dominant male in a power position, the supplicant beseeching an unmoved and harsh deity. Yes, she is an achingly vulnerable and sympathetic character, which makes her persecution even more reprehensible.

There are so many great lines! They just don't do this stuff anymore! Thompson to Davidson: "Your God and me could never be shipmates! And the next time you talk to him, you can tell him from me that Sadie Thompson is on her way to hell!" And to Horn and soldiers: "I'd race ya to the beach if it wasn't for these pesky heels!"

It's a tragedy that it was not appreciated at the time of its release, causing Crawford to underrate her own fascinating and emotionally raw performance. Stripped down to the repentant, she is far more beautiful yet it's interesting that this "purified" self is portrayed as unhealthy. That choice alone speaks volumes about the nature of true "spirit."

Today We Live (1933) ★★★★

Today We Live is one of Joan Crawford's most unusual films, both romance and action picture replete with air battle sequences. As Diana "Ann" Boyce Smith, a young Englishwoman caught in a love triangle in World War I, never before or after would she look so stunningly beautiful; I actually gasped in several scenes at her sublime close-ups. In the early and mid-'30s, she was indeed at her apex in this regard and here in particular, she looks more exquisite in the trench coats than in her Adrian dresses, the starkness of the suits and peaked hats accentuating her looks. Her performance, in turn, is delicate, understated and fine. Although frequently dismissed and treated as a glamorous clotheshorse, Crawford was extraordinarily gifted at conveying emotional nuances and certainly had the large and beautiful eyes that spoke volumes. Beyond the rhapsodic beauty of Crawford, the film has a feeling of poetry, particularly due to the effecting music, the moody black and white cinematography, the backdrop, and an odd lack of pronouns that forces the leads to talk in a kind of surreal haiku.

This French postcard depicts four scenes from the film.

Directed by Howard Hawks, the film is based on William Faulkner's short story "Turnabout" and concerns an American aviator Richard Bogard (Gary Cooper) who comes to England in 1916 to rent Ann's country home. (A woman was not in the original story, but was worked into the plotline so that Crawford could be cast). Ann has just learned her father was killed in the war and finds it difficult to watch Richard handling her father's guns and things in the study, finally breaking down a bit so that he apologizes. She plans to live in the gardener's cottage on the estate (which proves to be quite charming if not as spectacular and ornate as the house.) When Richard meets Ann bicycling on the grounds, he confesses that he loves her. (This is unbelievable, due to a lack of chemistry between the two, however lovely Ann is, and the brief span of time given to the development.) Ann says she loves him, too, and shortly he is joining the cause because of her. Meanwhile, Ann has a brother Ronnie (Franchot Tone) and childhood friend Claude Hope (Robert Young) who are both lieutenants in the war, and with this incestuous bond the trio has, she becomes engaged to Claude in Ronnie's presence. (Never mind that her chemistry with Franchot Tone is so smoldering — this being the film in which they met and fell in love — that all the sexual energy seems directed to the "forbidden fruit.") With the ongoing lack of pronouns ("Thought so. Your letters."), none of the dialogue sounds the least realistic and as the three brace for entering the war and try to seem British if not manage the accents (Crawford tries and intermittently succeeds), they are as stiff as wind-up toys. Not even the stiff-upper-lip-British are that stiff. But this idiosyncrasy adds to the strange beauty and "unreality" of this unique film and to the emotion and unreality of war.

While volunteering as a nurse, Ann reads that Richard has been killed in action and begins living with Claude outside of marriage. The scene in which Ann tells Claude, "No one in the world I love so much" is quite tender and beautiful with Crawford breathtaking, as usual. Then the pair feel bound to tell Ronnie ("no secrets"; how kinky!) and when Ann says, looking at her brother with big, solemn eyes from beneath a cap sitting fashionably on the side of her head, "We didn't wait, Ronnie," he merely replies, "I knew it." The whole sequence drips with "sibling" sexual tension, particularly when Ronnie grabs Ann's chin and kisses her. Meanwhile, Richard is alive and, learning Ann is in France, goes to find her. Their chance meeting in a hall brimming with war activity, however, ultimately proves to be a disappointment because Ann tells him she is "dead." He learns what that cryptic comment means when he shortly runs across a drunken Claude and is obliged to help another soldier carry the lad home. Ann opens the door at Claude's home. (Frankly I can't see how he has the right to be angry at her if she has "shacked up" with someone, given that he was presumed dead and barely knew her.) In any case, the war has turned the fate of all three.

The addition of Ann and the romance works well as a good motivation for a war-within-a-war in the story, the animosity of Richard toward Claude adding a precarious danger and opportunity for nobility. There are numerous exciting and surprisingly effective scenes of testosterone-laden air battles with Claude proving to be a happy idiot when set up by a bitter Richard to "show him some [real] war." The "kid" guns down planes as if playing a game. Meanwhile, as the men are in the middle of killing and ego proving, a teary Ann is worried about the way Richard looked at her last. ("His eyes. Hating me.")

Today We Live is a very unique and beautiful film with much to recommend it, however strange it may be. The performances are strong in spite of dodgy British accents. Crawford is amazingly true, as usual, heartfelt, eloquent and sincere, so that even when forced to say stilted dialogue, she convinces and resonates emotionally. She also has her enchanting giggle and girlishness yet and those Garboesque close-ups are to die for; she gives the film its necessary feminine element. Young is perhaps the weakest link, although one gets accustomed to his glibness as he is playing a somewhat naïve character, an example of tragically unprepared youth. Tone, who many reviewers admire, is strong in spots, although his pipe and blustery masculinity come off as extremely awkward and phony. The clipped shorthand of the speech, although a bit humorous, adds to the rhythm and peculiar beauty: "Sister. Mine." (Tone indicating Ann). "See better now. See lots of things." (Young) "He was here. Left this. Will come again." (Crawford) Or the best: "Tried. Tried terribly."

The one squeamish part is the cockroaches that crop up repeatedly, likely something Faulkner himself experienced in the war. In one scene Crawford handles a roach as Tone and Young look on eagerly, treating it as a plaything, and in later scenes, soldiers use cockroaches to duel the way some use chickens. Did Crawford really handle a bug or was it a fake?

In all, one of Crawford's most unusual film in which she gives a first-rate performance and perhaps the film I'd choose above all that displays like Hurrell the peak of her beauty.

Dancing Lady (1933) ★★★★★

Originally *Dancing Lady* was not one of my favorite Joan Crawford or Gable/Crawford films, but I now appreciate immensely its beautiful, black and white, Deco splendor, music and upbeat storyline. The script is based on James Warner Bellah's delightful Runyonesque novel. Crawford is Janie Barlow, a nice girl forced by circumstance to work in a cheap burlesque show. When she is busted in a raid, Franchot Tone as wealthy Tod Newton bails her out, because, of course, he's romantically interested in her. Hoping to get her eventually interested in marriage, Newton arranges for Janie to work in a show put on by musical director

PHOTO COURTESY OF NEIL MACIEJEWSKI

Patch Gallagher (Clark Gable) which would help move her up from seedy chorus work to Broadway. Patch gives her a hard time, but ultimately he falls for her, is impressed by her talent and moves her into the star spot. But jealous Newton conspires to sabotage the show. Guess who wins the lady's heart?

There are some marvelous scenes including the burlesque scene in the beginning when Crawford gets to show some of that charisma that made her a star — her flirtatious smiling and eye contact with audience;

Crawford and Gable, a magic duo. PHOTO COURTESY OF JERRY MURBACH

the gym scene between Gable and Crawford where they both glow in one another's presence; the sumptuous Depression era fantasy swimming pool scene where Crawford and Tone are both so attractive, she more than he (in my estimate — in fact, Joan with her sleek body and sculptured, porcelain face looks like an absolute goddess), and oh those party scenes with the wonderful singing and costumes and music — a world of

The "Let's Go Bavarian" number with Astaire — beer, beer, beer! PHOTO COURTESY OF JERRY MURBACH

elegance. Eve Arden makes a delightful cameo as a blonde impersonating a Southerner for an audition. My only objection is that Janie Barlow is too darn unconvincingly sweet when around Patch, continually approaching him with doe eyes and teary gratitude. But, of course, she looks lovely in her Adrian gowns, and her '30s dialogue ("I'm going up where it's art — uptown"; "scram"; and "so you're laying down") is a hoot. My other quibble is that Gable is too one-note gruff, shouting frequently, often abrasive. That's not the way I like to see him in a Crawford and Gable film, even if one knows he likes her.

This is a veritable MGM stew with everyone on the lot in the film —

Being chewed out by Patch. Isn't that always love? PHOTO COURTESY OF JERRY MURBACH

the Three Stooges and Nelson Eddy and Fred Astaire and Crawford and Gable and Tone! As for the dance numbers, Joan Crawford is a vivacious hoofer, but her dancing style in no way meshes with Fred Astaire's debonair ballroom elegance. A girl auditioning for Janie's spot, in fact, doing fouettés, is so obviously superior a dancer, in spite of the script's attempts to discredit her, that one can only imagine Patch's artistic integrity is prejudiced by his personal feelings for Janie. This was Astaire's debut, incidentally, and needless to say, he's a paradigm of style. The finale, while fun, pales in comparison to the spectacular Busby Berkeley extravaganzas that capped musicals like *42nd Street*, yet it's still joyous and wonderful and the final clinch with Clark and Joan always brings tears to my eyes.

Sadie McKee (1934) ★★★★

Excerpts from *Sadie McKee* are featured in *Whatever Happened to Baby Jane* to show Blanche Hudson (Joan Crawford) at the height of her stunning glamour and beauty, and indeed the remarkable thing about *Sadie* is Crawford's face. Crawford had a visage meant for cinema and to appreciate

The maid makes good.

this, it's important to see her in her glory days (in films like "Sadie") when the camera rapturously captured that delicate bone structure; fine nose; and wide, expressive, luminescent eyes. No mere glamorous clothes hanger, contrary to detractors, she could act when given the chance and here a whole range of emotions animate her features and eyes in various breathtaking close-ups. She is attired by Adrian in some of his most sublime

With Tone and Arnold. Note signature lipstick line. PHOTO COURTESY OF JERRY MURBACH

creations, striding like a thoroughbred race horse through sumptuous sets of unimaginable wealth. Crawford in *Sadie McKee* is an Art Deco goddess, the stuff of dreams. This is a Hollywood fantasy that has truly disappeared. You no longer find the panache and raw vitality that a star like Crawford exuded because these same dreams are no longer being manufactured by the studio as they were certainly in the 1930s. Crawford, with her sleek sophistication and earthy grit, was a wonderful heroine for Depression era girls, a real life Cinderella who caught the brass ring. So it is her jaw-dropping glamour that bowls one over in this film as it is meant to seduce. The shimmer of satin and voluptuous surroundings. The Deco nightclub. That face and sleek body like an Erte design.

The plot is rather annoying in that it requires Crawford to be virtuous and prove her virtue. Why are men not required to redeem themselves this way? Sadie McKee is a maid with amazing bone structure, working in the household of the wealthy Alderson family. Real life husband Franchot Tone plays the family's son Mike who carries the torch for her and makes himself a pest because she has attached herself to a ukulele-strumming scoundrel Tommy (Gene Raymond). When Mike insults Tommy at the family dinner table (tellingly as Sadie "waits" on them),

A lobby card depicting Crawford in my all-time favorite Adrian dress (and hers, too). PHOTO COURTESY OF JERRY MURBACH

he alienates Sadie and she runs off to begin a new life in New York City with her scamp boyfriend. A chance encounter with Opal (Jean Dixon), one of those ubiquitous, cheap, heart-of-gold types, leads the couple to a depressed boarding house with shared baths on each floor (there has to be depressed boarding houses to contrast with the palatial riches to come) and here the glossy, angelic Sadie (glamorous close-ups abound) has to feign discomfort over the one bed (not even daring to say its name, only nodding at it with her eyes), leading Tommy to gallantly sleep in a chair and sing the pleasing "All I Do is Dream of You" (which apparently became a hit song) to lull his gal to sleep. But a potent goodnight kiss afterwards as Sadie lies in bed implies tantalizingly the night might not remain chaste.

Basically Sadie is left dangling at City Hall, waiting to marry Tommy, when the wastrel runs into (and ultimately off with) a blowsy, Mae-West-type singer, Dolly Merrick (Esther Ralston) who offers him a job in her act. This leads jilted Sadie into chorus girl work and the drunken arms of a pudgy alcoholic millionaire, Jack Brennan (character actor Edward Arnold). As Jack is a good friend of Mike, Mike accuses Sadie of being a gold digger and a "little chiseler" when Jack comes onto her and she doesn't rebuff him. Given that Mike knew Sadie since childhood, the fact that he blames, insults and underestimates her, laying into her cruelly, makes him quite unsympathetic and overbearing and certainly not worthy of the noble miss. Or is it just a jealous pose on his part? In retaliation, Sadie marries Jack and moves into swank surroundings and swank duds without anything apparently required of her in return (maintaining her chasteness). Will she become the noble heroine and save her husband from drink? Who will win her heart?

Again, it's the brilliant, to-die-for sets (note the striped lamps in the Brennan living room) and Crawford's beauty that make this film. Those close-ups! Those eyes! Incredible! She is lit like a Madonna. Esther Ralston is a cute blonde who can't sing a note, reminiscent, oddly enough, of a very young Sharon Stone, and Raymond, scamp that he may be, is likable enough. Tone, however, rankles as both a character and actor, over-acting terribly and shaking his jaws when angry, although, like Sadie, he has the opportunity to prove his noble mettle. The film culminates in a fabulous nightclub scene (my favorite) where Crawford is Total Goddess in one of Adrian's most sublime designs (her favorite dress and definitely one of mine) — oh, that Deco age; nothing compares. If I had to choose between the three men for Crawford, I'd choose Clark Gable. But guess what? He's not in the movie. Oh, well.

A disturbing moment for me is when Brennan pulls Sadie into his arms at one point and kisses her, the shock registering on her face. I actually had the chills, the moment evoking every poor Hollywood starlet who had to sleep with an unappetizing big wig to get a break, undoubtedly as Crawford did. It still angers and stuns me that men with money and power think they can get any young beauty they so desire (and they're usually right), whereas women (who especially at the time of this film had few economic options) get flack for anything less than love. But then this is my sensitivity; the scene won't so impact most viewers.

Definitely worth it for the glorious eye appeal! A great example of Depression era fantasy.

Chained (1934) ★★★

The plot is as thin as crepe paper in *Chained*, but it doesn't matter, because the romantic and sexual chemistry between Joan Crawford and Clark Gable is at an all-time high and just delightful to watch. Plus, there's so much elegance, Art Deco '30s splendor, a giggly pool scene with

Crawford with Gable on a moonlit cruise, lighter than Springtime. PHOTO COURTESY OF NEIL MACIEJEWSKI

the dynamic duo, and a lovely sprint by the couple through high grass after a runaway foal. Crawford (at her lacquered, lovely best) plays Diane Lovering who is romantically involved with an older, married man Richard Field (Otto Kruger). Since his wife won't give him a divorce and Diane is even willing to be the "other woman" (which he doesn't think would be fair to her), he decides to send her on a cruise to Buenos Aires while he tries to get his wife to relent. On the cruise, Diane meets dashing rancher Mike Bradley (Clark Gable) and they start a shipboard romance.

Oh, Diane is trying to be faithful to the gentle, old nobleman at home and she is, but let's face it — you can almost smell Gable's cologne in this one, he looks so handsome. And Crawford in her Adrian gowns, lounging in the moonlight, sipping Sherry flips prettily, is indeed a thing of beauty (as she's intended to be). Plus the pair seem to be having such gosh-darn fun together and all their scenes together are the heart and meat and delight of this film. The pool scene mentioned above is particularly fun and features a child Mickey Rooney. Anyway, yes, Diane does fall for Mike and wants to come clean to the dignified Richard, but, meanwhile, Richard has achieved the grant of divorce and has his hopes set on Diane, so she decides to do the noble thing (glamorous suffering) and marry

PHOTO COURTESY OF NEIL MACIEJEWSKI

Richard, breaking it off with Mike. But then her path crosses with Mike unexpectedly (again, the film picks up!) and one sees that love is going to conquer all. (Dig those funky rain boots Diane dons, by the by, in her later encounter with Mike — designed to be worn over pumps!)

It doesn't matter if you know what happens — it's all romantic, glitzy escapism. Plus Crawford is so much fun to look at with her array of out-

Sweet Richard (Otto Kruger) is no match for dashing Clark Gable. PHOTO COURTESY OF JERRY MURBACH

fits — even her nails are something to see. Apparently cartoonist Milton Caniff was impressed by her striking look here as well since "The Dragon Lady" in his strip "Terry and the Pirates" was modeled after her (appearance only, not personality!).

It's all about chemistry and that's enough.

Forsaking All Others (1934) ★★★★

Forsaking All Others is a delight — a fast-paced, genuinely funny romantic comedy with a great cast who all do well with the material, resulting in sprightly entertainment that ranks with the best of the '30s screwballs. Clark Gable as Jeff Williams, Robert Montgomery as Dillon Todd and Joan Crawford as Mary Clay are all childhood friends. When Williams returns from a trip to Spain, he is gung-ho about proposing to Mary, whom he has loved since childhood. Unfortunately, he discovers that Mary is set to marry Dil, whom she also has loved since childhood. Jeff puts up a good face for Mary, his genuine love allowing him to put her interests and happiness first, but, meanwhile, a girl Dil had a six-month fling with in Paris blows back into the picture — Connie Barnes (the

COURTESY OF JERRY MURBACH

adorable Francis Drake). Connie is a '20s-type vamp that would knock any man sideways with her huge bedroom eyes, pencil brows, and svelte gown with décolleté, reminiscent of Bebe Daniels and Liza Minnelli. As Mary is all decked out in her beautiful bridal gown, a note is delivered which explains why the groom is late: Dil has married Connie. Now the fireworks begin as Mary is invited to attend a party with the new couple, the invitation evidently extended by Connie without Dil's knowledge, and it's all chic settings, tuxedos and sleek gowns in a game of love and war. But Mary isn't over Dil yet and it looks like she's going to make a fool of herself even if Jeff would like to change her mind with the aid of a hairbrush!

This typical romantic triangle is interesting here, due to the warmth of the main characters. Gable and Crawford are particularly delightful with that amazing onscreen chemistry (and, no doubt, off) (love when Joan sits in Clark's lap!), both at their lightest. Crawford is also outfitted in some of the wildest of Adrian designs. In one dress, weighed down with loops, it's a wonder her small frame was able to carry it, but she has fun playing with its appendages. (Her best outfit is a chic white suit with matching hat, hat worn at a rakish angle — a good outfit for the

Crawford as Mary Clay may be jilted at the altar, but she makes a lovely bride.

pratfalls she would find herself taking including falling into a pig sty!) The great supporting cast includes Billie Burke, Arthur Treacher, Charles Butterworth and an early appearance of Rosalind Russell. There are also MGM touches that are shameless and priceless like the picture depicting the three principals (Jeff, Mary and Dil) as children — each actor's adult head is superimposed on a child's body! Based on a stage play with Tallulah Bankhead, the screenplay was written by Joseph Mankiewicz. It's always possible to tell the difference when a film has had a source in literature, the script sharper and more sparkling. In any case, we all know who Joan is going to wind up with, but it's wonderful seeing her get there!

No More Ladies (1935) ★★★

Derived from a play by A.E. Thomas, *No More Ladies* is a cute, but somewhat static and stagy society comedy with haughty sophisticates waltzing around opulent Cedric Gibbons sets in high glamour and arch distress about marriage. In spite of glorious production values, priceless

Joan Crawford in classic Adrian with oversized bow sizes up Robert Montgomery's young prizefighting protégée, David Horsley, while Charlie Ruggles looks on.

character actors and leads who fill their tuxedos and Adrian gowns with requisite thoroughbred panache, there's a banality and insincerity that makes this film somewhat dull or forgettable, although it has its high points. The sheer elegance and sparkle of the stars, gowns and sets is a draw, for one. If only such glamour was still the norm! Supposedly, MGM was churning out this sort of thing because of the popularity of comedy-of-manners playwright Philip Barry (who went on to do *The Philadelphia Story*) on Broadway. Joan Crawford stars as Marcia Townsend Warren who falls in love with and marries, as described by her grandmother Fanny (the delightful horse-faced Edna May Oliver), "man-about-town, scamp,

PHOTO COURTESY OF NEIL MACIEJEWSKI

heartbreaker [and] worthless rake" Sherry (what else? it's the upper crust!) Warren (Robert Montgomery). Although pledging to be faithful when he takes the plunge with Marcia, Sherry shortly proves to be the same rascal as ever and Marcia, not one to take things lying down, conspires to give him a taste of his own medicine by inviting all his old flames to the house for the weekend and starting her own fire. Charades, anyone?

A sexy publicity photo of Crawford was incorporated into this colorful poster. PHOTO COURTESY OF JERRY MURBACH

Interestingly, George Cukor (although not listed in the credits) took over for director Edward H. Griffith midway and Crawford at first bristled at this motion picture novice criticizing her line readings, but came to really respect and appreciate him and vice versa. In that "butterfly lashes" phase of her MGM career, she looks incredible in the gowns Adrian designed for her and in the beginning she undresses to her undies — lace-lined, satin lingerie (naturally) (she did have an adorable body and great legs which were often showcased). At this point, she was required mainly to look gorgeous and chic (which she does, her hairstyle alternating from tight curls to loose with bangs, the style changing like her costumes), and she's particularly breathtaking dressed to the nines in a form-fitting ensemble with a picture hat. Given that the script doesn't offer much tour de force opportunity, she is actually quite good in spots (is that Cukor's influence?), such as when she tries to pretend all is okay with hubby again yet her pain and distrust shows.

Crawford and Montgomery get double billing, paired again as they frequently are, and have about as much chemistry for me as they usually do — next to none. One can well imagine Montgomery was better served playing a psycho, as in *When Night Falls*. I sympathize, however, with contract players like the two leads stuck in cardboard roles again and again, imagining their frustration at not being able to expand. Montgomery, as playboy Sherry, is doing the boyish thing, but the problem is he's not particularly boyish. Slightly paunchy with a receding hairline and good manners, he's not dashing or dangerous enough to explain why women are practically throwing themselves at him either. By contrast Clark Gable had a way with women and exuded so much virility and sexuality that even as a cad, his allure was undeniable. In some of their big confrontational scenes as husband and wife (which are never impolite or above tepid), Montgomery is as stiff as a martini whereas Crawford's own proletarian familiarity with struggle seems to leak through even when she looks to the manor born. Franchot Tone (who married Crawford at the close of this film) plays Jim Salston, one of the men Sherry cuckolded who believes Marcia deserves better (meaning, himself) and whom she uses as ammunition. Tone, as an actor, has always struck me as either too smug and gruff or unbearably hammy (as in *Love on the Run* and *Phantom Lady*). This is one of his better performances.

Once again it's the character actors who stop the show. Edna May Oliver, in fact, steals it and her dancing duet with Arthur Treacher (appearing like a breath of fresh air as "Ducky") is a huge highlight. These supporting actors are the cream of the crop, trained stage actors and genuine comedians. When stodgy Oliver (Reginald Denny) inquires cagily about Marcia, Fanny says, "You and Marcia — splendid. Why not Jean Harlow and Mahatma Ghandi!" And British culture (which did more to advance civilization than perhaps any other on earth) informs everything from the delivery and dialogue ("It was beastly of me!" "Right-o!") to the way characters play bridge as in Agatha Christie novels. It is rampant in the dry wit:

Fanny to the butler (as Marcia's weekend coupe is in full swing): "What's Mrs. Warren doing?"
The butler: "Well, after dinner she was in the conservatory with Mr. Salsten showing her orchids. Then she showed him the Japanese perbula."
Fanny: "Well, what's she showing him now?"

In sum, featherweight nonsense perhaps, but even the most mediocre of these MGM parlor hoohas is a class act. There's the genius of a designer like Adrian, an art director like Cedric Gibbons, character actors who come from English music halls and stage backgrounds, actresses and actors like Joan Crawford and Robert Montgomery who have more elegance in their pinkies than most do in their entire bodies and who embody an old-style glamour that simply doesn't exist anymore. (One dressing gown here is satin *and* fur-lined!) Gail Patrick, a beauty who resembles Julie Newmar and Paula Prentiss, appears as one of Sherry's paramours, Therese Germane.

I Live My Life (1935) ★ ★ ★ *(mostly for the character actors)*

Oddly, *I Live My Life* was immediately one of my least favorite of Joan Crawford's MGM output, although it has grown on me enough to "join the fold" of the acceptable, leaving no Crawford film in the dust in my estimate. It takes a long while to have any genuine moments, even so, and still proves largely unsuccessful, grating and tired as a romantic — let alone screwball — comedy. This is as much due to the miscast leads as to the stale and overdone premise. The basic story involves a spoiled society girl, Kay Bentley (Crawford) who meets an archaeologist while on vacation in Greece (once again, as was predictable in these churned-out products, via contrived and unconvincing "accident" meant to be cute as Kay, placing herself where she shouldn't be, slides down into the pit of his dig). When Kay appears to have sprained her ankle (another screwball touch as heavy as a sledge hammer), archaeologist Terry O'Neill (Brian Aherne) carries the sailor-suited miss down a mountain pass into town wherein she impishly reveals that she is not hurt, having feigned the sprain, and he abruptly sweeps her back up and carts her to the very spot where she started so she can walk down by herself. This show of "he-man-ship" evidently gets under the pampered princess' skin, as is always the case with pampered princesses, most film (and television) scripts having been influenced by *The Taming of the Shrew* as the quintessential male/female courtship. Like the caveman clubbing his woman and dragging her back to the lair by her hair, it's the uppity woman being bent to the man's will, because, we're told, that's what she really wants all along. In any case, there has to be resistance before the sapping of will, so Kay gives Terry a false name and identity (so I'm not the only girl who has ever done that?) and goes back to her socialite's whirl in New York, whereas Terry, figuring they kissed and it's now official, tracks her to America in order to marry her.

Aren't you laughing yet?

PHOTO COURTESY OF NEIL MACIEJEWSKI

Once in New York, Terry is turned off greatly by Kay's snobbish, vacuous friends who embody the usual broad stereotype of shallow rich folks (then who is funding the arts and most charities?) and when Terry gives Kay "what for" for "duping" him in Greece (after all, a kiss is a kiss and she's not a mere secretary, as she let on), she is a little more taken with him, amazed that he is putting her into her place (which also gives one of her servant's pleasure — a realistic stroke). Kay, however, is already engaged to someone all-too-willing to move into the seat of Vice President in her father's business but when she learns her father has become destitute, she once again pulls the rug from under Terry's feet and tells him she is going to marry her original beau, not him. He abandons her with the same swiftness in which he decided to marry her. This push-pull lasts practically until the final frame and in between, the leads are forced into some very unpleasant and strident temper tantrums played without an ounce of the intended humor or charm, although they have a few moments of at least the latter outside of these "big scenes."

I'm not in accord with those who believe Crawford didn't have the light touch necessary for comedy, since she acquitted herself admirably (and deliciously) in vehicles like *The Women, Susan and God* and *They All Kissed the Bride*, but here, she falls flat. I'm tempted to agree with those who believe Carole Lombard had the screwball genius to breathe life into even this forced farce, but I wouldn't promise it. In her glamorous Adrian gowns (a few bearing those over-the-top protruding edges that look like they could poke someone's eye out), Crawford is young, sleek and beautiful enough, although whose idea was the butterfly-wing eyelashes which are so artificial (even in an MGM universe that revels and depends on artificiality) so as to distract? Her problem is that rather than being witty as well as pretty, she's surly, spoiled, unlikable and downright unpleasant in her big "comedic" moments, as light as lead. Aherne is blond and handsome and speaks with the faux aristocratic accent like Cary Grant (and Crawford), but he isn't much of a comedian and sinks his funny scenes as well, never lending them any goofiness or aplomb.

Interestingly, there are some viewers who say the first half shows some aborted promise, whereas the whole thing doesn't start to sing for me until well into the second half. That's when the character actors take over. Reliable pros in their chosen personas, they give the film its only humorous momentum. Outstanding among these beloved players is Jessie Ralph as Mrs. Gage, Kay's grandmother and the family matriarch. Her moments are worth the whole film. If this supporting cast, including stalwarts like Arthur Treacher and Frank Morgan, was running the entire show, the premise, however tired, would come off based on their comedic deftness. But they aren't. Still, it's not unpleasant, if not entirely there, because the production values are grade A and the leads milk out a little chemistry eventually and Crawford does look mighty cute, particularly in the ballroom sequence. She does have those big, bedroom eyes even if they're weighted by even bigger lashes.

Extreme lashes. PHOTO COURTESY OF NEIL MACIEJEWSKI

What always impresses (and saddens) me — saddens, because it's sorely lacking from contemporary films — are the classical references made routinely for an "average" audience. No one even bothers to condescend to classicism or European culture at its best anymore, which I feel is symbolic in its own small way of the cultural decline that occurred when that "culture," in general, was looked on as "too biased" and rarefied for the masses. It's been a tremendous loss. If the '30s had anything, the era of Astaire and Cole Porter and P.G. Wodehouse, it was cultural élan, and even in lesser examples of its sophistication such as this film, it's still there in spades — enough to redeem *I Live My Life*, enough to lift benighted souls from the Depression.

The Gorgeous Hussy (1936) ★★¾

Based on the real life "petticoat politics" story of a Washington innkeeper's daughter, Peggy O'Neill (Joan Crawford) in the 1800s, *The Gorgeous Hussy* portrays an O'Neill who many viewers complained was not much of a hussy although she had four men snapping at her heels like frisky MGM puppies. Since Crawford offscreen had a love life that Casanova would have envied and was ranked very highly as a lover by notorious ladies men who should know, I'm sure she could tell tales that would curl the pigtails of any one of her suitors in this film. But instead of walking on the wild side and flashing her petticoats, this belle is demure, devoid even of the conniving undercurrent that Vivien Leigh wove seamlessly into her portrayal of Scarlett O'Hara. Of course she's not meant to be truly a hussy. Rather, the title is ironic (if it can be given that much credit), referring to the way gossipy women try to frame Peggy in order to chip away at her uncle, President Andrew Jackson (Lionel Barrymore), their political adversary.

Our pretty titular miss is preoccupied with politics and juggling beaus, the latter of which she is in no shortage. During a thunderstorm at a dance, in fact, two beaus fight over her and in order to ride out the night, two gigantic mattresses (where did they find them?) are set up — one for men, the other for the womenfolk. The scene with amorous Lt. Timberlake (a gorgeous Robert Taylor) in one bed and Crawford in its neighbor has all the sexual spark of a slumber party with cub scouts. Everyone is fully dressed and made up beneath the sheets, reminding me of the puppets "tucked in" in *Rudolph the Red-Nosed Reindeer*. Not even an undercurrent of scandal sullies this sleepover. The pair exchange a chaste kiss and speak of meeting in dreams, just as earlier Taylor chirped, "I dreamed that you smothered me with kisses that left little red hearts all over my face" as the pair moseyed along in a wagon with another of Peggy's admirers Roderick "Rowdy" Dow (James Stewart). At that time, they were accompanied by the requisite merrily singing slaves — so inherently good at harmony and quiet just long enough for the principals to state their dialogue before resuming their melodious chorus, so useful for Dixie ambience.

A tepid hussy.

Although Peggy has loved John Randolph (Melvyn Douglas) since she was "in pigtails," he gives her the rebuff in an earlier encounter, thinking her "not growed up enough" presumably (as Crawford tries unsuccessfully to look it), so she marries the dashing Lt. Timberlake who shortly gets killed in action, opening the way for more ardent suitors. Finally and briefly Peggy and John are given the chance to profess their mutual love

Crawford with Franchot Tone. PHOTO COURTESY OF NEIL MACIEJEWSKI

and marry, but upon Jackson's ascendancy to the presidency, their polar political sympathies drive them apart. Meanwhile, Jackson's morale is being punctured by the local hens who go for his weak spot by attacking his wife, Rachel (Beulah Bondi), a woman as crusty as her husband and ripe for material. After Rachel dies and Peggy takes over the mantle of supporting the president, she becomes the new target. She weds the man her uncle recommends (in his own political camp), John Eaton (the ever-smirking Franchot Tone, her real life husband).

Once she throws off the straight-jacket of dewy innocence and grating cuteness that hampers her earliest scenes where she is portraying Peggy as a youngster, Crawford becomes strong as an actor and character. One aspect of Crawford's screen persona I greatly admire and cherish then shines — her fiery spirit. One of her best scenes is in a ballroom where not only does she look glorious (and mite sexy) in a sumptuous low-cut gown (designer Adrian's hand again) but exudes the cunning and fire which finally spur the plot into life.

A candid shot of Crawford with Robert Taylor and Barbara Stanwyck during the filming of *The Gorgeous Hussy*. PHOTO COURTESY OF NEIL MACIEJEWSKI

Although my initial tendency was to underrate Melvyn Douglas, I've come to recognize and appreciate his smooth authority as an actor. Against an entire mishmash of MGM contract players who evidently kept the wardrobe people up to their eyeballs in lace, buckles and pancake makeup, he holds his own, becoming a sympathetic and likeable character. Barrymore is essentially a character actor and can be very good or very bad, depending on the way you look at it, at times hammy and almost burlesque, at other times wrenchingly poignant and brilliant. Here he is saddled with period makeup that makes him appear dipped in bleach, every patch of hair whitened. But his performance overall ranks with his best, recalling his irascible colonel in *The Littlest Colonel* with Shirley Temple.

In sum, in spite of the care lavished on *The Gorgeous Hussy* and some capable performances, the match never quite lights. It's like *Seven Brides for Seven Brothers* without the musical interludes, everyone behaving as if they're about to burst into song because of MGM's tendency to sentimentality and hokeyness and as far as historical accuracy, throwing the baby out with the bathwater. It recalls a comment Crawford made in *Conversations with Joan Crawford* that made me laugh — in which she referred to a film as one of those "let's-throw-everyone-on-the-lot-into-a-musical things." The ado might have been about much more than nothing if historical veracity were substituted more often for saccharine. Sidney Toler, best known for Charlie Chan, appears as Daniel Webster.

Love on the Run (1936) ★★★

Love on the Run, in the tradition of many screwball comedies of the '30s, has a light, frothy tone as it tells of newspaper reporter, Michael Anthony (Clark Gable), sent to cover the wedding of beautiful American heiress, Sally Parker (Joan Crawford). He winds up "fleeing from the press" with her when she leaves the groom at the altar. Naturally Anthony keeps his identity as a reporter a secret from Sally. Also on hand is Franchot Tone, Crawford's second husband, as Barney Pells, a fellow reporter. In the meantime, Michael and Sally inadvertently get caught up in international intrigue when someone hides a map in a bouquet of flowers she is handed at the airport as the pair are making a getaway (a fantastical scene where Michael pilots a plane and almost mows spectators down). Now Michael and Sally are also being pursued by dangerous spies along with reporters.

To be honest, Preston Sturges it ain't. Curiously, although Gable and Crawford are usually combustible on film, here their fabled chemistry is often just not happening, maybe because so much of the film feels forced. It does surface in moments as when they look at each other and quietly say, "Hello" at one point, both glowing — that moment drips with warmth and sexual sparks as does their embrace later in the story when Michael climbs heroically in through the bedroom window as Sally is crying. Pure romance! But the script too often descends into silliness and contrived, strained humor as when they break into Fountainebleau Place to hide out and meet the dotty caretaker who thinks they are the ghosts of Louis XIV and Mme. de Maintenon. There's also a moment where Crawford conveniently finds costumes in the back of a getaway car, giving her the opportunity to change into a glittering Adrian gown. But, at the same time, it's all pleasant enough with divine music ("Gone") from Franz Waxman.

Hair stylist Sydney Guilaroff once called Crawford "a glittering person; remarkably beautiful" and this film certainly captures her glow. To be honest, in the latter half of the film, some of her clothes were so dazzling (and she in them), they became worth the price of admission alone and there's a delicious scene where she tries to seduce the Baron who is about to kidnap her. Equally funny is Gable being asked to take off his trousers by the female spy. Let's face it — at this high-glamour phase of

Crawford's career, it's greatly about the clothes and her looks. Give in to it; she had panache like no one's business. One suit, in fact, went from incredible to more incredible, fitting her like a glove. When she struts with grace and élan across the room in this glossy ensemble, a hat with feather jauntily astride her head, her sunglasses with their own veil, it is one of Hollywood's truly great iconic moments. Where do you see glamour like that anymore? Nowhere! With the leading lady's chic charisma, her

Strangers on a train? Once again MGM brings out the peasant — or, rather hobo — props! Note Crawford's doe eyes here. PHOTO COURTESY OF NEIL MACIEJEWSKI

favorite leading man (Gable) and the general tone of lightness, *Love on the Run* is a worthwhile enough diversion — not the best of the screwball comedies, but respectable.

The Last of Mrs. Cheyney (1937) ★★★★

Based on a stage play by Frederick Lonsdale which had been filmed in 1929 with Norma Shearer, *The Last of Mrs. Cheyney* tells the story of a beautiful, sophisticated woman, Fay Cheyney (Joan Crawford) who charms her way into British high society in order to steal a pearl necklace. Crawford, attired in Adrian dresses and gowns that are glamorous and chic without being overdone, is enormously attractive and alluring here with elegant diction and poise, yet clearly seems a tad sad or depressed, her presence somewhat subdued. (It was not surprising when I learned that she was having marital problems at the time.) Nonetheless, she gives an assured performance with the excellent timing that was one of her gifts as an actress. Her strong face and crafty looks make her well suited for

The mark (Jessie Ralph) unwittingly displays the bait to con artist Mrs. Cheyney (Joan Crawford) PHOTO COURTESY OF NEIL MACIEJEWSKI

these slightly sinister parts; she has the appropriate edge to be a jewel thief. It was particularly wonderful to see her paired with another of my favorites, the debonair William Powell who plays Charles, her partner in crime in the film, ensconced in the household of the targeted wealthy family as a butler. Frequent co-star Robert Montgomery stars as Lord Arthur Dilling, the man whose eye Fay catches and who also has an eye on the goings-on.

Among the supporting players are some of the MGM's best character actors: Nigel Bruce as Lord Willie Winton, Frank Morgan (now best known for *The Wizard of Oz*) as Lord Francis Kelton, Jessie Ralph as the Duchess of Ebley (memorably charming in this small role) whose necklace Fay is slated to steal, and Benita Hume, Ralph Forbes and Aileen

Pringle as part of the band of thieves who are all disguised as servants. Fay has misgivings about stealing the necklace from a woman who trusts her, but decides to do it for Charles who, as one later learns in what comes off almost as an "in joke," taught Crawford the ropes when she was merely a "shopgirl" and thereby brought her from poverty into the upper echelons of society.

The film begins with Fay being discovered in the shipboard cabin and bed of Lord Winton. She is curled up asleep under a mink, which had interesting possibilities, that undercurrent of double entendre or insinuation always a strong suit in MGM's sprightly upper crust parlor dramas. Naturally the rest of the party of aristocrats (their "set") is more than amused when they walk in on Lord Winton and the duplicitous, comely Fay is discovered zipping up her dress (which she put on while Lord Winton remained chivalrously in the bathroom). Shortly, Lord Dilling is vying for Fay's attentions, along with every other red-blooded male in the cast, and the Duchess takes an immediate, uncharacteristic shine to her. She tells her this quite frankly when Fay is hosting an auction of large dolls that replicate each of the group, including herself. A fabulous line during this segment (and droll bit of foreshadowing) is when Lord Dilling wins the replica of Fay Cheyney and says to butler/thief Charles, "You needn't bother giving me Mrs. Cheyney, Charles. I'll take her myself." (Touché!) As in many of the MGM society films of this period, everyone speaks in that vedy, vedy, faux accent and the over-bright drawing room repartee can get a bit tedious and overwrought (Americans and Brits alike seem to use the word "heaps"), but this one is rescued from banality by the jewel thief intrigue. It's a great hoot to see all the servants/thieves lying around the sleek Cedric Gibbons sets, their "covers" removed, smoking and drinking and doing all the things they normally would out of view of their "marks." This joke is taken further in the denouement.

Crawford looks lovely skulking around in the dark as she attempts to steal the pearls, the light and shadows playing across and flattering her bone structure and expressive eyes. But deliciously, Lord Dilling is one step ahead of her and catches her in the act on her second attempt, giving her his own terms and conditions by which he won't turn her over to the police. As they say, never try to trick a trickster. However, Fay and Charles are about to play their own hand! Will Lord Dilling ultimately assure "the last of Mrs. Cheyney?"

Much of the dialogue is wonderful, particularly the attitude Fay takes towards herself, maintaining a dignity and poise under pressure and criticism that adds to the featherweight archness. The Duchess, enchanted by

Crawford in an Argentinean magazine ad at the time of *The Last of Mrs. Cheyney*. Note her magnificent eyes. Some say Bette Davis eyes — I say Joan Crawford eyes!

Fay early on, sees her as a kin spirit, a "respectable woman with the heart of an adventuress" which Fay later corrects, saying that she is really an "adventuress with the heart of a respectable woman." One of my favorite exchanges between Fay and Lord Dilling is the following:

> *Lord Dilling:* I called you up five times this week and each time I was told you were out.
> *Mrs. Cheyney:* What a shame.
> *Lord Dilling:* Were you out?
> *Mrs. Cheyney:* No, each time I was in.
> *Lord Dilling:* I thought so.
> *Mrs. Cheyney:* Twice I answered the telephone myself and told you I was out.

And this wonderful bit by Lord Kelton as Fay puts his boot on (the others assuming he is proposing to her): "It makes me feel almost primitive to have a lovely lady tampering with my feet." Crawford and Powell make a delicious duo and look more interesting together romantically than she and Montgomery. Both stars are that great combination of the proletarian and urbane. But since Montgomery and Crawford were so often paired in these films, it's intriguing to see their evolution from their young, tender days. Montgomery is showing just the shade of paunch, yet remains an emblem of grace under pressure (he pours sherry during one crisis), and Crawford has entered her notably thin stage, her eyes at their saddest. Love when she takes his cigarette from him and smokes it. Bruce and Morgan are so much like twins, I had trouble keeping them apart.

As an extra note: veteran director Richard Boleslawski died tragically before the film was completed and although he received sole directorial credit, the film was completed by Dorothy Arzner who would later team again with Crawford in *The Bride Wore Red*.

The Bride Wore Red (1937) ★★★★★

To my mind, *The Bride Wore Red* contains Joan Crawford's perhaps finest performance from the 1930s, certainly most underrated. As Anni Pavlovitch, world-weary cabaret performer who gets a chance to go to the ball, so to speak, (and wear her fantasy "red evening dress with beads") through an aristocrat's wager, she is flawless. She turns what might have been treacly, pedestrian "Pygmalion" material into something poignant and beautiful and heartbreaking. Making the dialogue ring with her own truth, she is also at her most seductive and bewitching. It is just one of the many instances that demonstrate the artistry Crawford possessed that was squandered in vapid vehicles and, despite her continued commitment and touch of glamour, eventually reduced to self-parody by an industry and era "no longer worthy of her," as *Reel Classics* aptly put it. She would have made an incredible Mata Hari.

Crawford in a love triangle — what else? — between Robert Young and Franchot Tone.

Based on the story *The Girl From Trieste* by Terenc Molnar and directed by Dorothy Arzner, the film opens at the chic Cosmos Club in Trieste where champagne flows freely under the chandeliers as Count Armalia (George Zucco) and Rudi Gil (Robert Young) watch roulette being played. Count Armalia wagers that "life is a great roulette wheel" and that nothing distinguishes one person from the next but the luck of the wheel at birth.

With Franchot Tone. PHOTO COURTESY OF JERRY MURBACH

To prove his point, he goes to the lowest dive in Trieste where, as Rudi departs, he tells the impressed owner to bring a girl to his table. He asks for the one who is singing. The camera cuts to Crawford as Anni. Hollow-eyed, jaded and yet incredibly glamorous in the flattering page-boy (why did she never wear this style again?), she is singing "Who Wants Love?" in her deep voice, a song integral to the theme. When she is brought to the table, at first wary, Armalia offers the amazed girl two weeks exactly at a hotel resort in Tirano in the Tyrol with a list of dressmakers and money for expenses. She is to masquerade as Signora Ann Vivaldi. "I had the good luck to be born rich," he tells her, to which she responds, "I had the back luck to be born." Awed by this unexpected opportunity, she seeks out the dressmaker and orders her dream outfit — "a red evening dress with beads!" (One of Franz Waxman's ironic lyrics in the earlier song is "love is a child believing stories of castles in the air.")

At the hotel Anni experiences a sort of rebirth, discovering a bird's nest outside her window, untold luxury and her friend Maria (Mary Philips) ensconced as the maid. The friendship between the women is wonderful, and a sure touch of Dorothy Arzner, as the two embrace and squeal

Anni learns table manners as Joan once learned them at Pickfair during her first marriage to Douglas Fairbanks, Jr. PHOTO COURTESY OF JERRY MURBACH

happily and Anni says she feels "like a fat woman with her corsets off." It is also a good way for Anni to measure her feelings against a trusted person of her own standing. The refreshing perspective of a director who likes and understands women is another reason this film works so well. Due to an earlier circumstance where the intended driver was delayed, Anni wound up riding to the hotel via donkey cart with postman Giulio (Franchot Tone, Crawford's then-husband). She was clearly enchanted by his abundant love of nature, although trying vainly to act superior to him. As Armalia predicted, Rudi doesn't suspect that "Ann" is not in his social class and becomes instantly smitten with her beauty and mystique, pursuing her in spite of his engagement to Maddelena Monti (Lynne Carver). Anni, having tasted the good life and desiring to bask forever in its warmth, decides she is not going back. Rudi is her ticket and she works her magic on him, hoping he will marry her, even though she loves Giulio. As she tells Maria, "If you saw a chance to come out of the gutter and live as you never dreamed you could live, to have the things you never dreamed could exist, you'd sacrifice anything to take that chance, wouldn't you?" But will her golden carriage turn back into a pumpkin when her time is up?

Crawford is simply sublime. There are some critics and reviewers who say this role is unsympathetic and cite Crawford's cynicism. Of course she is cynical, as Anni would be. How else do people denied by life and rank act? Like Julia Roberts' ridiculously sweet prostitute in *Pretty Woman*? I think not. Anni's longing and desperation is real, as are her warts. She does not descend into the impossible, mawkish nobility that infected characters like "Sadie McKee." Who can't understand why this girl would want to stay more than two weeks in the sun? One of the most moving scenes, in fact, is where she runs through a pine forest to the top of the mountain and stands looking out, breathlessly happy and in tears. When Rudi asks her why she is crying, she hides her face self-consciously and says, "I just thought that I'll be gone next week — and I just thought I'll never see the sun again." Even more poignant — when she sees a lake that she likens to a drop of jade and says wistfully, "I had a jade ring once." Crawford brings the dialogue and scene to its fullest wrenching beauty. Does Maria's life look appealing — over-worked maid cow-towing to her "betters?" Perhaps this role resonates so much because Crawford in real life knew hardship and we believe her. This is one of her most sincere and whole performances, more so than many of the rags-to-riches roles she played because it doesn't compromise. She skirts a wonderful, delicate balance between all shades of Anni, between the tentative, insecure, frightened, deprived Anni, somewhat shy and in love with a world she is seeing for the first time, conscious of her missteps, and the cynical and calculating Anni, never having had luck yet able to be a friend, bewitching and seductive in a sophisticated, worldly way people have forgotten how to be.

The peasants here, like the natives in *Rain*, are annoyingly shown as singing happily, the prevalent stereotype of the lower classes, indicating

Crawford as Anni in her red dress with beads (bugle beads), a dress that symbolizes hope and futility. PHOTO COURTESY OF NEIL MACIEJEWSKI

them to be unfettered by complex needs. Thankfully, Anni is human and even says cynically of Armalia when she's told he wants her to come to his table at the club in Trieste, "Oh, a count, is he? Come to stare at the animals in the zoo?" There are a lot of great touches throughout from the saucy music box figure of Crawford in the titles in form-fitting, extremely provocative dress perched on a mountain top to the scene where Anni tears up the note Rudi brings to her table and leans forward, showing cleavage (boy, a gay woman was directing this one!) and then can't figure out which of the many forks to use until the waiter, Giulio's friend, comes to the rescue. Amusingly she plays hard to get with Rudi, saying she's not accustomed to sitting at strange tables on demand when he invites her, a parallel against the early scene in Trieste. *(Spoilers!)* And when she finally does wear the red dress, her dream dress which is viewed as too gauche and a mark presumably of a scarlet woman (symbolic in itself of a crushed dream), and humiliatingly faces the aristocrats who now know her secret and throw her out like yesterday's garbage, she returns to her room and calls out for Maria. The pain on her face is only comparable to the sequence in *A Woman's Face* when she tells Melvyn Douglas, "Can't you all leave me alone?" It's a superb scene marred only by Maria's ridiculously trite speech as she comforts the sobbing Anni. For Anni in that moment, the dream is over. This is the fairy tale turned inside out, the fairy godfather's benevolence a cruel joke.

This is the last of seven films Crawford and Tone did together. Tone, in spite of the lederhosen, does a great job as Giulio. Their marriage on the outside was falling apart (and one sees a defeat and sadness in Crawford's eyes that one imagines was not all acting) yet it was one of the instances in which the couple have real chemistry onscreen. As Anni rides off into the sun with Giulio on the donkey cart at the end, both in peasant costumes (which pained me), it's hard to imagine if she's "choosing love" or forfeiting her dream to rise above her station, put in her "place." But one imagines there will be the breathtaking mountains for compensation.

Mannequin (1938) ★★★½

Mannequin, to my mind, is not essential Crawford, but still worthwhile with some splendid moments and performances that outshine the material. Joan Crawford plays Jessie Cassidy, a pretty young woman living in a Hester Street tenement with her mother (Elisabeth Risdon), ill-tempered father, and younger, wiseacre brother Clifford ("Dead Ends" kid Leo Gorcey). All that is missing from Gorcey is a white "crowned" cap, the sort that was popular during that era on "street kids." He spouts lines like "Gimme some grass, Mom" (referring to cabbage). Since Crawford has the stunning look of a Hurrell photograph, she seems as incongruous in the hardscrabble Lower East Side setting, largely Eastern European and Jewish then, as if she was superimposed there from another film. To escape her depressing life, Jessie runs away with good-for-nothing, handsome Eddie Miller (Alan Curtis), her childhood sweetheart who ostensibly is a carbon copy of her equally shiftless father. (Earlier, Jessie, bringing in the potatoes, frustrated by her father's laziness as her mother toils, snaps, "If you want these peeled, peel them yourself!") The city was then gentle enough to allow people to visit the Coney Island beach at night, swim and contemplate the stars. Coney Island was still in its glory and we see stock footage of glittering Luna Park as luminous Jessie lies on the beach. In yet another incarnation of roles played in *Sadie McKee*, *The Bride Wore Red*, and *Possessed* (1931), Crawford is a girl of character not content to waste her life in the gutter, committed to the man she loves. In spite of the repetitive formula, she gives a quiet, impassioned performance, particularly excellent in some monologues, and if her box office was slipping at this period, it's because of the string of similar roles, certainly not her talent. She is soft, gentle and sweet with beautiful, hauntingly sad eyes and portrays Jessie with simplicity, strength, sensitivity and honesty.

After marrying, Miller brings his bride to a sweet, three-room apartment and she is ready to pour her heart and energy into making a home for them, but it quickly becomes apparent that he isn't willing to do an honest day's work, allowing her to toe the line for both of them. The scene where Crawford sings "Always and Always" into Eddie's ear as they are dancing is one of the most touching in the film; she sings well and is achingly sensual. She understandably catches the attention of self-made millionaire John Hennessy (Spencer Tracy) and clearly there is an immediate charisma between them. Eddie shows his true tawdry colors by encouraging his bride to dance with the wealthy man, foreshadowing exploitation to come. John falls in love with Jessie at first sight and apparently her marriage status is not much of an obstacle to him. He asks her if she can fault a man for trying, sizing Eddie up fairly accurately as a scoundrel. "I want to see those three rooms of yours," he tells her. "I've been wondering what makes them mean so much more to you than anything I've got means to me." Following her with a bouquet of violets, he learns, at the same time Jessie does, that the Miller apartment is merely borrowed. With the original tenants returning, the couple is forced to move into more squalid surroundings similar to what Jessie "escaped." Then Eddie goes too far by suggesting that Jessie marry John for six months for his money. Crawford is superb in this scene as she digests the enormity of his betrayal. Eventually she does marry John, making it clear to him that she doesn't love him, but this changes as he showers her with adoration and love, even taking her to the too-cute cottage in Ireland, replete with Crawford in puffed sleeves and apron (whipping up a cake) and Tracy with clay pipe by the

Crawford is a shop girl — what else? — in love with a "no account" scamp. Ain't it always the way? PHOTO COURTESY OF NEIL MACIEJEWSKI

Displaying her shapely gams in a showgirl costume. PHOTO COURTESY OF NEIL MACIEJEWSKI

hearth (funny but since Jessie's father spoke with an Irish brogue, I wonder if history isn't repeating itself for Jessie with John as well.) As Jessie falls genuinely in love with her devoted new husband, all would seem well except Eddie continues to cast a dark shadow over her happiness.

Although pleasant enough with sensitive performances and some nice bits of dialogue that transcend the hokum, this isn't one of the finer

Crawford in sexy backless attire with Tracy. Off-screen she had a brief affair with Tracy, but found him to be a "mean bastard" who stepped on her toes and chewed garlic during love scenes.

Crawford vehicles, to my mind. She plays, as one critic put it, "tender, strong, heroic, and regal," but the "shopgirl" formula was running a bit thin and even the dialogue echoed earlier roles. The interlude where Jessie is working as a "mannequin" and modeling clothes seemed to sum up the contrived or shallow feeling to the film (recalling the fashion show of *Our Blushing Brides*). She also is allowed to look marvelously sexy as a showgirl, the job she assumes to support Eddie, in costumes bearing the mark of Adrian. Clearly she was very often used decoratively in these films, although hinting at having much more to offer. "Women are weak and men are strong. My mother wasted a lifetime of strength trying to prove that," she says at one point. With her eyes sultry, she delivers the line magnificently. Or her "Sometimes I feel kind of old" is breathtaking, showing this young woman whose marriage is already falling apart. Spencer Tracy manages to be tender and convincing at times, his underplaying well matched with Crawford, but I've never quite liked him, in general (and Crawford reports that he was "a mean bastard," having had a short-lived affair with him during filming). He always reminds me of Popeye and I wait for him to break open that can of spinach.

In all, a Crawford formula that was running thin, yet still has fine moments due to great performances by Crawford and Tracy.

The Shining Hour (1938) ★★¾

The Shining Hour has a "paint-by-numbers" (to use that chestnut) feeling about it, evidently one of the films that MGM cranked out replete with standard quality production team (i.e., Cedric Gibbons for sets and Adrian for costume design plus Joseph Mankiewicz and Frank Brozage as directors) and solid romantic leads, but in spite of worthy points, particularly the performances, it also suffers from a spotty script. Dialogue of panache and wit alternates with insufficient development in story, the most glaring example being the rushed ending. Still, MGM at its weakest has a lot of escapist glamour and kitsch to offer and this is no exception. Simply looking at a beauteous, dreamy-eyed Joan Crawford standing by a glittering seascape in long gown or hearing the refrain of a Chopin waltz played by Robert Young at various intervals as a key to his hidden emotions is classy and divine in the way films simply never are anymore.

Joan Crawford plays Olivia Riley, a presumably "morally loose" nightclub dancer who agrees to marry her debonair, wealthy farmboy suitor Henry Linden (Melvyn Douglas), even though she admittedly doesn't love him. As she tells him, "If only I liked you less and loved you more" (a line that alone had my head spinning!) Meanwhile, he has a brother David (Robert Young) who is rankled by Henry's pursuit of Olivia and takes every occasion to make nasty jibes about her character like a schoolboy who shoots spitballs at the girl he likes. The scene of a notably thin Crawford (oh, those stringent diets she was constantly on) in a nightclub doing a ludicrously airy and affected waltz in satin gown that brings both brothers to attention catches ours as well, in spite of its hokeyness, because of the electric vitality of her presence and the way she uses her eyes (eye rolling and use of eyes in dancing more common in the '20s and '30s). She is also soft and beautiful with a subtle seductiveness. After Olivia marries Henry, hoping for a more stable life, she is summarily brought home to meet the folks at their country abode (what else?) with its four-poster beds and stables (what else?). Although Olivia is warmly welcomed by David's tomboy-next-door wife Judy (Margaret Sullavan, a sort of June Allyson and Rosemary Clooney), she meets with open hostility (and the same script writer who provides David's smarmy remarks) by his sister Hannah (Fay Bainter, a sort of Mercedes McCambridge in *Johnny Guitar*). (Hannah after Olivia returns from horse riding: "Are you going to wash

With Margaret Sullavan.

up for dinner, Olivia? You know you do have that faint aroma of the stables.") Once again, Crawford is the odd girl out, deemed unsuitable yet defying her detractors.

> *Olivia:* May I have a drink?
> *Hannah:* There's a bottle of whiskey on the side board, David. I got it out this morning.
> *Olivia:* I mean a drink of water. But don't let me deprive you.

The Lindens are apparently one of those idle, "smug" old money families like those that populated Agatha Christie novels. (Aristocracy is always vedy, vedy British in origin as is our cultural history). They dress for dinner (what else?) and ride horses (what else?). And MGM spins that phony rolling backdrop when they ride in cars where no one really has to watch the road so they can converse and kiss and turn completely around without threat. Once down at the farm, Olivia and David's proximity makes clear that tragedy is in the wind as the star-crossed lovers furtively speak while "keeping up appearances" for those around them (who aren't the least bit fooled anyway). A loves B and B loves C and D wants blood and everyone suffers with dignity. What's to become of them all?

A notably thin Crawford trips the light fantastic. PHOTO COURTESY OF NEIL MACIEJEWSKI

The script, even though faulty, brims with wonderful exchanges. One of the most sublime, in my estimate, the reason MGM was MGM, is when Henry says to Judy, "You've become lovely to look at" and she replies, "What do you mean 'become?' I don't like that word. So gradual."

(Spoilers!) The growing tension culminates in a hammer-hitting metaphor as Olivia and Henry's new dream house (which they build nearby to the family homestead) goes up in flames and culprit Hannah stands cackling in diabolical glee. Self-sacrificing Judy, heartbroken that her David has designs on Olivia, throws herself into the burning building and little Joan/Olivia actually runs in and carries her out, both ladies suffering from smoke exhaustion and Judy badly burned (although only in the room for minutes). The most delicious part comes when David runs to Judy's side, first being summoned by Olivia who gives him one of those noble speeches of head-scratching logic, that both of them are not worth one Judy (why? at least they're sane), and then we have the kitschy pay-off as David "goes" to Judy. The would-be suicide is laid out in bed with her head swathed completely like a mummy save for an eye hole (yes, even her mouth is taped). Her eyes peering through their vent are fully made up with false lashes and mascara. Through the bandages she says with a quivering vibrato of self-sacrificial nobility, "Hello, David." You just want to smack her. All is expediently and unbelievably resolved with even the arsonist getting off easily, redeeming herself by urging Henry to "go after" Olivia. (It's okay — they have plenty of money. What's one less dream house?) Hattie McDaniel appears as the maid Belvedere.

Ice Follies of 1939 (1939) ★★¾

"Christ," Joan Crawford famously remarked. "Everyone was out of their collective minds when they made *Ice Follies*." Maybe. But there are a few aspects of this film, such as a gorgeous color sequence, that make it an interesting and desirable curiosity piece.

Ice Follies of 1939 was a film made by MGM supposedly when they were trying to edge Crawford out of her happy, little home to make way for a new wave of starlets by offering her sub-standard scripts the way they had supplanted Greta Garbo and Norma Shearer. Frankly, I don't agree that all the films made during this period were that dismal, particularly not her final MGM film *Above Suspicion*, nor were the scripts that much thinner than those she injected life into previously through charisma, class, and chemistry with Clark Gable. This is no exception. The story involves a skating team, Larry Hall (James Stewart) and Mary McKay (Joan Crawford), who marry, breaking up Hall's partnership with Eddie Burgess (Lew Ayres), but then the couple's relationship falters when she becomes a big movie star and his career stagnates. Bizarrely, it mirrored what was happening in Crawford's real life with her crumbling marriage to Franchot Tone (Tone's career did not match Crawford's success and although he supposedly loathed Hollywood, he was taking it out on her, so it seems).

Joan Crawford and Jimmy Stewart in *Ice Follies*.

Crawford is soft and appealing here, but Stewart actually made me actively dislike him. Whether telling Mary to "shush" or acting predictably disgruntled and unpleasant when she gets any opportunities that don't involve him or worse, in one particularly offensive scene, telling her to just "yes" him and don't ask questions (which backfires when he asks her if she's ever met anyone as great as him and she says yes), he seems to spout enough hot air to melt the entire rink. With stardom, Mary

The cast on the ice — out of their "collective minds," as our gal put it, but in color! PHOTO COURTESY OF JERRY MURBACH

McKay's name is inexplicably changed to Sandra Lee (hello?), she is given a Hedy Lamarr do and a glamorous wardrobe that looks quite a lot like Crawford's own wardrobe, including great furs and smart hats, but she is still reasonably sweet although she has less and less time for Mr. Man. Stewart then leaves her, saying he'll return when his career matches hers (how white of him), and in great MGM fashion, Crawford now is given the opportunity to apologize publicly before a room of Hollywood peers — in glittering gown, no less — for the unpardonable sin of success and nobly claim that all the glory, gowns, glamour, adulation and huge money mean less than her marriage, so she's turning her back on it all to go home. One can almost hear a choking sound in her voice. Stewart is elated and embarrassingly celebratory about it in a way that rivals Tom Cruise jumping all over Oprah's couch.

But of course, Mary does want to be a star (as did Joan Crawford — and why not?), so the film culminates in Mary manipulating the studio head to give Stewart a contract for an elaborate ice revue in which she stars along with real skaters — the Shipstad and Johnson Ice Follies — in a beautiful Technicolor sequence; Mary and Larry attend the film's premiere. Although the skating is annoyingly cute, it is worth the price of admission to see Crawford in color at this point in her life, and in the film-within-a-film, she does look especially glamorous and beautiful in the little blue skating outfit that shows off her gorgeous legs.

In all, worthwhile for the rare chance to see Crawford in color and a prime example of the way MGM tried to make women apologize for their success (although at the same time celebrating it).

The Women (1939) ★ ★ ★ ★ ★

I revisited *The Women* on the big-screen in New York City, ironically during Women's Heritage Month (supposedly). The saying is that, since the entire cast and even all the animals in the film are female, there aren't any Y chromosomes to be found onscreen. However, it was just the opposite in the packed theater which was predominately male (and gay). It's hard not to enjoy this wickedly bitchy satire about a well-to-do woman Mary "Mrs. Stephen" Haines (Norma Shearer) whose husband is having an affair with shopgirl and "man trap" Crystal Allen (Joan Crawford — who else?) and whose gossipy friends (particularly the sublime Rosalind Russell as Sylvia "Mrs. Howard" Fowler) thrive on scandal. The huge cast is superb with even the bit players excelling at delivering rapid-fire one-liners that hit their mark like a good left hook. Yet beneath the dizzyingly paced fun are horribly misguided messages aimed at women such as "[Pride is] a luxury a woman in love can't afford" and "A woman is compromised the day she is born," along with the notion that women's lives revolve around catching and maintaining a man and then accepting any behavior said man throws her way as part of women's lot. The film is so brilliant, however, and so chock full of talent that it stands the test of time in spite of these painful messages (which were indeed deeply internalized by women and still are to some degree). Among the supporting cast, Mary Boland as the Countess DeLave and the beautiful Virginia Grey as Pat are outstanding. Crawford as Crystal has actually comparatively little screen time, but her presence is so strong and vital that she comes off as a lead.

Crystal Allen (Joan Crawford) takes no prisoners. PHOTO COURTESY OF NEIL MACIEJEWSKI

An endless array of great lines, including these delivered by Crystal: "He almost stood me up for his wife" and "[W]hen anything I wear doesn't please Stephen, I take it off" and "There is a name for you, ladies, but it isn't used in high society…outside of a kennel" and — my favorite — "You noble wives and mothers bore the brains out of me. And I bet you bore your husbands, too." Next to the latter, my favorite lines are these:

The three heavyhitters: Crawford, Shearer and Russell — meow! PHOTO COURTESY OF NEIL MACIEJEWSKI

Sylvia Fowler: Oh, you remember the awful things they said about what's-her-name before she jumped out the window? There. You see? I can't even remember her name so who cares?

Crystal Allen: I'm having him dine at my place. It's about time he found out I was a home girl.
Pat: A home girl? Get her? Why don't you borrow the quintuplets for the evening?
Crystal Allen: Because I'm all the baby he wants, pet.

Films of the Forties

PHOTO COURTESY OF NEIL MACIEJEWSKI

Strange Cargo (1940) ★★★★★

Strange Cargo is, by far, the best of the eight films Joan Crawford and Clark Gable made together and coincidentally their last film. An interesting allegorical film that combines mysticism, romance, high adventure and drama, this underrated masterpiece tells the story of a group of hard-bitten convicts, men who have been cast out and essentially forgotten by life, who escape from a French penal colony on Devil's Island and undertake a perilous journey through the jungle. Becoming both competitive with and dependent on one another for survival, they find a chance at physical *and* spiritual liberation. This complex theme is handled beautifully and never becomes sanctimonious. Also on the journey is the enigmatic Christ-

Verne to Julie: "Grief ain't what I came after." PHOTO COURTESY OF JERRY MURBACH

like figure of Cambreau (the superb Ian Hunter) and a hardened dance hall girl Julie (Joan Crawford). With its smart dialogue, fine ensemble acting and intriguing tests of inner strength, *Strange Cargo* is deliciously moving and intense.

Crawford and Gable have their usual sizzling chemistry, evident even beneath their sparring. After Gable as Andre Verne encounters

Julie (Crawford) pleads with captor Marfeu (Bernard Nedell) to let her go.
PHOTO COURTESY OF NEIL MACIEJEWSKI

Crawford's sexy dance hall singer on the docks and grabs her ankle, the pair's relationship evolves from basic sexual attraction to deep emotional commitment and caring. Cambreau, through his own detachment and silent strength, is able to influence even the most ardent disbelievers and cynics (which describes all the characters, to some degree) to confide in him and behave responsibly. Most of the members of the jungle trek ultimately find themselves committing an unselfish act, an ultimate sacrifice for another, as they struggle to survive. Gable, while still a loveable rogue, shows dimensions to his acting that are breathtaking; it is possibly his finest hour. Crawford, spending the greater part of the film in muddy and (strategically) ripped dress sans glamour and seemingly without makeup, is eloquent in her simplicity and vulnerability and still strikingly beautiful and luminous. All of the characters become people one cares about.

One brilliant moment has Gable screaming to a drowning Cambreau, "I'm the only God you can count on now! I'm the Old Temple! Remember? You were right when you said God lives in me! God's in everybody! Gamby's God! I'm God!"

Verne (Gable) promises Julie (Crawford) he'll take her with him — from sewer to sewer. PHOTO COURTESY OF NEIL MACIEJEWSKI

A rich experience, both cinematically and thematically, *Strange Cargo* is one of the all-time great films. It deserves wider exposure and recognition as a classic film treasure.

Susan and God (1940) ★★★★

With *Susan and God,* Joan Crawford is at the top of her game and gets to show a slightly darker, more bitingly comedic side to her screen persona than she had previously (with the exception of *The Women*). She is excellent at the rapid-fire delivery as shallow socialite Susan Trexel (a role Gertrude Lawrence played on Broadway) who amazes and distresses her jaded set of friends when she returns from an extended trip to Europe and professes to have found God. Susan makes her over-the-top arrival on a speedboat, yelling, "You darlings! You darlings! You darlings!," arms extended as if to embrace the entire aghast group. Each line from this gushy, dizzyingly frivolous minx contains the edge of sugar-coated cattiness that is writer Anita Loos' (*Gentlemen Prefer Blondes*) forte, but the brilliant source is Rachel Crother's play. Susan's husband Barrie (Fredric March), meanwhile, drinks himself into a stupor and gambles, but still carries a torch for his wife. It's hard to know if he is to blame for her

PHOTO COURTESY OF NEIL MACIEJEWSKI

PHOTO COURTESY OF NEIL MACIEJEWSKI

behavior or she his (in the play, the former is insinuated, here the latter is). But Crothers nails the superficiality of the jaded rich who fixate on the latest trend or religion like a new hairstyle (think of Madonna's stint with Buddhism) without ever penetrating the surface of their own selfishness. Under the direction of Cukor, Crawford once again stretches herself as an actress with great results. Her vocal dips and inflections are superb, as is her timing, bringing high comedy to its full potential. She is hilarious as much as she is annoying. ("Where is your estate, Mrs. Trexel?" asks Leonora Hutchins, played by a young and goddessy Rita Hayword. Crawford as Susan: "Oh — [waving her hand vaguely] — uh — it's over there.") At times, one hears and sees that Crawford has a bad cold as she discreetly pats her nose with a handkerchief (MGM records reveal that she suffered from pneumonia during this period), but her energy and commitment to the performance never flags. Her Susan is funny, nuanced and theatrical.

Susan proceeds to take care of the souls of her friends by meddling in their lives, particularly their romantic affairs. Refusing a drink as she recalls her new commitment which prompts a friend to ask if she is on the wagon, she explains vapidly, "It's something much more spiritual than a wagon!" Meanwhile, her marriage is clearly on the skids and daughter Blossom (Rita Quigley) is neglected and shunted off to camp. As she probes into the broiling affairs of the people around her to their great annoyance, Susan trips herself up by announcing that "people can be made over" if they're really sorry, a manipulative line that Barrie overhears. He forces her to strike a bargain, whereby she will agree not to divorce him if he can remain alcohol-free for the summer during which time the three of them (Susan, Barrie and Blossom) will live together at their country home as a family. If he slips just once, however, he will grant her the divorce. She reminds him there will be no hanky panky as this "arrangement" is played out and, with distaste, the three hole up for the summer, taking their country retreat out of mothballs. Clothes horse Susan is still consumed with the superficial as she surveys her country home and says, "Oh, Barry, why didn't we ever do this place over or touch a match to it or something?" (Love Crawford in that oh-so-sophisticated white suit and hat with veil! Very chic!)

Susan and God, though odd, is loads of fun. The script, direction, cast and performances are strong and an added asset is the young, radiantly beautiful Hayworth. At its center, Crawford proves a delicious surprise. Adrian outfits her in beautiful dresses and a classical gown that drapes her body gorgeously, highlighting her alabaster skin and delicate beauty.

She looks like a Greek sculpture and the regal way she holds her body throughout lends a statuesque illusion. She is particularly lovely here. As movement leader Lady Wigstaff (a delightful Constance Collier) visits Susan and keeps her mindlessly preoccupied and embroiled in "work," Barrie loses his patience. He recognizes the toll their neglect has taken on Blossom.

In her fabulous white suit and hat with beekeeper's netting.

The last third when Susan is being cowed into the usual, MGM conversion to nobility (and aren't women the ones always doing the atoning for so-called "selfishness?") feels ingenuine and unbelievable. The women weep and the man rages but Susan's change of heart remains unconvincingly abrupt, perhaps because the marriage never convinces. Why does it need saving? The Trexels don't seem remotely suited or attracted to one another, save for rare moments such as when they share a sudden kiss in the kitchen or Barrie reminds Susan that he married her for her sex appeal, that intelligence had nothing to do with it. Most of the time they radiate intense dislike for one another. Susan is very uncomfortable initially when Barrie attempts to embrace her and no less so with her daughter's attempts at affection. Yet this family unit does undergo transformation as Susan realizes what really matters.

Susan and God represents a welcome change of pace for Crawford and she delivers a superb performance. Interestingly, both films she made in 1940 involved God. Among the highlights is a witty musical interlude in which the entire cast — singing! — "storms the Bastille" (so MGM!). Also features great, great work from character actor Marjorie Main as Susan's maid. A fine ensemble piece.

A Woman's Face (1941) ★★★★★

Out of Joan Crawford's multi-faceted, 50-year career in films, I'd rank *A Woman's Face* as containing one of her most fascinating and memorable performances. As Anna Holm, she is an embittered woman whose face had been horribly disfigured in a childhood accident, leaving her isolated and loveless, her anger channeled into a life of crime as a ruthless blackmailer. In the opening courtroom scene, with her face veiled, she is on trial for murder as a parade of witnesses tell their stories. Through flashback, we learn that Anna was humiliated by the blackmailers she employed. ("What would any man have to do with her?" asks partner-in-crime Christina Dalvik (Connie Gilchrist)). Ultimately she falls into the clutches of Torsten Barring (Conrad Veidt), whose obstacle to inheriting his family fortune is his 4-year-old nephew Lars Erik (Richard Nichols), the heir-in-line. Torsten manipulates Anna by pretending to desire her with a nefarious ulterior motive in mind. When plastic surgeon Gustaf Segert (Melvyn Douglas) corrects Anna's scar and gives her the opportunity to resume a normal life, Torsten has Anna installed as nursemaid in his family home where she is to murder the child.

This exciting and immensely absorbing drama is full of duplicity, malevolent double dealings and tension yet manages to also be deeply romantic — lit beautifully and in the style of German expressionism, imbued with classical touches and fine compositions. Director George Cukor forced Crawford to abandon all affectations and succeeded in drawing a performance out of her that is revealing, touching and powerful. Half covered in the "scar" makeup throughout part of this film, Crawford's face still magnificently catches the light and remains an enigmatic study. The anguish on her face and in her expressive eyes is astonishing and a window into the real actress. She is given a co-star worthy of her in the superbly sinister Veidt. He makes a powerful symbol of the rising tide of fascism in Europe and has a compelling attractiveness. His S&M-like control over Crawford is established through scenes of gorgeous composition such as when the camera slowly pans over remnants of fine dining with insinuating eroticism. It comes to rest on Torsten's fingers playing the piano and Anna lounging languidly, a figure of black and white, in a pale chair under the light, smoking a cigarette. A very subtle undercurrent of decadence is found throughout from the two women dancing together in the beginning under the proprietary gaze of Torsten to the insinuating use of the word "submit" in a courtroom scene.

Blackmailers have rounded educations. The "Wonder Girl" has also tried poetry, art, and alcohol. PHOTO COURTESY OF JERRY MURBACH

The nefarious Torsten Barring (Conrad Veidt) manipulates Anna (Joan Crawford) in a Gothic attic. PHOTO COURTESY OF JERRY MURBACH

Although he initially left no special impression on me, overshadowed as he is by the nefarious presence of Veidt, I've since come to value the quiet authority and charms of Melvyn Douglas. He's a subtle actor, gentle yet masculine and intelligent. There's a beautiful sequence where he runs into Anna at a party in the Barring household where she has assumed her new alias of Ingrid Paulson and examines her under a lamp (she is

A kinder, more physically beautiful Anna (Crawford) with a scarred soul.
PHOTO COURTESY OF NEIL MACIEJEWSKI

frequently under the spotlight). When he inquires into whether she has changed, since he last knew her as a "thief," she retorts, "Turn on your lights" and he says, "Unfortunately for humanity the light hasn't been invented that could look into that interesting heart of yours." Then, to her surprise, he says, "Let's say my hopes may have begun to be justified," his voice becoming soft, "because I know about your intelligence. I've seen your courage. And I — I have hoped."

Those great character actors (God, how I miss them!), including Marjorie Main and Donald Meek, bring colorful support to the superb leads.

One of Crawford's best performances. A great film. A must for all film lovers. She should've won the Oscar for this and she believed this omission is why she won for *Mildred Pierce* four years later.

When Ladies Meet (1941) ★★★½

When Ladies Meet (an ironic title since it pairs upcoming British import Greer Garson with MGM's reigning queen Joan Crawford) involves an author Mary Howard (Crawford) who falls for her married publisher Rogers Woodruff (Herbert Marshall) as friend Jimmy Lee (Robert Taylor) who loves her, too, conspires to rewrite that "last chapter" in

With Robert Taylor. PHOTO COURTESY OF JIM MAHONEY

her "pending novel" by having the two ladies — Mary and Mrs. Claire Woodruff (Garson) — meet.

Based on a play by Rachel Crothers, the film moves along at a sprightly clip with brisk, sophisticated dialogue and great double entendres, opening with Mary being kissed under protest by callow, dashing Jimmy in a room off her own crowded book reception. As she pushes him away and tells him their relationship is trivial, he tells her he wants her to marry him

Two of MGM's beautiful leading ladies meet — Joan Crawford and Greer Garson! PHOTO COURTESY OF JIM MAHONEY

and be the mother of his children. Crawford is clad in those strange, draping robes with the scarf pulled over her head that Adrian was obsessed with in this period; he used similar costumes for *The Women* and *Susan and God*. Mary's friend "Bridgie" Drake (the sublime Spring Byington), hostess of the event, barges in on the couple and sweeps Mary back to the reception, Jimmy in impish pursuit. Mary signs books generously for fans and he slips her a book asking her to marry him which she signs with a resounding "no." Ultimately Jimmy discovers the roadblock in his goal to win Mary's heart — her publisher. When he reads the manuscript for her new book, he disapproves to her baffled chagrin because in its story of a woman falling in love with a married man, he recognizes the true situation. Mary still hasn't written the last chapter, however, which means essentially the way her affair with Rogers is going to end. She puzzles out the various scenarios and struggles with her conscience. When Bridgie invites Mary to her country home for the weekend and Jimmy has a chance meeting with the vivid Claire Woodruff, he plans his ultimate coup — bringing Claire to the country house without telling Mary her true identity and having the ladies meet.

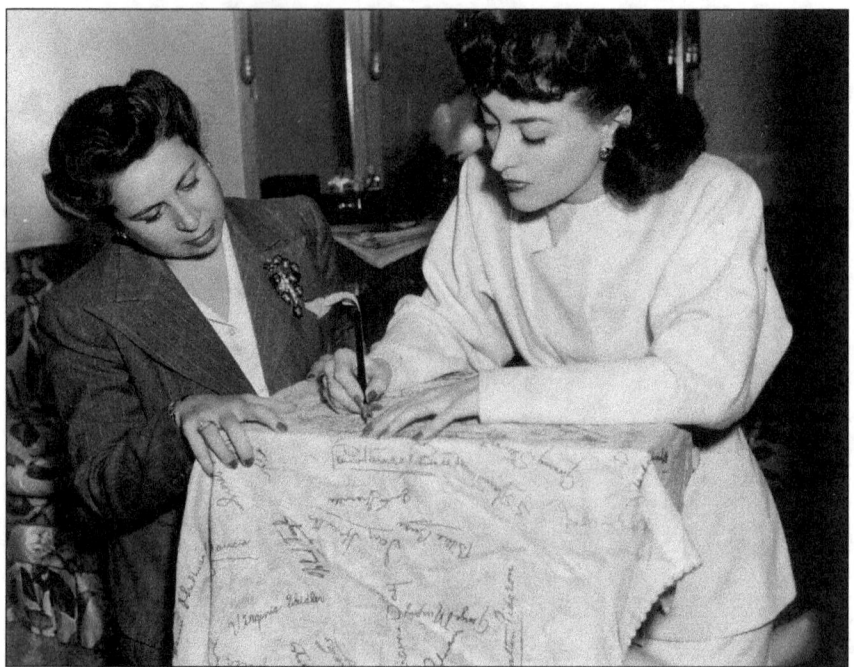

The beautiful star autographs a piece of fabric on the set. PHOTO COURTESY OF NEIL MACIEJEWSKI

Since Garson and Crawford are both extremely beautiful women, lithe and glamorous with exquisite bone structure and charm to spare, it boggles the mind what either of them see in the mousy, staid Rogers. Herbert Marshall might behave like a gentleman, but he in no way has the distinguished charm or looks of a Charles Boyer to explain his fascination. It becomes even more incomprehensible when his romantic rival is young, dark and handsome Taylor. It recalls an incident I once witnessed on the New York subway when a sexy black bombshell came on board, arm in arm with a tiny, fawning man resembling Truman Capote. When the pair exited, the entire car burst into laughter. What kind of after shave lotion does Rogers wear, anyway, the lucky stiff?

When Ladies Meet, while not even being one of the greatest of MGM's output, still has all the ingredients that made MGM an inimitable dream factory. There is such an array of talent assembled here from the wonderful Cedric Gibbons sets to Adrian's chic costumes to the oh-so-attractive leads and delightful character actors. Anita Loos also helped adapt the screenplay. Charm, sophistication and beauty on this level simply isn't to be found on the screen anymore. There are no Joan Crawfords or Robert Taylors or Greer Garsons anywhere — not by a long shot. The two women are wonderful studies in screen magic and allure. Garson is effervescent and enchanting, more lovely and sexy than I've ever seen her on screen (and she often looks good!) with those smiling eyes and long lashes. And she speaks French! Oh, behave! Love when she starts calling Jimmy "Jimmy Dimmy" to make Mary jealous. Crawford is equally beautiful, a paradigm of sophistication and elegance even with the way she holds her body or leans against a piano or lets her head and eyes roll romantically as if hearing inner music. She especially impresses me, this abused little girl from the wrong side of the tracks who exudes more élan, glamour and grace than any blue blood — an emblem of celluloid fantasy and perfection (love her pronunciations and the modulations in her voice!). Both ladies provide strong, sensitive performances.

One of my favorite lines is when Bridgie says to Rogers as he watches a swimsuit-clad Mary (such a cute suit, too!) swinging on a tree swing, "Never mind Mary. You have plenty of time for your last chapter." Another hilarious exchange is when Mary, after being asked about her book by Claire, says, "I just solved the last problem today" and Bridgie chirps, "Oh, did you, Mary? Well, well! I didn't know that! I saw you sitting around with a pencil in your hand, but I didn't know anything was going on — anything creative I mean." Oh, these character actors were gems! Byington made me laugh out loud! (Funny — Billie Burke seems to be her dithery substitute in other films). The layer of sexual sauciness is also a highlight such as when Mary tells Jimmy Rogers is interested in her intellectually and he retorts, "Oh, baloney!...He's nuts about you for the same reason I am and it's not because you're brainy!"

In any case, a fascinating confrontation between two of Hollywood's most luminous leading ladies — brunette and redhead — and a chance to appreciate the Golden Age of MGM and enjoy sophisticated banter, drawing room sparks between the sexes — plus piano playing, swimming, sailing and duets! "Here's bubbles!" as Joan says in *Rain*.

They All Kissed the Bride (1942) ★★★★½

They All Kissed the Bride is a delightful 1940s film starring a gorgeous Joan Crawford as Margaret "M.J." Drew, dressed to the nines in fashions from Irene. She inherits her father's trucking business and runs it with an iron fist until jaunty reporter Michael Holmes (Melvyn Douglas) comes

A take charge woman of the forties. Crawford wowed me with her beauty, lightness and glamour in this one.

around and upsets the apple cart by making her fall in love with him. It's a great battle of the sexes and a precursor of the glamorous yet steely business woman that would become Crawford's signature in *Mildred Pierce*.

I have a special affection for this film since it's the one that really got me hooked on Joan. Like Bette Davis, she is almost assuredly more known for her Grand Guignol roles, in which her former Hollywood glamour is but a macabre shadow (Hollywood never respected aging actresses, besides) or for her bitchy, later-day parts, and I'd always primarily enjoyed her in such roles when they were actually only a tiny segment of her lengthy career. This film wowed me in showcasing what a very beautiful woman she was, capable of enormous charm and versatility, this beauty at its apex in the 1930s, still strong in the 1940s and discernible even in much later years to the last. Here she gets to demonstrate a lighter touch

Playful in sexy lace black dress. PHOTO COURTESY OF JERRY MURBACH

when transforming from iron-fisted businesswoman (always in high style) to a lovestruck, weak-kneed, softer character. It's great fun to see her jitterbug and have one drink too many (dressed in an incredibly sexy black dress) and tell truckers that Michael called her "a beautiful baby."

Even better is that my first time seeing this film was on the big screen at a retro festival where it — and she — was dazzling. Here are some of the

Trucking tycoon Maggie Drew is weak-kneed for Melvyn Douglas.

things that make it a gem: Crawford's eye-popping, glamorous dresses and suits (the glitter of rhinestones alone is worth seeing); the hairstyles; the absolute panache with which she pulls this look off; Crawford humming and dancing with her trophy in the office after winning the dance competition and coming in disheveled; the "hot dog" double entendres; the opulent "Drew" home with the elegant sliding French doors that open into a grand living room; the chemistry between Crawford and Douglas that was understated and sexier than any ridiculous, panting, clothes-tearing scene put on film today; the wonderful character actors; Joan's jitterbug; beautiful Joan commanding the board room. This largely forgotten film of Crawford's is yet again proof of how magical movies can be and total heaven to watch. As a sideline note: Crawford took the role when its original star, Carole Lombard, was killed in an airplane crash. To her credit, she donated her entire salary to wartime charities when it was completed.

Reunion in France (1942) ★★★

Leave it to Joan Crawford to provide sex appeal and some kind of arc to her character in this essentially hokey production of *Reunion in France*. If you don't take it seriously, the film is rather fun, but please be forewarned that the goings-on and script are more than a little absurd.

According to some accounts, Crawford was embarrassed about appearing with co-star Philip Dorn, ostensibly because he was an ex-fling and she was newly married. She kept moving out of frame with him so they wouldn't appear in the same scene although they were doing love scenes. Exasperated, director Jules Dassin leaped down from the camera crane, the crane flying up, and yelled, "I'm going to punch you in the jaw." Crawford put down her purse and pointed to her jaw and said, "Go ahead." Dassin could only think of one thing. He yelled, "Let's break for lunch!"

Crawford plays a spoiled French woman Michelle de la Becque (she is of French ancestry, although she speaks intermittently with a deliciously clipped British accent — love the way she says "registry") who is engaged to Robert Cortot (Philip Dorn) and heading an exclusive dressmaker's salon. When asked by Michelle why the Rajah's silk isn't in the line, one of her employees sarcastically replies, "Our shipments from India have been rather uncertain since the war" to which Michelle responds, "The war. You should have told me and I'd have had the silk brought in in a diplomatic pouch!" Her insulated world turns upside down, however, when she discovers that Robert may be working for the Nazis and stumbles across an injured RAF pilot, Pat Talbot (John Wayne — yes, John Wayne), whom she takes into her home for safety. And Joan slides into the French Resistance movement with only a passing smudge to sully her glamour.

The Nazis can't prevent Crawford from being a fashion icon! PHOTO COURTESY OF NEIL MACIEJEWSKI

Oh, what can one say about this movie? What can anyone say about Crawford, finding herself in a blitz, running back home to see if the Renoir is still in place? Or having the wherewithal and chutzpah to remain dressed to the nines in fashions from Irene while supposedly destitute and as bombs fall over her beloved country? The Nazis are also considerate enough to transport her entire wardrobe when they move

Crawford on the set of *Reunion in France* with hubby Phil Terry. Note the gender-appropriate leg positions. PHOTO COURTESY OF NEIL MACIEJEWSKI

her to smaller quarters, even though some very bad art hangs on the wall (a great contrast against the Renoir) and she is now reduced to being a dress fitter's assistant (without ever complaining, mind). What about the outrageously thick, Austin-Powers-like accent adopted by Reginald Owen as a Gestapo agent (oh, he is so sinister but almost campy,) and the fact that Crawford allows him to kiss her against a wall so that Pat can make his escape? Or the "bumbling Nazis" who allow two sets of people to engineer relatively mindless escapes (actually, a fair amount of suspense and tension is evoked in the finale)? Or stand mutely as Crawford shows them her contempt (and don't we love her for it — Joan vs. the Nazis!)? Cheesy real footage of France during the occupation is woven into the mix. Anyone who has seen *The Sorrow and the Pity* knows that this story is taking major liberties with reality. But then, I gave in to the occasional shallow excesses and enjoyed that incredibly sexy, low-backed dress with the covering of black silk that Crawford wears in the opening scene when she deliberately knocks over a glass of water during a political speech so she can kiss Robert on the balcony and tells him, frivolously, "Let them fight [the war] in there!" Oh, if it were only that easy, Michelle!

I actually got used to the idea of Joan and John — er, Mike and Pat, as they're called here — as a romantic couple. The Duke and Mildred Pierce (before she was "Mildred Pierce," of course). Who'd have thought? Yet they have a definite chemistry, Crawford always seeming to like these big lugs and notably flirtatious in Wayne's presence. Emerging sheep-faced from her closet where he is hiding and blushing, Pat says, "Like going to sleep in a flower bed." Looking mighty fetching in her smart hats and suits, "Mike" responds, "If you're that crazy about my perfume, I can let you have some." "Won't do," Pat insists. "There's something soft and cool about those dresses — like perfume, like you." (Oh, behave!) Now Michelle is ready to do everything and anything for the glory of her mother country, having grown up overnight and with a strapping man to nurse back to health and a boyfriend of dubious political loyalties. As if a war isn't enough to handle, Crawford always is up to her "mad" hats in men!

In a letter to actress Lotte Palfi, dated September 1, 1943, Crawford gave her own consensus of the film: "*Above Suspicion* is not a good picture I am sorry to say. However, it is far superior to that stinking *Reunion in France*."

Natalie Schaefer who played Mrs. Howell on *Gilligan's Island* and Ava Gardner both appear briefly. A fine performance from our gal and close-ups reveal once again what a fragile, porcelain beauty she possessed.

Above Suspicion (1943) ★★★★½

Above Suspicion was Joan Crawford's last film with MGM before she left for greener pastures and more challenging opportunities at Warner's. Contrary to the general myth or consensus, this film, based on a novel by Helen MacInnes, is actually more satisfying and entertaining than some of her earlier MGM output (and later work) where the scripts were as thin as gossamer even though her charisma (or chemistry with a delicious co-star like Clark Gable) helped one overlook it. To my mind, *Above Suspicion* is an escapist delight with a great cast (led by Crawford, Fred MacMurray, and Basil Rathbone), a swift pace and tongue-in-cheek lightness, all packed into an economical ninety minutes. Surprisingly, Fred MacMurray and Joan Crawford have wonderful chemistry together and are quite engaging and believable as Richard and Frances Myles, a pair of

American newlyweds improbably hired by the British Secret Service to act as spies in Nazi-dominated Europe during World War II. The idea is that the couple will be "above suspicion." The silly idiosyncrasies of MGM; the tunes and absurd oversized rose on Crawford's hat as "signals"; the assassination scene; the assorted kidnappings and disguises; the enthusiasm of the amateur sleuths in unraveling clues and their general cool

Crawford in a publicity photo, looking like a glamorous deer in the headlights. PHOTO COURTESY OF JIM MAHONEY

under pressure; the incongruity of having MacMurray as a professor at Oxford — it all rolls smoothly along with nothing to be taken seriously. Along with moments of genuine suspense and a sweet affection between the two leads, there are some fun musical interludes where Crawford plays the piano and, together with MacMurray, sings. Frances also has a charming tic — she twists her ankle when nervous.

Interestingly, the hard-shelled dame image most commonly associated with Crawford's screen work is actually not representative of the great bulk of her career. She ran the gamut during her 50-year run as an actress and it's delightful when she plays "out of the box." Here, she has the "classic Crawford" face in place (the one that would become best identified as her "look" henceforth), but her personality has the lightness of her MGM roles and a sweet, kittenish quality that is very winning. Highly enjoyable entertainment. This was Conrad Veidt's last film.

Hollywood Canteen (1944) ★★★★★

Call me sentimental, but this valentine to the troops centering on two soldiers who spend three nights at the Hollywood Canteen before returning to duty was not only enjoyable — unabashedly simple and corny as the storyline is — but also deeply, deeply moving. One reason it tugs the heart is the startling and painful comparison between the respect and gratitude shown the troops by the cream of Hollywood, Warner's biggest stars, in the '40s and the attitudes of current Hollywood where such a showing of love and support would be unimaginable; instead, you have big hypocritical capitalist film stars bashing the country or even going to foreign countries and committing open treason by talking against us to the enemy. Pretty shameful. It doesn't matter if you're for the war or not, but soldiers are dying out there and deserve our support. It's amazing to see the United States when it was a truly united front in this respect — not into self-abasement, but actual pride and patriotism, simple displays of caring. In any case, this bouquet to our troops is both moving and goofily hokey kind of like Judy Garland's hairstyle in *Meet Me in St. Louis*.

The two soldiers who get to have their wildest fantasies come true and rub elbows with big stars at the Hollywood Canteen are Corporal Ed "Slim" Green (Robert Hutton) who is on medical leave and has a mad crush on Joan Leslie (playing herself) and his buddy, Sergeant Nowland (Dane Clark). Improbably (but does it really matter?) Slim wins a date with Joan Leslie, since he is the one millionth soldier to enter the Canteen, and falls in love with her. Meanwhile, this plot is a throwaway device to showcase some great musical numbers and variety acts and an amazing roster of stars playing themselves as volunteers at the Canteen. It presents a superb time capsule of the period. Stars include the Andrew Sisters, Sydney Greenstreet, Barbara Stanwyck, Dennis Morgan, Ida Lupino, Joe E. Brown, Peter Lorre, our gal Joan Crawford (of course), plus Bette Davis and John Garfield who founded the Canteen. The Hollywood Canteen was established during World War II as a place where soldiers on leave in Los Angeles could have a good time with food, drink and dancing, and as a plus, rub shoulders with movie stars (and employees from the film studio) who functioned as waiters, busboys, and dancing partners. The surprise here is seeing so many stars in their unimaginably dewy youth. All the women look stunning and have a fresh, charming friendliness about them — you actually see the "regular girl" in these actresses, including Alexis Smith and Jane Wyman (was she really that cute?). Downright startling is a young Kitty Carlisle (you mean she was a girl once, too?), now a grand dowager in her nineties. Particularly surprising is Bette Davis. Although her voice is affected, as are the carefully modulated voices of most of the actresses, she comes across as more attractive and natural than I've ever quite seen her — sparkling, warm, and even sexy. She is actually rather pretty, the first time I've truly glimpsed her womanly charms.

PHOTO COURTESY OF JERRY MURBACH

The stars, by and large, are very likeable and full of warmth. Of course, the dialogue is clearly scripted although they are "playing themselves" and you don't believe for a minute anyone is "candid," but no matter. There's still a pervading sense of kindness and giving — of everyone pitching in — that is genuinely felt. Among the stand-outs in the variety acts (and variety is always a mixed bag) are Carmen Cavallaro whose virtuoso piano interpretation of "Voodoo Man" sounds like a tango dance (wow); Patty Andrews of the Andrews Sisters, a great, all-around entertainer with a voice like a white black woman and personality of a Fanny Brice; and flamboyant flamenco from Rosario and Antonio. It's hard to say if such huge production numbers went on in the Canteen normally, but I doubt it. Still these stars really did interact with soldiers which was undoubtedly thrilling and our gal Crawford more than did her part in the war effort, even substituting her rose garden for a victory garden (which betrays the lie of Christina's claim that she hacked roses in the middle of the night). Also on hand is a gorgeous brunette Janis Paige playing a studio employee posing as an actress.

Meanwhile, the two soldiers' starry-eyed enthusiasm is hokey, but undoubtedly a nice fantasy for the troops watching whom this film salutes. Our gal makes her appearance in a dress with a huge kitty decal on the shoulder. She has bangs and shoulder-length hair and is sweet and girlish, not having entered yet into the hard-boiled roles at Warners. When Nowland says, "I'm off women for the duration," Crawford (whose back is to the camera) turns around and asks, "Isn't that an unfortunate attitude to have at the Hollywood Canteen?" She offers to dance with him and he says, "Has anybody ever told you you look like Joan Crawford?" to which she replies, "Why, yes, my husband has." (That was Phil Terry she was referring to, my favorite of her husbands!) It's a wonder why the focus would continue to be on Joan Leslie when so many other delectable women like our gal are on hand. Once again, Crawford's huge, beautiful eyes amaze me and like the other women in this film, she glows, exuding warmth and friendliness. Nowland almost passes out when he realizes he's with the Real McCoy.

Even if the romance between Joan Leslie and shy "Every Soldier" Slim is evidently a fantasy, taken to the hokey extreme where he goes to meet her parents and, like the proverbial "girl next door," she lives in a house with a white picket fence and sheep dog, stern parents assessing the new boy and Leslie almost as shy and flustered as her soldier-man — it's still a sweet idea, putting young soldiers on an accessible scale with young film stars. You almost believe it — again, that goofy and moving quality like Garland's hairstyle in *Meet Me in St. Louis*. Bette Davis has the last word, addressing the troops openly as she looks in the camera, revealing the unabashed patriotism and participation in the war effort that was a source of pride for most Americans, "You've given us something we'll never forget and wherever you go, our hearts go with you." The hearts at the Hollywood Canteen were in the right place.

Mildred Pierce (1945) ★★★★★

Mildred Pierce is a fabulous film on all counts with superb performances particularly from Joan Crawford in the title role (she won the Oscar) and Ann Blyth as her monstrous daughter Veda. This was Crawford's triumphant comeback role (and what a comeback!) after she was edged out of the safe womb of MGM and languished at new studio Warners without a suitable property until *Mildred* turned up. As the oft-told legend goes, Crawford was so eager to nail this part with its biographical parallels that she ate humble pie and auditioned (unheard of for an established star), gained a few pounds, and also championed Ann Blyth (who subsequently has always spoken warmly of her) when Blyth was considered "too sweet" to play Veda. Director Michael Curtiz was very hard on Crawford at

Shady dame on the waterfront, Crawford's most iconic role and my personal favorite. PHOTO COURTESY OF NEIL MACIEJEWSKI

first and supposedly growled when she showed up in a "little cotton housedress that she'd bought off the rack at Sears," "You and your damn Adrian shoulder pads! This stinks!" and then ripped her dress from neck to hemline, only to discover Joan's shoulders were still there. This sent the star running to her dressing-room in tears. But she ultimately earned his deep respect — and whatever he might have thought about shoulder pads, never has Crawford sported more of a linebacker look than in *Mildred*, which became part of her iconic image.

Based on the phenomenal, hard-hitting novel by James M. Cain, *Mildred Pierce* tells the story of a housewife's rise from waitress to restaurateur in Southern California after leaving her unemployed, philandering husband Bert (Bruce Bennett) and finding herself a "grass widow with two small children to support." Basically Mildred is willing to do anything

Weird, misleading tag line. It was Mildred who was surrounded by scoundrels, none the kind of men she should have or want. PHOTO COURTESY OF JERRY MURBACH

and everything to win the love of her ungrateful daughter Veda — perhaps even murder — and, meanwhile, the men in her life are pretty slimy, too. This tale of ill-fated ambition and maternal obsession is given a richly atmospheric, glossy black and white treatment and still maintains the sordid underlayer and cynicism of the novel.

The casting was fortuitous. Crawford is a superb Mildred, her performance admirably restrained. She looks suitably taut beneath the surface, evolving by necessity into a glamorous and calculatingly sexy hard-shell dame, making a sublime entrance as a silhouette on the smoke-filled docks. Ann Blyth has a sneering, fresh-faced insolence as a great counterpoint to her suppressed rage and suffering. Wonderful support comes from Jack Carson as Bert's oily yet genial ex-partner Wally Fay with romantic designs on Mildred and Zachary Scott as caddish Monty Beragon whom Mildred marries. What a classic! The stunning black and white cinematography; a stellar cast with great dynamics; Crawford's allure and strength (suffering in sable — the only way! And those shoes!); riveting story; and delightful, stalwart character actors like Eve Arden (as Mildred's wisecracking — what else? — friend Ida) and Butterfly McQueen (as her high-strung maid — what else?). All in all, classic Crawford. Classic film noir. Not to be missed.

Humoresque (1946) ★★★★

Humoresque is one of cinema's sublime masterpieces. It has a rich, complex script penned by Clifford Odets (based on the Fanny Hurst novel); superb performances; gorgeous black and white photography by Ernest Haller (love especially that shot through a wine glass); impeccable, beautifully drawn characters; believable emotion; glamour; and music — music throughout that is close to heaven. The violin solos are played by Isaac Stern. It is as haunting, sophisticated and classily romantic as Hollywood ever gets.

Gritty Paul Borae (John Garfield) overcomes his humble background in the slums of New York City (largely Eastern European then) to become a concert violinist, generously aided by his mercurial patron/love interest

PHOTO COURTESY OF JERRY MURBACH

Mrs. Helen Wright (Joan Crawford). He exposes the vulnerability beneath her facade of sarcasm, bile and alcohol, and she longs to possess him. The dynamics between Garfield and Crawford are complex, volatile and intense. Crawford not only looks beautiful in exquisitely tasteful Adrian, but her performance is perhaps her best ever — understated, unaffected and genuine. It is in films like this that one sees why Crawford was Crawford. Although she doesn't appear until thirty minutes into the film, once she does, she dominates seamlessly. There are numerous

PHOTO COURTESY OF NEIL MACIEJEWSKI

dazzling close-ups where a range of emotion and story are conveyed on the faces without a single word. The ending when a distraught and inebriated Crawford walks on the beach in the moonlight towards the sea in her glistening, rhinestone-studded black gown to the strains of Liebestod from Wagner's Tristan and Isolde is one of Hollywood's greatest. It reaches a crescendo as in the music. Oscar Levant is on hand as well to provide comic relief and brilliant piano solos as Borae's best friend Sid.

Among my favorite exchanges in a film brimming with wonderful dialogue:

Paul Borae to an inebriated Helen: "Drink your coffee."
Helen Wright: "Here we go again. Only a man who doesn't drink thinks that black coffee sobers you up."
Sid: "I envy people who drink. At least they know what to blame everything on."
Helen: "If it's so simple, why don't you drink?"

According to Frank Miller of *Turner Classic Movies,* Joan Crawford was attracted to John Garfield's brazen masculinity. On their first meeting, he said, "So you're Joan Crawford, the big movie star! Glad to meet

PHOTO COURTESY OF NEIL MACIEJEWSKI

ya," and pinched her breast. She bristled at first, but then smiled and said, "I think we're going to get along just fine." Apparently, they got along swimmingly!

Possessed (1947) ★★★★½

Possessed begins with a pale, disoriented woman (Joan Crawford) in a plain, but impeccably cut black dress, wandering the streets of Los Angeles, murmuring the name "David." This is film noir and the wonderful camera angles and black and white cinematography, the German expressionism, all lend to the off kilter feeling of the story which describes Crawford's mental state. The woman winds up in a hospital where her story emerges through flashbacks.

Apparently Louise Howell (Crawford) was having an affair with bachelor David Sutton (Van Heflin), but although Louise is becoming increasingly fervently attached, David is ready to cut the cord. He reminds her that he never pretended to love her — this after they've just returned from "swimming." Oh, that beautiful code language! This rejection sends Louise over the edge. After he boats her across the water to the house

As nurse Louise Howell (Joan Crawford) breaks with reality, her employer Dean Graham (Raymond Massey) sets his romantic sights on her. Some people just ask for it, don't they? PHOTO COURTESY OF NEIL MACIEJEWSKI

where she is employed, we learn that she is a private nurse for the ill wife of wealthy Dean Graham (Raymond Massey) and that the delusional Mrs. Graham believes Nurse Howell is having an affair with her husband. When Mrs. Graham is found drowned in an apparent suicide, Mr. Graham eventually makes known his growing love for Nurse Howell and begs her to marry him. Louise's heart lies elsewhere, but he convinces her to give the marriage a go. Initially Graham's daughter Carol (Geraldine Brooks) rejects Louise, believing her responsible for her mother's death although Louise insists that Mrs. Graham was "more ill" than Carol realized. (Wonderful touch since Louise is "more ill" than she realizes). With time Carol accepts her new stepmother, but the plot thickens when Carol begins a relationship with David which becomes serious and threatens Louise's sanity. Like a bad penny, David keeps showing up.

Joan Crawford gives a powerhouse performance in *Possessed* (for which she earned an Academy Award nomination), making Louise's emotional state properly edgy and palpable, but the script never satisfactorily explains why Louise is as she is except in terms of irrational gender mumbo jumbo. The male white coats in the hospital comment on her condition as she languishes in a stupor, no less, with howlers like: "Beautiful woman, intelligent,

Fatal attraction. PHOTO COURTESY OF NEIL MACIEJEWSKI

frustrated. Frustrated just like all the others we've seen." Hello? No wonder she's frustrated if this is what women face in way of medical care. Crawford deserved an Academy just for keeping a straight face during that speech. Certainly love can make people insane, but would unrequited love for David so upend Louise? Is Dean attracted to unbalanced women?

In spite of some irrational rationale, *Possessed* is an A-quality, entertaining and extremely watchable film with intricate twists, turns and ironies and solid performances from Crawford, Heflin and Brooks. Both Louise

Louise is a problem David can't solve. PHOTO COURTESY OF JIM MAHONEY

and David are self-absorbed characters, suitably matched as antagonists. Brooks as Carol also has a fascinating duality to her personality like Ann Blyth in *Mildred Pierce*, able to appear sweet and almost viperish as the plot demands. At times, viewing things from Louise's perspective, it's impossible to discern what is real and what is delusional as the drama enfolds. In my initial viewings, my sympathies lie completely with Louise, but after seeing it on the big screen recently, it struck me that Louise was a bit of a stalker and David, cad or no cad, had promised her no rose garden. Still, seeing Louise become "very objectionable" is part of the fun.

Entertaining melodrama, in spite of unintentionally amusing psychobabble, with Crawford in full command of the screen, if not (according to the script) of her wits.

Daisy Kenyon (1947) ★★★★

Although *Daisy Kenyon* (based on the exquisite Elizabeth Janeway novel and produced and directed by Otto Preminger) might appear to be a "slight" film, essentially concerned with a love triangle, it is distinguished by intelligently drawn, complex characters, particularly that of the title woman; fine performances; and a fascinating portrait of 1940s cocktail lounge sophistication. Joan Crawford is excellent in the titular role, a magazine illustrator in New York City who is juggling two men and unfulfilled. One is Dan O' Mara (Dana Andrews), an unhappily married attorney who seems to care for Daisy and respect her on some level, but will never offer her security or commitment. Daisy and Dan (as embodied by the principals) look good together and appear suited on a superficial basis, but one doesn't want to see her wind up with this man who — as is so typical of this type of do-gooder — sees fit to go to bat for the world's unfortunate (defending a Japanese decorated veteran whose farm was legally stolen after World War II, a politically unpopular victim) as he neglects his own wife and family. His long-suffering wife Lucille (Ruth Warrick) is portrayed — offensively, to my mind — as a shrew as

Greenwich Village love triangle. PHOTO COURTESY OF JERRY MURBACH

if not supposed to object to his coldness or infidelities or somehow to blame for them. In one scene, she picks up the extension when he is on the phone with Daisy and interrupts them. He grabs the phone from her and in a stroke of overt emotional abuse, tells her he never thought she was worth killing before but does now, a scene witnessed by his teary youngest daughter who is herself being abused by the mother. An inter-

On the street where she lives. PHOTO COURTESY OF JERRY MURBACH

esting subplot: pain and abuse trickle down. Dan is a charming, selfish bastard, on some levels, but so multi-dimensional and fleshed out, as he was in the novel, that he retains a flawed humanity.

The other man in Daisy's life is mild-mannered Peter Lapham (Henry Fonda), a decorated Army officer and former Yacht designer. He is smitten with Daisy in a puppy dog, essentially passive way, since his heart still belongs to the wife he lost five years ago and not whole-heartedly to Daisy. Hanging his head, he tells her when dropping her off from a date at 3 a.m., "I love you." She is startled and doesn't quite believe it or return it. At one point she says to him, "You're using me, sort of" and he responds, "Yes. Aren't you using me?"

The situations might be familiar, but the script and dialogue is not predictable and is sharp, literate and realistic. When Peter asks Daisy if she loves Dan, she says defiantly, "Yes, I do love him" and he responds,

"But it isn't enough or I wouldn't be here, would I?" And later, Daisy to Peter: "Don't ever expect one person to replace another one, Peter. It might be disappointing." Or Peter of Dan: "Funny thing is I like him." There are also wonderful shots, such as that of Daisy forlornly alone in her apartment after Dan leaves or the gorgeous image of Daisy and Peter reflected in the window as it is pouring outside. Frequently the weather is

Sultry pose with Henry Fonda. PHOTO COURTESY OF JERRY MURBACH

troubled — either storming or snowing — perhaps reflecting the tumultuous psyche of the characters. Daisy attempts to be alone, running to a cabin in the woods, but the two men tail her for a final confrontation in which she must choose. She attempts to flee in her car, but has an accident in the snow and must return on foot. Fate pulls her back.

Crawford was a remarkable beauty, her appearance continually evolv-

Two suitors battle it out for Daisy as she looks off and thinks of England.
PHOTO COURTESY OF JERRY MURBACH

ing to suit the times, but I love her look in the '40s especially when perhaps at its most iconic, a lushness mixed with maturity. The tailored dresses with shoulder pads and longer hair pulled back from her ears suit the strong, yet glamorous woman she represented. One can see her freckles here, which is nice. She also has one of those dignified, assertive lines, defying her status as a sexual outsider or "other woman," so typical of Crawford and the reason she resonated so strongly with women and continues to remain a powerful role model: "I'll do my own thinking, thank you, and my own existing," she snaps at Peter.

An interesting, fine, vastly underrated film with superb performances from the three leads. A scene at the Stork Club features John Garfield and Walter Winchell. Peggy Anne Garner plays one of Dan's daughters.

Pet line: Peter to Daisy, picking her up: "Were you ever carried over your own threshold before?" Daisy: "Not sober, darling!"

Flamingo Road (1949) ★★★★★

Flamingo Road is one of my pet favorite Crawford films. She plays Lane Bellamy, a carnival dancer who is stranded in a small town where she falls in love with local deputy/political candidate Fielding Carlisle (Zachary Scott) and runs up against corrupt, deliciously unsavory Sheriff Titus

A great ad from *Movie Life*. What a dame!

Semple (Sydney Greenstreet) who has the weight (no pun intended) and power to run her out of town. Many of the players from *Mildred Pierce* reunite, including director Michael Curtiz, Max Steiner who scored the film, and stars Scott and Crawford.

Oh, this is delicious in a way they can't get right anymore! Sydney Greenstreet was such a wonderful character actor with that wheezing

Crawford and Greenstreet are worthy adversaries! PHOTO COURTESY OF NEIL MACIEJEWSKI

laugh like a braying mule and heavy-lidded eyes like a toad about to strike the unsuspecting fly as he sits with his pitcher of milk in swank nightclubs or on his friendly porch with the overhead fans. He exerts very little effort but manages to be villainous just the same. Crawford narrates the opening and makes a superb "entrance" — at least, aside from her initial appearance during the voiceover and her bit in harem

Even with the diminutive flamenco dancer in center stage, Crawford as Lane Bellamy — road house worker/former carnival girl — shines like a goddess. No mistaking the star here.

girl get-up on the carny stage where she wriggles in veil and silky pants. Scott, sent to check out the abandoned carnival tent, hears music — the lush "If I Could Be One Hour with You [Tonight]" sung throatily by Crawford and parts the flaps of the tent to find her gams in light as the rest of her (sprawled across a couch) is in shadow. She is crooning this song and sits up abruptly. Then the flirtation begins. With her becoming light hair (this softer, toned down look the way she should have gone as she entered her mid-forties), Crawford is the intriguing combination of contrasts that make her so fascinating and powerful a star: elegant but earthy; seductive but girlish; assertive but demure; vulnerable but no one's fool. Her face registers emotion marvelously, making her a natural for romantic melodrama, and whether slinging hash at a two-bit diner or

The "stray cat from the carnival" on Easy Street — er, *Flamingo Road* where minks are always off-the-shoulder. PHOTO COURTESY OF THEO POUROS

sprawled across a satin-draped bed in a glamorous gown at her Flamingo Road digs, she is always impeccably made up and lit. She captures the essence of Lane in the novel, including the "dusky" voice (very kittenish and languid, yet I wonder if she had a cold). It is one of my favorite Crawford portrayals.

A tremendous showdown of worthy opponents as Crawford, never weak-spined, takes on Greenstreet. Also on hand is David Brian as Dan Reynolds, here a refreshingly likeable character, although still bristling with physical power. The black and white cinematography is beautiful and the dialogue witty and snappy, too — Brian to Crawford: "I'm crazy about you, Lane. What's your last name?" Or my favorite — Crawford to Greenstreet when he professes to never forget anything: "You know, Sheriff, we had an elephant in our carnival with a memory like that. He went after a keeper he'd held a grudge against for almost fifteen years. Had to be shot. You just wouldn't believe how much trouble it is to dispose of a dead elephant." Gorgeously composed scenes include one of Lane and Field by a lake, the romantic build ending with Lane throwing her cigarette in the water, the camera cutting to the quiet ripples and glitter as the leads embrace. Another scene that had the entire theater laughing (because they "got it") in a retro showing in New York is when Lane confronts Titus at Lute Mae's. As Greenfield's corpulent form fills the foreground in the frame, Crawford appears, draped in sable wraps, as a dark shadow in the background, outlined in the doorway, this tiny woman managing to radiate a palpable threat, a testament to the "virility," as it was once termed, of her screen presence. Love the jail scene where the jailbirds in the women's dorm act and sound like saucy chorus girls from a Busby Berkeley musical. And Gladys George as Lute May Sanders, who runs some sort of house of ill repute that lends Crawford employment (just what do those "girls" do anyway?), looks like old Hollywood's version of the madame with the heart of gold, down to the peroxide curls.

Get your popcorn and enjoy!

It's a Great Feeling (1949) ★★★½ *(five for Day's songs and Joan's cameo)*

It's a Great Feeling was a showcase, as it were, for a young Doris Day and an attempt by Warners to duplicate the popular Bing Crosby/Bob Hope team with Dennis Morgan and Jack Carson, although it evidently didn't quite work, as pleasant as the film may be. Hollywood also spoofs itself in this sprightly musical comedy and many of its brightest stars appear in cameos, reminding one of the magic and excitement that existed when the studio system was in place. It was indeed like its own kingdom with a mystique and glamour unknown today. The film is in Technicolor, too, which has never been improved upon, giving every frame the hue of impressionist paintings. The nonsensical plot concerns a "little country girl" hailing from Gurkey's Corners, Wisconsin, Judy Adams (Day), who works in the commissary as a waitress at Warner Brothers and wants to be in pictures (what else?). Jack Carson, about to direct himself in a musical called "Mademoiselle Fifi," because no one else will direct him, might be her ticket, but it won't be a straight path. Along the way in Judy's pursuit of stardom, she runs across real stars (their cameos often comedic), including Sydney Greenstreet, Danny Kaye, Gary Cooper, Ronald "Ronnie" Reagan, Eleanor Parker, Patricia Neal, and my own personal favorite, our gal Joan Crawford. Crawford claimed Jack Warner originally wanted her to play Day's sister, to which she replied, "Come on, Jack. No one would believe that I would have Doris Day for a sister." However, *It's a Great Feeling* remained one of Crawford's own favorite parts. The book *Conversations with Crawford* reported her as saying, "The first comedy I'd done in ages, and I loved every minute of it. Marvelous therapy, after doing all those heavy parts, one after another, starting with 'Mildred.'" Indeed she is a delight here and one of the highlights, fleeting as her appearance may be.

Judy arranges to deliver lunch to Jack Carson personally, then locks his door and launches into a frontal attack of melodramatic acting and posing. A picture of Joan Crawford is prominent in Carson's dressing room, the photos of Warner stars sprinkled throughout the lot. Day is cute, but has a squeaky, tomboyish wholesomeness that is a little overdone. They are going for the young ingénue here, of course, yet this June Allyson cornpone belies the tremendous abilities Day had as a songstress and musical comedy star. Although occasionally strident as a dramatic actress, she was near flawless as a musician, more sophisticated than her image ever fully allowed her to explore. It nonetheless came out in her singing and delivery. Carson decides he can use Judy to his advantage by having her pose as the "secret" Mrs. Carson for Dennis Morgan so he'll appear in Carson's picture. It's a great scene and Day is wonderful in it. Carson climbs a tree so he can coach her from the window. When Morgan finds out their game, he demands, "What did you promise her to get her to do this?" and Carson wittily responds, "You know, a part in a picture, usual malarkey."

Crushed by the insincerity of Carson, Judy decides to take the train back to Gurkey's Corners, yet a guilty and somewhat amorous Carson and Morgan conspire to get her back. There's the small matter and running joke that no one wants to be in a Carson picture, you see, so perhaps the "little country girl" would fill the bill as their much-needed leading lady. Hollywood looks pink and tropical and beautiful with sets being pushed around and no garbage or decline. It's interesting to see it in its clean and prosperous glory days before it became physically sordid

Joan is in a triangle again — at least picture-wise! WARNER BROS.

(although undoubtedly it was still Hollywood Babylon on other levels). At the train station, there's a funny bit as the attendant tries to find information about the apparently obscure Gurkey's Corners for Judy in a series of heavy tomes. Carson and Morgan vie for Judy's attention, so they can subvert her from running home and marrying local sweetheart Jeffrey Bushdinkle and succeed in convincing her to give it and them another shot.

The cameo with Joan Crawford happens fittingly (pun intended) at a swank dress salon where Judy is being shown some possible outfits for her debut. Crawford, turned out impeccably with a mink wrap (or is it sable?) draped around her shoulders and auburn hair, looks gorgeous in color, making one rue that they didn't give her more color films. She is chic and petite, appearing tiny even against Doris Day, proving how very small a woman she really was. She does a great, funny spoof on her

Mildred Pierce role (Carson having been one of her co-stars) and double slaps both Carson and Morgan. When Carson asks what she did that for, she smiles charmingly and says, "I do that in all my pictures!" Day gushes how much she loves "Miss Crawford."

Meanwhile, Judy, in an effort to interest studio bigwig Arthur Trent (Bill Goodwin), is made to be everywhere he is in a variety of guises, always flashing him a toothy Colgate grin and batting her eyelashes until he is dizzy. She becomes so over-exposed that finally they have to disguise her as an exotic French woman Yvonne Amour, whose background the publicity department dreams up. Again, a photo of Crawford in *Humoresque* is seen on the wall in this scene as the details are worked out. Day proves her moxie as a theatrical/musical lead when pretending to be Yvonne in brunette wig (so Arthur won't recognize her), singing in a terrible French accent. Trying to read her lines from the back of the fan she sports, she finally gets discombobulated and confused and flies off the stage, her wig coming off at the same time. It's absolutely priceless. Again, it's fun to see the alleged workings of the studio system with all the commissary waitresses working the room as the big band plays. Arthur Trent now sees the blonde that was making him nuts and wants nothing to do with her. Will the "little country girl" take the train back to Gurkey's Corners, Wisconsin, or will she get her chance to join the stars at Warners?

Aside from Joan's delightful cameo where her beauty and comic timing is given a chance to shine, Day's numbers are high points. It seems Day would've been better served, one can't help think, if she had been made less cutesy, although certainly her popularity acknowledged her talent and proved they were doing something right. But too often Day was given a prim, buttoned-up look and image that strait-jacketed her. Here, in one scene in a bar where she is watching a wrestling match, she looks absolutely wonderful and far sexier in a sophisticated Lana Turner '40s style hairdo and padded shoulders. It suits her very well and seems more in line with her sophisticated, sensual singing style, although her cute, feisty, wholesome appeal did well by her, too. She could belt when necessary, but never threw it away showily like some singers; rather, as she put it, she preferred to whisper in your ear.

All in all, not a great film, but fun nonetheless with its cameos (particularly our gal Joan), songs and gags. Good for family viewing and a rare chance to see my favorite actress Crawford appear with another of my longtime favorites, Day. Claire Carleton as Judy's saucy roommate Grace is also a highlight.

Films of the Fifties

The Damned Don't Cry (1950) ★★★★★

The Damned Don't Cry is a first-rate, gripping crime drama and film noir, based on the Bugsy Siegel-Virginia Hill story, seemingly combining all the stock Joan Crawford prototypes from her films — with the exception of musical star — and rolling them into one. Not only does Joan revisit all her past film types, but she swims and wears mink, too! She's a brassy riot as this no nonsense, tough talking woman taking on the boys and making it in a man's world. It is simply my favorite of her 1950s films and one of the best films of its kind with evocative black and white cinematography, superb shots and angles, script, direction and performances all gelling beautifully.

Joan plays hardball with a gangster!

As in *Mildred Pierce*, the story is told in flashbacks as the body of a murdered gangster is found in the desert, his home movies featuring a fashionable socialite and heiress known as Lorna Hansen Forbes, and a distraught, mink-clad woman arrives at a ramshackle house on the outskirts of oil derricks. We learn that the woman is Ethel Whitehead (Crawford), a working-class housewife who had been saddled with a weak

Socialite Patricia Longworth (Selena Royle) sets up the newly-christened "Lorna Hansen Forbes" (who else?) in the dangerous underworld.

husband of no ambition (Richard Egan) (shades of *Mildred Pierce*) and who reached her limit when her six-year-old son Tom was run over by a truck while riding the bicycle she scraped to buy him. Ethel then headed to the Big Apple where with a will of iron and the use of her feminine wiles and sex appeal, she rose from cigar store girl to a dress model for a randy group of out of town buyers (where the models are required to "date" the salesmen, along with putting up with outright harassment). The businessmen prove to be part of an illegal bookmaking racket, and Ethel sleeps her way to the top of this empire, beginning with a spineless accountant, Martin Blackford (Kent Smith) to the ruthless blond head of the ring, George Castleman (David Brian) and including the dark, sleek West Coast gangster Nick Prenta (Steve Cochran). In order to aid Castleman's operation, Ethel is transformed into Lorna Hansen Forbes, fur-lined socialite and mistress of Castleman. Although Ethel is "moving up" in the world, she is also digging herself in deeper with duplicity and danger which culminates in her being sent to the West Coast and hired to keep Castleman informed about Nick. At this point, Ethel, horrified at the turn events have taken, is in over her head.

Crawford makes the whole sordid enterprise taut and entertaining

A fun publicity shot with Crawford and two of her male leads, Steve Cochran and David Brian. PHOTO COURTESY OF JERRY MURBACH

and is mesmerizing onscreen, walking across a room as if she owns it. Although Ethel is as "tough as a 75-cent steak," Crawford injects this hard-shelled dame with enough verve, style, chutzpah and charm to make one root for her. Her cheeky, sexy confidence in certain scenes helps roll the plot along. Although accused of being often paired with weak men onscreen at this juncture in her career, this is not the case with David Brian. He not only achieves a palpable electricity and edge in his dynamics with Crawford, but also brings a fascinating brutality and realism to his role. His voice is as sinuous and deadly as an asp. Fortuitous casting! This type of man is recognizable — powerful, large, impeccably dressed and a ruthless sociopath. You know not to mess with his kind — unless you're Ethel Whitehead. As the accountant, Blackford is so weak, Crawford could eat him for breakfast (and love when she snaps at him, "Don't talk to me about self respect! That's something you tell yourself you've got when you've got nothing else!") Prenta is appropriately handsome and hunky, the sort she would understandably fall for and protect.

In all, it's Joan at her gritty, spunky best.

Pet scene: Crawford telling off mobster Brian in his office. In heels and rose-covered hat she's a full head shorter than him. It is this kind of role that makes Crawford Crawford, a woman far ahead of her time and absolutely in a league of her own. (Incidentally, some scenes of *The Damned Don't Cry* were shot at Twin Palms, Frank Sinatra's landmark first home in Palm Springs, and Crawford swims the length of his spectacular pool in the film.)

Harriet Craig (1950) ★★★★

In this remake of the 1936 Rosalind Russell film *Craig's Wife*, Joan Crawford appears in the titular role as the emotionally scarred woman whose abandonment issues cause her to have a neurotic need for order and control over her household and its inhabitants. As always in these Crawford films where audiences are invited to perceive her character as the heavy, my sympathies are with Harriet, a woman who might lie and manipulate, but evidently needs to in order to have any influence, living as she does in her husband's childhood home under the shadow of his mother's memory and with his biased boyhood servant in tow. Harriet also apparently loves hubby Walter (Wendell Corey) and shows him affection, insecure as she may be and questionable as her deceits may be. When she returns to her home, however, and finds full ashtrays and Walter's clothes strewn about, I could well understand her chagrin, especially when she has to pick up after him. Isn't there common courtesy in keeping things neat when co-habiting — or is it me? Personally I've always found chaos disquieting, not "comfy." Furthermore, looking at languidly competent yet careless Walter and the cool but efficient Harriet, it's clear that Harriet is the more capable as far as keeping things running. According to backstory, she was also successful on her own in business, but relegated herself to her current position as homemaker and wife in order to have a security she doesn't entirely trust.

Crawford is excellent in the role — sexy and adorable even with the severe hairstyle, but also conveying a certain rigidity and cold authority that underscores her coating of charm and exposes her fear of losing control. Backstory also tells us that she blames her father for her mother's mental breakdown and does not want the same to happen to her.

Corey, in the role of affable husband (dwarfing Crawford in some scenes), is meant to be viewed as a loveable sheep dog, yet in spite of his so-called affection, I found him contemptible on some level. His patronizing attitude toward Harriet (driven as it is by lust) can be summed up by his comment, "Wives may be a little extra trouble now and then, but they're mighty handy gadgets to have around the house" while Harriet's

Walter Craig (Wendell Corey) confronts the "little woman" Harriet (Joan Crawford) across the beautifully appointed table as the "poor relation" looks on. Crawford's severe hairdo is surprisingly sexy, accentuating her fine and delicate features.

philosophy is, "Husbands must be trained." Wasn't this exactly the attitude that was being passed down in that era in reality between the sexes because of the imbalance in power — for men overt, for women covert? Meanwhile, all the minor characters (including the delicious Ellen Corby as Lottie, cowering when she breaks a cup the way Mrs. Bucket's neighbor does when handling the china in the Brit comedy *Keeping Up Appearances*) are drawn expressly to indict Harriet for her unreasonableness. It only stokes my sympathy for Harriet who like Eva in *Queen Bee* finds herself the outsider in her own home even though superficially in control.

Rather than finding fault with Harriet for her behavior (except for her interference in a budding romance between her doting cousin and

Walter's business associate, which was undeserved), I wonder: Why does Harriet's mother's psychiatrist probe Harriet on her marriage when Harriet is consulting her about her mother's condition, even asking Harriet whether she has children? Why does she look at Harriet as if she has two heads when Harriet volunteers that her father left at age fourteen and probably caused her mother's "disassociation" a statement the psychiatrist

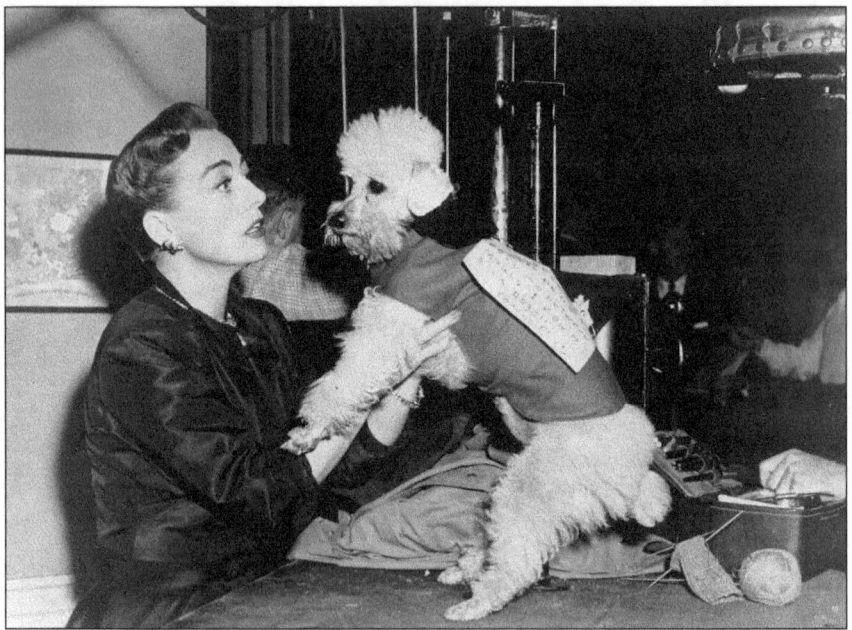

Adorable candid of Crawford with her beloved poodle Cliquot, her ball of knitting not far off. The sign on his back reads: "Please do not feed me between meals. I was a sick doggie. Thanks. C.C."

then pooh-poohs in her clinical, dispassionate voice? And why does Celia Fenwick (Lucille Watson) develop such an immediate camaraderie with Walter during a card game that she, too, feels entitled to quiz him about whether he is happy in his home and why he has no children? Not a very delicate hand in this script at times.

Apparently Vincent Sherman (whose relationship with Crawford always struck me as questionable, distasteful as he was about boasting of his conquests, for one) used Crawford's own quirks and story in the film. At one point Harriet even mentions that she worked in a laundry as a kid, true of Crawford.

Basically *Harriet Craig* rankles me, being at heart another attempt to frame a dominant woman with the real complaint being that husband was supposedly denied his "right" to wear the pants in the family. Even when one learns that Harriet lied about her ability to conceive children, fatherhood being very important to Walter, it fails to strike me as diabolical, but more a necessary evil; otherwise Harriet would not have had her own preference honored and she'd be carrying the babies. How necessary lying and manipulation become when one has few outlets for power, as

Another great candid of Crawford with her stand-in on the set of *Harriet Craig.* Two hands reach for Cliquot. COURTESY OF WIDE WORLD PHOTOS

was the case for women in the 1950s. In the scenario presented in this film, Walter is given an opportunity to go on business to Japan for three months, a prospect which frightens Harriet, so she approaches his boss to sabotage it. The act is viewed as an outrage (or meant to be), but think if it were Harriet going on a three-month sabbatical for business? In "Ice Follies of 1939," hubby James Stewart left his wife because of her career demands and jumped with hysterical joy when she publicly denounced her career to return to him. Double standards never sit well with me, so I see Harriet's point of view in at least resenting such a protracted separation.

(Spoilers!) In any case, well acted and worthwhile, but yet another cautionary tale to keep women "in their place." Ultimately, however, although I felt sorry for Harriet alone in the great house at the end, particularly when she bursts into tears, it seems almost fitting since one sees a calm come over her as she surveys what is now completely hers. Sister, sometimes you're better off with the Ming vase.

Goodbye My Fancy (1951) ★★★ *(mostly for Eve Arden)*

In *Goodbye, My Fancy,* Congresswoman Agatha Reed (Joan Crawford) accepts an invitation to spend a weekend and receive an honorary degree at the Massachusetts college from which she was expelled twenty years ago, Good Hope. Although she's in the midst of an election and her wisecracking personal secretary, Woody (Eve Arden — who else?) thinks it's sentimental hogwash, Agatha is eager to see her old love, James Merrill (Robert Young), now the president of Good Hope, and the very reason she was expelled (she stayed out all night with him and, even though they were engaged to be married, ran away afterwards so his chance of becoming president would not be compromised). Meanwhile, another old fling of Agatha's comes onto the scene (Crawford is forever in the midst of romantic triangles), a photographer for *Life* magazine, Matt Cole (Frank Lovejoy) whom Agatha had romanced in China during the war. Sent to cover the festivities at the college, he also is intent on picking up where he left off and discovering why Agatha ran out on him five years ago. The third complication is the "free speech" film that Agatha wants to show the students that upsets the conservative money bags who control the college and could cost Jim his position.

Goodbye My Fancy was originally a Broadway play by Fay Kanin and many of the scenes and players have a stage-bound feeling, particularly the shrill and hyper Lurene Tuttle as Ellie Griswold, Aggie's former roommate. (She might not have been in the original Broadway cast, but you'd never know, because she performs as if playing to the back row, a bizarre contrast against Crawford's cold sophistication.) This being the third and final film that Crawford did with director and lover Vincent Sherman, it is refreshingly light fare compared to the actress' other '50s films and not campy, but neither does the "message" quite have the impas-

Crawford co-stars with Eve Arden once again and this time our gal Joan is a Congresswoman! Did you think she wouldn't be?

sioned impact it aims for, nor the star much lightness. There are several things that hamper its effectiveness. For one, Crawford often seems to be reciting lines (albeit with feeling) rather than convincingly inhabiting the character, as she usually does even with mediocre scripts. In some of the emotional scenes, she is overblown and artificial (although, by far, not the only offender) and the sanctimonious "hallowed halls" music doesn't help. She exudes potent enough sexuality and that classy "cocktail dame" charm that I like in her strapless cocktail dresses, tastefully provocative gowns and ankle-strap shoes, lighter and cigarette always in hand (perhaps because Crawford often needed to do things with her hands), trim body carried with dancer's pride, but is also somewhat forbidding. In her scenes with old co-star Young, however, she becomes warm and genuine, more tender and girlish, and loses some of the steel that penetrates elsewhere. By contrast, she has no chemistry with Lovejoy, not even the hint of buried interest, and so the very premise that she is chasing a dream with the debonair Jim at the expense of a worthier relationship with Matt rings false. Jim resonates clearly as her true love. The most gorgeous scene in the whole film, in fact, heartfelt and moving, is when she meets Jim again in their special place and discovers he kept the note she wrote him twenty years ago. As he begins to recite it, she completes it for him, the words of Walt Whitman:

Goodbye, my fancy!
Farewell my dear mate, dear love!
I'm going away, I know not where
Or to what fortune, or whether I may
ever see you again.
So goodbye, my fancy.

Crawford is eloquent and sincere in this scene, her husky speaking voice pleasing, and never has she spoken a lovelier line than when she adds, "Hello, my fancy," looking at Young. The potential for the "right" film was all there, but unfortunately short-circuited!

Aside from these scenes between Crawford and Young, Arden, who only seemed to improve with age, makes the film and is attractive enough to deserve her own love interest (no such luck).

Agatha: If I feel like acting like a kid, I'm going to…I'm going to cry. I'm going to be sentimental. I'm going to walk barefoot down memory lane with ivy entwined in my hair. And if you don't like it, you don't have to look.
Woody: I'll bring my dark glasses along.

Another great line is when Woody tells Aggie that she can't marry when she's smack in the middle of an election campaign and Aggie responds, "There's quite a difference between a busy life and a full one."

The hunger for "truth" by these college girls (like escapees from the cast of "Bye Bye Birdie") never quite resonates, although it's a timely and timeless problem. And not a single character catches the irony when Ellie ultimately shows her support but stresses that it's important for her husband to think it was his idea. After all the bluster about the importance of free speech, we see that it is okay for girls to think as long as men take credit for it. Heigh-ho! Back to the black boards!

In all, *Goodbye My Fancy* is a refreshing change of pace for Crawford which doesn't quite work, but is nonetheless entertaining and worthwhile with a great Eve Arden and beautiful chemistry between Crawford and Young.

This Woman is Dangerous (1952) ★★★½

Contrary to popular myth, Joan Crawford looked quite attractive and sexy, as opposed to harsh or "mannish" in the majority of her 1950s films, as *This Woman is Dangerous* demonstrates. She was no longer the ingénue, obviously, so her look was "mature," but her face still revealed the natural beauty she possessed of great bones, beautiful profile and large, expressive eyes, plus she kept her trim figure throughout her career. The last film in her Warners contract, *This Woman is Dangerous* is, by the same token, not as dire as its reputation, although evidently cheaper in budget than its sister "gangster" film, *The Damned Don't Cry* which also featured David Brian as a sociopath and Crawford as his unfortunate lover.

The plot concerns an elegant ex-jailbird Beth Austin (Crawford) (she was in the pen for extortion) who is the girlfriend of a dangerous, pathologically jealous gangster, Matt Jackson (David Brian). He, along with equally unhinged and antagonistic brother Will (Philip Carey), form a notorious band, The Jackson Brothers. Plagued by headaches, Beth is losing her sight and has to undergo a critical eye operation in Indiana, although even her hospital stay threatens loose trigger Matt who calls obsessively to check up on her and hires a private detective to track her moves. It's always interesting to me when Crawford is given "flaws" in her films (*Humoresque, A Woman's Face*) and they're intrinsically bound with her character's fate. In this case, it's rather touching and well done when her vision is slowly restored and she gets to see surgeon Ben Halleck (Dennis Morgan). ("I've been looking at you, Mrs. Austin," he says. "In many ways, you've opened my eyes.") This romance is handled sensitively and puts Crawford in familiar territory, that of being torn between two men — what else? — and tearily willing to sacrifice her own happiness out of loyalty to her original beau — what else? The key question is posed by Ben: "Do you love him?" We want these two lovely people to redeem their pasts and find bliss with one another. But will Ben accept Beth, warts and all, when he knows the truth about her past?

Morgan as the surgeon offering Beth and himself a second chance at life and love is extremely appealing, gentle and kind, so I rooted for their romance, even if it was rushed and only marginally more convincing than the one between Beth and Matt. Still, I enjoyed their dynamics and wanted more. The scenes in the hospital, although criticized for hokeyness, are actually genuinely tender. Particularly good moments include Beth saying, "I suppose it does have its advantages, drifting in the dark. You don't have to face realities" and Ben giving her a single rose, which

Crawford once again tangles with a psychotic David Brian in *This Woman is Dangerous*. PHOTO COURTESY OF JIM MAHONEY

she identifies by smell, the latter scene working on the appeal of the two actors alone and Crawford's ability to project a sympathetic dimension to even the sketchiest of characters. One sees for a few minutes the jaded woman in Beth who would like to believe but has fallen too far. The hope presented by this scenario — that an essentially good woman who has gone off the track somewhere in life can find love and be redeemed — is one of my chief loves of classic films, the unabashed sentimental idealism, the raw cathartic emotions.

The real monkey wrench in the production is Brian whose gangster is so brutish and relentlessly one note that it's inconceivable why a classy, gentle-spoken woman like Beth — extortionist or no extortionist — would

With handsome Dennis Morgan, Dr. "Feelgood."

even fall for him. They go together like oil and water with no believable chemistry, although Crawford gives everything a game try, as she always does, oozing a lightly flirtatious charm in his direction while he always appears one step short of psychotic rage. He is given a few powerful moments, however, such as when he throws a liquor bottle from a speeding camper's window, attracting the notice of a highway patrol cop who he then murders in cold blood. (And Beth is interested in him for what reason?) The action culminates in a creepy, but fascinating scene where this fanatical, brutish infant comes to the hospital operating room to murder the surgeon as he is in the midst of an operation. This woman is not particularly dangerous, but the man definitely is.

All in all, a fairly good film with sensitive performances from Crawford and Morgan, good melodrama, and nice touches. Like *Rain*, this film is much better than Crawford or some critics ever gave it credit for. And who can resist fabulous trailers like these:

> *EVERY INCH A LADY… till you look at the record!*
> *Part of her was Ritz — part of her was "racket" — all of her was exciting!*
> *Beth Austin — stylish dame with a stylish name — who lived by jungle law in a big city and clawed her way to where the money was…!*

Sudden Fear (1952) ★★★★★

As in *Midnight Lace* where Doris Day — plagued with threatening phone calls — might've curtailed trouble by simply hanging up instead of shrieking hysterically into the receiver and building to a histrionic meltdown that convinced everyone who was previously on the fence of her instability, Joan Crawford might've spared herself a whole lot of fear by going to the police at the onset. But then the world would be short of two deliciously fun thrillers with leading ladies who are both fearful and fashionable.

Sudden Fear is the superior of the two, although both are highly entertaining. Crawford not only stars, but co-produced this top notch noir, showing further evidence of her boundless talent. She, in fact, carries the film, as she so often does, this time with two strong and well-cast co-stars, Jack Palance and Gloria Grahame. With a tight build-up of suspense; gorgeous, glossy black and white cinematography; and a riveting score, the whole thing works every time.

At the start of the film, Myra Hudson (Crawford), a playwright and heiress, is attending rehearsals for her upcoming Broadway play *Halfway to Heaven* and finds the leading man Lester Blaine (Jack Palance) lacking as a romantic hero. According to Hudson, he doesn't seem to be the type who would make "every woman in the audience sit right up and go, 'Mmph!'" (Funny how Crawford's films always seem to mirror her own life, since she, too, wasn't thrilled with the choice of Palance as a co-star, although his oddly sinister face makes him perfect as the "heavy" and

Myra Hudson (Joan Crawford) fears the honeymoon may be over.

their off-screen tension adds wonderfully to the friction; she was also put off by his method acting which included French kissing during their love sequences.) By chance, Hudson and Blaine meet on a train going from New York to San Francisco and begin a whirlwind romance. The pair marry and the older-but-not-wiser Hudson is eager to introduce her new husband to all her society friends, many of whom are suspicious of him — like her attorney, Steve Kearney (Bruce Bennett - who played Crawford's husband in *Mildred Pierce*.) As the merciless hands of fate (and the screenwriters) have it, Irene Neves (Gloria Grahame), Lester's ex-girlfriend, is at the party on the arm of Junior Kearney (Mike Connors — yes, "Mannix"), Steve's son. Like two cats in heat, the conniving pair secretly meet and hatch a plot to get at Myra's millions. When they learn that Myra plans to leave the bulk of her estate to a foundation with only $10,000 a year for Lester, they scheme to kill her and make it look like an accident before the will is signed — a tight deadline of only the weekend. Myra, however, learns of this nefarious plan when she leaves on her Dictaphone machine and the pair's conversation is unwittingly recorded. This begins her state of sudden fear. After a sleepless night, she hatches a foil for this dastardly duo worthy of one of her own plays.

Sudden Fear is exciting fun, using the sort of nail-biting, manipulative

Her clenched fists and clenched jaw speak volumes. Crawford and Palance are a study in chiseled visages.

devices of an old radio play and much of the acting relies on Crawford's facial expressions; her silent screen days prepared her well. Although underrated and at times accused of being phony as an actor, Crawford was a consummate professional and often achieved an emotional truth and naturalness onscreen, inhabiting characters fully. Her characters are vulnerable and human — and therefore, somehow real — as is the case with Myra. Ultimately, in spite of a glamorous and capable facade, she's so human, one wonders if Myra will carry out the ingenious plan she's concocted, which adds to the peril of her predicament. Palance is perfectly villainous and Grahame is in her element as the brash, slightly tawdry and sexy tart (what else?) who likes rough sex and oozes danger. It's also delicious fun watching Crawford walk from one area of Pacific Heights to the next and then run up and down the steep hills of San Francisco in high heels and a mink — after falling down a flight of stairs, no less, with little stain to her glamour beyond a few beads of sweat. That — and the glass of milk — are some of the great quirks that make classic films like this one divine fun.

Torch Song (1953) ★★½ *(five for "bad film" fans)*

Just as *That Touch of Mink* is perhaps single-handedly to blame for Doris Day being inaccurately dubbed a "professional virgin," *Torch Song* deserves top honors for advancing the largely unfair "mannish gorgon" caricature of 1950s Joan Crawford. In this case, it bears some weight, although as with all stereotypes, it's not the whole story. Though petite and ultra feminine in garb, in this evidently emotional return to her old alma mate MGM, Crawford comes off as so ironclad that she resembles the drag queens who impersonate her. Yet the fear beneath the abrasive posturing is touching. Bios reveal that she was frightened to be dancing again after so many years. Crawford spent the first twenty years of her career at MGM and, even if his business interests came first, Louis Mayer was one of her deferred-to "father figures." As tacky as *Torch Song* is, even in later years, she continued to overrate it. In his book describing their friendship, Carl Johnes recalled how hurt she was when Carol Burnett lampooned it. "I did more in that picture than just show off my legs, for God's sake," she snapped, to which he added as an aside, "although, frankly, that's the only thing I could remember." MGM rolled out the red carpet for Joan, but *Torch Song* is no homage with, as one viewer put it, "retina-scorching colors," a plot out of bad dinner theater, and clunky musical numbers. What more could a bad film lover want?

Yes, this is one of Crawford's rare color films — full blown Technicolor. God, how I miss it! The star even has her hair dyed red, since one must make full use of the color wheel. Some laugh at the surreal hues, but I love them, even if, in this case, sunglasses with high UV protection are recommended — completely opaque ones for the "Two-Faced Woman" number.

Our titian-haired gal is Jenny Stewart, a tyrannical musical star who is secretly lonely — what else? — and vulnerable — what else? — beneath the alligator hide. She cries herself to sleep at night as you learn in one scene where she is swathed in a day-glo lemon robe that billows around her like a swirling dervish. When one piano player quits, having earlier given her an opportunity for a great line — (as they ride in a taxi and the driver asks his address, Jenny cracks, "Any

Crawford as Jenny Stewart: "[Her] mouth belongs to an angel but the words that come out of it are pure tramp."

dark bar") — she inherits another, Tye Graham (Michael Wilding). The problem is he's blind. She bristles at him and is shortly ready to give him the heave-ho when he dares to give her musical advice ("Why don't you find yourself a nice seeing-eye girl?"), but soon she is fumbling about with her eyes closed to understand what his life is all about. Like a great soap opera twist, Tye has actually loved Jenny since reviewing

Where the line between Joan and drag queens becomes dicey. PHOTO COURTESY OF NEIL MACIEJEWSKI

her in one of her first performances back when he could see, and he's still carrying the "torch." Her earlier sweet image is implanted on his mental retina. Yeah, right.

Jenny is one Crawford character who is not successfully softened and perpetuates the common negative stereotype of the star which tends to obscure the considerable charms that brought her popularity in the first place. Crawford, in fact, was blessed with many natural assets that ensured her ascent. Aside from a face that photographed well from any angle and those eyes and her vitality and charisma, she had a beautiful, trim body — voluptuous without being huge-breasted, toned and sleek like a dancer, with especially shapely legs. She wore clothes like a model and knew how to hold herself and move. Besides which, she had talent and a committed work ethic. Unfortunately, like so many women who are judged by their looks and deemed worthless as they age, apparently she felt she "needed work" pre-MGM comeback to compete with youth and that meant augmentation. In *Torch Song*, she thrusts out torpedo breasts that could puncture an eye like the protruding collars on her old Adrian gowns. They overpower her slim hips and add to the drag queen illusion particularly when she's lip synching. Her natural body and her own singing voice (opposed to the dubbing by India Adams) would have been preferable. A scene where she actually does sing over her own supposed early recording of "Tenderly" is much better than the big phony, dubbed production numbers.

It's not that you can't see that Crawford's a real woman, mind, that I say she resembles a drag queen; it's that she's strait-jacketed (excuse the Joan pun) into this rigid parody of womanhood that the 1950s imposed on all women as a backlash against their successful takeover of male-dominated jobs during the war. She's overblown and playing a tough barracuda on top of it. Any "naturalness" doesn't stand a chance because of the strident musical numbers with stiff, though competently executed, choreography (as bad as any Susan Hayward was forced to do in the '50s). I don't feel it's all her fault that she comes off as campy and in the same position with those peculiar pressures, many of us might have eaten crow to stay on top. I don't fault (as some do), but applaud Crawford's (and Bette Davis') desire and efforts to prevail and hang on in an industry that sought to discard them when they were no longer youthful. I'm grateful to them. Apparently Crawford disliked lousy roles as much as anyone, although her judgment remained clouded on *Torch Song* due to sentiment.

Still, many scenes are responsible for the bitchy caricature that persists today of Crawford, although, in reality, she enjoyed a good working relationship with the majority of her co-workers and certainly her crew. In one instance, she requests a party and snaps, "Get the usual gang." We see that the "usual gang" is all male leaving her the lone — er — Queen Bee in their midst as if to disallow any female competition. At this gathering, however, with her harsh countenance, striding around irritably, she seems to exude as much testosterone as the rest of them — her frilly cocktail

"Gratefully, Jenny Stewart": Jenny's warm interaction with her fans mirrors Crawford's own cherished relationship with her public.

dress incongruous, although she has those same dreamy, sensual eyes that seduced audiences in countless films like *Our Blushing Brides*.

The best scenes are the ones between Jenny and her mother (Marjorie Rambeau). They lend Jenny and the film some dimension, as does the easy rapport she displays with her maid Ann (Maidie Norman). (Interestingly, Rambeau was her co-star in an earlier film *Laughing Sinners* which was based on a play called *Torch Song*.) Another scene, in particular, which moved me is when Tye is upbraiding a tear-stained Jenny for the tough hide she developed in an industry that is going to throw her out as she gets older. I'm sure that whole speech hit home for Crawford and it shows on her face. More biographical/"in jokes" are present. Tye's seeing eye dog is named Duchess (a nod, I suspect, to Crawford's nickname in her biggest MGM musical, *Dancing Lady*); and Jenny's warm interaction with her fans mirrors Crawford's own cherished relationship with her public to whom she, like Jenny, believed she owed her all and gave it accordingly. I also genuinely adore the line by Jenny's parasitic boyfriend Cliff Willard (Gig Young): "I'll curl up in front of the fire with a good book or a bad girl."

In any case, *Torch Song* is trash, but that's not necessarily a negative. My dance teacher once said, "As a performer, it's your job to fascinate." And Crawford in color in quintessential self parody delivering lines with deadpan in the way only she can is something to behold. Besides, I'd rather curl up with a bad girl any day!

Johnny Guitar (1954) ★★★★

Johnny Guitar is a Nicholas Ray western that has developed a cult following, gaining its earliest avid appreciation in Europe among the New Wave directors like Francoise Truffaut and Americans like Martin Scorsese. Although not one of my favorite Joan Crawford films and although never particularly drawn to westerns, in general, *Johnny Guitar* is distinguished by several fascinating factors — one being style, including creative use of color (Tru-Color was the method used, unnaturally vibrant and saturated) and another being the non-traditional gender roles and situations. Women here are in power and the men, by and large, although comprised of many "western" stereotypes like "the kid" and the strong, enigmatic and silent stranger (think "Shane"), essentially defer to them.

Michael Kupperman's superb *Johnny Guitar* portrait which nails our gal's grit to a T! CARTOON COURTESY OF MICHAEL KUPPERMAN

Crawford plays Vienna, the owner of a casino (supposedly won brick by brick through sexual favors, or so it is implied), who is maintaining her hold on a boomtown that promises greater expansion with the upcoming railroad. Her nemesis is

Crawford goes a tad butch, but, then, she owns the business in the town and is calling the shots. PHOTO COURTESY OF NEIL MACIEJEWSKI

Emma (Mercedes Cambridge) who loves the Dancing Kid and despises Vienna for having romanced him and also for supposedly being involved in a stagecoach robbery that took the life of Emma's brother. The hatred between the two women, which extended off-screen, is palpable, contributing an intense psycho-sexual drama to the plot. Crawford was beginning to take on her harsher "steel rose" look at this point, her lips done up in her

Color is used to great effect in *Johnny Guitar* and the heroine naturally wears white (and — not pictured here — plays the piano, as Crawford often does in her films).

mid-career signature red "smear" and with the film's saturated color, they seem to leap from the screen. Like McCambridge, she, as a formidable force in a one-horse town, has taken on an appropriately "butch" look with short hair and is often shot from low angles. Without her usual high heels, she is tiny, but nonetheless mighty, her stance dominant in typical cowboy fashion, a holster slung around her hips. Exteriors show wide vistas of clay mountains in shades of rust and burnt orange, and interiors are steeped in the same clay colors with green and red, giving everything a rustic look. The characters wear colors significantly, too, with Emma and "boys" in, as Vienna puts it, "funeral colors" (black), as Vienna sports a flowing white dress when her enemies come to confront her. Johnny Guitar nee Johnny Logan (Sterling Hayden) is Vienna's former lover, come to town to help her against her adversaries; once a sure shot, he has traded in guns for a guitar. He wears pink.

Incredible scenes here include the conversation between Crawford and Hayden when they discuss their relationship, which is orchestrated to a sublime and perfect pitch. The dialogue below had me jumping in my seat in glee. The pair have completely exchanged a-typical gender dialogue. Hayden's goofy sincerity and Crawford's steely detachment make it a hoot:

Johnny: Don't go away.
Vienna: I haven't moved.
Johnny: Tell me something nice.
Vienna: Sure, what do you want to hear?
Johnny: Lie to me. Tell me all these years you've waited. Tell me.
Vienna: All those years I've waited.
Johnny: Tell me you'd a-died if I hadn't come back.
Vienna: I woulda died if you hadn't come back.
Johnny: Tell me you still love me like I love you.
Vienna: I still love you like you love me.
Johnny: Thanks. Thanks a lot.

The plot builds in intensity as the undesirables are targeted and intimidated, interpreted by many as an allegory for the McCarthy hearings in which fear of communism led to witch burning hysteria and testimony. To add to the oddness, the film culminates in a romantic clinch between Crawford and Hayden as Peggy Lee sings on the soundtrack. Not for all tastes perhaps, but definitely one of a kind and audacious.

Female on the Beach (1955) ★ ★ ★ ½

As I long suspected, *Female on the Beach* is delicious, overwrought, trashy fun of the best kind — the kind with the later-mid-career Joan Crawford in strappy heels tangling with a beach stud. Crawford stars as Lynn Markham, a wealthy gambler's widow who leases a beach house in Balboa, California sight unseen so that she can be "alone." Oh, if it were only that simple, Joan! Unbeknownst to Markham, the prior tenant — also a rich widow — was either pushed or fell to her death from the balcony, and the broken railing remains as warning. Enter boy-toy and beach bum Drummond (Jeff Chandler) with bulging biceps and chiseled face — in fact, he enters Markham's kitchen in the morning with his own key. Markham sizes him up as a gigolo pretty rapidly and tries to give him the heave-ho (at least she gets back the key), but damn, if the insolent bum won't move his boat from her harbor. What's a lone woman to do? This one climbs over the side of his boat one night in Barbie doll dress and heels and let's him put his greasy paw on her and kiss her. "I've left a mark on you," he says, referring to the smudge of grease on her arm. "You'd

Crawford once said, "Never love anything that can't love you back." But when it comes to beach studs, does she take her own advice? (Note Joan's coordinated shoes and shirt.) PHOTO COURTESY OF JERRY MURBACH

leave a mark on anyone," she responds silkily. "I wish I could afford you." And this after she's been warned by a local detective that "a woman alone on the beach is a target." (If they can't bind our feet, we get the warning to curtail our movements!)

Oh, this is a watchable, entertaining hoot and a half. There's the snaky music and Chandler in his striped tops and tight bathing trunks and

What's a specialty dancer with great gams to do when no one will allow her to read her erotic poetry the way she likes her coffee — alone?

Crawford in a whole array of cocktail-dress ensembles that she sports while merely sashaying around her home alone. She protests, but it doesn't take long for the muscled beach stud to weaken her better instincts and make her love him, especially when he tears her dress one night in a frenzy. In spite of warnings from the cop and the suspicious blonde bombshell (Jan Sterling) who was her real estate agent and who also loves the bum and in spite of finding a diary behind a brick in the fireplace that pretty much spells out the trouble between the prior tenant and said stud muffin and in spite of telling Drummond herself that he is "about as friendly as a suction pump" and comparing him unfavorably to two species of animal, Markham marries the guy. Then she worries whether he is going to kill her.

For years it's been the older man with the young bimbo and you've got to hand it to Joan for turning the tables. Naturally a woman alone is perceived as a threat to society, thereby, she must be threatened, but before she's getting sloshed and staggering across the beach in stilettos, Crawford isn't afraid to call a beach bum a beach bum. Pushing fifty at the time and moving into that more severe look that she would adopt, she was still basically very attractive, but that exaggerated makeup and those hairstyles weren't doing her any favors! This hairdo here is one of my pet

Crawford as Lynn Markham with Jan Sterling, a less-than-honest real estate agent (so what else is new?).

peeves for her — what's with the heart-shaped part? And why does she adjust her night shorts on camera after rising from the bed in this one? Dare anyone ask? Don't ask. Just enjoy this totally delicious sand- stud- and-soap camp gem.

    Pet moment (of many): Joan in Lolita sunglasses and shorts sunning on the docks when Jeff Chandler swims over and has the temerity to hug her. As he rubs her back while holding her and tells her he thinks she's lonely, her eyes and mouth are working (oh, the silent screen expertise!) in hungry response to the touch. When he lets her go, she says frostily, "I hope you don't bruise easily, Mr. Hall. I'm not enjoying this!" Oh, Joan! You're a hoot! This is why we're all still watching!

Queen Bee (1955) ★★★½

I'd seen *Queen Bee* several times at retro festivals and frankly had only vague memories of it. Revisiting it, I found it completely different than I expected and also at variance with what I've read about it. Based on a novel by Edna Lee, the story centers around Eva Phillips (Joan Crawford),

Crawford as Eva Phillips, defying the red-blooded to look away — that means you! PHOTO COURTESY OF THEO POUROS

a superficially gracious, manipulative woman married to a wealthy mill owner, brooding alcoholic Avery (Barry Sullivan) whose scarred face has earned him the nickname of Beauty. When ingénue Jennifer (the mealy-mouthed Lucy Marlow) comes to stay with the family in their surreally extravagant Southern mansion at cousin Eva's request, she walks right into the hive of dark secrets with Eva administering the stings left and right.

Although much is made of the severe look Crawford adopted during the '50s, here, at approximately fifty years old, she looks quite lovely and exudes charm, vitality and feminine seductiveness, garbed in Jean Louis fashions (which seem to change minutely) and apparently much of her own jewelry. Crawford is such a powerhouse presence at this stage in her career that all she has to do is enter a room to command full attention. The rest of the cast float like satellites in her orbit. She also (gotta love her) makes us understand why Eva feels so trapped and lonely in this house and the opposition she's against, which a lesser actress would not have done. When Eva surveys her family's glum, malevolent faces in the living room as they fall silent upon her entrance and says, "My, how cozy you all look," one can't help rooting for her defiance. To my mind, she's the most sympathetic character in the film and becomes more so, not less so, as the plot progresses.

Ultimately the family's dirty laundry is aired, such as it is. Carol Lee (Betsy Palmer), Avery's sister, is secretly engaged to Judson Prentiss (a perpetually surly John Ireland) who apparently had a tryst with Eva in Chicago ten years ago. For some unexplainable reason, Jud seems to feel much animosity towards Eva over this affair, presumably because she left him for Avery who left Sue McKinon (Fay Wray), his fiancée, "at the altar" for Eva. According to embittered Avery, Eva "tricked" him into marriage by pretending she was pregnant and engaging his nobler family sensibilities. This jilting resulted in fragile Sue going off her nut. All too predictably, the two men blame Eva for having seduced them with that double standard going back to Eve and Adam and the apple. She is tarnished as the temptress as they wallow in self-pity and resentment. Eva tries to seduce Jud again (off-camera Crawford was having an affair with Ireland) as his engagement to Carol is announced and fails, but when she hints to Carol Lee that Jud is not lily pure, it so upends Carol that Carol hangs herself immediately. What fragile grapes grow on these vines! It seems the other women are more emotionally imbalanced and given to madness than the script wants us to believe Eva is.

In fact, in spite of the attempt to frame Eva as the catty troublemaker deserving of scorn, Crawford gives her enough dimension and emotion to be understandable, to my mind. When she slaps sugary little Jennifer as Jennifer gloats over a coup for Carol and Jud, it's delicious. Hypocritically, "good girl" Jennifer has already made the moves on "long-suffering" Avery. Eva fails to seem "villainous," much less evil, to me, since she periodically lets show her own isolation and seems genuinely eager to connect with Jennifer. She also has some conscience. When Eva discovers that Carol

Crawford keeps the men in line in *Queen Bee*. PHOTO COURTESY OF NEIL MACIEJEWSKI

has committed suicide, she smears the mirror with cold cream and refuses to look at herself in the mirror thereafter, although to my mind, her behavior was not responsible for such an extreme reaction. The much-heralded scene with the riding crop is not particularly violent and is actually almost poignant. As Eva pushes a few items on the floor with her crop, she doesn't go haywire but explains bitterly to Carol where her acerbic sting originated (the self defense), at one point saying, "You don't know the things they made me do, trying to protect myself." Only Dunaway in *Mommie Dearest* committed herself to cross-eyed histrionics in her caricature of Crawford (many images culled apparently from Crawford films), although Crawford herself, preferring to be liked onscreen, never allowed even her hardest characters to be quite without sympathy.

Consequently, the most disturbing thing about *Queen Bee* involves the mentality embodied by lines like "If she were mine, I would beat her" said by Jud of Eva (imagine a woman making that implication to a wife about her husband) as if under any circumstances, wife beating were justifiable and spouses were "property." This sort of misogynistic message was rampant particularly in the 1950s with the female sexual aggressor being inevitably punished and massacred like the lesbian vampire hellcats in Hammer films at the birth of women's liberation. Even more disturbing is that audiences are being asked to accept (and do) that Eva's adultery is worthy of her being burned like a witch and is, in fact, a worse crime than the diabolical murder that husband and ex-lover plot against Eva. It feels more unfair, in fact, when one sees that Eva is genuinely eager to reconcile with her husband and reveals the real shocker that he has not been "her husband" to her for quite some time, making his anger at her recent flirtations all the more puzzling and hypocritical. It is even hinted that apparently he tried to kill her by automobile in the past which led to his scar. Who is the truly scary person, I ask?

Besides, how can anyone not like a woman who spouts lines like: "Do sit down, Jud. I never thought of you as a gentleman." And: "Jen, you really must learn to join in conversations. Otherwise you give such a mousy impression." And: "Really, that Dr. Pearson, he's so absurd. He actually trembles when I talk to him. You'd think he'd never seen a beautiful woman before." And my favorite to Ty Harding: "Don't tell me you're finally going to succumb to my fatal charm."

In any case, I'll take the sassy sister Eva (as played with such exquisite bitchery by Crawford) any time. A preferred ending would have been for Eva to get a chance to rebuild her marriage and for Jennifer to get one more double slap and be sent packing.

Pet moment: Crawford kittenishly wrapping a telephone cord around Ireland's neck.

Autumn Leaves (1956) ★ ★ ★ ½ *(five for Joan's performance)*

In *Autumn Leaves*, Joan Crawford is Millicent Wetherby, a middle-aged typist who believes that love has passed her by, until she encounters a twitchy young man, Burt Hanson (Cliff Robertson) in a diner as "Autumn Leaves" plays on the jukebox. The young man, clearly a decade her junior, is persistent in his romantic pursuit of her and although rightfully guarded and skeptical at first, she eventually succumbs and marries him. The romance begins with much charm and promise. It seems too good to be true — and it is.

Autumn Leaves has strong, believable performances from both Crawford and Robertson, but I had a few issues with the messages. (Don't read further if you've never seen it, since there will be spoilers). For one thing, the moment Burt comes onto the scene, there are major red flags from his

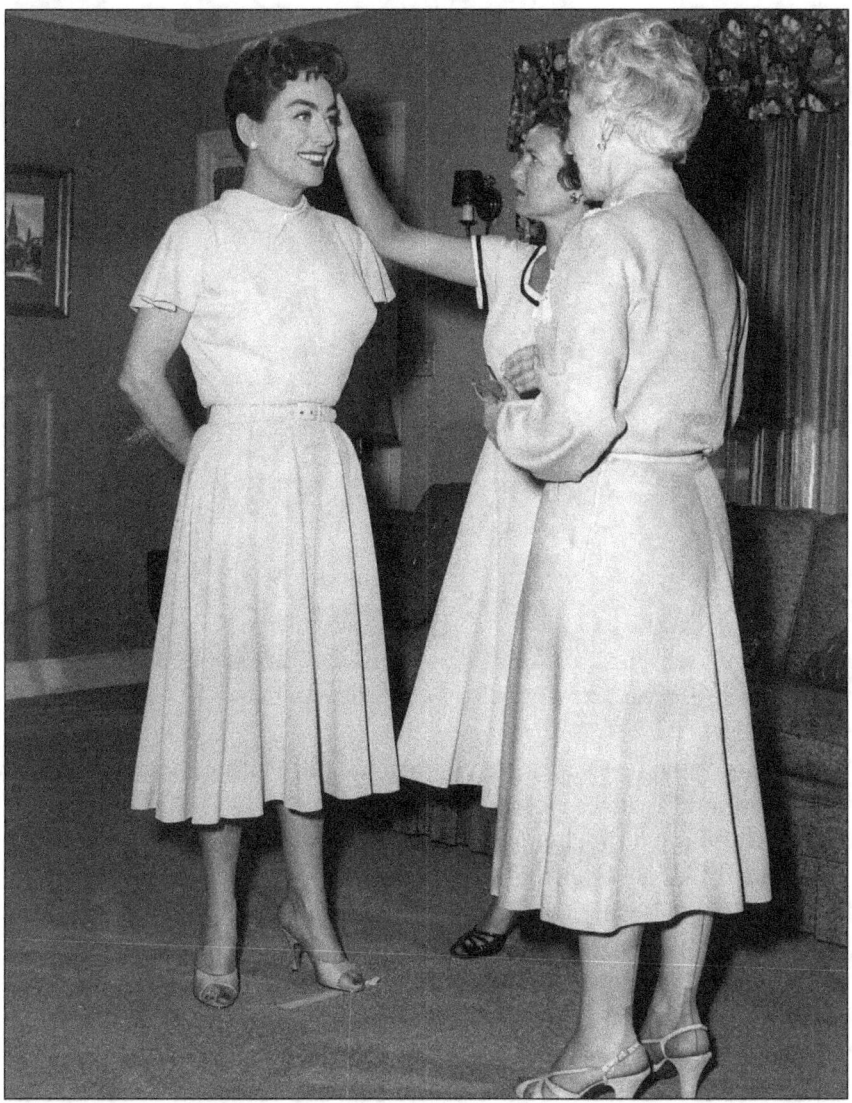

Cute photo of Crawford on the set of *Autumn Leaves*. COLUMBIA PICTURES

glassy-eyed stare alone. For another, who ever said it was sane or advisable to try to "reform" a pathological liar and psychotic? To my knowledge, it's never been done yet. If your romantic partner throws a typewriter on your hand and blackens your eye, my advice is to pack your bags and run, not enter into an equally psychotic pretense with him that all is rosy. But poor, desperate Millie sticks by her man loyally and is determined to see him

With Lorne Greene. PHOTO COURTESY OF NEIL MACIEJEWSKI

to the bloody end — shock treatments and all. Oh, that's another thing. His treatment involves electric shock therapy, almost as inhumane as a lobotomy, to my mind, but apparently quite acceptable at the time.

    The first half is better than the second with everything moving along in a genuinely pleasing and then gripping fashion, but the minute Millie emerged as a victim, it pleased me less. I didn't want her to end up with this lunatic. No woman should be that desperate or heedless of her own well being. Having "missed the boat" because she was nursing a sick father, she seems to be sliding into a caretaker role once again with her troubled husband. Most disturbing of all is the perverse eroticism about a scene showing battered Millie, hand in sling and sunglasses hiding her black eye, canoodling with Burt as if the ardor is undimmed in spite of the pain being inflicted. Since she is so clearly capable, smart and attractive and he looks nutty enough to eat flies, even if she hasn't touched flesh in twenty years, what does she see in him? Is his technique so phenomenal that she would risk life and limb for it? When he comes out of the institution with half-cocked grin and gleaming eyes at the end, supposedly cured, I didn't believe it for a minute. An early scene of the lovers in the surf is a gorgeous metaphor for the danger to follow with Millie in literally over her head.

During the 1950s, Crawford adopted those heavy eyebrows plus a much shorter hairstyle, and here, although her face is beautiful with a great smile, she has the overpowering brows. In the '50s, in general, however, she was much more feminine than popular stereotype admits in the majority of her films, although often handed sub-par material. *Autumn Leaves* gives her a chance to show her stuff and her performance is solid and superb. A scene at the pool where she surveys her own figure in a suit with insecurity and shyness is very real and touching as are so many other moments. There is a lovely, off-kilter shot of her sitting on the rocks above the surf. What Crawford expresses by eyes and face alone never ceases to astound me.

In any case, it's an absorbing, moving and basically entertaining melodrama and tension is balanced with moments of great fun such as when Crawford confronts Burt's family. ("Your filthy souls are too evil for hell itself!") One of Joan's finer, non-campy, latter day performances, but doesn't send a good message to women.

The Story of Esther Costello (1957) ★★★★

The Story of Esther Costello holds one of Joan Crawford's finest latter day performances and demonstrates how criminally she was underrated and mishandled throughout much of her career by being handed substandard scripts when, given the chance to showcase her talent properly, she was a very fine actress indeed. The film begins in Ireland when a little girl, Esther Costello (Janina Faye), is left blind, deaf and dumb after accidentally setting off explosives in a root cellar. When a wealthy American socialite Margaret Landi (Crawford) visits Ireland on vacation and runs across Esther, now a young woman (played by Heather Sears), unkempt and crawling around like a wild animal, she is horrified by such neglect and ultimately convinced to take the girl under her care. Working with Esther to learn how to communicate simple needs, Margaret succeeds in making breakthroughs and later sets up a charitable foundation to raise money for further research and aid for the blind. Margaret's wild success in this fund-raising enterprise attracts the attention of her husband Carlo (Rosanno Brazzi) from whom she is separated. Carlo insinuates his way back into Margaret's life and love, but shortly it becomes clear that his motives are not sincere. Not only is he in league to squander and embezzle funds from Margaret's charitable organization, but he is also taking more than fatherly notice to the shapely, young Esther.

Beautiful candid of Joan Crawford with Rosanno Brazzi on the *Esther Costello* set. PHOTO COURTESY OF THEO POUROS

Although this is a fine drama with overall strong and even stellar performances, there are a few implausible and dubious choices in the script, none of which sink the film however. For instance, it is questionable whether Esther could have survived the magnitude of the explosion that opened the film, rather than merely being left blind, deaf and dumb. There is also a scene in which Margaret discovers Carlo intently watching Esther undressing from another room, unaware that Margaret has returned, and Margaret angrily wraps Esther in a towel and shakes her, saying, "You little fool!" Esther is left shaken and bewildered by this sudden rage on the part of her benefactress, and afterwards Margaret begs Carlo tearfully to go away with her alone and abandon the foundation. She wants to also get Esther out of the picture by placing her in college. This seems cold and out of character on the part of the benevolent Margaret. She comes across as far too competent and confident a woman to be reduced to such desperation and even cruelty by a man she had already separated from once. The ending is also an unfortunate misstep (without going into details here), needlessly drastic. Yet somehow the integrity of the performances and the serious issues raised by the script, including the corruptible nature of

Crawford, Brazzi and Sears filming the banquet/betrayal scene of *Esther Costello* with director David Miller. PHOTO COURTESY OF THEO POUROS.

charitable foundations, overcome any far-fetched film contrivances and keep things believable. Only the ending truly disappoints.

Crawford is amazing as Margaret Landi. In the opening sequences, she is almost too sweet and benevolent yet when Rosanno Brazzi enters the scene, her performance takes off. The scene where Margaret first notices Carlo's designs on Esther is devastating. Crawford proves herself to be at the peak of a mature and considerable talent. She hits all the right notes, as the saying goes, and allows the action to pack a punch. This is one of her performances that surely warranted an Oscar. Heather Sears is fine as the young girl and Rosanno Brazzi is well cast as the husband, suave and handsome enough to make a great oily manipulator. But Crawford is the best of them all. She also looks terrific, her charm and charisma right on the money for fundraising success and a parallel to the similar role she undertook for then-hubby Alfred Steele's Pepsi product.

Crawford with former co-star Brian Aherne. They first appeared together in *I Live My Life* (1935).

The Best of Everything (1959) ★★★

The Best of Everything is based on the novel by Rona Jaffe and its popular fiction roots show. With a wonderful splashy opening song by Johnny Mathis and the sight of young, pretty Hope Lange as Caroline Bender answering an ad (hilariously promising "the best of everything" in a secretarial career) at a posh Manhattan publishing house, the film revolves around three young women seeking their fortunes in the Big Apple. The three central characters (all of whom start in the typing pool at Fabian's Publishing and come to share a cold water flat) include Lange as impeccably and jauntily suited Caroline (she really does wear a suit well), the woman with the most smarts and dignity of the three, who quickly demonstrates

FILMS OF THE FIFTIES

A lovely shot of Crawford as Amanda Farrow.

a natural aptitude and moxie for the publishing business; impossibly gorgeous Suzy Parker as aspiring actress Gregg Adams (Parker, a top model of the time, seems way too glamorous, sophisticated and beautiful to be lost in the typing pool or ignored by casting agents); and Diane Baker as chirpy, annoying, naive April Morrison, fresh from Hicksville and willing to swallow any hook or line that is thrown her way. Her main goal is to marry.

Two women (Crawford and Lange) with business suits and buns confront one another on the mean, mean floors of Fabian's Publishing. The two were probably no happier to confront one another on the set.

The usual soap opera commences, but it's fun stuff with lots of dish and dirt. Although the attitudes towards women remind women of why the feminist movement began (sexual harassment tolerated by the resident lecher, Mr. Shalimar, played with alcoholic panache and humor by Brian Aherne; all women with careers looked on as "hard" and having missed the boat in romance; double standard between men and women), honey, anyone who has seen the inside of a secretarial pool today can tell you things haven't changed terribly much beyond — cosmetically — the sexual attitudes. The secretaries storming the Bastille in the morning, brimming with gossip and tales of engagements, are much the same today, and Joan Crawford is believable as tough editor Amanda Farrow who gives her "girl" a hard time (and in her short time onscreen, she really does command it). She has her share of unintentionally hilarious lines, too. (When she retires to pursue a love affair, hoping it's not "too late," she later returns and announces, "It was too late for me.") And what man today would hand his girl socks to darn with she cheerfully happy to comply?

The interesting thing about Crawford — who although in a minor role is one of the reasons this film has retro appeal — is that, even when playing a fearsome boss-lady, she's rawly human. As Doug Bonner astutely observes in *PostModern Joan*, "As a viewer of her craft, one doesn't know where artifice begins and autobiography disappears as she emotes for the screen." Having just lost fourth husband Alfred Steele, she was in a fragile state during shooting, but too pro to let it show onscreen. Amanda Farrow's prototype hasn't changed much either. Bosses still "test" their subordinates with the same tactics, yet one can appreciate the older woman feeling threatened by younger competition. Like many mentors, she feels she needs to prepare these girls for the rough knocks in life she's experienced (so doomed to backfire and alienate). Amanda is vulnerable but feisty and tough, and her strong emotions and the fact she doesn't suffer fools gladly is what makes her (and Crawford) enduringly resonate. "I have one small corner of your life. I've never asked for more," Amanda tells her married lover, "and I will not settle for less." Then she adds this favorite howler: "Now you and your rabbit-faced wife can go to hell!" And who doesn't want to say, "Oh, shut up, shut up" like Amanda when the chipper April bubbles over about an invitation to a shower?

Pet line (besides the ones mentioned above): when the busload of employees are en route to the company picnic, singing, April chirps to Caroline, "This is going to be fun — don't you think?" and Caroline says, "I'd rather be shot."

Films of the Sixties

PHOTO COURTESY OF NEIL MACIEJEWSKI

Whatever Happened to Baby Jane (1962) ★★★★★

Whatever Happened to Baby Jane has been as much a part of my pop culture history and childhood as *The Wizard of Oz* and *It's a Wonderful Life*. How many rubber rats and fake dead canaries have I served to friends on trays and how many times have we repeated the line, "Butcha are, Blanche! Butcha are in that chair!" Funny that as time goes on, "Baby Jane" actually disturbs and frightens me more than amuses in the way the horror genre (which I've always selectively enjoyed) became temporarily taboo when I was grappling with my own mortality. Perhaps it pains and haunts me to see two powerhouse leading ladies made into a freak show as elderly "has-beens" with parallels (slight) to their real careers. Or is

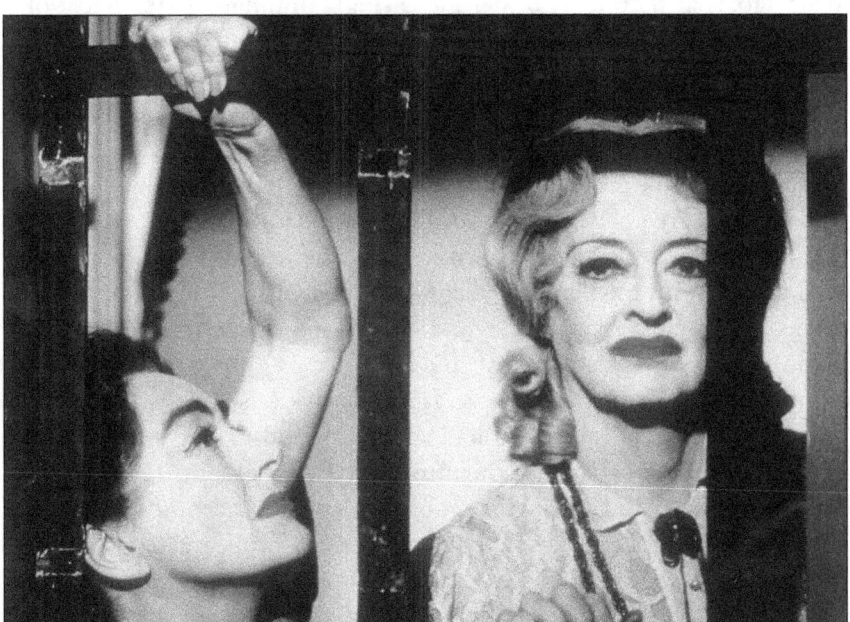

A great shot of the two screen legends, co-starring at last! Crawford gets in some lovely profile, in spite of her debauched role, and note the nail polish!

it that Davis, dubbed "screen sadist" tortures Crawford, dubbed "screen masochist?" Still what other opportunity is there to view these two legends and real-life rivals playing opposite one another in a battle of wills? (No, *Hollywood Canteen*, in which both appeared as themselves pitching in for the war effort and still in their dewy youth, doesn't count.) Although neither would admit it and stories are legion about off-screen antics, I suspect they rather enjoyed themselves! In any case, *Whatever Happened to Baby Jane?* is a deeply disturbing and unsettling film, in spite of whatever camp elements audiences read into it, with absolutely brilliant acting and an equally brilliant script. It is chilling, sometimes hilarious, and full of superbly realized characters, a hive of dysfunctional families from hell suspended in their own private hell behind closed doors.

Originally a novel by Henry Farrell, *Whatever Happened to Baby Jane*, like *What's the Matter with Helen*, is the macabre side of Hollywood ambition, the undercurrent of resentment, jealousy and stunted emotional growth beneath an industry that uses and discards as it freezes and projects beauty and immortality. Two sisters — one a former child star of vaudeville, Baby Jane Hudson, the other a major film star of the 1930s, Blanche — share a home in which Blanche, crippled in a car accident years ago, is at the mercy of her increasingly unhinged sister. Most of it concerns the helpless, beleaguered Blanche trying to escape from her Gothic prison (teeming with old memories and familial bitterness) and escalating sadism at the hands of Baby Jane who is macabrely trying to stage a comeback.

In an ensemble piece of extraordinary acting, Bette Davis is a stand-out as Baby Jane. True, she has the "showier" role and Crawford, in a softer part, confined to a wheelchair, is painfully sympathetic and certainly superb as well, communicating whole passages of drama with her facial expressions alone, but Davis is riveting. Beyond the dumpy, slovenly, mannered high camp element that delights the audience, Davis gives us a woman who is emotionally as much a cripple as her sister physically is. Sometimes childlike, she veers into pathological cruelty and malice with no more conscience than a baby tiger. The often-imitated moment when she sings "Taking a Letter to Daddy" to a polite but appalled accompanist, Edwin Flagg (a deliciously quirky Victor Buono), her pancake makeup and ringlets grotesque and debauched, is astonishing. One sees her as "helpless" as her sister in a sense — helpless against herself and her illness, monstrously and pathetically trapped in the mindset of a spoiled six-year-old.

Clips from early Joan Crawford and Bette Davis films (Davis' ironically used to demonstrate her inability to act) reveal the two stars at the peak of their youth and glamour. (Crawford's early clips are from *Sadie McKee*, by the by, in which she was exquisite.) Though in her sixties at the time of this film, required to deteriorate and lit without softening effects, Crawford's beauty is still notable, her doleful eyes reminding me of the coquettish vulnerability of her flapper years. As Vivian Sobchack noted in "The Leech Woman's Revenge," sadly, in this ageist culture, the aging

Canary. It's what's for dinner.

woman has been scapegoated and abhorred as the symbol of a general fear of aging with no male counterpart existing, older women tragically seen "not as a resource, but as a 'problem.'" The open scorning that continues to thrive could use an "extreme makeover." This particular film ironically started a wave of Grand Guignol horror films depicting aging and "macabre" actresses, punished and marginalized by Hollywood for growing older, yet given "new blood," according to some interpretations, through these arguably demeaning but substantial roles.

Nothing Blanche did (as in the surprise twist revelation which I won't give away) justifies or excuses Baby Jane's horrifying mistreatment, nor does it make her somehow more culpable for that treatment. Baby Jane was a selfish little monster, as demonstrated in the eerie opening vaudeville scenes, and deserved a good kick in the pants. One sympathizes with Blanche and wants to see her escape and Crawford, beautifully underplaying, makes us feel every desperate moment.

The supporting cast is uniformly magnificent. Buono is fabulous as the corpulent mama's boy (even he has a backstory, adding to the portrait of Hollywood decadence and delusion). That "pansyish," sullen mama's boy, trapped in an unhealthy symbiotic relationship with mama, was a popular fetish of the '60s and reveals the underlying prejudice regarding women (again!) (mothers yet still a popular scapegoat in psychology as fathers earn little rancor for their parental shortcomings), homosexuality, and obesity. Maidie Norman (who also played Joan's assistant in *Torch Song*), such a welcome presence in films, is wonderful and heroic as Elvira, their maid, her sensitive face and warmth giving strength and presence to her characterizations. Even the young actresses who play Jane and Blanche as children (Julie Allred and Gina Gillespie, respectively) are superb. And speaking of children, Bette Davis' real-life daughter, B.D. Hyman, has a bit role in this. She can't act worth a damn and comes off sullen, spoiled and snotty and it works brilliantly, a perfect counterpoint to Baby Jane.

(Spoilers!) I like to think Blanche survives at the finale; it remains ambiguous. (Couldn't the cops have given her an ice cream? Interesting that things come full circle with Baby Jane offering Blanche an ice cream as she had in the beginning.) Ultimately, Crawford, once again, is a "female on the beach," but this time there's no attractive boy-toy as the menacer.

An amazing film, a masterpiece of horror and characterization with two great legends co-starring at long last and an ensemble supporting cast that meets them full throttle.

The Caretakers (1963) ★★★½ (mainly for Crawford and Stack)

The Caretakers obviously was intended as a plea for mental health care reform, using shock tactics like those anti-cocaine propaganda films aimed at teenagers during the 1950s, as schizophrenic Lorna Melford (Polly Bergen) winds up in a psychiatric hospital under Dr. Donovan MacLeod

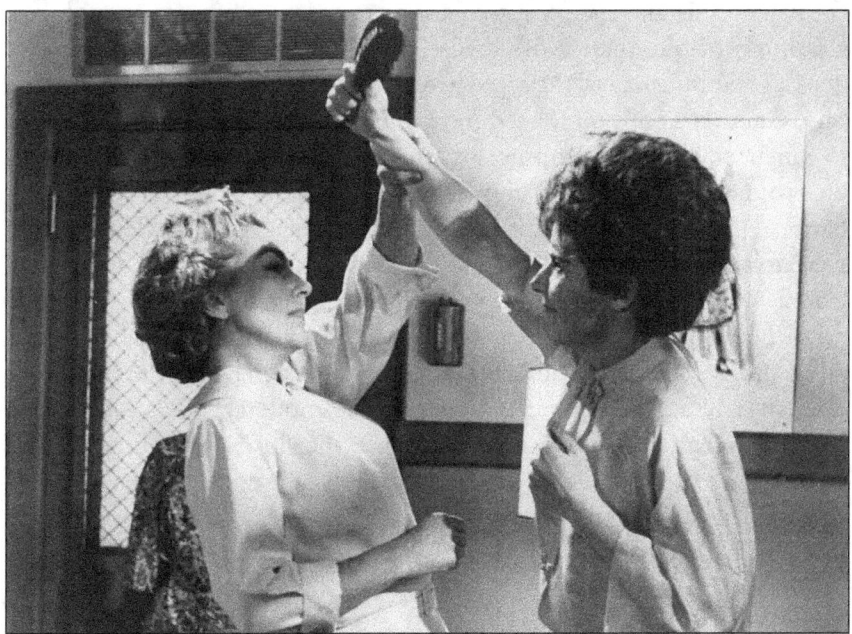

A hairbrush is a lethal weapon in an asylum, but Joan knows how to handle 'em.

(Robert Stack) and in the "snake pit" of group therapy. Dr. MacLeod is trying hard to revolutionize and humanize patient "care" but is up against an intractable old guard who view their charges as fundamentally dangerous. Stack, whose sonorous delivery recalls *The Untouchables*, manages to do well even with stock speeches like, "Every patient in this hospital is a human being, entitled to respect and dignity. We are the caretakers of their hope." Maybe, but it's hard to take his or the film's plea seriously or even sympathetically with the campy troupe of actresses who play the "patients" in the "group" and hipster music that converts some scenes into bad "women in prison" moments. Still, in spite of a lurid presentation and heavy-handed metaphors, there are several things to recommend this film, including fine characterizations and performances from Stack and Joan Crawford as his opponent, Lucretia Terry, R.N.

There are obviously viewers out there who seem to delight in "campy" Joan and misinterpret many of her non-campy film roles as such (because there are actually relatively few "camp" films in Crawford's canon in relation to her lengthy career). These viewers insist on trying to slate all Crawford's work and her persona into a narrow, largely untruthful, parodied image. Evidently much of this is residue from *Mommie Dearest* (and there are those who mistake the film itself for a credible biopic even though it is full of more holes than Swiss cheese and liberally spoofs her films) but it does a great injustice to the real actress' complexity as a woman and artist. She is neither campy nor one-dimensional in *The Caretakers*. She manages to convey some human conflict and maintain enormous presence with an unfortunately relatively small role. She also is quite beautiful with a very flattering hairdo and she and Herbert Marshall as Dr. Jubal Harrington, her partner at the hospital and another representative of the "old guard," lend a touch of elegance and grace to the proceedings. Unfairly, to my mind, because of their age, they are meant to be viewed as "old hat" when, given the unpredictable and sometimes violent behavior of the patients, their view actually seem much more credible, moderate and sensible than that of "touchy feely" MacLeod. Oh, yeah, the '60s were coming on and youth ruled! All "establishment" was suddenly "the enemy" to be quashed. As in the overall "big picture," it seems the baby was being summarily and foolhardily thrown out with the bathwater.

The Caretakers has a feeling of "beat" as in Alan Ginsburg's *Howl*, maybe due to the jangling, hep-cat score by Elmer Bernstein which I disliked intensely, but the black and white cinematography is tense and effective. Basically a haunted Lorna Melford (Bergen) (resembling Judy Garland) winds up tripping out in front of a movie screen like Hayley Mills' Siamese in *That Darn Cat* two years later, creating a movie within a movie for the unsuspecting audience. She is summarily transported to the nut house where MacLeod proves himself a non-traditionalist by offering her a cigarette in her room (ironically, this would now seem dreadfully out-of-date and misguided). He wants to give patients the option for a "day hospital" where they could survive in their own apartments. A sanctimonious lecture to his nurses explains his deadly important theories, "In a group something exciting happens. The group fights to be normal, fights in some remarkable way to destroy the abnormality in each person, in each brain. I think it's because the group as a whole, the people in it, begin to realize that they need and care for each other." Really? Meanwhile, his "group" — which includes a nymphomaniac Janis Paige, a "mute" Barbara Barrie, and a bizarrely lit Ana Maria Lynch (who seems to be superimposed in the room from a silent film) — break into cat fights, try to attack nurses with sharp objects, and — worse — "do the twist" when not hurling insults or dumping bottles of rubbing alcohol and other medications into a makeshift punch bowl so they can all get drunk when supervision is on the wane. Sure, they're ready for the "real world!"

Lucretia, meanwhile, believes they "can only be handled through the intelligent use of force" and, having once been attacked herself by a homicidally-bent patient, she tries to "protect" her own nurses by teaching them judo (sounds in order to me!). This training allows her Nurse Bracken (Constance Ford, meant to be the forbidding "Nurse Ratchet" of the ward) to actually save her own life when a patient attacks her, although she is incomprehensibly brought to task for it by the do-gooders trying to overtake the hospital, and also affords Crawford an opportunity to show her trim shape in a leotard with snazzy chiffon scarf. Lucretia is not presented as a villain, however, rather we see that she and Dr. Harrington made the hospital what it was and believe they are right. Amusingly, Crawford gets in "Pepsi" placements, although they are subtle as in "Where's Waldo," the product featured at a hospital picnic in which these loose gun wards are questionably entrusted near hot grills. (They're fine, folks — until someone criticizes them or makes a wrong move. Then you have them wild-eyed and paranoid again and ready to run in front of another movie screen or, in the case of Barbara Barrie, prepared to set the hospital on fire. Don't worry. They can all be brought onto an even keel by the reassurance that they're "wanted" and "loved." Just have a coat ready to put out the fire.)

Crawford and former co-star Marshall share a very nice moment as she surveys the picnic from a hospital window and observes, "This isn't a hospital anymore — it's MacLeod's private country club" at which point he becomes introspective, recalling himself at the same age as MacLeod. As they both recognize they might be losing their hold on the hospital and Lucretia's iron-clad views are thrown into some doubt, she puts her hands on the doctor's shoulder. This was indeed touching, since Marshall was her former co-star from *When Ladies Meet* and quite ill in this film, and in consideration of this, Crawford allowed him to shoot all his scenes first. Although presented as recalcitrates to change, the pair (much more suited to one another than they were in *When Ladies Meet* when the difference in age was more pronounced) strike me as much more attractive and appealing than the younger set and unfairly maligned by the script.

Overall, nice performances from Crawford and Stack and a moving appearance by Marshall, but the group reeks with hamminess out of a stock company and the metaphors are as dense and heavy as concrete. (When one patient keeps a bird in a cage — in a cage, get it? — we all know this bird is going to meet an untimely metaphoric end, although at least it doesn't end up on a tray). There are extremely effective moments, outside of the fine acting from the two aforementioned stars, such as when Lorna gets attacked by male orderlies who look like the Jets in *West Side Story* moving en masse towards her to the hip discordant music. The explanation for Lorna's psychosis, replete with childhood repressed memories, is also as hokey as a $3 bill, but it foresees the "me generation." And there's a genuine sweetness when MacLeod reassures Lorna that she is completely safe. (Let's not fail anyone in school, either, okay, doc? That's mean!)

Ellen Corby and a very young Robert Vaughn also appear.

Crawford's last legitimate screen appearance before the horror flicks and a worthwhile, respectable one.

Strait-Jacket (1964) ★★★★ *(for sheer nerve)*

Strait-Jacket is a camp classic, as compulsively watchable as a train wreck, and succeeds on the inspired combination of showman/director William Castle, an impish, Hitchcock-wannabe, and star Joan Crawford, so off-the-charts and "committed" in her performance that she defies one to look away. Usually Castle has a gimmick like "Percept-o" wired seats for *The Tingler* and "Illusion-o" 3-D glasses for *13 Ghosts*. This time he has Crawford. I saw this film on television as a little girl and would say it's good fun for all ages; I remember laughing at the same bits then.

Joan Crawford stars as Lucy Harbin, a woman who has just been released from an asylum for killing her husband and his girlfriend with an axe. She is now planning to reunite with daughter Carol (Diane Baker) who had witnessed the brutal slaying as a child. Everything is going smoothly…until the heads start rolling again (literally).

Strait-Jacket is elevated to memorably gleeful heights for many reasons, not the least of which is Crawford. In fact, her performance is the chief fascination. Although it is sad to see our gal reduced to such an undignified role, she plays it straight and gives this B-picture her all, per usual, actually managing to imbue her character with some vulnerability and genuine pathos in the midst of the sensationalism. She runs a schizophrenic gamut of emotion from maniacal fury to sadness to lasciviousness to fear to everything in between, often in the same scene, yet her performance is grade A and sympathetic. At times, she is reminiscent of her likeable, vulnerable character in *Autumn Leaves*. Her first meeting with daughter Carol is a feat of incredible acting, all without words — Gosh, but Crawford was great at that! (Why didn't they give this woman more A work? She's almost wrenching with believable pathos.) Her bizarre attire when transforming back to the Lucy of twenty years ago includes an unflattering black fright wig and an armload of clanking bracelets and

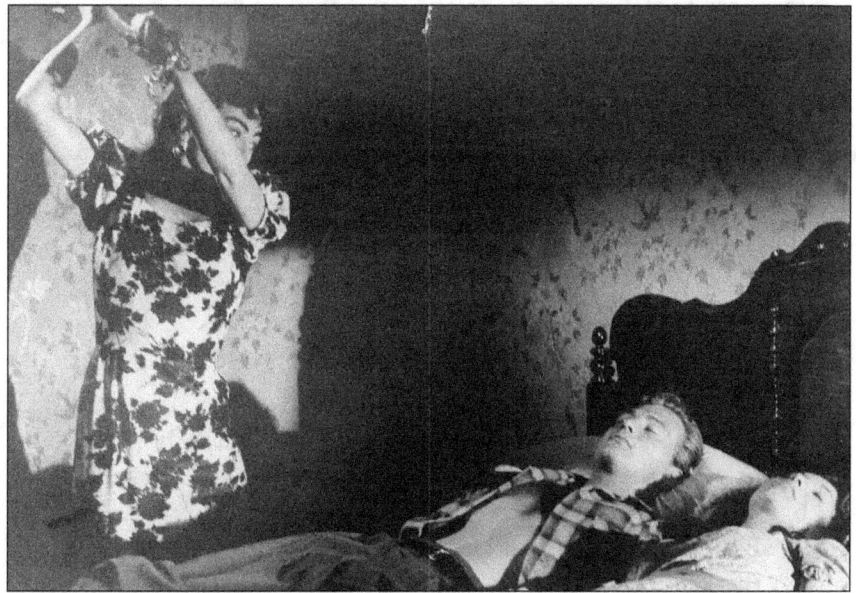

Christina, bring me the axe! This film inspired the infamous axe-wielding sequence in *Mommie Dearest,* not reality.

she is garishly lit (oh, what these ladies of the silver screen didn't have to endure to keep working after a "certain age!"). Playing at forty, we don't care that we don't believe her, but she fares much better when her makeup is toned down and she uses her natural hair, appearing more normal then as opposed to partially deranged. Actually, she has a "killer" body (no pun intended), remaining trim and shapely, and even with the harsh lighting and gonzo attire, her beauty is discernible. Diane Baker works well as Carol and Rochelle Hudson stars as Baker's aunt.

Which campy moment to relish? The beginner's luck with which Crawford is able to chop off two obviously wooden heads with one blow in an early scene? The amazing coincidence that daughter Carol locates a dress and jewelry in a store identical to that worn by Lucy twenty years ago? The scene where Crawford saucily lights a match on a phonograph record? Or when looking like an aging hooker, as one viewer put it, she makes a play for her daughter's boyfriend out of left field and equally out of left field (for the other cast members) sticks her fingers in his mouth? Or what about the Pepsi CEO who is as wooden as the Indian in a cigar store and who was given a job simply as a political perk? Painfully he recites his lines and mercilessly he is dispatched. Even in the "saucy Lucy" scenes that are worth the whole film, pushing the camp stratosphere to deliriously delicious heights, Crawford communicates amazingly without words. Her delivery transforms nothing lines into something (Doctor: "How do you spend your time?" Lucy: "Knitting.") Her encounter with her daughter's boyfriend's family (once again, Joan is being judged and found lacking!) is another acting tour de force! Or my absolute favorite — the denouement in which two Lucy-Harbins-as-Mildred-Pierce-with-a-hatchet appear and the "real killer" is unmasked.

A campfest of the highest order.

I Saw What You Did (1965) ★★★

In *I Saw What You Did*, Libby Mannering (Andi Garrett) and Kit Austen (Sarah Lane) are teen-aged girls left unexpectedly home alone overnight when their parents' babysitter cancels out at the last moment. Libby is entrusted to look after younger sister Tess (Sharyl Locke) and Kit is allowed to visit until 11:30 p.m. sharp, but hardly have the cats turned the key in the lock when the mice begin making prank phone calls to amuse themselves. Kids! Libby ickily mimics an adult by saying breathily, "I saw what you did and I know who you are." It becomes even ickier when she says this to someone who (a) was in the shower (sexual overtones); (b) is making out with his girl (sexual overtones); and (c) just murdered his girlfriend (big red flags). With the distinct look and feeling of a 1950s sitcom, it's almost like *Leave It to Beaver* or *The Patty Duke Show* — with bloody stabbings. The wholesome aspect is kind of fun, nonetheless, with the two leads not very strong in the acting department but — gee-willikers — they're appealing. And showmeister William Castle — who else? — is at the helm and, although he doesn't use his trademark gimmicks, at the time of the film's release theaters had seatbelts to strap in frightened audience members.

With all the phony giggling these two girls do, as they foolishly target victims who give them a rise (Libby mistaking the reaction of murderer Steve Marak (John Ireland) and breathing, "Oooh, he wants a date!"), you just want to smack them silly or show them a 1950s propaganda film about cocaine with Ray Milland. Castle makes yet another Hitchcock homage with *Psycho* fresh in his mind and, being the impish adolescent that he is, steals the shower scene outright, replete with the black-and-white blood going down the drain. But he gives it an amateurish zeal that's much more fun! In Castle's version, the poor actress is *fully clothed* and has to pretend to die against the tiles while water streams down her face (try doing that one and not gagging), then gets summarily thrown

Everyone seems to have trouble by using the phone, including our amorous gal who listens in on extensions! PHOTO COURTESY OF NEIL MACIEJEWSKI

through the plate glass of the shower door by a streaming-wet Ireland. (He's nothing if not thorough!) At this point we all believe she's dead. With impeccably bad timing, Joan Crawford shows up as his amorous neighbor turned blackmailer Amy Nelson, ringing his bell and insinuating herself with seductive desperation. With Crawford giving her all to a part not worthy of her (what else is new?), Amy manages to have a touching pathos and, to my mind, sympathy (after all, she just wants a love muffin and only Steve will do), but she soon tries the loose gun's patience when she spies on him and threatens to go to the police with what she knows unless he marries her. (After she believes this posture really worked, one feels for her). (Did any Miss Lonelyhearts ever have it this bad?)

Reunited after co-starring ten years earlier in *Queen Bee*, Crawford and Ireland have a touching chemistry — that is, up until the point where he — *Spoilers!* — knifes her (ouch) or maybe it's my own romanticism since he and Crawford were lovers when they last shared a freezing soundstage and in his autobiography he was quite sentimental about her. One senses that he cares about her here, as he apparently did, so they have some nice moments — er — until he sticks the you know what into her gut. Crawford has a lot to offer onscreen (damn, but did Hollywood waste mature actresses), although she descends into camp as the script requires. Still, she's poignant at times and looks good with her trim figure and '60s beehive, but she's wearing a necklace (obviously to deflect attention from poor lighting) that's like a chandelier. How could she sneak around Steve's house in that?

In any case, Steve soon has two dead dames on his hands and wants to tie up loose ends (he's thorough, as I said) by doing away with the other nosy pokers. Our cute kids go from bad to worse when they drive to Mr. Tall, Dark and Dangerous' house with the youngster Tess in tow. (Last time Libby will be in charge.) This is when Amy (who is still breathing at this point with irrational designs on Steve) corners Libby in the bushes and calls her a tramp, the stuff some Joan fans eat up — and would any film from this era be complete without someone calling someone else a tramp? But it only gets worse for our mischievous misses as terror comes right to their doorstep.

This was a popular film in its day and it's not hard to imagine. It's not a bad little film, very entertaining, and Crawford and Castle aren't a bad team. While still maintaining vestiges of a bygone glamour (albeit with a scar, as Ireland put it), our gal makes these films more memorable with her sassy presence than they have any right to be.

Berserk (1968) ★★¾

Berserk is another of these degrading B-pictures the legendary Joan Crawford was handed in her later career (so many of the great female stars of the prior decades were reduced to such an unworthy fate) and another in which she approaches it with 200% zeal. Hey, her fourth husband left her

It's a circus, not a charm school!

in debt and she needed the money. Plus, as Joan herself attested, she wanted to be known as an actress, not just someone who hawked Pepsi products. But the results with the cheesy production values are moderate camp.

I suppose aficionados of camp and B-films will debate the fine points as to whether *Strait-Jacket* or *Berserk* is the "better" of two essentially schlocky films; my vote is for *Strait-Jacket* which is actually really good in spite of the odds, mainly due to Crawford. Like *Strait-Jacket*, I'd watched *Berserk* on television as a kid and enjoyed it. As an adult, it holds up less well, however, due primarily to the stock footage of circus acts (as incongruous against the set as the vintage news reels in Woody Allen's *Zelig*) and the absurd impossibilities about some of the actual murders. It might be my imagination but Joan Crawford, in spite of keeping her head held high, actually looks more embarrassed in this one and I'm sorry for her. But she still gives it kick and there's fun to be had.

Crawford plays Monica Rivers, owner of the Great Rivers Circus, which is being plagued by a series of grisly murders. Even as the credits are rolling at the get-go, it's hard not to laugh as our gal pushes clowns around and smacks a camera man who has come to photograph a ridiculous murder during a high wire act in which the rope snapped and then, as if alive, wrapped itself around the victim's neck to hang him! Valiantly

Left to right: Frank Hawkins (Ty Hardin); Monica Rivers (who else? dig the unlit cigarette in her hand); Angela Rivers (Judy Geeson); and Gustavo (Peter Burton) discuss Angela's part in a knife-throwing act. (Sound familiar? Our gal did the same act in *The Unknown*.)

trying to inject some glamour into this film, the star had costume designer Edith Head provide her leotard and shows off her still-good legs at sixty thereabouts. Older and sterner or not, she's still a beautiful woman. But with her beehive, bull whip, and boy-toy (Ty Hardin), the latter currying her affections to the fury of sometimes-lover/business manager Dorando (Michael Hough), it only adds to the camp, especially when Crawford is bothering to act and boy-toy isn't. I smell the hand of a drag queen in the writing of this one, particularly when the killer spouts the immortal line, "Kill! Kill! Kill!" (What else?) And who can resist the moment when, sitting next to Hardin in a truck, Crawford gives him a saucy look that could start a forest fire or her "hard to get" attitude with this stud young enough to be her son at least! (Oh, thank you, Joan, for turning those tables and doing it with such iron balls!)

Horror films of varying degrees of quality were the rage in the '60s and early '70s, particularly grisly ones, so there are many close-ups of victims' faces, and all the innocuous acts (like performing poodles) are just warm-ups for the gory mishaps of the more dangerous ones to follow. In case you might forget it's a B-picture, there's even a cat fight — between two women, not lions.

Although attempts are made to generate suspense and suspicion, the unmasking of the killer is such a non-issue that it's actually used as a clip in the documentary *Joan Crawford: The Ultimate Movie Star*. (Talk about spoilers.) Not a bad film actually and the star really is a hoot, but it truly saddens me that she is remembered more for these horror films or even worse, *Mommie Dearest* (a camp travesty full of holes and blatant inaccuracies), than for her glory days at MGM when she was at the height of her beauty, glamour and charm or for her many sterling performances at Warners, MGM, and other studios. It does a great disservice to this hard-working dynamo who even in later years was capable of delivering (as proven by television outings like *Della*). However, would we want to be deprived of such camp gems from Crawford, even if a questionable use of talent? I think not!

Judy Geeson plays Monica's daughter Angela. Watch for Pepsi placements — they stand out in a crowd.

Films of the Seventies

PHOTO COURTESY OF NEIL MACIEJEWSKI

Trog (1970) ★★ *(for Joan's presence!)*

First of all, let's put to rest a nasty urban legend. Joan Crawford was not forced to dress in a car on the moors, because the budget was so low in this film. According to *Trog* producer Herman Cohen, she had a huge caravan. As he says in an interview on the website *Herman Cohen: The Man and his Movies*, "I have reason to remember that well [the caravan]! We were out on location and it was quite chilly out, and I was told by my assistant that Joan was deathly ill in her caravan. I had my car take me there immediately, I went in to see her and she was saying [huffing and puffing], 'Oh, Herm…oh!…get me a doctor…I can't work.' I told her I'd do it, and I turned to run out. On these caravans, the door is low, and I ran and smashed my head against the top of the door [frame] — knocked myself for a loop! Joan jumped up and yelled, 'Oh, Herman, Herman, darling! Come here, lie down!' She got a cold compress for my head — 'You rest! I'll work!' — and within an hour, she was on the set! She forgot that she was sick, now that she was taking care of me!"

Clearly, Crawford as anthropologist Dr. Brockton had a bad cold during the making of *Trog* which one can hear in her voice, particularly in the early scenes. The film begins with fair enough promise as a group of intrepid young males go spelunking in a cave where the dark shadows and increasingly foolish behavior of said lads foretell that something wicked is about this way to come. Sure enough, the bowels of the earth hold a primitive secret. Look, the sets aren't bad, they're actually quite good, but couldn't they have afforded a better ape suit? Out from the darkness comes the "creature" to beat the spelunker into mincemeat. Unfortunately, this isn't nearly as terrifying as it sounds, since the troglodyte is actually a husky man (Joe Cornelius) wearing a terrible rubber ape mask (with bad teeth), moccasins (Neanderthals wore booties?), and convenient longish fur around his loins while the rest of his body is his birthday suit. It isn't exactly a costume on the scale of *Gorillas in the Mist*. Perhaps Trog dressed in the car on the moors.

Anyway, Dr. Brockton naturally is intrigued by whatever the surviving spelunker witnessed down below. Funny, the cave itself didn't appear so terribly inaccessible that a "missing link" could go missing for long, but what the hay! How many generations of Loch Ness monsters can escape notice? The congested Crawford looks quite good, conducting herself with dignity — at first (one of the many things I love about her), and managing a slight British accent — at first (which she eventually drops, save for the occasional odd pronunciation like "pro-gress"), but she isn't quite

Well, it's not Clark Gable!

as nimble around some of the prolonged textbook speeches which fail to sound like anything but written dialogue (it would take Richard Burton to salvage them). It's amusing to see her manage words like "hypothesis" and "Neanderthal" as well, which she does by the skin of her teeth. And what can anyone do with lines like: "Cliff kept talking about something he'd seen in that cave — something that terrified him — almost as if it had escape from another world!" Still, Crawford plays it straight (as does everyone — what else?), although I confess to giving a shout of laughter when this woman who allegedly wrote *Social Structures in Primates* enters the cave wearing helmet and full makeup. She then takes an even more hilarious photo of said troglodyte in an action pose.

The ridiculousness of the plot only increases. The media, public and Dr. Brockton swamp the cave site and Trog emerges and smashes an unwitting cameraman. Not wishing to see the "most valuable scientific evidence we have in existence today" destroyed, Dr. Brockton nabs her rifle with tranquilizer and puts the menace to rest at her feet, adding this howler, "Hurry! We need a net!" Then, shades of *The Story of Esther Costello*, the good doctor and blonde daughter Anne (Kim Braden) take the female anthropologist's approach to rehabilitating missing links, which is to treat them like toddlers (oh, those terrible twos!) and introduce social skills through wind-up dolls, trucks, rubber balls, and plenty of positive reinforcement. (Crawford never had a worse moment in film than when she has to look all warm and fuzzy over this wretched excuse for a beast's lame learning curve.) She also feeds him her proscribed diet of fish and lizards, the lizards notably rubber (another lapse in the budget), and dispenses bad parental advice to Ann as the poor girl approaches this thing that left several men already in tatters: "That's right, Ann, darling. Never show fear, only trust."

Naturally, the world of science is going to have its opponents and Sam Murdock (Michael Gough) is one of them. He's also my favorite character in the film, the only person with a shred of sense and conviction (Gough is a horror veteran and imbues the necessary vitality). Rarely will I side with a man, particularly when he feels threatened by a woman, but in this case, Dr. Brockton's idea of "therapy" seems liberal to a fault, as bad as Cher saying she didn't want to be "too bossy" as a mother. Of course, Sam's motives for opposition aren't exactly concern for mankind. "That female quack had made herself the star of the whole show," he growls. "You'd think the sun rises and sets on Dr. Brockton...I would much rather see a dignified, qualified man at the head of the clinic."

The folly of Dr. Brockton's intentions take full rein when (a) she and her adopted charge play ball in the park and he mangles a German shepherd (this leads to a session in court and more painful speeches for our gal, the accent long-gone by now) and (b) my guy Sam tries to put a monkey wrench, pun intended, in the works by trashing the lab and letting Trog loose to take the blame, which fatally backfires (what else?). Soon our Hunchback of Bray Studios is mangling the butcher, if not the baker and the candlestick-maker, and heading for the playground to kidnap a cute little blonde child (Chloe Franks). Favorite line (from Dr. Brockton): "Please, Trog, let me have the child. Please?" And: "I implore you to let me go back with my hypo-gun!"

One imagines they were aiming for *King Kong* here or *The Thing From Another World*, but the attempt at emotional significance falls far short — about as short as Trog's loin cloth. Plus, as in *King Kong*, I side with civilization. The sight of Crawford giving one teary look at the spectacle around her and then walking wearily to the horizon is rather moving, her tears ostensibly not for the ape-man but because it's her last film. Having followed her canon from her early flapper days to this last gasp, I can only feel grateful for the legacy. This isn't exactly her shining moment, granted, it's not even good (although there is a nifty dinosaur sequence), but she's still imminently watchable; she gives it a game shot; and she shows us the élan, grace, great bones, beauty, dedication, and charm she still possesses in spades. Thanks, Joan.

Television

The following reviews of Joan Crawford's television work do not include her numerous guest star appearances as herself on television shows like *What's My Line, The Mike Douglas Show, The Tonight Show, The Tim Conway Comedy Hour, Girl Talk, The Lucy Show,* and *The Hollywood Palace*, to name a few. (Yes, I have *The Lucy Show*, but, again, Crawford is playing herself there — or, at least, Lucy's version of Joan the Star, not a "role," however scripted it may be.) It's nigh high impossible to create a comprehensive list of Crawford's work, since she was very active with charities; commercials; print ads; guest star bits on game shows, comedy shows, and talk shows; as well as many radio appearances and dramatic and comedy readings that sometimes included recreations of her film roles. In addition, she did a number of shorts such as *WAMPAS Baby Stars of 1926, Hollywood Snapshots, The Stolen Jools,* and the like during her career. Somehow she found time to also pose for publicity shots and endless photographs — let's not forget her work for Pepsi as an active board member and ambassadress! This was one busy woman. Reviews of those appearances I've been fortunate enough to see are included beneath the title of the episode or film.

1950s

The Revlon Mirror Theater: "Because I Love Him" (1953)

I was thrilled to obtain this early television work of Crawford and was especially pleased at seeing her in this medium while she was still relatively young (approximately 47, depending on when you believe she was born). She looks especially beautiful, her delicate bone structure and big, coquettish eyes striking, plus she is trim, demure and petite, her hair thankfully more flattering and soft than the strange dos she often adopted in the '50s. Her character, Margaret Hughes, a housewife whose doctor (William Ching) informs her that her husband (James Sealy) has only a year to live, gives her ample opportunity to be loving and warm and exude that kittenish charm Crawford possessed that is so alluring.

The plot is the usual melodramatic kitsch and barely five minutes have gone by before Crawford, given the disturbing diagnosis, is all desperate tears and choking voice, doomed to suffer "because [she] love[s] him!" Good grief. Now she has to make this year count for the doomed hubby (who, shades of *Dark Victory*, is not to know he is doomed — someone is always kept in the dark about these things, of course!). Crawford gets to wear some lovely ensembles, suffering always glamorous in Joan World, often recalling *Susan and God* in her facial expressions. It's clear that she and her doctor are on much warmer terms than most people enjoy with their physicians, indicating an outside friendship. An amusing moment comes when, after learning of the vague fatal disease (damning x-rays — what else?), Crawford delivers this howler, "I ought to send out new invitations [for my party Saturday night]. Make it a combination anniversary — and wake!" Not only is handsome hubby told nothing, the couple seem to discuss little else of major impact, leaving out significant info like — er, he will be dead within a year and er, he knows she told a baby broker (Ellen Corby) to cancel their planned adoption of a boy.

The couple lives in luxury with canopy bed and fireplace in bedroom and Crawford gets to be the sexy "little woman," straightening hubby's tie, although trouble is on the horizon on all fronts. "Madame, if there's any available, I want the last of the stock in this firm," hubby says as they canoodle. "You own it all," she says. But then Margaret is thrown several left curves. The twists in this plot let me down (curses!) and left me unhappy, although I suspected these developments and won't add spoilers here. Amazingly, husbands are always shown to be so unemotional and of few words or is it that Joan could out-act her male co-stars on far too many occasions (true even of Clark Gable in early years)?

In any case, beautiful chance to see Crawford in her first foray into television drama (as far as I know!).

The General Electric Theater: "The Road to Edinburgh" (1954)

I appreciate how Crawford tried to create distinct characterizations from relatively thin or well-worn material even if she relied on her stock repertoire of techniques and ample charm. Clearly she was a woman who depended partly on feminine allure for survival; I'm sure that great smile and those eyes aided her often. It certainly helps to have good looks if you're going to be in front of a camera and the camera exploited hers blatantly, but clearly she was equally concerned with her craft. Here Joan is Mary Andrews, a journalist on the road to Edinburgh who unexpectedly gets a flat. Her Mary seems to be a pleasant, light-hearted woman. There is already humor in how incredibly expressive Crawford is while merely driving as if thousands of light thoughts are dancing through her brain. Sure enough a man (John Sutton) comes along to help the hapless little lady with the tire (what else?). She becomes flirtatious and adorable with her Good Samaritan, recalling her nubile blonde Val in *This Modern Age*. What a coquette!

Laying on the Southern (seemingly) hospitality with a spatula, our gal offers the stranger — who is a widower, he offers, to her widow — a ride. He accepts the ride, doesn't accept her open palm hand. Bad call. Already we know this is going to be a bumpy night. Sure enough, they've just pulled out onto the deserted road (what else?) at night (what else?) when our Strange Man reveals that he just got out of prison after seventeen years — for killing a woman. Uh-oh. He offers to leave the vehicle, but Mary fears that if she pulls over, he will do away with her. Oh — it's the old dumb situation where our damsel in distress could end her misery easily but chooses to prolong it because she is following a script that requires white-knuckle suspense and blatant foolishness. He also says he's 42, but looks 50, so already we know he isn't to be trusted.

This is a particularly fun episode with a very sexy exchange between Sutton and Crawford, dialogue dripping with double entendres (all said with a straight face and no trace of irony!):

She: "You know you're intriguing me."
He: "As a reporter or as a woman?"
She (giving him the wary Joan eyes): "As a reporter." (As always, Crawford's timing is delicious!)

And my favorite when Tall Dark Stranger becomes suddenly randy (out of left field — what else?), saying he hasn't been close to a woman in seventeen years (uh-oh!):

He (moving suddenly closer to her and fondling her face and hair): Beautiful hair.
She (voiceover thought, eyes frantic): I can't stand this any longer.
He: High cheekbones.
She: I'll scream if he doesn't stop!
He: Lovely blue eyes.
She: He wants me to lose my self control. *(No, Joan, don't do that!)*

Then our gal picks up an American soldier (Chuck Connors), delighted she's found help. Actually she now has two strange men in the car instead of one, but it's Joan — always a triangle!

The script does have its intentional humor, like that sway in the bridge, to levy the tension and it's such overheated kitsch that, like *Female on the Beach*, it's the kind of guilty pleasure to be watched and savored over and over! Too good!

Ronald Reagan hosts the episode and Sheila O'Brien (of *Sudden Fear*) designed Crawford's ensemble.

The General Electric Theater: "Strange Witness" (1958)

This is another episode I anticipated with great relish. It co-stars Joan Crawford with author Thomas Tryon (who wrote *The Other*, for one) and opens provocatively with the couple in a passionate tryst in front of the fireplace. This love scene is notably more torrid than one is used to seeing Joan in the throes of and frankly the fact that her shoes are off is more suggestive and sexy than most graphic scenes; it goes to show how they were pushing the envelope in the 1950s. Anyway, it becomes quickly established that our heroine, Ruth Marshall, is cheating on her attorney husband John (John McIntire) with David (Tryon). David, needless to say, is no angel. He appears to be somewhat of a heel, after John's money, as Ruth probably is. John interrupts the love birds and one can well appreciate why Ruth was cheating on him and has cheated on him repeatedly throughout their marriage, as he later tells David. He's homely and an old fart, to boot. "As a playmate, she's one thing," he says of the comely Ruth to David. "As a steady diet, as a wife, she becomes a dangerous and sometimes degrading habit." (And what is he? Clearly no prize.) My sympathies are with Ruth.

As the storm rages, David abruptly shoots John and now Ruth is in a panic, although David insists that this is what she wanted. As always with a Crawford character, Ruth is essentially human and not good with crime. There is the classic tears-glittering-in-eyes-without-falling that Crawford is so good at. Classic Joan stuff. She is in an absolute panic and quickly David reveals his true colors as a ruthless scoundrel. Meanwhile, the doorbell rings and a guest arrives — it's John's friend Chris with the sonorous voice (Sidney Blackmer who played Roman Castevet in *Rosemary's Baby*). This presents a potential threat — with one exception. Chris is blind.

This is a wonderful suspense episode, better written than some of the television fare offered in these vignette programs. Crawford is very pretty

Crawford and Tom Tryon in a steamy clinch in *Strange Witness*. You know if it's Joan, there's always a Third Man.

here with the sexy, kittenish voice, and gives a solid, great performance almost reminiscent of her dramatic range in *Possessed* (1947), although confined to the half hour. It's a great opportunity for her and makes me rue she didn't do much more television drama.

The General Electric Theater: "And One Was Loyal" (1959)

These short dramatic TV episodes can be hit or miss, evidently supplied on a weekly crunch, and this one is definitely above average. It's well written and exceptionally well acted with nice production values. I actually had to watch it twice, probably because of a scattered attention span, since it opens at an art gallery with our gal Joan Crawford looking quite glamorous in a mad hat and elegant dress and then shifts to back story. It's fun to see her in those outrageous hats on screen and not just at Pepsi functions. She plays Ann Howard and in this initial appearance, she uses the Continental broad A's that she occasionally adopts to convey society women. She runs into an old acquaintance, George Manson (Tom Helmore), at the gallery and graciously arranges to meet him after the show. George, evidently amazed at her appearance and/or success, reflects on how they originally met.

Apparently George ran across the Howards, a Colonial couple, in the jungles of Asia and had to depend on the kindness of these strangers to put him up. "Do you have any whiskey?" the rough-hewn Roger Howard (Robert Douglas) bellows, a grim foreboding. When George says that he does, he is invited to stay and introduced to Roger's wife Mary, whom he is informed is mute, due to an accident. Crawford shyly makes her appearance, clearly wary of her boisterous husband, looking lovely in her simple attire, her face resembling its look in the late '30s. Here she has a superb tour de force opportunity, as she is introduced to the kindly stranger, obviously hungry and eager for a friend or warm exchange. She reveals a whole progression of thoughts with her face alone as if reflecting on the happy possibilities of the advent of this stranger, her years of silent film experience aiding her beautifully. Her ability to convey so much text without words always amazes me. "You know, for someone who doesn't talk, you communicate remarkably well," George tells her. (I'll say!) In any case, one learns Ann paints and immediately the stranger takes an interest and asks to see her work which she welcomes like a life preserver thrown her way. The two have an immediate bond, he being a writer, a fellow artist. Ann's intentions are felt without words, Crawford's warmth and charm a sort of natural seduction. At one point, desperate as she is for the milk of human kindness, she takes George's hand lovingly when he invites her to his large house in England with the elderly housekeeper, hinting pointedly that the stay could be indefinite. Having already read the situation between Ann and her husband without yet knowing the worst of it, George has an understanding with this lovely but unfortunate woman who is clearly unhappy.

The extent of the sadistic abuse Ann has suffered at the hands of her husband becomes known as the evening progresses. Eventually George will learn how Ann lost her voice and that she endured four years of hell in her marriage. (Crawford's own span with marriages was four years, ironically — when are these ironic coincidences not cropping up in her work?) Anyway, Roger meets his end after a delicious (rubber) snake invades his room (what else?) and he lunges for Ann. The ambiguity is in who was actually responsible for this planted serpent that ultimately led to Roger's death.

This is not only a solid half hour drama with rich and well defined characters, given authenticity by sharp performances, but it is also extremely satisfying. It's a wonderful acting opportunity for Crawford and she acquits herself beautifully. All the longing Joan shows makes the scenes come alive and the furtive, unspoken romance between George and Ann is very touching. She also gets to thrive in a happy ending, beautifully turned out in ankle-strap shoes and elegant dress, her personality sweet and appealing and soft, her voice restored. A wonderful TV opportunity for Crawford and a rewarding half hour of good storytelling.

Woman on the Run **(1959)** *Not available for viewing.*

On Trial: **"Strange Witness" (1959)** *See previous page for review.*

Zane Grey Theatre: **"Rebel Ranger" (1959)**

Crawford's role as gritty frontier woman Stella Faring, to my mind, is one of her finest pieces of television acting. She is very beautiful with that exquisitely delicate bone structure, but styled naturally here as befits the role, and it allows her character to be unfettered, quiet and developed. In a nutshell, Stella is a widow with a young son, Rob (Don Grady a.k.a. "Robbie" on *My Three Sons*) who has come to reclaim her frontier home, but unfortunately, trouble comes in the form of a whole pack of men — one, in particular, Cass Taggart (Scott Forbes), claims to have the deed now and wants her out. But it's Joan — she ain't goin'! Oh, Joan, I love you!

Long before Gloria Steinem or even Emma Peel on *The Avengers* showed beautiful, capable females who didn't play the fool, there was Crawford. Without ever losing an ounce of femininity and never short on charm, she makes a wonderful role model — a real rebel on the range, alright! When Taggart grabs her arms threateningly, she merely raises the steaming kettle in return and then goes to the window and says, quietly, "The evening's come on gentle in this valley" as if in secure possession of her homestead.

After her son shoots Taggert and Taggert mistakenly believes she did it, he says, "What kind of a woman are you?" (a great line) and later as she tends to him in his convalescence, "You sure do a thorough job — shoot a man, bind him up, look after him." Crawford then says one of my favorite lines in the show: "There's food for you in the oven — beans and side meat but they're nourishing!" This not only has a wonderful female heroine portrayed with dignity and moxie, but it's well written with solid characterizations — a good portrait of a woman fending for herself alone. There is genuine chemistry between Crawford and Forbes, too. More great dialogue comes in the cheeky exchange regarding Stella's late husband: "When you're a woman alone and you've never had a home," Stella says, pointedly, "you'd do most anything to get one. It was a fair trade. I wanted a home and my husband wanted a family." I can't blame Taggert for wanting to make a "fair trade" with this sexy pioneer dame.

1960s

Zane Grey Theatre: "One Must Die" (1961)

Zane Grey Theatre, based originally on the stories of Zane Grey and narrated by Dick Powell, was a fun Western show, nicely produced. Evidently scripts ranged from solid (as with "Rebel Ranger") to thin going and idiotic, as with this one, but the opportunity to see Joan as twins (one good, one "bad" — what else?) is a blessing from the Joan gods and makes highly entertaining viewing. In fact, the only thing more I could have wanted (oh, we always want more!) is Joan as twins in a feature length film (or two), maybe one circa 1940, her own *A Stolen Life* or something. But, thankfully, we have "One Must Die."

When John Baylor (Philip Carey) from Boston drives up to the Hobbes homestead on horse-drawn buggy (our gal peeking mischievously out the window), he has a premonition that his life "will never be the same again." Why would it? We all know what he's in for. Apparently his father was a good friend of the dying Thaddeus Hobbes (Carol Benton Reid) who wants to leave his entire sizable estate to daughter Sarah, the demure one, and cut out sister Melanie, the "forward" one, entirely. John meets both lasses, Sarah first, and Crawford plays the "twins" without changing makeup, wanting to work "from the inside out," no doubt, as she stated (see review for *Portrait of Joan*). She obviously relished and dug into this opportunity. Looking incredibly young at age fifty-five approximately, she makes her Sarah very soft and demure, soft-spoken, doing needlepoint, no less, and yet nonetheless flirtatious. It's Joan. It's a good-looking man. Tellingly Sarah gets that ooky spooky look on her face when sister Melanie is mentioned. John seems quite taken with this appealing woman.

Shortly he meets sister Melanie in the library, initially mistaking her for Sarah, since they are dressed identical. (No, it's not just the Crawford family who wears look-alike clothes!) When Melanie whirls around, she has a different dynamic than the other shy miss. This sister is more confident and bold and immediately I like this one a little more. She recalls the young Joan with a frisky charm that is overt but not gauche. She seems playful. "I like tall men," she tells John. Both sisters have beautiful Joan eyes, of course (Crawford's eyes really stand out — I've said it a million times and say it again — man, what eyes she had!). Anyway, John gets one good kiss in with Melanie before he puts a stop to her aggressive come-on. Melanie wants the money and the man and has the same weird look when Sarah is mentioned that Sarah had when her name came up.

Strangely enough, other people even get odd when Melanie is mentioned, not wanting to indulge in "gutter gossip" (hello?) and her own father shudders at her name. There is an indication she is kept "locked up" and one wonders if confidence and sexual boldness is seen as a form of insanity in women. But as Melanie confronts her bedridden father, one sees her maniacal side. Crawford goes over-the-top, eyes gleaming, brandishing a riding crop like Eva Phillips in *Queen Bee* and, like Eva, she appears to be an odd girl out again, shafted by her own family. At least, that's as it *appears!* "Why don't you die?" she screams at poor daddy.

Oh, this is all delicious fun with a head-spinning, head-scratching resolution! Pet moment: Joan throwing a kerosene lamp! If only Crawford had been given more A roles throughout her career to prove her moxie — she evidently and understandably craved them (and deserved them). As is, she makes B and even Z pics riveting grand fun!

The Foxes (1961) *Not available for viewing.*

Your First Impression (1962) *Not available for viewing.*

Route 66: "Same Picture, Different Frame" (1963)

Gosh, do I miss high quality dramatic shows like *Route 66* which were wholesome and suitable for the whole family, but suspenseful. Of course, I only caught it on reruns, its original air date being in the early '60s. The stories were more character-based and devoid of gore. Crawford guests as Morgan Harper and, yes, she looks good with her trim body and great bones, but she's clearly pushing sixty, so it causes a chuckle when she's described as "one of those handsome mid-forty jobs." Oh, Joan, you never let up, and for that we can all be grateful! Two handsome studs, one blond, one dark, are regulars on the show and it's quite amusing when Crawford in jodhpurs gives the dark one, Linc Case (Glenn Corbett) an up and down look — as she's leading a horse, no less — and gets that spark in her eyes. Basically, Morgan is being terrorized by a scarred mystery man named Eric (Patrick O'Neal). He's a great villain with dark sunglasses and a big shot gun. Villains always are more effective with scars, sort of symbolic, I suppose, of their damaged psyches — much more menacing if their eyes are covered with shades. In any case, soon Morgan is leaning heavily on the kindness of Linc and giving him the eyes, and he is reciprocating by being her protector.

Crawford invests her many monologues with her all, replete with MGM pronunciations, the latter lending an interesting idiosyncratic touch. There's a cute sub-plot involving the blond Tab Hunter type, Tod Stiles (Martin Milner) and a sixteen year old girl which makes an odd and amusing contrast against his partner's situation with the much older Crawford. This is another good, solid, dramatic opportunity for Crawford with lots of soft-focus close-ups. She gets to do a long phone monologue (always a strength), ride in a convertible (it's a prerequisite for being on the show — they all do), bawl, wear opera gloves, and play yet another strong, gutsy, slightly acerbic gal — tough but tender and take charge. A mildly amusing moment is when Linc asks her if she'd like to have dinner with him, saying she must be hungry, and she replies, "Top drawer of the filing cabinet there's a bottle. Shot glasses should be there, too." But Joan has the last laugh, because she then refuses both the drink and the dinner invitation. You know how to handle 'em, Joan!

Della (1964) a.k.a. *Fatal Confinement*

This was apparently going to be the pilot for a series called *Royal Bay*. It contains very fine work from Joan Crawford in the title role, a woman named Della Chappel who has had much influence and old money in Royal Bay, but now finds that a corporation, Delta Industries, wants to buy off her land. An arrogant young attorney, Barney Stafford (Paul Burke) comes to her imposing, sequestered residence in the wee hours, at Della's request, to talk the deal over with her. She says no, but asks him to try to change her mind. Meanwhile, he runs across her ooky-spooky daughter Jenny (Diane Baker) and becomes smitten with her and shortly convinced that her mother is holding her prisoner there, preventing her from a normal life. Jenny encourages this impression by saying, "Mother doesn't like people much. I think she hates them." Now Barney has become Della's opponent, but Della has an iron will.

It's too bad that Crawford wasn't being offered film work on a caliber such as this, but at least she found a worthy outlet in television. Not only does she have the opportunity to show her stuff with some very powerfully acted and convincing monologues, but she looks absolutely beautiful and exudes that touch of Old Hollywood glamour and class. My favorite moment in that vein is when she comes into town in Royal Bay, something Della hasn't done in years apparently according to the script — and man, does Crawford look like all that. She's chic, carries herself like a queen, has the sleek body, and is wrapped in chinchilla, no less, with opera gloves. Wow. It would've been nice to see this woman in a romance with someone, rather than all the focus being on the daughter.

Very good Joan TV mystery/melodrama. And I must say I was not on the side of Delta Industries whatsoever, as the script possibly intended viewers to be. People are squeezed out of their hard-earned properties all too often with eminent domain clauses and I'm in favor of land and preserving history, not overdevelopment. Also it irritated me that the "domineering" woman is seen as an obstacle and nuisance whereas the domineering man as some kind of hero. Meanwhile, thank God for Crawford who holds her own against rooms full of smug, swaggering males and yet remains every inch a lady. She still knows how to be coy and sexy when she asks for a light. In color.

The Man From U.N.C.L.E.: "The Five Daughters Affair" (1967)

Crawford looks wonderful with her bee-hive and tasteful attire in this *U.N.C.L.E.* episode in which she cries (of course), defies a baddie, throws off some witty lines with absolute panache, and gets dispatched for her pains all too quickly. She's so good that it makes one rue the way she was

Crawford in "The Five Daughters Affair," an episode of *The Man From U.N.C.L.E.* that was released theatrically in Europe as *The Karate Killers*.

criminally wasted as she got older when her emotional power and skill as an actress had ripened. It's a great kick to see her on one of the best and swingiest of the '60s spy series! Love the kicky music, too! Miss the excitement of "guest stars" — in color!

Journey to Midnight **(1968)** *Scenes deleted*

The Secret Storm **(1968)** *Not available for viewing.*

Journey to the Unknown **(1969)**

Love these horror anthologies that sprang up in the Hammer/Amicus/ *Dark Shadows* era, although they ranged in quality and cheese factor! *Journey to the Unknown*, a British production with American guest stars, great scripts and top-rate production values, is not only ghoulishly fun, but far above average, doing justice to the genre. It's perhaps the best of the best. The executive producer, Joan Harrison, by the by, was an associate of Alfred Hitchcock. Interestingly, the titles look a lot like *Dark Shadows*. As usual, they consist of good, old-fashioned chillers and classic scenarios — the ones here of more psychological bend with intriguing, well-written scripts — and tongue-in-cheek humor.

Joan Crawford appears as herself, making an extremely attractive hostess. She looks beautiful and well-turned out, as always. Love the beehives on her, highlighting her stunning bone structure. She performs with dignity, having learned to read well during her many radio show experiences, and has a clear sense of humor, playing into the ooky spooky, campy quality of it. Entering into a dark library ("a warehouse of human knowledge," as she puts it), she lets us know that "even such peaceful places contain unimaginable horrors, especially for women alone." Yes, I'm sure you know, Joan, having been "menaced" onscreen yourself in plenty of scripts. You can still hear the kittenish, girlish voice from her early years. Love when she says, "I must go now," looking over her shoulder meaningfully. Too funny.

The first episode stars Joan's old co-star from *Autumn Leaves*, Vera Miles, as a writer of murder tales who is trapped in a dark, old library and transported into the past when the killer she is researching claimed his fourth victim — a librarian in that same library. Again, it does justice to the fun premise and Miles is kind of cute. The creepy library has been done before and it all began to feel very familiar; in fact, I think I've seen this same plot stolen wholesale for another similar horror omnibus. Naturally, the woman goes skulking around in the dark while the homicidal maniac is unleashed, but it's fun and effectively unnerving and suspenseful.

The second one, even better than the first, features Patty Duke who did her share of horror flicks. (*You'll Like My Mother* comes to mind.) She barks out her lines like she does in *Valley of the Dolls*, but she's great in this genre, because she has a sweet face yet a hard, cynical edge. The script was wonderful in this one, another classic, with the girl fresh from a sanitarium being haunted in the "real world" in a seaside setting. Good characters as you try to figure out who the loony is. Joan gets to shiver when she introduces this one! (Oh, Joan, you're a hoot!) No one can top the Brits! Wish they still made series like this!

Night Gallery (1969)

Once again, I'm reminded how much television has declined. *Night Gallery* has now been gorgeously restored on DVD and holds up as being exceptionally produced, written, acted, and filmed with color that was like a painting (no pun intended, since the series always began with a "gallery" of paintings). The "Eyes" segment, which was part of the pilot, follows a superb episode with Roddy McDowall (always so good at playing bad boys, particularly ones rotten to family members). Crawford's episode was a young Stephen Spielberg's directorial debut, and certainly already showed his remarkable talent. He won over even our gal who was soon going to him in tears, dependent on his input after initially feeling wary of the neophyte. Crawford looks magnificent in blue with her red hair coiled on her head in a '60s beehive (very flattering, highlighting her regal glamour); there are several moments when you see the angle of her head and it's as noble and magnificent as any of the sculptures her character, Miss Menlo, has in her 5th Avenue penthouse (an apartment house built by Miss Menlo where she was installed as the only tenant). Crawford once again is playing a difficult diva — in this case, "an imperious, predatory dowager," as she is described by Rod Serling at the start. Miss Menlo, however, is blind and will do anything for a few hours of sight. She blackmails her doctor (Barry Sullivan who played "Beauty" in *Queen Bee*) into doing an operation which would give her twelve hours of sight and take the sight of a criminal, Resnick (played by Tom Bosley). We're meant to see this as greedy and Sullivan does a great monologue (oh, the writing is so good here — like the stage!) about "the idle rich — a little something to relieve the boredom." Miss Menlo reminds him that her "abiding concern, Doctor, and my singular preoccupation is myself." She adds, "I want to see something!," her voice swelling magnificently. Crawford was truly gifted with timing and makes nearly every line resonate.

Naturally things aren't going to go so simply. But, meanwhile, we're treated to some beautiful cinematography and imaginative shots and montages as weasley Resnick prepares to sell his sight for the $900 he owes his shady colleagues. Resnick — like a simpering mouse — tells the doctor, "I'd still like to be able to cry out of them [his eyes]." I guess we're supposed to feel sorry for him, but frankly, I was on Joan's side. I felt she was far more important than this nothing of a man who was up to no good anyway. Crawford's lines are superb and delivered superbly — they almost vibrate. "When I see, I shall drink up Central Park" begins one fabulous monologue. "My eyes will take pictures." And this, what she wants to see: "COLOR!" The problem is that, after the operation, when she has carefully undone the bandages around her eyes (shades of *A Woman's Face*), there is a blackout! Almost reminiscent of his later work *Schindler's List*, Spielberg then shows Crawford in her orange suit stumbling around against a black matte background, the only visible figure; in *Schindler's List*, he had a little girl in red, the only splash of color in a black and white landscape. Poor Miss Menlo has been deprived of her big and brief moment — the Faustian deal, allegedly. The next day she opens her eyes to find she still has some remaining sight and can see the sun for the first time through her plate glass windows. Mesmerized, she walks toward it, amazed by the color. The glass is already partly shattered from the night before. The vision begins to dim and Miss Menlo is alarmed, her eyes filling with tears as only Joan's can. "I want the sun!" (Great line!) In order to reach out and grab that fleeting sun, Miss Menlo crashes through the plate glass. (Strange, it reminded me of the role that brought Crawford to fame in the 1920s - *Our Dancing Daughters* in which her character, Diana, wants to "hold out my hands and catch [all of life] like the sunlight." So Joan — so very, very Joan that there are these eerie coincidences in her work.) Above average. Crawford deserved an Emmy, as did Spielberg.

1970s

The Virginian: "Nightmare" (1970)

I wasn't familiar with *The Virginian* prior to learning Joan was a guest star, but apparently it was based on a 1901 Owen Wister novel of the same name and was also television's first feature length Western. It is set in Medicine Bow, Wyoming and stars James Drury in the title role. Anyway, it's in living color and Joan Crawford looks fabulous, playing Stephanie White, a woman who marries wealthy eligible John (Michael Conrad) and is now in line to inherit his business, a fact that gains her rootin' tootin' enemies including an "Injun" woman Natawista (Rachel Rosenthal) who looks like Mr. Bean, the British comedian, in drag and is about as wooden as — well, a wooden Indian nickel! Oh, what a delicious role this is for our gal! She gets to run the gamut from coquettish sexuality (yep, in her sixties at the time, she still definitely had it) to strength to ribald laughter to tears and even do a mad scene, don a gun, and slap someone (all good Joan stuff)! She also thankfully gets kissed by not just one, but two men (one of whom earns the slap after she willingly enough seems to submit to the embrace), ensnared in one of her romantic triangles, this time with believable dignity instead of camp. Stephanie is not your "gal next door" and can shoot and ride as well as cook. Go, Joan!

Crawford demonstrates what an exceedingly beautiful woman she was to the end, interestingly much of her younger "faces" asserting themselves in her older being as if life comes full circle which perhaps it does. At times, especially in the beginning in her becoming ringlets and period attire, she recalls *The Gorgeous Hussy*, other times one sees those beguiling doe eyes from *Our Dancing Daughters*. Against all the big, strapping men on the ranch, she is smoked out as tiny. She wears clothes exceedingly well, even the frontier hats coming off as smart and fashionable on her. Her eyes look blue green and are notably emotional and expressive and huge — like wells. God — does anyone have eyes like that on the screen anymore? Did they ever? Thankfully, television provided — for the most - a dignified outlet for her talent since film had turned her into a caricature, as it did all older actresses.

Once again, our gal is odd woman out, haunted by scandal and trouble. "I've never brought luck to any man I ever loved," she says and sure enough, the men start falling — not just in love, but to tragic ends — left and right and soon she is implicated in murder. A woman with a shady past (what else?), tarot card reading is rumored among her dubious vices! She is called "Steve" by her husband, an affectionate moniker like the one John Wayne gave her ("Mike") in *Reunion in France*. She tries to defend herself against her detractors (what else?) with dignity (what else?). Acquitting herself nicely in the acting scenes, she particularly "shines," to use that cliché, in a bedridden scene in which she appears to be genuinely crying as she relays her story (perhaps recalling her loss of Alfred Steele?). Amusingly, however, this touching moment is followed by a schizophrenic burst of diabolical suspicion and rage. Her mad scenes are much more wrought and shameless like something out of *Strait-Jacket*. These men folk are always trying to convince the women folk that they're unbalanced, ain't they?

No fear, folks. The Virginian comes to the rescue of the damsel in distress who is no wilting violet in spite of her occasional fragile baleful looks. While getting to run through an entire gamut of emotive highs and lows, plenty of range (no pun intended) and close ups, Joan also gets carried by the Virginian! Great to see! Probably as much fun to play!

The Name of the Game: **"Los Angeles 2017"** (1971)
Not available for viewing.

Journey to Murder **(1971)** *Not available for viewing.*

Beyond the Water's Edge **(1972)** *Not available for viewing.*

The Sixth Sense: "Dear Joan, We're Going to Scare You to Death" (1972)

Oh, this is so '70s! *Night Gallery* was a fun spooky show narrated by Rod Serling. There's a cheesy quality about these, yet the special effects are neat — typical made-for-TV quality like *How Awful About Alan, Picture Mommy Dead* and *Crowhaven Farm*. When our gal's car crashes, she finds herself at the mercy of hippie kids like something out of the Manson clan who practice ESP and live in a crumbling mausoleum of a house. That's what happens when kids are home alone! Apparently Joan Fairchild lost her daughter by drowning ("Why did you let me die?" the waterlogged apparition asks) and the bad hippies want to test their ESP powers by scaring Joan to death, knowing full well she has asthma. Can she outwit them? Crawford is older and frailer here, looking obviously ill, yet projects strength, poise and class. She also still has a sexy, kittenish voice. She is overly tense and on edge, her acting a little off, but I take into consideration that she was probably not altogether well. It's great to see her, anyway! (Joan, you are missed!)

Book Reviews

"Love with Joan Crawford might be a strenuous business, perhaps a little difficult at times. But well worth the run."

James M. Cain
Author of Mildred Pierce

The following are book reviews of Joan Crawford biographies, autobiographies and novels and plays that were made into JC movies. Please note that this does not represent a complete book list, only works I've obtained and read at the time of this writing. Books with "Joan mentions" will not be included, only those books that were either the basis for one of her films or where she or her work is the primary focus. Also any book not available in English or adapted into a film not available at press time (as is the case with some silents), will not be reviewed.

Fiction Made Into Film

Above Suspicion by Helen MacInnes (Written 1939) ★★★★

Above Suspicion, the novel by Scottish author Helen MacInnes, is an entertaining, light yet surprisingly incisive spy thriller about a young British couple from Oxford, Richard and Frances Myles, who are enlisted as undercover agents at the onset of World War II. (MacInnes' own husband was a don at Oxford.) As in the film version with Joan Crawford and Fred MacMurray, they are hired precisely because they appear "above suspicion," although their mission is not without risk. Like the contemporary series *Maisie Dobbs*, MacInnes manages to capture the devastation and horror of war with only a whiff of graphic brutality. She also has a gift for presenting a far-ranging perspective on the depressed situation in Europe that enabled German citizens and others to be taken in by propaganda, although simultaneously gripped by a climate of fear. There are many superb touches such as when Richard and Frances visit a torture chamber and later hear cries coming from a Jewish alley, although they are prevented from investigating by Nazi officers, or see the simplicity of the peasants and farmers. ("It was pathetic, [Frances] thought, that 'Tyrolean' clothes, bought in the smart shops of large cities far away from the Tyrol, should be better-looking than the originals they copied. It was the tragedy of city hands being more skillful in cutting better material, of colors more carefully blended with the sophisticated designer's eye.") Like their film counterparts, Richard and Frances Myles have an enchanting, loving relationship with Frances matching her husband in brains, wit, nerve and athleticism. Their romance is pure champagne. ("[Richard] felt that wave of emotion which came to him when he looked at Frances in her unguarded moments; and he had the bleak horror which always attacked him then when he thought how easy it might have been never to have met her.") The action builds to a great cat-and-mouse chase and satisfying conclusion. This novel ranks among the best of the World War II vintage novels I've read.

    I enjoy both film and original novel. The film did a great job in capturing the flavor of the novel and its characters while adding many hokey yet fun MGM touches. The book affords a more realistic window into Europe at the early stages of Nazism with its grim implications, but both versions are fast-paced and escapist with courageous, charming protagonists.

All the Brothers Were Valiant by Ben Ames Williams (Written 1919)
★★★★★
Filmed as *Across to Singapore*

> *"The fine old house stood on Jumping Town Hill, above the town. It had stood there before there was a town, when only a cabin or two fringed the woods below, nearer the shore. The weather boarding had been brought in ships from England, ready sawed; likewise the bricks of the chimney. Indians used to come to the house in the cold of winter, begging shelter. Given blankets, and food, and drink, they slept upon the kitchen floor; and when Joel Shore's great-great-grandfather came down in the morning, he found Indians and blankets gone together."*
>
> Ben Ames Williams, *All the Brothers Were Valiant*

The basis for the film *Across to Singapore*, Ben Ames Williams' *All the Brothers Were Valiant* is a swift-moving, colorful tale of blood brothers, treachery, and high adventure aboard a New England whaling ship commanded by the youngest and possibly last of five brothers. It was turned into the aforementioned film, which had as assets the appeal and beauty of a youthful Joan Crawford and Ramon Novarro in major roles, but unfortunately and inexplicably, the book's strong plotline/narrative was insipidly altered and bolloxed by MGM, draining it of its strength, clarity and impact. The original story made far more sense, principally, and is told with much color, atmosphere and great characterization. Additionally, Ernest Torrence is completely miscast as one of the central characters, Mark Shore, which throws the entire substance and slant of the story off. The Mark Shore of the novel is a dashing, sexually magnetic hellion, better embodied by an earthy, heroic heartthrob like John Gilbert, Tyrone Power or Clark Gable. He is a Long John Silver, dangerous and reckless but enormously charismatic and attractive, a weaver of mesmerizing tales and easily influential to men and women both. ("There was a splendor of strength and vigor about the man, in the very look of him, and in his eye, and his voice, and his laughter. He seemed to shine, like the sun.") Torrence, although spoken of fondly by Crawford as "the lamb of the world" and often cast as a crusty sea dog, is no matinee idol, to put it mildly.

Most significantly, Mark Shore's attraction should be palpable enough to sway Priscilla (played by Crawford), the damsel of the tale. Instead, he is repulsive to her and fairly dastardly which makes the other liberties in the plot — namely, the forced betrothal of Priscilla to Mark — head-spinning and confusing. The original story, then, is essentially ruined, but the film still gets by — loopy as it may be — on the strength of heart throbs Crawford and Novarro.

The novel sets things up quickly. Matthew Shore of New England began a log when his five boys were young, chronicling their valor as whalers on the high seas, which each son maintains in turn. Three of his sons perished in acts of bravery and, as a matter of ritual, entries in the log end with the line "All the brothers were valiant." Now the fourth son Mark has disappeared while his ship watered at the Gilbert Islands and is presumed dead, and the whaling bark, the *Nathan Ross*, is put in the command of youngest brother, Joel who hopes to locate Mark, even though the two had a longstanding enmity. Close-lipped salt Asa Worthen puts the craft in Joel's hands and before setting off on a three-year cruise, Joel cajoles childhood sweetheart, Priscilla Holt, "a gay and careless child" six years his junior, to marry and accompany him. Crawford, then barely out of her teens, perfectly embodies Priscilla with her doll-faced beauty, petite and shapely figure, and vivacious personality. She also brings the right combination of sly sexuality and innocence. The "dainty, sweetly proportioned creature, built on fine lines that were strangely out of keeping with the stalwart stock from which she sprung" is prone to hero worship and makes the transition from girl to woman through the action-packed whaling adventure. Actually, all the major characters go through rites of passage (literally and figuratively) to prove their mete — or valor. The "shuddering, bloody, oily work" of the whaling industry quickly sickens Priscilla and thrust into Joel's constant companionship, he begins to wear on her as well. Then "lost brother," Mark Shore, swings onboard at Tubai, quickly mesmerizing the men and Priscilla with his colorful and exotic tales when he was "not three pagans, but six" and felt "back at the beginning of the world." His enticing romance with a "little brown girl" with the "eyes of a deer" during those days when he was presumed dead, which even stirs slow-blooded Joel who knows "the witchery of those warm, southern nights," led to swashbuckling adventure and bloodshed surrounding a pearl-filled lagoon. Maliciously, tantalizingly and fatally, he taints the atmosphere onboard with the rumor of hidden pearls, "sweet as a woman's skin," and all hell breaks loose. The ship is in mutiny.

Like Long John Silver in Robert Louis Stevenson's *Treasure Island*, bad boy Mark is as seductive to readers as he is to the characters in the novel. His story within a story is truly beguiling and exciting, including a fabulous passage where, in a stupor like classic private eyes on a case, his senses scrambled with fever, he sets off swimming after a boat that has hijacked his little brown girl and gets his breast and sides rasped raw by a shark beside him which he confuses for the girl. Later he throws a marauder on the hijacking ship overboard and sees "a fiery streak in the water where I dropped him. That shark was not so squeamish as the one I had — embraced." The story within a story, Mark's adventures while presumed lost, are, again, altered unaccountably by the film. An uncredited and adorable Anna Mae Wong serves as "the little brown girl," but her significance and role in Mark's character development fails to materialize with major elements in the backstory removed. The chief bollox the film makes is the forced betrothal of Priscilla, which changes the relationship of the three central characters. Inexplicably, Joel is shown as almost villainous when he forces Priscilla, the woman he allegedly loves, to go through with a betrothal to his brother — a wedding that was arranged without her knowledge, in fact — in spite of her teary protests! He even takes her *against her will* onboard! In the novel, however, he is genuinely noble and a man of great integrity, always kind to Priscilla, only moderately stern when her safety is at risk, and although at odds with his brother, he still shows wonderful character and kindness in that direction as well. Mark, also, is reckless, but ultimately not a scoundrel and because of the goodness of both characters, the finale is stirring and moving and has both heart and spirit. Blood does out!

In sum, a great adventure on the high seas with men of genuine valor and a fair maiden who becomes a woman. The film with an adorable Joan Crawford and Ramon Novarro fails miserably to faithfully translate the plot, resulting in loopy confusion and weakened narrative, but still succeeds on the appeal and glamour of its two young stars and silent film innovations.

The Best of Everything by Rona Jaffe (Written 1958) ★★★★

Rona Jaffe's *The Best of Everything* is far superior to the film version, capturing with humor and realism (and an astuteness that still is relevant) the experiences of five "working" girls — or rather, "career girls," as they were then called — who come to work as secretaries in a large publishing house in New York City. Jaffe knew this world well and it shows. The backstory behind the novel is as fascinating and fun as the novel itself, since Jaffe, a recent graduate from Radcliffe, progressed from file clerk to associate editor in a house similar to the one she describes in her novel and wrote *The Best of Everything* after being introduced by chance to producer Jerry Wald (of *Mildred Pierce* fame). When Wald was told flippantly by an editor that Jaffe would write the book on "working girls in New York" he was seeking, Jaffe set herself to the task. Wald agreed to produce it, resulting in a huge publicity campaign for a book that hadn't yet been written. Jaffe typed all 775 pages on a manual typewriter. The finished product became a runaway bestseller, feverishly read by and influencing scores of young women.

A sort of *Sex in the City* of the 1950s, *The Best of Everything* gets into the minds of its five fresh young things, capturing their adventures, ambitions and most especially their sexual/romantic longings and relationships with a sensitivity and frankness that was perhaps groundbreaking at the time. The dialogue is achingly real with situations recognizable to most girls, even if morality has changed (to debatable degrees). Some things, in fact, never change. Jaffe is hilariously spot-on about interminable blind dates and office parties, reminding me not only of dreadful and dreaded office affairs (once accurately described by a friend as "like a meeting that just broke up"), but those God-awful stretches of time with the wrong person. Some of the lines are wry masterstrokes: "The coffee shop, which doubled as a bar at night, was brightly lighted now and crowded with girls and women who all seemed to be talking at once at the top of their lungs. Six at a time would be jammed into a booth, hunched over their hamburgers and dissecting the other office personnel with venom or hilarity." The story alternates between its five protagonists, but the central heroine is Caroline Bender, a savvy, sweet and sophisticated go-getter, who I suspect is most closely a composite of Jaffe herself. It is her capable presence that opens and closes the novel. The other four consist of April Morrison, a farm-fresh, naive stunner who lightly pursues acting; Gregg Adams, a sweet but depressive actress who develops a fatal attraction; Barbara Lemont, a single mother with a Mona Lisa face who becomes a Beauty Editor; and the staunch, level-headed, predictable Mary Agnes, the Louella Parsons of the thirty-fifth floor.

It's interesting, and a sign of the times, that the young impressionables here, all of twenty or twenty-one years of age, often wind up in affairs with older, allegedly dashing men who become tutors of a sort. There is something inherently sexist in that, the imbalance of power so the man can be "in charge," and it's unfortunate the reverse is not shown here (older woman, younger man) and yet it's realistic enough. Also interesting is the way the girls, in general, are depicted as much more focused on love, security and a domestic future then men, which was how they were undoubtedly trained to be with men seen as their "protectors" and love and marriage as their life's "beginning." The scenes of one girl having to undergo an abortion are especially heartbreaking and haunting with so little options for her to keep the child without marriage. Jaffe, like a number of female writers, also tends to endow men with a sensitivity that they in reality often don't possess, although her male characters are well drawn and believable enough. The figure of Amanda Farrow, bitchy and threatened editor who goes through secretaries like nylons, fascinates me as much as she does gullible April. Depicted as cold and removed, she actually seemed a deal more interesting than her guileless sisters. Gosh, I remember as a child reading things like this depicting "sex" and the way "girls think" and being completely baffled as to this twisted sexuality where, to my mind, men were getting the better deal. All the more incomprehensible that the beautiful female should be the one desperate to get hitched or viewed as a "noose around the neck" rather than the reverse. It still baffles me that all the myriad vagaries of one vast group of people of same sex should be presumed to be sexually attracted to their opposite gender and that each group should be supposed to share gender-based social traits, completely oppositional to one another.

None of the actors in the screen version match their book counterparts very well. The film doesn't capture the sophistication, intelligence and complexity of the novel or the progression the girls make to more knowing young women; certainly the sexual frankness is missing or made ridiculously florid and melodramatic. Hope Lange has some of Caroline's savvy, but is so physically unlike the book's Caroline that they seem like different people. Diane Baker, although often a good actress, is too precious as April and too cutesy, not the stunning blonde with a model's profile described. She remains annoyingly chirpy without capturing the bitter cynicism that shatters April or the recklessness that overtakes her. Richard Aherne is wonderful as office lecher Mr. Shalimar, seedy, yet poignant, and Crawford is a far cry from the youthful, chic, frosty Ms. Farris of the novel, yet brings a maturity, bitterness, and pathos to the role that allows her to memorably steal the picture. Her venom-dripped "Now you and your rabbit-faced wife can go to hell" is worth the whole film.

In all, compulsively readable "chick lit."

The Caretakers by Dariel Telfer (Written 1959) ★★½

The Caretakers is more sordid and shocking than any Sidney Sheldon novel — distasteful and hard to read at times, but even more disturbing is that the horrific exploitation and abuse taking place in the fictional "health care" institution (i.e., insane asylum), Canterbury, is completely plausible (author Dariel Telfer claimed to know first-hand). In typical potboiler fashion, it follows a host of different characters from fresh young things beginning nursing training to intractable old guard intimidators and various inmates and doctors, people teeming with hidden passions. My Signet paperback edition's cover (with its racy semi-nude photo and depictions of hospital philandering) boasts "[a] shattering novel about nurses, doctors, and patients in a state hospital where emotions readily explode, where lust leads to rape, hate to murder." Michael Korda, who edited the book at publishing giant *Simon and Schuster*, once noted that it was the first novel to sell six figures, "marking," as he quipped, "the start of the decline of the book industry." Not so laughable, actually. The film's "noble reform" slant is less in evidence in the book and there are no "heroes," dubious as the screen "heroes" may be. Aides and affiliates bear mute witness to shock treatments where a patient's head must be held to prevent the neck breaking (a treatment sometimes used to "punish" intractable patients into docility) and assist in "packing" others in icy sheets where these helpless mummies must remain, strapped flat to the bed, for 72 hours. Slowly, each nurse-in-training learns to see no evil, hear no evil and speak no evil. When a young reporter, Mike Stewart cries, "It's medieval torture, the Dark Ages all over. What are you trying to do, kill people?," Donovan Macleod (played by sonorous Robert Stack in the film version), the head of staff who allegedly "cares," responds, "Not at all. It's excellent therapy" even though he barely believes it himself.

One suspects Telfer has incorporated some of herself into Kathy Hunter, the young woman who comes to Canterbury for her training at the novel's opening. Through Kathy's eyes, we begin to see the grim realities of Canterbury, although as other characters fill the landscape, we learn their stories and inner conflicts. Kathy becomes roommates, friends and eventually rivals with another new affiliate, Althea Horne, a gorgeous violet-eyed blonde. There is the stock-in-trade, mousy and middle-aged Millie (what else would she be called?) who desperately needs this job, various doctors (all of them lusting after the females surrounding them), brash news reporter Mike Stewart (sent to evaluate funding needs), and steely Lucretia Terry, "the final authority on almost every phase of hospital routine." With her "large ash tray piled high with cigarette butts," "lashing assertiveness," and secret longing to be loved like other women, Terry is par for the course for the older Joan Crawford who plays her onscreen. Laughably, she is described as wearing shapeless dresses, while Crawford's incarnation was actually dressed to the nines, far more stylishly than any hospital administrator. (A hospital picnic scene with "soda pop" gave Crawford a chance for Pepsi placements in the film.)

Rounding things out are the wrenching stories of several patients, a few likely based on Telfer's own experiences. A baby-faced blonde Mary Elsie is sexually exploited by Portuguese visiting physician Dr. Andreatta who makes nightly visits to her room and resolves "not [to] leave this one until another just as tempting" comes along. When her husband visits and heatedly attempts to embrace her in the visiting room, setting her off, one sees that she is saddled with someone boorish enough to be part of the problem. Reasons subscribed to psychosis are decidedly "1950s," for the main — resident lesbian Madge develops a barbiturate problem when her relationship is quashed by the institution and is promptly committed; syphilis leads to "mental degeneration" for a pre-teen patient; Mary Elsie becomes unhinged after the loss of her baby. If these inmates have not already had a complete mental break, the barbaric "cures" in store for them will guarantee it. One suspects many people were committed and subjected to treatments for reasons having nothing to do with illness; certainly real people like Frances Farmer are a testament to that. Kathy finds "worst of all" those patients aware of how forgotten they are, "lost, lonely faces staring out the windows of Hydro between treatments."

True to sexist form, female characters are drawn as cut-throat and competitive with one another, Kathy and Althea incomprehensibly obsessed with the stoic, cold Donovan who eschews romantic complications. Althea longs to get her "hooks in" and marry him (it's the '50s! what else?) and the shared obsession drives a wedge between the two girls — the rivalry becoming downright psychotic. Treachery abounds on all levels, however. Even supervisors like Lucretia (decent beneath her hard-nosed exterior - so Joan, so very Joan) overlook troublemakers for political reasons and fear for their jobs. In a troubling environment, everyone is troubled. As Kathy puts it, Donovan reminds her "that I must never forget I was on probation as long as I worked in a hospital. I was not a free moral agent. I could not make decisions or offer advice to supervisors and doctors or even criticize them."

The film certainly lessens the seriousness of the institution's and staff's failings, making it more of a contest between a liberal new guard led by Donovan and the traditional led by Lucretia. Occasionally the campy inmates play with matches or free symbolic canaries, as Lucretia teaches her staff self-protective judo (Crawford's opportunity to show some leg and a chiffon scarf!). The book, in contrast, lays on one act of inhumanity and degradation after the next, depicting an overflowing and understaffed hospital, a problem that has mushroomed beyond their control and dissolved into widespread abuse. In one heartbreaking scene, a male ward is described where the rare film night creates excitement for hours afterwards and where desperate men "clutched small possessions, a rubber band, a sliver of soap wrapped in toilet tissue, a ragged magazine, a banana skin, some shreds of tobacco. These trifles gave them a feeling of independence and inner security." Naturally these pathetic treasures are confiscated by unfeeling staff. Donovan's speech to his students is a far cry from the noble promise of Robert Stack's in the film ("We are the caretakers of their hope"). In the book, Donovan paints this portrait: "They [patients] are the living dead who know only how to die, and we must not forget for one instant that this is an appalling national waste, a spiritual waste if you like. We must do all we humanly can to be the right kind of custodians." (Bring on the ice and electricity!)

All plot points boil to a fever pitch, ending in various tragedies, as the cover promises. There is no real moral compass. The attitudes towards women are appalling. "I've failed as a doctor," the love-stricken Larry Denning tells Althea, "but as a man I can succeed…I've got to help you the only way I can now." "His way" of helping her forget Donovan is driving her to a secluded spot, ripping off her clothes and violently raping her. Incredulously, when Donovan and Kathy see Althea emerging from Larry's car in ripped clothes, clearly attacked, their concern is not that she was hurt, but that she had sex. The news spreads throughout the institution and, amazingly, Althea angsts over being thought a "whore" or "slut." No stigma or even attempt at criminal prosecution is made against Larry. He even tells Althea, "If you feel I raped you, all the more reason for us to be married." Hello? A similar caveman-style attack is made on Kathy by Donovan — which she invites sacrificially by disrobing in his apartment. Rather than apologizing for his brutality, he offers to marry her afterwards since she had been a virgin! Why would women want to marry the men who raped or brutalized them? And how is it such unstable and dangerous doctors don't have their license removed? Perhaps Donovan's thoughts later when he has his beloved Althea in his apartment where "she could not escape him" reveal Telfer's own attitude or those of the times: "He would confess that he had simply lost his head [re Kathy]. There was nothing strange in that; many men had experiences they were ashamed of when they lost control of themselves." When mentally imbalanced Mary Elsie is sent home because she is pregnant, thanks to Dr. Andreatta's exploitation, her husband visualizes bearing her down to the floor and stamping "the life out of every inch of her contaminated, impregnated body." The aggressive, he-man pursuit, now known as stalking, is Telfer's idea of the romantic male and the double standard is firmly in place. It's no wonder these women go off their nut!

In spite of the tangled web of hormones and that silly gravity like cocaine propaganda films of the fifties, *The Caretakers* manages to be occasionally sobering as a believable record of horror (some of it — like the sexism — unintentional). It is said there are no atheists in a cockpit. Apparently God isn't found in a cockpit either — or a "snake pit." In an atmosphere of literal insanity where every day "something new and unexpected and devastating" happens, inmates and employees alike are dehumanized. Abuse of the vulnerable in such homes remains a problem most foul.

Claustrophobia by Abbie Carter Goodloe (Written 1926) ★★½
Filmed as *I Live My Life*

"Claustrophobia," the basis for the Joan Crawford film *I Live My Life*, was published in the April 1926 edition of *Scribner's Magazine*, more evidence of the devotion that once existed to literature in this country, and won an O.Henry Award that year. It is illustrated with sketchy pen and ink drawings of society types.

To be honest, "Claustrophobia" bares only the thinnest resemblance to the Crawford film, which calls into question the effort involved on my part in tracking it down so zealously. It is a cute story, but patently thin, and seems almost suitable for one of Crawford's "Dancing Daughter" flapper films with young moderns and their foibles in love. The basic plot involves a man, Phil Warner, from "Bye-low Ranch" in Idaho who is having severe second thoughts and trepidation about his impending marriage to a New York society girl named Rémy Cosgrove. The couple met while the spoiled, headstrong Rémy was visiting mining properties with one of her "set," John Carlisle, in Snake River country and came upon Warner's ranch. The attraction between the two was immediate.

> *His thin, tanned face, his supple, hard body, slim-waisted, narrow-flanked, so different from the well-fed, well set-up New Yorkers she had known, exercised a curious fascination over her. An impersonal note in*

his attentions, a politeness untinged with gallantry, piqued her. As for Warner, the unexpected advent of this girl, her youth and seductiveness, the aura of wealth and power about her, dazzled him, who had never been dazzled by such things. It was as though he had plucked a star from the blue...

Evidently Warner fears the fact that he is abnegating his own life to fit into Rémy's design. With typical male chauvinism, he believes they might have had a real marriage if she had been willing to follow *him* and adapted to his world; rather, he was being swallowed by hers. Part of his feeling of suffocation comes from the fact that he was alone and unattached and living in the wide open, wild spaces of the West, but now has been transported to cramped New York City with "a thousand damnable conventions." There is that confusion at the modern girl, which seemed so prevalent a topic during that period (do things really change?). ("In the beginning, Warner had sometimes thought Rémy too direct, too brutally forthright in her manner. It was a note in her youthful ultra-modernism which he hadn't particularly liked.") Desperately and abruptly, he tries to break the engagement on their very wedding day. After Warner compares their relationship to passage on a boat that has been found unseaworthy and thus should be canceled, Rémy retorts, amusingly, "You can't cancel a passage when it's time to haul in the gang-plank! It's too late — no steamship company would stand for it, Phil."

Ultimately, stating that she didn't want a man who didn't want her, the cool-headed Rémy comes up with an ingenious idea to save face before Society and her people with this last-minute cancellation of her wedding. Nothing will be said, but she won't show up at the altar! It will be far less humiliating if she appears to "throw over" the man than the truth. Warner is relieved and all plans go underway until the hour when he anxiously awaits being stood up at the altar. Throngs line up to witness this "fashionable church wedding." ("White-gloved policemen waved up the gleaming limousines in unending line and dispatched them after the lordly fashion of well-subsidized policemen at a wedding. The halting, curious crowd pressed close about the awning, beneath which richly dressed women and men in frock-coats and high silk hats passed into the Church of the Heavenly Angels.") The suspense mounts and Warner counts the minutes until his freedom, thinking it will soon be over. It soon is. As he glances down the aisle, he sees Rémy coming toward him on the arm of her father. Ultimately and triumphantly, she pulls the last coup (and her sass is likeable) by showing up, after all, and getting her man.

This is a cute story with likeable characters, although one wonders if indeed either of them love each other or if Warner merely has last minute jitters. For her part, Rémy is evidently attracted and repelled by Warner, as she admits to herself, but more attracted than repelled and his very unmalleable character is what appeals to her. Perhaps opposites attract.

The film *I Live My Life* is one of my less favorite Crawford vehicles, its comedy strained and strident and lacking in charm, but like Rémy in the story, Crawford's Kay Bentley (her name in the film) is spunky, flippant, modern and cute. In her sassy, little sailor suits and fetching gowns, Crawford is certainly in all her cute, youthful glory with those big eyes and butterfly-wing lashes. She is also irritating, surly and unpleasant in her "comedic" moments, the pratfalls falling flat. Brian Aherne as Terry O'Neill, the Warner character (if he can be called that), is reinvented as an archaeologist and equally out-of-step with the screwball antics. Fortunately, there are those always-reliable character actors to keep the ship from sinking entirely — their contribution and Joan's plucky charm and beauty, plus MGM's posh gloss and world of elegance (including Crawford's sleek gowns), help even this labored film sail.

Daisy Kenyon by Elizabeth Janeway (Written 1945) ★★★★★

Daisy Kenyon, adapted into a 1947 Joan Crawford film, tells the story of a magazine illustrator, Margaret "Daisy" Kenyon, who is torn between the love of two men in New York circa 1940. This description, however, hardly does justice to the phenomenal complexity and beauty of author Janeway's prose, her ability to make every character and scene come alive with sensuality, immediacy and dimension. At times, her writing is so breathtaking that I had to stop to contemplate a passage as if a landscape. Janeway's own pedigree (she was judge for both the Pulitzer Prize and National Book Awards and book reviewer for The New York Times) shows in the braininess and sophistication of her characters. The novel achieves both depth and a moving romanticism like the film *Now Voyager*.

At the opening of the story, Daisy is inhabiting a Greenwich Village studio walk-up with her Angora cat Mac and steeped in an eight-year affair with a powerful, married partner in a law firm, Dan O'Mara, although she maintains her independence and self-respect by supporting herself. Dan has dropped in unexpectedly, using his key, as she is getting ready for a date, the scene setting the tone for their intense yet conflicted relationship. As in the film, he tells her he must break their own date with her friends for next weekend and she is chagrined with his continual unreliability.

Fighting tears, she tells him she is "through," but he disarms her by saying if she means it, he'll leave, meanwhile, pulling her in his arms and playfully unzipping her housecoat. Stamping on his foot, physical wrestling part of their sexual play, Daisy slowly breaks down as they argue. Dan holds her wrists together (a telling detail) and says he'd like to get a later train. Then he picks her up and carries her presumably to the bedroom as Daisy, laughing and crying, says she's tried to stop loving him and will someday, and Dan says, "All right, darling...stop sometime — next year, next week, but not right now." The date (whose waiting cab Dan steals as he departs) is Pete Lapham, an editor for one of the magazines Daisy does illustrations for. Pete and Daisy, oddly connecting, wind up marrying. This new development sets in motion the turbulent dynamics of a romantic triangle.

Along with evocative passages that recreate an entire world gorgeously ["In the morning the birds were more uncertain than usual, for the sun was a source of light through the pearly mist, felt but not seen, an intuition growing into certainty, but never a palpable scientific fact"], there is equally stunning dialogue and characterizations. The story builds to strong dramatic arcs, exploring the heights and depths of each character's emotions and psyche.

Hard to witness are the scenes involving Dan and his wife Lucille. The O'Maras are stuck in a loveless hell, keeping up appearances at business dinners ["Mrs. Gaylord turned and smiled and opened her mouth to include Lucille in the conversation. Lucille braced herself and waited."]. Love has gone out of the marriage for Dan, yet he is as complicit in maintaining a charade as he derides Lucille for being. Unfaithful and emotionally cold to his wife, at times overtly cruel, he has effectively isolated her. Her pathetic attempts at self-preservation backfire, worsening her degradation. Monstrous as Dan's behavior is, he is so fully realized and multi-faceted that he never becomes one-dimensional. With Daisy, Dan has a deeper bond and respect, a relationship of equality and substance on many levels, although he shatters that trust when his grief over her abandonment turns ugly. Meanwhile, Pete becomes a soldier and the book details the impact of World War II on all their lives.

The film, although in no way achieving the book's depth, succeeds in maintaining the essence of characters, tone and story. Since I saw the film first, I pictured Henry Fonda as Pete, although I had a completely different vision of Daisy (who is described in the book as a "tall redhead"), despite Crawford's excellence in the role. (And as a Crawford fan, I'd have no one else as Daisy!) In both versions, characters smoke and drink a lot, always mixing or imbuing highballs and cocktails — even, in the book, serving one in the hospital! Key changes have been made, however. *(Spoilers!)* Where Dan only forces unwanted kisses on Daisy in the film after she has married Pete, he rapes her in the book, this act the nadir of his decline and the narrative's (and Daisy's) pivotal arc. Removing this detail critical to the story's dramatic peak, the

A scene from the film with Dana Andrews and Joan Crawford. Her spacious Greenwich Village apartment with fireplace is described as a "hovel" by Dan. PHOTO COURTESY OF JERRY MURBACH

film invents a car crash as a substitute crisis, a weaker event. The rape's tragic impact on Daisy is illustrated in the novel with poignant realism. Troubling, however, was Daisy ultimately equating Dan's horrendous act with her leaving him as if the hurts or "sins" were of equal caliber; they are not even marginally morally comparable. The resolution, however, is moving and satisfying.

Daisy was a character I fell in love with, and Dan's emotion when he was about to lose her I felt in my own gut:

> *The lamp had gone from the big table behind the sofa, which was now covered with newspaper and a lot of miscellaneous items — candlesticks,*

cigarette boxes, brandy glasses — that Daisy was carefully wrapping in more newspaper. [Dan] stopped in the door. This was beyond words. The only thing that came to him was the voice of his intuition saying faintly, "Always believe me. Never doubt me again."

She heard him and turned from her work. He looked at her carefully. Her hair was messy, her face was dirty, she had no lipstick on, she looked very tired and certainly not beautiful at all. I will never see her again, he thought, and something broke inside of him.

Daisy Kenyon, film and book, offers a fascinating window into a sophisticated, intellectual, cocktail lounge era New York with a strong, sexy heroine who has become one of my favorite characters in literature.

Dancing Lady by James Warner Bellah (Written 1932)
★★★★★★★★★★ *(the sky's the limit!)*

Dancing Lady by James Warner Bellah was such a beloved and special reading experience, I almost can't rate it or put it into words. Apparently, Bellah was best known for his westerns and became a pal of director John Ford, working with Ford on screenplays such as *Fort Apache* (based on "Massacre," one of his own stories). With *Dancing Lady*, he has created a plucky, sassy heroine who completely captured my heart, a girl who has much in common with the actress who played her, Joan Crawford, and a similar hard-working, indomitable, life-affirming spirit. Abandoned by her mother at an early age and growing up in the tenements, Janie Barlow goes to work while still underage, but the smell of greasepaint is in her blood and she's willing to work hard to give her dream a chance. From burlesque to Broadway, Janie makes the rounds with other colorful chorus girls of the early '30s, the storytelling both a slangy shorthand and deliciously sophisticated. Never have I encountered anything quite like it, its dialogue far wittier, snappier and sassier than the best of its kind — at times recalling the inventive dexterity of P.G. Wodehouse, but completely its own breed. One girl at the Cockatoo "buttonholes" Janie (going under the moniker "Janice") her second night in a show by saying, "You look as if you washed — how do you play the man racket?" Bellah pulls you into the era of Pantages, forty-cent special dinners, vaudeville houses, nightclub acts, fast-talking guys and dolls quick on the intake, even mentioning a movie marquee with Joan Crawford and Robert Montgomery on it, a popular box office draw of the time! In many ways, through brave, brassy and beautiful Janie — the "Kid," as small time vaudevillian "Patch" Gallagher calls her — he shows the human spirit in the face of defeat, reminiscent of Crawford who rose like a phoenix from the ashes again and again in her personal life and career, a very American story (as Janie observes when she's doing a dead-end job in a factory — and no doubt Crawford echoed: "Whatever they made you do they couldn't stop you from planning.").

The story spans several years in Janie's life from rags to riches, back again and everything in between. Along with the gunfire, delightful, sassy retorts ("I came here to see you." "Well, you've seen me — "), there are scores of tiny masterstroke exchanges that made me laugh out loud, such as when Janice (nee Janie) goes to audition for "lord of the theater world" Anton Langefeld (who "saw himself at times in velvet and silken hose, with a black Dane at his feet and the arms of the Duke of Valentinois on the leather chair back behind his shoulders — watching the rack crush slowly and terribly while he talked luncheon with his cook in quiet preoccupation"). He says, "I suppose you're just a brainless little tart like all the rest" and Janice replies, basing this on a remark an acquaintance told her regarding "the Scopaic eye and the serene abdomen" –"Scopas was the first lad who could sculpt an eye properly. Greek boy." Loved by four men, "each in his own way," Janie rolls with the punches, remaining a hoofer at heart even when they try to fashion her into a "high artiste," moving in the high and low echelons of society and seeing the pathos in both clearly.

There are wonderful, timelessly resonant speeches along the way about art, love, and suffering, among other things, such as when Anton pleads with a disillusioned Janie: "Love can be two things. It can be a tornado or it can be a gentle summer breeze that blows over you — that you come to feel gradually. They call it 'learning to love,' I suppose…Can't you trust in that — and wait for your summer breeze?…Don't tell me it hasn't come at the right time — tell me it has." or "There are two strings in any art… One confuses them too frequently…You pull one for money and you pull the other, I suppose, for your immortal soul." The relationship between Patch and Janie is a delight, set up beautifully at the start:

> "Listen, punk, I'm here on business, see? Try not to be a sap. You got feet and you're light and slim and your hands are small. If you wanta come down to Mendelhauser's and get a real tryout with me, say so. I get a room and a music box there when I want to, and don't get the idea you're gonna get kissed for your trouble, because you ain't."

Janie leaned over him. "Now you listen to me," she said. "I don't like you and I never did. I can't have you thrown out of here, but I would if I could. I'm not going to Mendelhauser's with you, or anywhere else, and if I never see you again I won't cry about it."

He threw his head back and laughed in her face.

"Swell!" He hit the table with the open palm of his left hand. With his right he took hers and shook it.

"That's the way I like to hear a woman talk. It's a bargain then — about nine o'clock?"

When, over coffee, Patch taps the back of Janie's hand with his finger and tells her he always liked her, it's sexier and brings a lump to the throat more than any sledge hammer panting and pawing love scene. It's divine.

The film version uses bits and elements of the original story, maintaining a few of the original characters, but eliminating others and liberally reinventing the story for brevity. Patch Gallagher, a bit less loveable and consistently caustic and irritable in his film counterpart, seems to be a combination of several characters from the novel, although basically reflecting Patch. Janie in the book begins as a mere teenager and doesn't conjure to mind Joan Crawford physically, but the film is its own experience — gloriously black-and-white Deco, filled with wonderful music, and meant to be an answer to the superior *42nd Street* while possessing its own unique charms. Perhaps Tod, as portrayed by Franchot Tone, is the closest fit, but not quite. It doesn't matter. They each enchant in their own unique way and the final clinch between Crawford and Gable always brings tears to my eyes.

I can only sum up *Dancing Lady* this way: It's delightful, it's delicious, it's delectable, it's delirious, it's de-limit.

Flamingo Road by **Robert Wilder (Written 1942)** ★★★★

The film *Flamingo Road* is surely a favorite among Joan Crawford fans and I'm no exception. The juicy face-off between Crawford and Sydney Greenstreet is a delicious highlight, but Crawford is particularly entrancing and sexy as carnival dancer Lane Bellamy, a breezily seductive Southern minx and "orphan" of sorts who is unfairly railroaded by corrupt Sheriff Titus Semple to clear away potential romantic complications she poses for his political candidate Fielding Carlisle (Zachary Scott). When he tries to run her out of town and she rebels, sick of running, Titus becomes her ruthless adversary. ("I shoulda, he thought, vomited an' spit her out the first time she lit between my teeth.") In the original novel, Lane Bellamy is Lane Ballou, as enchanting as her film counterpart; she is also only a teenager which makes her all the more vulnerable and winsome, yet somehow, even with the age discrepancy, Crawford has captured her essence, including the "dusky voice." Scott makes a great Fielding, even if older than his fictional counterpart as well. The casting of Sydney Greenstreet as Titus seems fortuitous. I can't imagine anyone who could've filled this character's boots or gallon-size pants. His lethargy is perfect, since Titus is described as "imperturbable as the great, heavy clouds which piled up in the west every afternoon." As he sits on his porch under the ceiling fans with his pitcher of milk, he is like the bull frog with heavy-lidded eyes about to strike the unsuspecting fly.

The novel begins with deputy sheriff Fielding discovering Lane at an abandoned carnival lot in Truro, Florida, and taking her under his wing. He finds her oddly disarming and brings her to the Eagle Diner where shortly he has obtained for her a job and a place to live, however unglamorous. She is deeply grateful and falls for him. Meanwhile, Field has been under the wing — or thumb — of Titus because of Titus' close relationship with Field's late father, a judge, and shortly Titus reveals his hand. He has engineered for Field to become senator. Because of Field's involvement with Lane, who is not on the "right side" of the tracks, Titus destroys the poor girl's chances of getting any employment in Truro and thereby forces her to join the local and "respected" brothel, Lute-Mae's. There Lane meets and enchants Dan Curtis, another player in the political arena, who is responsible for bringing her to the "right" side of town, Flamingo Road. But, as Lane in the film puts it, "You don't know how much trouble it is to dispose of a dead elephant." (Ironically, this choice bit of dialogue is not found in the book.)

The novel is both juicy and moving, and as can be expected, much more detailed than the film. The movie, however, has a romantic poetry with artful lighting, high wattage stars Crawford and Greenstreet, and the song "If I Could Be One Hour With You" sung so memorably and throatily by Crawford (a luscious touch). Only Lane in the book maintains this romanticism. Although the book's characterizations are deeper and the themes a bit less sugar-coated, the film maintains the essentials, much of the dialogue and most key scenes (not surprisingly, since author Wilder co-wrote the screenplay). Needless to say, Lute-Mae's is a whorehouse — high-class, but a brothel just the same. This is never indicated in the film, but Gladys George's peroxide curls and world-weariness say it in Hollywood's secret code language. A scene in which Lane resigns herself to a life at Lute-Mae's is particularly heartbreaking after she is examined dispassionately by a doctor to ensure that she is disease-free. She imagines that sex with "clients" will be like being raped.

> *Across the double bed was spread a powder-blue evening gown of cheap silk and beside it a pair of blue slippers. A twisting, ironic smile tugged at the corners of her mouth as she examined the pitiful finery. Both shoes and the dress had been worn, and Lane wondered by whom and for how long. Hurriedly she switched on the lights… The semidarkness had been filled with forebodings, and for a moment she had felt hopelessly alone and frightened…*

This lamb among wolves in an alien city has an impressive, innate breeding, however. Lute-Mae forms an unprecedented bond with her and Dan, decades her senior, determines to provide the security she deserves with a fanciful home on the most desirable street in town. Meanwhile, with the charming "carnival kid" earning respect and unexpected clout with the constituents who gather at her tony address (which threatens Titus' hold on them), Dan becomes the "big bear" Titus sets out to skin. A deliberately perverse scene, not in the film, is when Titus looks at himself naked in the mirror, glorying in his self-abasement.

Oh, it's the deep, dark South, alright! We all know it's not just gentility and mint juleps! The book doesn't even give us a particularly "feel good" ending; instead we're left hanging with an ambiguous outcome after becoming so invested in the appealing Lane. (Gee, this role was eerily perfect for Crawford — and a scene where Lane devours books to develop herself is uncannily spot-on). I'll take the film finale with Crawford/Lane walking off to the horizon, teary-eyed but hopeful, head held high with all its melodramatic, soapy magnificence and cinematic panache. Still, the novel paints a potent portrait of political corruption and meanness with a memorable, poignant heroine and a corpulent, colorful villain who has the weight (pun intended) to destroy lives while barely stirring from his porch.

Grand Hotel by Vicki Baum (Written 1930) ★★★★

Grand Hotel (*Menschen im Hotel*), the novel on which the famed 1932 film was based, is a superb window into the intersecting lives within an opulent hotel in Berlin prior to World War II. The hotel itself is brought to life with breathtakingly vivid detail and each character is drawn richly with descriptions at times wells of implication and insight (one of my favorites, although not a prime example, being "Schweimann's eyes crept like little gray mice out of the red cavities where they lived"). Vienna-born author Vicki Baum took a job as a parlourmaid in a hotel for six weeks to gather material for the novel and her research paid off. The iconic character of Dr. Otternschlag who sports only half a face ("a souvenir from Flanders," as he puts it), immortalized in the film for saying, "People come and go. Nothing ever happens," reflects the big picture, a relic of World War I steeped in emotional and spiritual apathy that leaves him waiting fruitlessly for a "message" in one of the grandest hotels of Europe, the superficial atmosphere of culture and ease belied by one-armed lift operators and portraits of dead game in its "drearier recesses." It is a portrait of beauty on the brink of collapse much like the ballerina Grusinskaya played by Greta Garbo in the film, a famed dancer who has lost her audience but remains desperate to keep up appearances and stay as she once was. On another level, *Grand Hotel* is an entertaining soap opera, teeming with intrigue and unexpected twists and romance. Whether describing the pursuit of the cat burglar on a crumbling ledge of the hotel or the inner workings of a character's mind, Baum creates an immediacy that makes compulsive and fascinating reading.

> *He saw men in dress coats and dinner jackets, smart cosmopolitan men. Women with bare arms, in wonderful clothes, with jewelry and furs, beautiful, well-dressed women. He heard music in the distance. He smelt coffee, cigarettes, scent, whiffs of asparagus from the dining room and the flowers that were displayed for sale on the flower stall. He felt the thick red carpet beneath his black leather boots and this perhaps impressed him most of all. Kringelein slid the sole of his boot gingerly over its pile and blinked. The lounge was beautifully illuminated and the light was delightfully golden; also there were bright red-shaded lights against the walls and the jets of the fountain in the Venetian basin shone green.*

Although naturally more in-depth, the novel has the same main characters as the film and it's hard not to picture their movie counterparts when visualizing them. The amazing cast of the film did justice to their essence, even with certain details at variance. One of the kinky quirks of the novel is that each character is often naked at some point. In fact, stenographer Flammchen runs through the hallway completely nude at the peak crisis after an aborted sexual encounter with her boss Preysing, this vision falling into dying bookkeeper Kringelein's arms. Crawford's Flamm wore a flimsy, see-through nightgown in this scene in the film, which communicated the intent, if less graphically. Most prurient and intriguing is that the suave jewel thief known as the Baron (played by John Barrymore in the film) is a sensual beast who loves flowers, stroking and even licking their petals like an animal when alone. Sometimes if left alone in showrooms, he smells and licks the upholstery of cars. He's amiable, which Barrymore conveyed beautifully, yet also apparently ruthless, the charming immoral; he falls instantly and madly in love with Grusinskaya whose pearls he is about to steal (and whom he observes in her frail nakedness), but unlike the film, in the novel he is at first willing to throttle her to cover his tracks until she stirs his compassion. Flammchen, played so enchantingly by a young, radiant Joan Crawford onscreen, has the beauty and joie de vivre Crawford possessed in spades particularly at that period in her life. She is described as having a little golden curl that hangs over her forehead, long legs, a "remarkably slender waist," and is "a magnificent example of the female form — of that there seemed no possible doubt." Careless of the attention she attracts in the lobby, "it was evident [Flamm] had her cares and as evident that those cares weighed on her as little as the lock of hair which from time to time she blew into the air off her forehead." Each character is given dimension. In both book and film, Flamm is pragmatic, charming and light in spirit, although at the same time prey to wolves like Preysing (played by Wallace Beery) due to financial need; Crawford was wonderful in creating a natural, nuanced girl and her Deco beauty and glow, plus her decent-girl-willing-to-sell-herself, enabled her to steal the film from her formidable co-stars effortlessly, most notably from Garbo. Preysing, in turn, is much more sympathetic in the book, although crossing a fatal line with his lust for a secretary who is his daughter's age just as he crosses his first corrupt line in business.

Grand Hotel, the novel, has many moments of deep beauty, each character managing to resonate with humanity at various points and the ending, even with its tragedies, is satisfying. One of the most touching and unforgettable characters, again, is Dr. Otternschlag, the emotionally and physically scarred ghost of the lobby. In a piercing monologue, he calls himself a "suicide," yet he still waits, hoping to be needed and wanted, miserable yet unable and unwilling to exit, watching the revolving door.

Humoresque **by Fannie Hurst (Written 1920)** ★ ★ ★ ½ *(five stars for film)*

Fannie Hurst's *Humoresque* is a short story (the titular one of a collection), not a novel, a slice-of-life about a hard-working Jewish family's prodigy violinist whose success may be cut short by war, thus, the subtitle of the story: "A Laugh on Life With a Tear Behind It." The wonderful character of Helen Wright (played with such memorable cynicism, passion and beauty by Joan Crawford in the film), wealthy patroness of Paul Borae, is not in the plot whatsoever. Her addition to the film was brilliant and took the story into another direction altogether, her intense dynamics with Paul and pathos exquisite like the vibrato of the violin. The original story, though dense, is a slight, somewhat schmaltzy and vivid photograph of early immigrant struggle with lots of Jewish ethnic color. Hurst has an incredible vocabulary, using words like avoirdupois and oleaginous (these in the same sentence, no less), her breathless style refreshing if not for all tastes. An American Jew who often wrote about the struggles of common people, she was dubbed "Queen of the Sob Sisters of American Letters" by literary critics. Her words seem to pan humanity like a camera on a dolly, creating a rich stew reminiscent of Alan Ginsberg's *Howl*. I wonder if he was influenced by her work.

> *By that impregnable chemistry of race whereby the red blood of the Mongolian and the red blood of the Caucasian become as oil and water in the mingle, Mulberry Street, bounded by sixteen languages, runs its intact Latin length of pushcarts, clotheslines, naked babies, drying vermicelli; black-eyed women in rhinestone combs and perennially big with child; whole families of buttonhole-makers, who first saw the blue-and-gold light of Sorrento, bent at home work round a single gas flare; pomaded barbers of a thousand Neapolitan amours. And then, just as suddenly, almost without osmosis and by the mere stepping down from the curb, Mulberry becomes Mott Street, hung in grillwork balconies, the moldy smell of poverty touched up with incense. Orientals whose feet shuffle and whose faces are carved out of satinwood. Forbidden women, their white, drugged faces behind upper windows. Yellow children, incongruous enough in Western clothing. A draughty areaway with an oblique of gaslight and a black well of descending staircase. Show-windows of jade and teas and Chinese porcelains.*

In Hurst's *Humoresque,* Leon Kantor, son of a Lower East Side (Allen Street) shopkeeper, develops an impassioned desire for a violin on his fifth birthday, which his mother secretly purchases with her hard-earned savings, and becomes a world-class violinist, fulfilling her dream as well as his own. The film takes the genesis of the boy-from-the-slums-becomes-virtuoso story, keeping the flavor, and fleshing out its own fascinating spin from the bare bones. The Jewishness is eliminated, Leon Kantor simplified to Paul Borae. This was very common in Hollywood and, to my mind, not particularly objectionable, allowing a more neutral landscape of characters to appeal to the widest audience, most immigrants eager to assimilate in those days and many Jews finding success in Hollywood in spite of anti-Semitism. The film, for once, exceeds the original source, turning a richly detailed, but simple tale of sentiment into a work of art. It is Hollywood hitting on all ten cylinders.

Humoresque is not only one of the greatest films ever, but contains one of Joan Crawford's most breathtaking, iconic, flawless performances. Rarely has she been more fine and understated in her work. She drips glamour. She pierces the senses. Who can forget cynical yet vulnerable Helen Wright drinking herself into oblivion, full of bile and pain yet wistful, looking out into the key lights in breathtaking close-up as she sings "My Sweet Embraceable You," throwing a glass at her reflection in the windows? Or that ending? Wow. Crawford is divine as Helen; she's to die for. Her chemistry with John Garfield (impeccable as Paul Borae) is searing. A rich, kaleidoscopic but simple portrait of a violinist has been turned into pure movie magic.

Interestingly, "Gina" (played by Joan Chandler in the film) does appear in the original story as the sweet potential love interest, but she is an opera singer and minor character.

Johnny Guitar by Roy Chanslor (Written 1953) ★★★★★ *(rootin' tootin' Wild West fun!)*

> *Handsome Johnny Guitar looked the place over and said to Vienna, "What do you do for recreation?"*
> *"I ride," she said.*
> *"I ride, too," Johnny replied. "Got an extra horse?"*
> *Vienna looked at him coldly. "I ride alone and I sleep alone. I don't like men."*
> *"What do you like, Vienna?"*
> *"Money," she said.*
> *Vienna had come from the honky-tonks of Tonopah, Johnny from the Mississippi river boats — both looking for suckers. But lynch-law and*

> *love sat in on their game. And when the chips were down, they had to play the cards as they fell. He drew to his hand and there was a gun in it; she drew to hers...*
>
> Roy Chanslor, *Johnny Guitar*

If the back jacket (above) sounds good, it gets even better! Roy Chanslor's paperback edition is dedicated to Joan Crawford and has a brief introduction (and endorsement) by our gal (signed). Like Crawford, the novel doesn't disappoint and neither does the character of Vienna. Not since Emma Peel and Crawford has a woman been so sassy and "fascinating," as Crawford accurately puts it in her introduction. The fact my gal thought so makes me admire both of them all the more. *Johnny Guitar* is a wonderful, romantic paean to the West with interesting, fully-fleshed characters (even the minor ones), a great hero and heroine, and a sense of nobility and soul that actually brought a tear to my eye. While the film is loads of quirky fun with a cult following, it has never been one of my favorites, Crawford being styled too butch in it for my tastes (although her performance is electric), a stereotype many carry of her which is actually hugely inaccurate. But the novel is superb and ultimately moving, while not skimping on a sense of fun. With its gritty women who can ride and shoot as good as men and tough, carousing cowboys who often are as sentimental and full of longing as women, it paints a romantic portrait of frontier living, particularly its loneliness, which probably isn't far from the mark. Chanslor's ability to get into the hearts and minds of his characters and make human beings out of them, while the narrative runs on classic lines of high adventure, is what makes it so special.

Johnny Guitar opens well with the town drunk spinning fabricated legends about his past and "the fine bold woman in black pants and red silk shirt" who rides into town. Already the latter is given a touch of myth. This audacious woman who sets tongues (and hearts) on fire is Vienna. She has a stud between her legs, not the mare, just to shock local prudes. Through Johnny Guitar's eyes (another enigmatic and bold character), we meet her ("the most remarkable-looking young woman [he] had ever seen and he'd seen a good many"). With her short, curly, dark hair with its lustrous sheen; tight, grey riding breeches that reveal long supple legs; jeweled bracelet; large eyes; and the thirty-eight Smith and Wesson strapped on her boyish hips, she rather fits Crawford to a T, particularly her strength, although I visualized a young Sean Young. And this: "Her mouth was wide, her lips full and red, bold red, painted, but there was no rouge upon her oval, olive, small, foreign-looking face." So much for those who think Crawford re-writes the source material exclusively to suit her; often times, she rather is following it religiously, even with her appearance. In any case, Vienna is rumored to be the gal of a notorious outlaw, The Dancing Kid, but she runs a saloon called The Bills (with many denominations lacquered beneath the wood of the bar) and is too proud to give any man a tumble. Johnny Guitar, a gambler, sets his

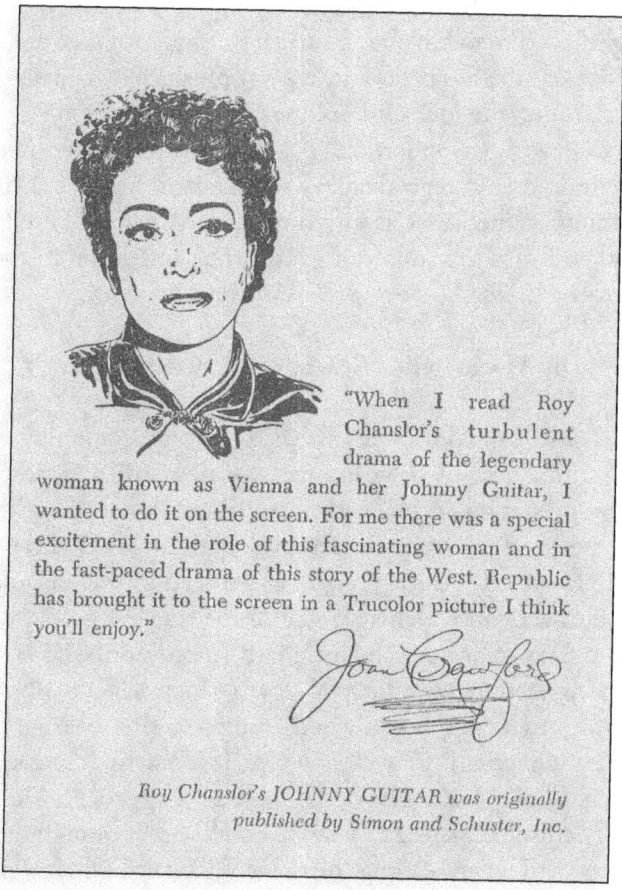

Our gal endorses the book.

odds on her and together — although she resists and fights his amorous attempts and he is gallant enough to stay respectful — they fight off lynch mobs engineered by jealous rabble rouser Emma Small. Even Emma has backstory that makes her somewhat sympathetic. Great details make the setting almost palpable, such as when Johnny Guitar eats stew made of elk. There's a keen sensitivity to women, to their distrust of men based on bad experiences, and to the vulnerability they faced in a wild land. Their grit and concessions to femininity seem real enough. No one is quite as he or she appears, and the romance between Johnny Guitar and Vienna, their mutual bravery and eventual real love, has a kind of poetry.

And what about these great witty lines: Of Emma Small — "Sheriff Boggs, Small and his wife, riding side-saddle like a lady, but not looking like one, were riding up to the hitching post" or "Vienna was halfway down the stairs, one hand holding her peignoir about her, the other her thirty-eight" or "'I'm talkin' about Turkey Ralson. Trot him out.'" Or: "Bull Moose unlocked the heavy door by the simple device of putting the barrel of his gun against the lock and pulling the trigger."

In any case, a truly wonderful Western — simple, but with many layers that make it unique. It reawakens a lost idealism that was as much a part of the taming of the West as anything else. When Johnny Guitar and Vienna ride off into the sunset, it brings the same lump in the throat as when Dorothy in *The Wizard of Oz* finds home.

Letty Lynton by Marie Belloc Lowndes (Written 1931) ★★★½

Marie Belloc Lowndes' *Letty Lynton*, based on the infamous Madeleine Smith poisoning case of 1857 in Glasgow, Scotland, is a downer — disheartening and depressing — and yet another illustration of the horrible, restrictive position allotted females in a "man's world" (these prejudices reflected in law) and societal pressures that lead to tragedy and unhappiness. The film version which starred a drop-dead-gorgeous, vampy Joan Crawford in the titular role actually greatly improved the book, its positive finale more in keeping with the real story (which had a reasonably happy ending, Smith marrying happily and living to a ripe, old age). The Letty of the novel is affectingly only eighteen years old with a child's immaturity, emotions and guilt. Like Crawford, she has "large, deep-blue eyes" and a "delicately chiseled, perfectly formed oval face," although one does not picture Crawford when reading the novel. Like far too many girls, Letty's immense beauty and sexual allure is her downfall because of the passion it inspires in men who feel they can buy or own beauty like lords of the kingdom. "Her naturally wavy hair was of that exquisite and unusual tint the French call blond centre…[E]very movement of her lissom young body was unconsciously graceful, easy, and free," we are told, the latter statement an irony. The "lovely Letty Lynton," as men and women in her hometown village of Thark refer to her, not only attracts "almost every man she met," but women, too, "were softened and subjugated." The girl's "less pleasing attributes were masked by a sweet temper, and what old people call 'a pretty manner.'" However, Letty is the daughter of upwardly mobile, enormously wealthy, and old-fashioned parents, John and Alice who are very conscious of their social position; Alice is also emotionally cold and, in many respects, blatantly unloving to her daughter, preferring and favoring her son, Bob (another eerie parallel to Crawford's life where emotionally withholding mother Anna blatantly favored son Hal). This cold, forbidding, and dishonest snobbery — whatever its root may be-- is the cornerstone of the tragedy that ensues.

There is a prescient of what is to come even as the story opens with Letty finally able to spread her wings and explore her budding sexuality, as any healthy girl does, after being sheltered by her parents who, not wanting Letty mixing with townspeople, don't invite young people around. Letty is learning to exploit her desirability or play with its power in the way children play with matches, delighted by her power over men and yet somewhat frightened by it. The opening scene reveals Alice Lynton's unforgiving bias against her young daughter as she blasts Noel Maclean, a "staid Scot" double Letty's age who is employed at the Lyntons' chemical factory, for making overtures to Letty, tellingly adding, "Not but what I expect it was a good bit Letty's fault." Her husband reminds her the girl is only 18. Later the shocking depth of this animosity or lack of feeling for Letty will expose itself when Letty is brought before a jury on charges of murder and Alice refuses to offer support. With intentional irony, Lowndes tells us that Mrs. Lynton is described by even those "who did not much care for her" as "an excellent wife and mother." She is, in fact, without tenderness or mercy for Letty and will be more worried about her own shame than as to whether or not her daughter hangs for murder.

Letty is not remotely attracted to the stolid Maclean, but enjoys breaking his reserve and having the upper hand in that way. She has a "sick terror" that her "foolishly worded notes" to Maclean are going to be discovered by her parents and sobs when she is told she must write him to break everything off. Her father and loyal, loving housekeeper, Mrs. Squelch ("Squelchy" as Letty affectionately calls her) have compassion for the girl's dilemma, Mrs. Squelch regarding Letty as her own child. After being forced to "break" with Maclean, Letty runs across the half Swedish, half British Axel Ekeborn, a handsome rake who immediately is attracted to the beauty and shortly passionately in love and lust with her. She notices that he has beautiful teeth, but does not "notice that he also had a loose-lipped mouth, characteristic of its owner's idle sensuous nature." Mutually attracted to one another, Letty determines to meet him again and soon they are having passionate trysts in the barn (which, however steamily portrayed, evidently involve only kisses, not actual sex). Axel is an extremely ardent and persistent lover, whispering to her in French, crushing her to him (Lowndes frequently lapses into purplish prose), having an almost hypnotic sexual effect on Letty as he does on many women. He deceives her by telling her that he is of an important background and, meanwhile, he is carrying on an ardent, if contemptuous affair with his landlady's daughter, the hardscrabble and completely smitten Kate Roker. Although his feelings for Letty are genuine, he is more than a little swayed by her wealth as much as her exquisite looks. He enjoys with a "fierce, animal delight" the passionate response he rouses in Kate to his caresses, but otherwise cares nothing for her. Letty, fickle and alluring as she may be, is also relatively inexperienced, her dalliances made all the more exciting by the subterfuge parental disapproval forces her to adopt. The addiction of these passionate flirtations cause her to get well in over her head.

The whole novel teems with deception, although the style is somewhat stilted which detracts at times. Kate has deceived herself that Axel is going to marry her, although he is at times blatantly cruel and openly scorns her. She then channels her pain and rage towards Letty, since Axel is her only salvation in an otherwise drudge existence. Axel has deceived Letty about his social position. Letty is dishonest with each of her admirers, intoxicated as she is by her burgeoning sexual powers and the idea of love. Infatuated and influenced by Axel initially, she becomes distracted by other admirers when he is called back to Sweden for an extended period and meets the much-older but respectable Lord Tintagel. Tintagel is widely encouraged and nurtured by her family as "suitable." Caught up in the whirlwind of romance and social expectation, Letty is soon betrothed, but Axel has no intention of letting go. He holds her love letters threateningly over her head, which could be seen as "breach of promise" if she doesn't marry him and bring disgrace to her family. In an agony of misery and unreasoning terror, Letty sees suicide as the only way out and secures poison from her father's factory, intending to end her own life. Then she comes upon another solution to rid herself of her cruel tormentor — murder.

Although Letty remains sympathetic, her situation wrenching, her lovers are less so. Lord Tintagel is downright icky. Loathing "fast girls" and believing "no man's lips ever touched hers," this older man is wetting his lips (so to speak) at the idea of possessing a young virgin, expecting chastity even while he is a "man of the world." Maclean's still waters run deep and dirty; he becomes monstrous in the finale. Axel Ekeborn has a "brutally cruel vein in his nature." At one point, in order to manipulate her, he presses Kate to him until she "could have cried out with the bruising pain." He is also willing to blackmail Letty and impose himself, at one point taking her arm in a grip that hurt. Passionately in love with her, he is nonetheless insecure and ruthless.

The enormity of Letty's fear of her mother is revealed early on when, returning from an illicit assignation with Axel in the barn, she sees a light under the door of her bedroom:

> *There came over her a feeling of intense terror; indeed she was so frightened that she sank down and rocked herself to and fro in an agony of fear.*

The great irony and tragedy is that the love letters Letty so dreads her parents seeing immediately come into the hands of the police and are read in Court, making her drastic step for self-protection all for naught; although torrid, they prove disappointingly tame, too. She has committed the ultimate crime for nothing. The bloodthirsty townspeople, in fact, suspect (and hope) something more scandalous has been omitted from this correspondence and Dr. Powell, the Coroner who is biased against Letty, has to assure them otherwise. The town is also prejudiced against Letty, believing her to be a grand girl who stole a humble girl's lover, hope for her guilt, and "in their inflamed imaginations, see her swinging."

(*Spoilers!*) Although she will be acquitted, Letty's fate is still disturbingly unpleasant. Her father, shockingly, takes it upon himself to call off her engagement to Lord Tintagel. Then, because there is scandal attached to the family and animosity in the town, the Lyntons decide to spend the time abroad. However, Letty is not to go with them. Her father instructs her to marry Maclean and live in New Zealand with him. Letty is terrified and tells him that she hated Maclean even kissing her, but "with a touch of brutality she has never yet heard in that voice which had always been kind and indulgent to her," he retorts, "What does that matter?" To my mind, this is a form of pimping, even if allegedly he wants to protect Letty from the aftermath of the trial. Also deeply disturbing is his reaction when Letty asks him how he could break her engagement with Tintagel — he feels a "physical shrinking" from his child and demands how he could do otherwise. Why such a reaction? Is it because of the disgrace? Or is it because Letty's quasi-"impurity" is more damning than murder, that repellent worldview that treats female sexual autonomy as a crime? Maclean becomes villainous, no longer Letty's worshipful slave. He "crushes her to him" and says, "You are going to be mine — all mine, and only mine. If you ever look at another man, I will kill you, Letty." The logical thing would be to refuse to marry him, but evidently girls had few chances to survive economically without marriage. The poor girl was actually a slave of sorts all along, powerless legally and socially beyond her sex appeal.

One can't help feeling the observation of her father's solicitor Mr. Kennington is on the money:

> *Poor little girl, poor foolish little girl! If she had been his daughter, she would never have got into this dangerous scrape. But then his wife was very unlike Letty's mother. Mrs. Kennington was a soft, cushiony woman whom her children went in all their troubles.*

Love on the Run by Alan Green and Julian Brodie (Written 1936) ★★★★★

> "*Douglas plodded up Mayfair's smuggest avenue. On either side of him bulky town houses flung silent taunts at the Spirit of Architecture... When Douglas came to the corner opposite the church, he had to push his way through a throng of curious onlookers until, reaching the curb, he was stopped momentarily by a bobby. He produced his invitation, one of the many granted to the press of the world, and was permitted to cross the thoroughfare.*
>
> *As he reached the opposite pavement, something made him glance to the right.*
>
> *It was the turning point of his life.*
>
> *All other eyes were focused on the crowd entering the church; his alone saw the little side entrance halfway down the cross street. And he alone saw emerge from it a girl in bridal costume. As he watched, she ran down a little flight of steps and, veils streaming behind her, disappeared into a taxicab.*"
>
> Alan Green and Julian Brodie, *Love on the Run*

The film *Love on the Run* has its moments and rewards for fans of its stars (Joan Crawford, Clark Gable, and Franchot Tone), Crawford's utter chic and élan being one of them, but is no heavyweight against other screwball comedies of that era. The original novel, published in the March 1936 *Cosmopolitan*, however, is an absolute delight of the first magnitude — light as a feather in the vein of P.G. Wodehouse with intersecting characters and stories and dry humor, telling of a runaway aristocratic bride aided by a journalist. It also reveals how fascinated America and England were in aviation at a time when aviation was still

Fabulous illustration from *Cosmopolitan* by Mario Cooper, spanning two pages.

in its infancy and aviators, both male and female, were taking derring-do maiden voyages across the world. The bride, Lady Beatrice Chesingham, and her gallant "knight," Douglas Anthony, make their getaway via a robin's egg blue Karp-Kloppenburg plane (pinched by Douglas from a German baron and baroness), the story capturing the daredevil spunk of flight. In screwball fashion, as in the film, the bride, posing as the baroness (who is locked in a hotel bathroom with the baron), is handed a bouquet of red roses before the flight and discovers that it contains a map of fortifications. Thereby, the baroness was most likely a spy, the plot growing ever nuttier and enjoyably escapist. Spiriting Lady Beatrice away from an unwanted, impending marriage to the Duke of Gloughm, Douglas promises to travel with and help her "get wherever you have to go for safety" if, without revealing her whereabouts, he can write daily news articles about her and her escape. Meanwhile, rival reporter (and Douglas' best friend) Barny Pells, super-sleuth Chief Inspector Cables, and growing numbers of police and gendarmes are hot on their trail.

I miss classical stories like this one, told in traditional literary fashion, be they comedy or drama or horror. It was what made stories exciting to me and inspired me to want to do it myself. "Love on the Run" is completely realized; it's written with élan and love of language (including intelligent — not dumbed-down — vocabulary) and tongue-firmly-in-cheek. If you want proof of how degraded our once-sublime culture has become, look no further than the quality of literature and dearth of it in today's magazines when once the short story was revered with romance, westerns, mysteries, literary, and every type of entertainment under the sun packed into one issue, enhanced by gorgeous (hand-done) artwork and design, and no base-level language to get the points across. In fact, stories retained their individuality without the language watered down to banal, colloquial sameness and crudity. In "Love on the Run," turns of phrase have delicacy and wit. The plot is a corker, shades of Evelyn Waugh and Nicholas Blake in the escalating inanity and fun. Sophistication is now about as extinct as the do do bird.

The banter between the leads recalls *The Thin Man* (and D.L. Sayers' Peter Wimsey and Harriet Vane), proving there were many romantic couples who had it in this period, with one of my favorite bits below:

> *Douglas and Beatrice found deck chairs and settled back placidly to watch the lights of Cap d'Ail slide by the port rail.*
>
> *Beatrice sighed. "Heavenly, isn't it?"*
>
> *"Mmmmmm. It's practically perfect."*
>
> *Beatrice detected a shade of emphasis he had placed on the word "practically." "Something missing?" she asked.*
>
> *"I don't know whether it's missing — or just concealed," he said vaguely.*
>
> *"My, how mysterious."*
>
> *He nodded. "It's probably better that way."*
>
> *"Better to be mysterious?"*
>
> *He nodded again.*
>
> *"Why?"*
>
> *"Because it's one of those things you either understand — or you wouldn't. Explaining it is needless. Superfluous."*
>
> *"Should I know what you're talking about?"*
>
> *"I think so. At least, I hope so."*
>
> *"Do you know?"*
>
> *"Yes, I know." Then he added gloomily, "And what's more, I think I know what it will all come to — a neat sacrificial-suicide on the altar of delusion."*

Or this bit of unabashed romanticism:

Her hand went to his lapel. He couldn't tell whether the gesture was tender — or just defensive. Neither could she.
Beatrice looked up at him. "The moon will come back," she said slowly. "It always does."
"But tonight won't. It never does."

One of my favorite scenes involves Barny Pells stumbling on a den of German spies because he was following the baroness (the real one — not Lady Beatrice impersonating the baroness). The baroness quickly concocts a ruse to throw off the reporter. The agents begin rapid whispers, some of them in favor of slitting Barny's throat (unbeknownst to him), instead of going through with the baroness' elaborate pretence, but she wins out and a deliciously absurd séance is concocted in the dark:

Almost at once the shuffling sound occurred not many feet to Barny's left. But at the same instant came a duplicate sound from his right. In unison two voices spoke. "I am here."
Adolph broke in. "There has been some confusion. Who is with us?"
"I," spoke the voice at Barny's left, "am Napoleon Bonaparte of Corsica — the great General."
"And I," came from Barny's right, "am Arthur Wellesley, Duke of Wellington — the greater *General."*
"Great heavens!" said Adolph. "this is most embarrassing."
"Not for me," said Napoleon.
"Certainly not for me," said Wellington.

The whole thing dissolves into name calling and a scuffle between the phony generals and each saying, "Why, you — !" Total silly fun. The finale of the novel, too, is a precious, brilliant and witty exchange of telegrams between all parties — as perfect and spectacular an ending as fireworks.

Amazingly, Lady Beatrice and Douglas really do hijack a couturier truck where the lady finds samples of the latest Parisian designs in the back and returns, "her arms laden with billowing organdy and crepe." (So it's not just an Adrian-inspired moment for Joan? In the film, she also climbs over the front seat to investigate the fashions in the back and returns in a sparkly Adrian dress — what else?)

Surprisingly, although in the film he annoyed the b'Jesus (a word Joan once used, spelled that way) out of me, Franchot Tone actually seems a fairly good fit as Barny, the alcohol-guzzling rival newshound, but the recalcitrant bride played by a to-die-for-glamorous Crawford onscreen (with character's name changed to Sally Parker) seemed tailor-made for Carole Lombard (although, being terribly biased, I'd keep my gal anyway). Neither does Douglas (renamed Michael in the film) quite bring to mind Clark Gable. Unfortunately, too, the screenplay takes liberties with the plot, most grievously omitting the priceless séance mentioned above. One suspects, however, they wouldn't be able to do justice to it, anyway, since the overall result of the film is tepid.

In all, a superb example of Golden Age magazine fiction at its best, screwball lightness with a little adventure, romance, humor, and innocent fun — turned into a film that fairly flattened it all with the exception of a few good moments and the incomparable sight of Joan Crawford at her most sophisticated. (Oh, that lost art of sophistication!) In fact, Crawford's iconic Hollywood glamour sums up what the story has — pure pizzazz.

Marry for Money by Katharine Brush (Written 1937) ★★★★
filmed as *Mannequin*

Katharine Brush's story "Marry for Money," the inspiration for *Mannequin*, appeared in the February 1937 issue of *Hearst's International Cosmopolitan* and, as standard in the Golden Age of magazine fiction, was beautifully laid out with lavish and gorgeous, slightly racy illustrations by John La Gatta. It differs from the movie, although the core is similar.

Jessie Cassidy (portrayed by an incongruously airbrushed Joan Crawford in the film version) comes from the slums in Dorchester, Massachusetts, where her parents "had nine children in the small hot rooms in the back [of a restaurant]…and *in the alleyway.*" (emphasis added). Does it get any grittier than that? (Couldn't help picturing the authoress churning out this steamy stuff.) A tall girl, Jessie makes an early marriage to a fleshy, slow-witted school friend Ernest "Hippo" Braun and has to sleep with men to survive while still in her teens, sexually exploited even by Hippo's father who gives her enough gifts to enable her escape. After a series of checkroom jobs and some exploitive landladies, at age twenty, she becomes a showgirl in Gerald Howell's "Indiscretions of 1928." Her signature frock was black satin.

> *She was almost beautiful by that time, anyway. She had a figure beautifully proportioned, and she had that skin, like French-vanilla ice cream, and she had that heavy autumn-colored hair. Her eyes were hazel. They were commonplace, but she had long thin eyelashes that she could*

thicken with mascara and black, noticeable eyebrows straight and swift across her face, and a good nose, and a full mouth. It was enough.

As in the film, she does many costume changes in her show, occasionally wearing towering head pieces. Jessie's story actually tallies with Joan's tales from *Conversations with Crawford* on what it was like to be a showgirl in a good revue. "She went to many parties after the theater, and she met many men, and she had never even dreamed of such prosperity...Every day Christmas."

Jessie meets a good-looking good-for-nothing, Harry Skarsen (renamed Eddie in the film, but well embodied by handsome Alan Curtis). He spends her money extravagantly, even after the show closes, and soon the Golden Goose isn't laying any more eggs. After behaving moodily, Harry finally brings up Ben Hertzig, a wealthy man from Jessie's chorus girl days who had a penthouse like a nightclub and a thing for her. Jessie remembers Hertzig's "kindly, ugly face and a big nose and scant black hair. He used to run his hand across his head, from right to left, to smooth the single lock that tried to cover all his baldness." (And this is the basis for the Spencer Tracy character!) Harry and Jessie are back in the grim surroundings she escaped, which she regards "uncomplainingly," thinking it temporary, but Harry then hatches his scheme. Jessie should marry Hertzig for his money, then divorce him and "in the generous settlement Hertzig would make upon her, and on the lifetime alimony he would pay...they could live like a couple of kings."

Since Harry suggested it, it "was done." Ben snaps up the chance to marry Jessie and, as they work on her divorce from Hippo, he works on

One of the beautiful illustrations by John LaGatta.

her trousseau, which they select together from Veronique's, an exclusive dressmaking establishment. "[Ben] knew precisely what he wanted Jessie to wear, and how he wanted her to look — he understood that her flamboyance needed framing without accent." He selects costumes for their sail to Paris and for the races and all the glamorous nights they have planned. (Makes Jessie seem like a beautiful possession, to my mind.)

Jessie learns that Ben, as she thinks of him now, once had a plain-looking wife who died of pneumonia. She is swept up on the whirlwind honeymoon preparations like "a full-length movie packed into one reel." Money is fun and Paris is grand, she discovers, and Ben proves generous and kind and sweet, making her feel both grateful and guilty. Meanwhile, she sends Harry postcards from all the hotspots in Paris with careful messages.

Finally the stock market crashes and, bankrupt now, Ben gives Jessie the chance to leave him. She sobs, but refuses while he's down, inwardly wrestling with herself, feeling this is only temporary and hoping still to reunite with scamp Harry. Seven years later she's still in this "arranged" marriage, since Harry predictably deserted her. Ben and Jessie's circumstances become reduced, they both are forced to work, and she becomes a mannequin at Veronique's. She no longer thinks about Harry; if still in love with him, she doesn't want to know it. A certain pathos, but not an entirely unhappy ending.

Although well-written and probably accurate for those Depression era days, the old "beauty and the beast" theme irks me, as if it's okay to judge a woman by beauty but women should look past it in men — in fact, embrace beasts. If beauty is only skin deep, why is there a double standard about homely women?

The film isn't one of my favorites, although Crawford is sensitive, beautiful, soft and mournful-eyed in it, making a suitable Jessie, and some of the dialogue is fine. Still, these shop girl roles were wearing thin for Crawford at the end of the 1930s.

Mildred Pierce by James M. Cain (Written 1941) ★★★★★

James M. Cain was one of the great pulp fiction writers of the early 20th Century and a number of his novels made successful transitions to the screen. *Mildred Pierce* struck me as a departure in style, being much less terse than most of his work, and made such an impact that for awhile, I wanted to open up a chain of restaurants. It tells the story of a put-upon housewife with "really beautiful legs" in Depression era California who leaves her shiftless husband and climbs from waitress to restaurateur to win the love of her monstrous daughter Veda. Her love, in fact, is almost an obsession, rising to mythic, Faustian proportions. ("[Mildred] knelt beside the bed,...took the lovely creature in her arms, and kissed her, hard, on the mouth.") The kiss becomes a potent symbol; Mildred sells her soul for Veda, yet remains sympathetic and real. Her passion for Veda is also symbolic of her own unattainable goals. She envies the child's snobbism "which hinted at things superior to her own commonplace nature" and fears it; beneath it is a "cold, cruel, coarse desire to...hurt her." Also startlingly believable (though seldom depicted) is her favoritism of one child over the other, Mildred's guilty relief when the favored child is not the one "taken" by illness. Although the story is often viewed as an indictment of bourgeois values and upwardly mobile ambition, Cain was mirroring a hidden side of human relationships — incestuous, twisted, complex, unseemly, the discontent and skeletons in every soul.

Since a determined Mildred makes her way in a man's world during an era of limited alternatives for females, the story is a favorite of women's studies classes. After becoming "the great American institution...a grass widow with two small children to support," she uses her sexuality and ability to cook as survival skills, too inexperienced for any other work. Initially she sleeps with lecherous admirer Wally (unlike the film where she rejects his advances but uses his friendship) so she won't have to break open her Scotch and can get $6 for it. She is baser in her sexuality than the film Mildred, in fact, but like her cinema counterpart, her motives have Veda at its core. In both versions, oily Monty Beragon insinuates his way into Mildred's life and shortly mirrors the same parasitic snobbery as Veda, as well as her cool contempt and treachery. He again symbolizes Mildred's failure to realize her ambitions and, in film and novel, Veda and Monty verbally deride her.

In one scene, the novel's Veda, smoking, maliciously relays Monty's intimate jibes about her mother including, "Never take the mistress if you can get the maid."

One of the wonderful illustrations inside book depicting Mildred (Joan Crawford) with Veda (Ann Blyth) and Kay (Jo Ann Marlowe).

> *For some time Mildred found [Veda's] taunts nothing but a jumble... Presently, however, words began to have meaning again, and she heard Veda saying: "After all, Mother, even in his darkest days, Monty's shoes are custom made."*
> "They ought to be. They cost me enough."
> *Mildred snapped this out bitterly, and for a second wished she hadn't. But the cigarette, suddenly still in mid-air, told her it was news to Veda, quite horrible news, and without further regret, she rammed home her advantage: "You didn't know that, did you?"*

The film gave Joan Crawford one of her most iconic roles, her triumphant comeback, and an Academy Award. Some readers argue that it changed Cain's intentions, which I would greatly contest. While glossing over some of the more explicit seediness and toughness, as so many Hollywood films of the time did, it nevertheless captures the sordid undercurrent, cynicism, and tensions of the characters beautifully. It maintains the genesis of the relationships and themes with a dream cast; stellar black-and-white photography; pivotal confrontations; and a moody Max Steiner score. The hugest difference in the film version is the addition of the murder, but it doesn't eclipse the story of ill-fated ambition and maternal obsession. Both versions have shock endings, the novel's as hard-hitting and harrowing, if not more so, without a murder. Interestingly, the film shows a washerwoman on the courthouse steps in the final frame, a symbol of oppression in the face of "justice." Some view it as a backlash against female mobility, Mildred being "punished" for leaving her conventional role and returned to "housewifely" duties, but I see it as the unforgiving pull of fate. Cain used this theme of desperate individuals "breaking out" but being caught in fate's cogs in many of his novels, the oppressed unable to free themselves by tainted motivations. Mildred, however, while ostensibly "restored" to Bert, is also forced to end her thankless obsession.

Crawford is a superb Mildred, her performance admirably restrained. She looks suitably taut beneath the surface while as glamorous and icily sexy a hard-shell dame as celluloid dreams provide, perfect for film noir. Ann Blyth has a sneering, fresh-faced insolence as a great counterpoint to her suppressed rage and suffering. Apparently James M. Cain must've approved of the leading lady, since he said, "Love with Joan Crawford might be a strenuous business, perhaps a little difficult at times. But well worth the run." Sounds almost as good as the original film ads.

Not Too Narrow…Not Too Deep by **Richard Sale (Written 1936)**
★★★★★

Not Too Narrow…Not Too Deep is a quiet masterpiece, made into a fascinating film of equal caliber starring Clark Gable and Joan Crawford, an allegorical, thought-provoking tale of spiritual redemption and liberation on the high seas as a motley band of convicts escape a French penal colony accompanied by a mysterious figure called Jean Cambreau. Succeeding as both a brilliant adventure tale and a deeper philosophical exegesis, this novel is as resonant today as ever, its rich, beautifully presented themes neither narrow nor shallow, but infinitely moving and complex. Who is Cambreau? This question takes on many profound layers with no simple answers. While the action remains fast-paced and thrilling, the ideas are equally so, eschewing fear-based, fire and brimstone notions of religious faith. Fascinating especially that this novel was written in 1936 prior to World War II and contains a fascist German character, Carl Weiner, a seditionist, yet it presents a possibility of hope for even the darkest dregs of humanity. It's not fatalistic, even when showing predetermination. Interesting, too, is that the toughest of men become weak when stripped of their defenses; all flesh is weak when faced with mortality, no matter how tough the shell. "You've lived your life believing in your flesh," Richard Pennington, the professor convicted of peacetime espionage, tells Philip LaSalle, the narrator. "You were a doctor, weren't you? Could you ever touch the power behind the flesh, the vital force which quickened the flesh and marked it a man instead of a corpse?…No. That is why I lost my belief in death's finality." LaSalle's plea to Cambreau epitomizes the eternal search:

> *"Then what dies?" I said, straining. "Tell me what dies!"*

The film is an excellent — although not entirely faithful — adaptation. Initial disappointment that no bar dancer Julie (played in the film by

Beautiful, but misleading cover art.

Crawford) appears in the novel quickly evaporates as the story progresses and proves its merit. In the novel, there are no principal female characters, in fact. A Negress, a local prostitute — dragged along for purposes of sexual gratification by George Verne (the rough and virile convict played by Clark Gable in the film) — makes only a brief appearance before she is eliminated from the plot again. Thankfully, Crawford was added to the film and holds her own as gritty, sexy Julie, her chemistry with Gable heating up the screen and working beautifully into the story. Although non-glamorous and wearing seemingly little makeup, she looks beautiful and luminous and is quite appealing and nakedly expressive, a fitting motivation for Verne's redemption. Another fun addition is Monsieur Pig played by Peter Lorre. Gable has possibly his finest hour as Verne (and is much more attractive than the book's description) and Ian Hunter is perfect as the indomitable, enigmatic Cambreau, his face radiant. The film has punchier lines than its original source; it deserves recognition as a Hollywood classic.

Not Too Narrow...Not Too Deep is a first-rate adventure story and drama; it is also a seminal philosophical book about spirituality. Like the film version, there is nothing sanctimonious about it. Rather it remains a breathtaking exploration into the nature of true faith and power, a power that comes from within through the depth, compassion and resilience of the human spirit.

One Man's Secret by Rita Weiman (Written 1943) ★★★★½
Filmed in 1947 as *Possessed*

"It would not have occurred to Dean Steward that six months after his wife's death, he could ask another woman to marry him.

> *He was standing at his study window when the knock came that proved to be destiny. At first it was lost in the splash of waves against the rocks, a rhythmic sound at once soothing and stirring. Or it may have been his absorption in the view, the swordlike streak of gold that followed sunset, the waters foaming where they hit below the window, the islands that dotted Long Island Sound glistening like amethysts in the afterglow. Today high tide was at twilight, the hour he loved best. He did not hear the knock at the door.*"
>
> Rita Weiman, *One Man's Secret*

Rita Weiman's *One Man's Secret*, which became the 1947 Joan Crawford film *Possessed*, carries many essences of the film, but differs in significant points, most notably that the story is told from the point of view of Dean Steward (Dean Graham in the film), husband of invalid Pauline, whereas the film was clearly centered on Pauline's nurse, Louise Howell (Crawford) (Gladys Mayden in the story). The storyline is also significantly different in Weiman's novella. In the film, nurse Howell is "possessed" by her love for architect David (Van Heflin) and fears that she was responsible for the death of her charge Pauline when Pauline is found drowned off Long Island Sound. In the story — **spoilers**--Dean marries Gladys six months after his wife's suicide (she jumped allegedly from her balcony, although she appeared to be recovering from a debilitating illness that rendered her an invalid and incapable of being a "wife") and his son Wynn, with whom he is close, has an instant hostility towards Gladys. As it turns out, Wynn's room was next to his mother's and he heard conversations between Gladys and Pauline, leading him to believe Gladys drove his mother to suicide by insinuating that Dean was in love with her. This suspicion, wrested from Wynn, haunts Dean and he finally begins to suspect that it is worse than his son imagined, that Gladys likely pushed Pauline to her death from the balcony. The story continually notes Gladys' strong and white hands "always suggestive of sculpture to Dean."

Gladys is described attractively and Crawford is a credible fit for the character, give or take a few details. ("Dean had never learned her age, but he judged Gladys Mayden to be in her early thirties. She had an untouched virginal quality. There was petal smoothness on her olive skin and in the glass of brown hair brushed back from her ears in soft wide waves. Her mouth, without a sign of rouge, was nevertheless crimson and firm, chiseled like her hands…Sitting there by the fire, in a round-necked brown sweater that hugged her breasts, a tan tweed jacket swung around her shoulders, and that anxious look in her eyes, she seemed more human than he had ever seen her.") Crawford has a soft essence in the film, yet definitely the psychological torment that grows in the character of Gladys, clearly troubled from the onset. The rocky cliffs and water, which figure so significantly in the story, are used to great effect in the film, "troubled waters" (literally) another motif, water being a symbol of sexuality in dreams.

Interestingly, — *(Spoilers!)* — in the film, Louise Howell, although driven to murder, does not murder Pauline; she murders her unrequited love David. In the story, Gladys indeed killed Pauline, hatching the plot with a man who was her tormentor since a child and is still blackmailing her, although it is unclear as to whether they are having a relationship. It is insinuated in the story that Gladys genuinely loves Dean, in spite of her treachery, which always makes things wrenching. Both film and story are gripping and well told with an evocative setting and great Gothic angst. Raymond Massey as Dean in the film is surprisingly bland, as compared to Dean in the original story, yet I couldn't help picturing Massey as I read. Crawford is magnificently wrought and appealing in the film, her vulnerability befitting the character, and kudos to her for the changes in storyline that make the woman more sympathetic and not the alleged overt villainess. That said, I confess to being wholly sympathetic to Gladys of the story, on her side and pained by her tragic downfall. She is the cornered animal hunted down by men (as it turns out). Unlike the film, where Dean's daughter has an initial hostility towards Louise, in the story his son has the animus. Then Dean's friend, Max, an attorney, closes in on poor Gladys in the finale, stripping away all her defenses until the tortured soul jumps from the balcony, the thing coming full circle. When, in this final showdown, Weiman makes an allusion to law (Max) vs. criminal (Gladys), it is impossible, in my estimate, not to intensely dislike the self-righteous and ruthless Max, pressing mercilessly on a woman who is clearly frightened and tortured. In fact, Weiman, to her credit, makes Gladys not a stock "evil character," as so many authors of this sort of story do (although I personally am always sympathetic to the stigmatized female anyway), but tragically vulnerable. In one breathtaking moment this defenselessness pierces especially. Dean threatens that if what he suspects is even close to true, he'll kill Gladys on the spot: "Her answer came, and there was no life in it. None at all. 'I almost wish you would.'"

Backstory increases my sympathy for Gladys and makes me rue the men who do her in or "bring her to justice" in a way that somehow seems more cold-blooded than the crime itself. Apparently she was an impoverished girl, living a hellish life under the thumb of her mother. It seems inconceivable why Wynn would find it so reprehensible that a poor girl would "scheme" to marry his father. Why shouldn't she want to better her chances, particularly given that Pauline is infirm and initially not deemed likely to recover? If Gladys' story is true, the man who hatched the scheme for her to marry Dean and masterminded Pauline's murder has been tormenting her since age sixteen. The girl was a victim, whichever way you slice it, and there is no real glory in seeing her driven to tragedy. Crawford's reworking of plot is much kinder. Yet Weiman, as noted above, seems to also retain sympathy for Gladys and remnants of that sympathy are found in Dean's protective reflex towards her even with the knowledge that she was responsible for his wife's murder.

Again, *One Man's Secret* is found in an issue of *Cosmopolitan* magazine in the Golden Age of magazine literature and illustration. Boy, has "Cosmo" nose-dived and become shallow trash, a huge contrast from its incarnation in the glory days. In this issue, there are no less than twelve pieces of fiction, all gorgeously and lavishly illustrated, including a novel, two serials, and several novellas. Articles are varied and there are many fascinating ads and references to the war and women's involvement in it. The entire issue is a treasure and is proof of how lucky writers like Rita Weiman were able to make a good living from freelance writing with short stories, a reality that is hard to imagine in today's market when magazine fiction is practically nonexistent and certainly not showcased with such love and care. In all, *One Man's Secret* is an excellent Gothic potboiler and romantic suspense piece turned into a memorable film of similar ilk which provided a role for Crawford that resulted in an Academy Award nomination.

Our Dancing Daughters (Novelized) by Winifred Van Duzer (Written 1928) ★★½

This movie spin-off was definitely designed to appeal to the flaming youth of the time, particularly Joan Crawford fans, and it's an interesting window into her flapper era personality, a completely different persona than the latter era one most familiar today. Obviously the usual cheesy pabulum was being fed to young "frills" of the day, as a list of popular romance novels on the back jacket proves. The descriptions are now quaint and amusing: "Sally's Shoulders: The story of a girl who bore all the family burdens and how she eventually found happiness. Honey Lou, or the Love Wrecker: This is the story of the first year of Honey Lou's married life and how it almost came to grief through the efforts of a 'love wrecker.' The Petter: Because life seemed just a gay series of petting parties to 'Merry' Locke, she did not recognize the Real Thing when it came along." We're told these "romances caused a tremendous sensation when they first appeared as newspaper serials." Interestingly, in one of Crawford's early letters, she breathlessly and romantically promises a boyfriend to stop "petting parties," pledging her heart to him! Yep, girls evidently lived up to the images they were fed and *Our Dancing Daughters* is more along that line, its jazz baby role model embodied by Crawford who in her flapper days was cute and doe-eyed and brimming with pep and hey-hey exuberance, always itching to dance, feet ever moving.

Winifred Van Duzer's novelization of the film that launched our gal to stardom stays pretty much on course, stretching a story that's mostly champagne bubbles anyway about the romantic affairs of three "bright young things" led by spirited Diana Rand (Crawford) who revel until dawn at the Yacht Club. Although some of the dialogue is inexplicably altered, the kinetic frivolity of our modern maiden, down to poses struck in the film, is recreated. Diminutive Diana wears the "highest heels ever worn on Main Street" and "when anyone save Daddy Seymour Rand ventured to address her as 'Half Pint,' 'Small Change' or 'Demi Tasse,' she was likely to toss back, 'Be yourself! I'm nineteen, I guess!' Then she would flash her gamin grin and rush out to have another lift put on the high heels." (Just how high can they go, one wonders?) There are also numerous references to Diana's "level gray eyes," but as Joan says in *They All Kissed the Bride* — "My eyes are blue!" Her relationship with her parents is more like friendship; they love, champion and adore her.

> *Then with a flourish Diana removed the wrappings and placed the statuette on the table, standing back with her look of delighted awe. "There! Don't you love it, ole Daddy dear?"*
>
> *He looked from the figurine to the girl and in a twinkling she assumed the pose of the little bronze dancer — head back, short hair streaming, her whole body alive with joyous movement.*

She also is the center of action and attention with her party mad set and frequently begged by the crowd at the Yacht Club to do eccentric solo dances. Diana's feminine yet tomboyish appeal and frankness is a contrast to her rival Ann Evart, a blonde "fairy-like creature," daintily petite, even tinier than Diana, and whose childlike fragility and helplessness masks amusingly nail-hard calculation. Ann is a delight, although meant to be the villainess. It's hard not to sympathize and root for her, though all the girls are easy to care about. Ann and her mother Hanna are on the wrong side of the track and their desperate and somewhat devious attempts to get on the right side make one ache. They are have-nots, continually foiled in their attempts to belong, scorned by society, their grim lodgings contrasted with the more lavish homes of the other girls. One can't fault Hanna for wanting to place daughter and herself on Easy Street by any means — who wouldn't? What options did women have then but to be gold diggers? Playing the baby act to appeal to men (an amusing irony in itself), Ann inwardly rebels against it, her duality a hoot. ("I'd like to throw something — and at him, too! He thinks I'm all chalk and water, the poor idiot!") Ann's relationship with Hanna is tense and fraught with resentment (eerily like Crawford's own sadly fractured relationship with her hardscrabble mother Anna).

Ann is not only exploited by Hanna, but also by male sidekick Freddie Sheldon, a brother under the skin who is far more callous than she (using her for fun, then discarding her when she becomes a nuisance while she seems to genuinely love and regard him as a soul mate) yet he comes to no "punishment." Only the immoral behavior of girls bears consequences — this double standard in spite of some rather suffragette attitudes from Diana. When her heartthrob Benny Black supposes that "a girl can drink and carouse and wear no clothes and still be a good girl," Diana cuts him off with, "Oh! Men like you hate to see all your pet prerogatives taken over and improved on by those you've always considered your inferiors — by women. That's it, isn't it? Huh! Tabasco sauce!" (This same Benny draws pictures of Diana's feet, depicting them with mercury wings, its quaintness reminding me of a Lord Peter Wimsey mystery where he intimidates a drug dealer by dressing as a Harlequin!)

The third "daughter" is Beatrice Sheldon, sister of Freddie, whose parents are forbidding and repressive, causing her to sneak around and dress like a frump, although her face is "rounded and exquisite, with long, dark eyes, lips a bit too full for beauty." Her eyes, as Benny observes her in the opening chapter, show "banked fires, sullen, dangerous…" She is "weighted by a beaten spirit," yet rebellious, and wears provocative clothes beneath her "eighteen-ninety" look. She is doomed and punished by the book for having had a prior sexual experience, which her paranoid husband Norman holds cruelly over her head, keeping her in a state of fear and submissiveness after initially pretending to accept her "past." The men, in fact, come off uniformly bad. Freddie is an out-and-out bounder while Benny and Norman are both priggish stuffed shirts, judging girls harshly on their virtue, though strong Diana holds her own with Benny. It's unsure whether the author intended it, but Norman strikes me as a stern, repressive extension of Beatrice's parents. In fact, he's downright scary, his jealousy a form of emotional abuse. Thus, the romantic quandaries. Beatrice loves Norman, but is judged by her past; Ann is forced by her mother to compete with Diana for Benny (and temporarily succeeds); and Diana loves Benny but is judged by her exhibitionist behavior which belies her sensible nature. (The most amusing line comes when Diana, comparing herself with a provocatively attired Beatrice, reflects that "often she [Diana] gave herself over to sinuous hula postures.")

It's interesting that both Beatrice and Ann are leading "double lives" on some level, repressed and with difficult parental relationships, whereas Diana, exuberant and cheeky, remains true to herself, likes herself, and expresses that self freely. Diana's healthy self-esteem evidently stems from her wholesome, supportive relationship with her doting parents.

Basically, this novelization of *Our Dancing Daughters* is silly tripe, an earlier incarnation of *The Best of Everything*, with sensible girl faring best romantically and less sensible ones suffering grief. It was ostensibly popular at the time due to the razzmatazz movie with our bubbly, flaming gal; festive Deco visuals; and youthful cast (and I still love those slinky beaded dresses!). But on paper it's transparently thin. It does its intended job, though, recreating the blazing, frenetic spirit and hokey cautionary tone for young "moderns."

The film, although thin story-wise, is more of a brilliant time capsule of the flapper era with spectacular visuals and a sensational Joan Crawford in a role tailor made for her then-personality and life (she won scores of Charleston trophies at the Coconut Grove and was a belle much like Diana at dances). Equally sensational is Anita Page as Ann. It's hard not to fall in love with these winsome, big-eyed, spirited flappers. Their energy is life-affirming and infectious. As Benny puts it, "You crazy kids! Spending yourself in the glitter!"

The book is illustrated with photos from the film.

Out of the Dark by Ursula Curtiss (Written 1963) ★★★★
Filmed as *I Saw What You Did*

Several of novelist Ursula Curtiss' thrillers were adapted into films as is the case with *Out of the Dark* which was the basis for schlockmeister William Castle's *I Saw What You Did*. Like the film version, the book begins with a sticky sweet scenario of children, including fourteen-year-old Libby Mannering, being left alone before the babysitter arrives as their parents go out for the evening. Unfortunately, the babysitter cancels and the five Mannering children, along with Libby's polite but knowing new friend Kit Austen, are now unsupervised. Sure enough, with the cats away, the mice play naughty and it begins to storm, no less (why wouldn't it?). With twelve words, "I know who you really are and I saw what you did," spoken in breathy tones to impress Libby, Kit makes a prank phone call that unleashes a reign of terror. At the other end of the line in one of her calls is a psychotic killer who lives under an alias in their New Mexico town (Curtiss herself lived in New Mexico). Now he's mad. He's real mad.

Although the film achieves a slightly creepy and sordid undercurrent, this disturbing aspect is much more pronounced and undiluted in the novel. There isn't that kicky '60s sitcom music to distract and killer Foxy

Birucoff (alias Leonard Whelk) is drawn with much more sociopathic detail. Bizarrely enough, since, for whatever reason, these uncanny parallels to her real life crop up in so many Crawford films, in the novel the killer's foster mother took in washing, as had Crawford's mother — a not-so-unusual situation and thus coincidence? The isolated country setting with its stretches of deserted road and bucolic underbrush and Curtiss' pacing are highly effective. I actually refrained from cheating. Her writing is observant and fun with lots of cheeky wit. Great touches include her depiction of family dynamics, such as the mayhem between the untended children when baby Tess "feeling herself abused and not caring by whom, sought with a grim hand for the goldfish in its cloudy bowl." And who can't love the brashness of the scene when this same tyke, feeling in a position of power with no authority figures around, demands an egg: "At five, with her tangled curls and small blue jeans and cowboy boots, she looked much too diminutive to withstand authority. Libby knew better, but she stood in front of the stove, defending it as though it were her virtue..." Few books depict children as cruel. Curtiss shows them as neither cruel nor sweet, but complex, not wholly formed people. Even her description of a heifer who is frequently allowed inside this discordant household by the kids shows sharp, knowing wit:

> *She liked popsicles and bread and peanut butter, and although she did not particularly care for having her tail twisted she allowed Tess and the boys to ride her; their company was better than none. When she had had all she could stand of the children she retired to the chicken house, butting the door open with her dehorned head, and lay down contentedly among the fluffy black bantams. The peacock withdrew his tail in horror, but the bantams had been hopping in and out of her grain dish for months and were old friends.*

The suspense is well handled with some nice turns of phrase ("He saw her shadow first, aimed at him like a weapon, and then, with the intense curiosity of fear and hatred, her belted raincoat and kerchief as she moved closer into the light at the far end of the bridge") and, as always, humor ("And although he was almost dense enough to be exhibited, [Fingaard] was eminently respectable, and highly regarded"). Humor in horror is like that give in the bridge.

The film does a competent job of adapting the book, although it's the usual Castle homage to Hitchcock, hammy and silly fun with as many unintentional laughs as chills. John Ireland is effectively sinister as the murderous menace (with his craggy face, how could he not be?), his name simplified to Steve Marak (actually I appreciate Curtiss' use of ethnic European names) and the blander-than-bland Mannering parents seem to have stepped right off the set of *Father Knows Best*. (What a great contrast they make to emotion-intense Joan; Crawford famously said, "If you want the girl-next-door, go next door." Well, here she *is* the *woman* next door, but this dysfunctional broad doesn't come over for sugar!) Although Sarah Lane is in line with my vision of Kit, as described by the book, she comes off as much more innocuous and innocent in the film. Fiction counterparts have interesting character dimensions. Adults and children do what they must do, not necessarily what their true feelings dictate; their own feelings are reckless and sloppy and instinctively self-indulgent which is pretty damn honest. There is no amorous neighbor in the novel, but Crawford's Amy is a nice addition to the film, a box office drawing card. I enjoy her tender chemistry with former co-star (and lover) John Ireland (palpable, even if he - er - sticks it to her). She lends a touch of old Hollywood glamour to the proceedings, although it's tiresome that better outlets weren't provided for her talents than these all-too-tiny and minor parts requiring her to inevitably call someone a "slut" in the way only Joan can. People now make fun of her adaptation to a situation she had little control over. If an actress of a "certain age" wanted to work (and why not?), there wasn't much choice but to be reduced to Grand Guignol. Trust me, even though Crawford gave her all as a pro, she was under no delusion this was *Mildred Pierce*, as her detractors foolishly try to imply. Be that as it may, she's a highlight and with that beehive and chandelier around her neck, what's not to love?

A great page-turning corker with realistic, non-sanctified child protagonists — just the thing for a thunderstorm.

Possessed (Fictionalized) by Jean Francis Webb (Published August 1947) ★★★★

This dramatization of the 1947 film *Possessed* appeared in Screen Romances, the original film being inspired by a Rita Weiman story (also reviewed here). Louise Howell, a nurse in care of "successful, important, rich" Dean Graham's invalid wife Pauline, is in need of healing herself and unrequited love for cold, indifferent, "unpitying" engineer David Sutton allegedly triggers her fragile mental state. Although entertaining, the dramatization underscores some of the absurdities of the script, such as when the doctors examine Louise, catatonic and murmuring "David" incessantly, and ask her how she feels. (The story flashbacks to how she came to be that way.) She stammers, "I feel," but is unable to say much more. "You can't find words. You want to, yet you can't," the doctor says. Then turning to his colleagues, he spits out this hilarious mumbo-jumbo, "Marked thought blocking. Almost complete mutism. We'll try narcosynthesis." Or worse: "She said herself, sir, that before she met him, she never felt anything keenly. Lack of emotional response. Typical schizoid detachment." And now you know why all these women wound up in madhouses with a diagnosis of schizophrenia. Someone in the script department thought this crackshot "analysis" sounded convincing.

Webb's fictionalization, oddly enough, made me realize that not just one, but two women were raving with sexual possession (and you wonder why women are still suffering from low self-esteem with these cultural messages?). Yellow wallpaper indeed. Louise is fatally attracted to David. Pauline, meanwhile, continually raves that Dean is having affairs with his nurses. When later Dean asks Louise to marry him shortly after Pauline commits suicide, one wonders why so many stories of this period posited that a nagging wife needed to be "disposed of" — a misogynist contention in itself. And those water/sexuality images! In no way do you believe that Pauline's jealous delusions were justifiable, but the story hasn't a trace of irony as to why Dean is continually attracted to imbalanced women. Does it give him some sense of control? In fact, he admits to knowing that Louise was disturbed for some time, yet, weirdly, brings her back to the very house where Pauline committed suicide, the source of part of Louise's paranoia. It's like those screen characters who go into the dark house or alley while a murderer is loose — alone. That he could think this would "cure" her is — well, irrational. (Where are the men in the white coats?) Still, Dean is definitely the hero of the piece, genuinely caring and long-suffering (as we're meant to think). Meanwhile, David keeps cropping up in Louise's life like a bad penny.

Some of the dialogue is really fun, as it is in the film, such as when Louise corners David in the library again after marrying Dean:

> "*Oh, David! It's wonderful to see you! Aren't you going to kiss me?*"
> *He shrugged. "I had no plans, one way or the other."*
> "*Do you know how long it's been since you said I love you?*"
> "*I love you is not a phrase you bandy about in Washington, D.C.*"

(Don't be so sure about that, David!)

Again, those "disturbing" messages to women, painting them as hysterics, and yet, there's some relief in that Louise's aggression won't be judged or "punished," given that she's off her nut (sexually aggressive women often, otherwise, are made "examples"). Her bad behavior, in fact, is really the source of entertainment in the story, although its root cause is never explained. Her hysterical laughter when stepdaughter Carol and David fall in love (the script's excuse to rub salt in her wound) and show up at a restaurant together, her feverish imaginings when left alone in the house, her high-pitched scene with stoic yet increasingly fearful David… One understands why Louise wants nothing to do with doctors who she fears will put her away. At the finale when Louise has gone over the edge, these well-meaning white coats tell kind, faithful Dean Graham, who nobly still loves her, "She won't recognize you, Mr. Graham. She's insane." Then continue, "In a biblical sense, we may say that such a person as Mrs. Graham is possessed by devils. It is a psychiatrist who must cast them out. She can be restored." (Although obviously some kind of "intervention" is necessary with this "caretaker," those connotations are a tad sinister, aren't they?) And whatever happened to upend Pauline? Troubled waters?

Happily, however, the "gentle, strong fingers" of Dean Graham are there to reassure Louise that "rescue was [there], that she need not be afraid." Such fairytales of the "male rescue" have screwed women up for centuries now, but it's a happy ending for Louise nonetheless. Crawford's complex and powerhouse personality are perfect in putting the whole thing across. As Louise, her behavior is "very objectionable" and, being an audience catharsis, we love her for it.

Pretty Sadie McKee by Vina Delmar (Written 1933) ★★★

Liberty, in which *Pretty Sadie McKee* ran in serial form, was an exceptional magazine, priced at five cents in 1933 and a fascinating time capsule. Author Vina Delmar is depicted (amusingly looking only about twelve years old) and it notes: "Her transformation from a movie usher to one of the best known writers in America within a few short years has been phenomenal." *Sadie McKee* with Joan Crawford in the title role, was a fairly faithful film adaptation, close to the tone and storyline of its source, although the outrageous tag on the magazine's front page boasts "The Story of Another 'Bad Girl.'" Sadie McKee is far from a "bad girl," sexist as *that* term is. The entire issue of the magazine, in fact, with its wonderful array of illustrated stories, speaks volumes about where women were at and inadvertently gives a clue to the social mores Joan Crawford was up against. Even more interesting to me than *Sadie* was a story by Adela Rogers St. John, a name come familiar to me because of her incessant and annoying gossip concerning Crawford, particularly her infuriatingly misogynist notion that Joan liked to be "treated rough" by men. This unsavory claim of women's inherent masochism was actually planted in popular culture *by* men, perpetuated like negative ethnic stereotypes, a sophisticated form of brainwashing that enabled abuse. All this notwithstanding, St. John's story, although a tad schmaltzy in line with popular taste of the time, was very well written, involving a famous starlet of Jewish origin whose parents are finally invited to visit her in Hollywood where the mother overhears inflammatory gossip about said daughter in a beauty parlor. One imagines similar talk was spread about our gal and, in fact, Crawford's name is in Harriet Parsons' gossip column ("Joan Crawford supervised the furnishing of Franchot Tone's new apartment. Which either indicates a newly awakened interest in interior decoration on Joan's part — or something less impersonal. Take your choice"). Women were definitely between a rock and a hard place; having scant economic/social freedom and dependent largely on men, they were also vilified for vanity, pettiness, ambition (even if through men), and promiscuity, although simultaneously valued primarily as sex objects and forced to occupy a smaller world, in some ways. In *Pretty Sadie McKee*, Sadie's mother dreams that her beautiful daughter can rise above her station and marry the wealthy Michael Alderson yet when it is clear Sadie's heart belongs to good-for-nothing Tommy and Sadie is going to run away with him to New York, Mrs. McKee can only stress, "Be sure and marry him first thing in the morning." In other words, even if this boy would doom Sadie to a hardscrabble life that her mother wanted her to escape, she'd rather see her daughter bonded to him than unchaste.

In the first installment, sweet and faithful Sadie follows her beloved boyfriend Tommy to New York after he runs into some trouble with the law and can't find employment locally. Wealthy Michael, whose parents once employed Sadie's mother as a maid, is strictly in the periphery. Descriptions are telling regarding gender. Of Michael: "He was rich and handsome and carried himself so that bereft of fine clothes the world would still know him for a gentleman." Of Sadie: "Her dark hair fell in thick curling masses to her waistline, and her eyes were deep blue and they looked squarely and bravely out into the world. Her mouth was red and soft, and she was beautiful." As seems to be the theme in the stories of this period, parents — in this case, Sadie's widowed mother — scrape for their children, poor but proud and honest. As in the film, Sadie and

Tommy find a room in a cheap boarding-house for $7 a night after eating at a drugstore soda fountain. This is 1930s New York, all right. The sandwiches and coffee they order cost forty cents ("[Tommy] had figured it would be thirty for what they had had, but this was New York"). And: "[Sadie] was thinking now that apparently five dollars a week was very cheap for a room in New York." Readers are left hanging as, having reg-

An example of the exquisite layout and illustration characteristic of magazines in the Golden Age, this one by James Montgomery Flagg.

istered for the night under Mr. and Mrs. Thomas Wallace and unpacked, Sadie faces Tommy in the tiny room with its one narrow bed. Quite an effective cliffhanger!

Part 2: Part two of the serialized *Pretty Sadie McKee* finds our fair heroine afraid and out of work in New York City, living "in sin" with no-account boyfriend Tommy in a shabby hotel room in a building filled with show people (what else?). (Amusingly, above each story is the "reading time," this segment clocked at "32 minutes, 5 seconds!" Down to the second, no less! I imagine a room full of readers clocking their time. Unfortunately, I failed to clock mine, but believe I was far ahead of the race.) As in the film, Sadie is noble to an irksome fault, dutifully pursuing work to the point of exhaustion, foregoing the movies (even though they are only fifty cents) because that change can be used for food, and saintly in a way that is almost a vice, although one still cares about her, naturally. This segment offers a portrait not only of Saint Sadie (embodied onscreen beautifully by a beauteous, sweet and radiant Crawford), but of all the desperate souls in the Depression, anxious people vying for the same low-paying job, many of them young. Although heavy-handed perhaps, it is nonetheless poignant. Just as Sadie has failed to find work, she runs across man trap Dolly Merrick, a successful singer living in their hotel. Dolly is barely twenty and a violet-eyed blonde, which already gains her my sympathy. Part Two ends with Dolly ringing the doorbell of Sadie and Tommy and setting her eyes on Tommy, this after Sadie had been told that Dolly "[has] gotta have every man she sees."

Part 3: The third installment of *Pretty Sadie McKee* really establishes the socially straitened position of women in the early '30s, not that it's changed altogether. As in the film, Sadie is noble to a self-abnegating fault, finding herself "living in sin" with Tommy in the big city and, with the advent of vaudeville star Dolly Merrick into their cramped space, Tommy quickly strays. Sadie recognizes "man-trap" Dolly's charms as Dolly sings the blues for them: "Her lids were a pale violet, and her skin was white and it would be soft. Her voice was frail and lovely." Soon Tommy is predictably coming in late and putting on airs, but poor, noble Sadie is determined to hang on to him and "take care of" him and "pick up the pieces when he fell." One finds her self-sacrifice or foolishness impossible to admire. Her friend Opal sees what's up and tries to couch the blow for Sadie when Tommy runs off to Boston with Dolly. But Sadie soon packs her bags to follow him after getting a coveted fourteen-dollar-a-week job, which doesn't make Tommy respect her any better. ("You're going to try to boss now that you've got a lousy fourteen bucks a week coming in, huh?") After Sadie confronts Dolly and Tommy — now in Dolly's act — in Dolly's dressing room at the vaudeville theater they're playing in Boston and has no luck in convincing the recalcitrant to return to her, she retorts, "What is pride anyhow but the thing women claim they have when they haven't got the guts to go after the man they want?" Why are women always encouraged to be selfless?

Meanwhile, Sadie is keeping up a brave and false face for her mother, acting as if she and Tommy are married and doing well. She returns to New York and shares her flat with Opal, the rent now reduced to $3.50 a week, her salesgirl job gone in her absence, and Opal convinces her to get a dancing job at Roquette's where it isn't necessary to know how to dance. Sadie becomes aware of the drawing-card of her own beauty while employed at this nightclub. Here's where the age-old and horrific position of women becomes unwittingly illustrated. Sadie, clad in "a few inches of feathers and tulle," is told not to object to the men who grab at her, even if they nearly rip the mantilla of her costume, to "smile" and speak "pleasantly" to them always. Girls, we're still being fed this tripe. The chorus girls also have to sing self-effacing lyrics, including "Our brains are not extensive, but our tastes are so expensive," which Sadie finds amusing (unsurprisingly). Meanwhile, Sadie considers the other girls to be "bums," aside of a fifteen-year-old (sadly, to my mind) employed there. She seems completely incognizant of the fact that these girls looking for a way to get "new dresses and pretty trinkets" likely have no other way of acquiring much of anything. As cliffhanger in this installment, she has her mantilla indeed ripped (and noble Sadie offers to pay for this — surprise, surprise — although it's not her fault) by the unappetizing alcoholic Jack Brennan whom her boss orders her to "sit with." Go to any go-go bar and see how little things have changed! Female chattel, anyone? The Crawford film is fairly faithful to this story and does a more than competent job of bringing it to life, the characters well represented by each actor.

Beautiful and racy watercolor illustration by James Montgomery Flagg.

Part 4: The July 15, 1933 installment left a bad, lingering taste in my mouth. The illustrations in the issue, as always, are phenomenal and surprisingly risqué, showing clearly outlined breasts; one story depicts an orgy. A subheading lists *Pretty Sadie McKee* as a "Vivid Story of Another 'Bad Girl.'" Hardly. With scant economic options and a Depression, no less, girls had no choice but to compromise themselves with unhappy liaisons for survival; how does this make them bad? And how absurd is it that a girl should be called "bad" for being sexual? Aren't men and women both sexual beings? This segment illustrates Sadie's plight clearly in this regard; she is beset upon by an unsavory, alcoholic millionaire Jack Brennan at the nightclub where she dances and she doesn't reject his advances because she knows her financial prospects are dire. He continually repeats that her name is Sadie and announces that he likes her and is going to marry her. It seems her feelings on the matter aren't an issue; he knows he's in the driver's seat. Meanwhile, rather than finding Jack offensive, Sadie's companion Gilbert Fenlon looks coldly on her as a gold digger. He glares and asks, "What's your racket?" at one point, to which she returns, "What's yours?" Ironically, he is worried that Sadie is going to "take advantage" of Jack when clearly Jack has the "advantage" in the bargain. Sadie returns to Jack's sumptuous home with him, as in the film, and waits there all night as Gilbert continues to glare at her and make remarks like, "I hate to see birds shot on the ground." As Kay Pierce says in *Mildred Pierce*, "Aw, you're breaking my heart!" Gilbert makes an attempt to talk Jack out of his boast of marrying Sadie, but fails. Disheartingly, Sadie assesses her situation:

> Jack Brennan had said he was going to marry her. He was big and bloated and the whites of his eyes were bloodshot and more yellow than white. He wasn't nice to look at but he had money. She had never pictured herself with money and had never felt a yearning for the great things money could buy…if she couldn't have Tommy, what difference did it make, then, which man she took?

Gilbert, meanwhile, promises to keep her "from roping [Jack] in." What a guy! They sit in Jack's house all night and the next morning, sober Jack still wants to marry beautiful Sadie. He kisses her full on the lips and she "wanted to push him away and run out of the house." She feels he has a "right to kiss her," though, thinking of "clean beds" and "getting her mother out of Griswold's kitchen." She "closes her eyes" and "offer[s] her lips again." (Crawford depicted this agony well onscreen and certainly had the radiant beauty.) This says it all. Slavery came in all types. What a downer! The next issue promises to reveal her answer.

Queen Bee by **Edna Lee** (Written 1949)
★★★★ *for writing (zero stars for latent misogyny)*

> "You awake in the night, I thought, in a place where you've never been before and will never be again and you are as nothing. Nothing, cradled in the vast womb of night and suspended between two points — the place from which you come, the place to which you go. For a moment you lie staring into the dark, your mind as blank as an idiot's. Then memories one after another begin to thrust their way up from the subconscious like sentinels who, having slept, spring to attention again."
>
> Edna Lee, Queen Bee

Edna Lee's *Queen Bee*, the novel which became a cult classic film with — and because of — Joan Crawford in the title role, is delicious trash or Southern Gothic, reminiscent of Daphne du Maurier's *Rebecca* in plot and style with elegant, beautifully turned purple prose. Like *Rebecca*, it also has, disguised beneath the honey (pun intended), ridiculously misogynist attitudes towards women tellingly enforced by women (author and narrator). Still, it all goes down like wine (at first), beguiling like "Queen Bee" Eva Avery's light, musical, laughing, soft and husky voice. Both novels suspensefully relay the story of a sweet, young thing sent blindly to live in an impressive and imposing house haunted in some way by the allegedly malevolent and controlling presence of another woman, a great beauty initially presumed to be admirable, wife of a seemingly severe and emotionally cold man who the sweet young thing ultimately falls in love with. Then we're to believe that mean man's mean attitude and misery is all the fault of said beauty (misunderstood? oh, that excuse!) because trophy wife has been unfaithful or is just too damn uppity and spoiled. Either way, she deserves, according to author logic and attitudes towards women deeply ingrained in worldview, to be violently murdered for her sins, particularly for oppressing hubby and the lives around her. Her demise frees the sweet, young thing to marry wronged husband and be the dutiful, loving, less flashy wife he deserves or, in the case of *Queen Bee*, inherit the children. Basically it is about the innocent's awakening, particularly sexual, and the competition literally being killed off so she can guiltlessly have — in some form — the "brooding" male who initially frightened her and all the spoils her own lack of materialism allegedly makes her more worthy of. It is also an ugly cautionary tale to women to not get too full of themselves.

In *Queen Bee*, character Ty McKinnon sets the general thesis before innocent Jennifer as she is en route to her aunt's palatial home, explaining his theory about queen bees: "There are women like that, you know. Millions of them. It's a whole social order. Queen-Beeism. And you find them everywhere. Not just in the South — although more in the South because every little girl on every shabby little street down here is raised to believe that she's so damned wonderful that the world must be served to her on a silver platter." Meanwhile, Jennifer, while puzzling over this quirky remark and not realizing its intended application to her aunt, observes and likes "feeling very small behind his tallness and…the way he walked, in leisurely fashion, yet with such surety, as if it never occurred to him that he might fail to get his way. He was nice, I thought." Apparently Queen-Beeism in men is okay.

Edna Lee does a great job of capturing the lushness and paradoxical nature of the South, entrancing with homey details about lifestyle and landscape. Readers see it all through Jennifer's eyes and, like her film counterpart, she is an annoying ingénue, initially in her innocence puzzled by the palpable animosity tirelessly directed towards her "shining," lovely, sweetly prattling aunt by all and sundry at the seemingly delightful abode but eventually, as she is handed books about bee behavior (hint, hint) and innocuously witnesses seductive liaisons, some involving aunt of the three-note laugh, and in particular when illicit feelings of her own are flamed towards brooding Beauty, she begins to share hostility for the aunt she had hitherto pledged to befriend. Meanwhile, as Eva is vilified for her unfaithfulness (abused verbally and apparently sexually by the men who fall prey to her wanton ploys — no matter, she is incapable of being hurt, we're told), Jennifer and Beauty begin a flirtation that grows increasingly bolder (never mind that Jen is Beauty's niece which makes it incest). Revising her initial fearful impression of the intractable, wounding and wounded uncle, Jennifer secretly prays for their love and bears witness to more and more "stinging" machinations, the pent-up emotions and frustrations leading to the dream-prophesized and implied (by endless metaphor) violent "climax" (pun intended). Thus, as millions of women are abused and murdered by their husbands across the world, it is posited in *Queen Bee* that it may be well deserved, in fact the only viable option for maligned hubbies whose uppity wives won't grant divorce and are too good in bed, besides, to abandon immediately.

The influence of Margaret Mitchell's *Gone with the Wind* is easily discernible in both the characterization of Eva Avery (lacking the dimension, complexity and admirable strength of Scarlett O'Hara) and especially Beauty Avery with his mocking tones and habit of bating women, a rake of sorts like Rhett Butler supposedly desirable to women because of this brooding, rough, cheeky sexuality (the exact cheekiness condemned in women) and his incongruous tenderness with children. Meanwhile, dangerous sexuality in women, the author warns, is not desirable as it is in men. Eva Avery is painted as a sociopath of sorts, not because she tortures animals, kills prostitutes or poisons guests with elderberry wine, or drives recklessly like husband Beauty under the influence of alcohol. No, she's branded as "a bad thing bred so deep in the blood and bone it can't be got out," as the scary metaphorical song sung by Beauty *to his children* goes ("Some day I'll kill her and deep, so deep, I'll bury my lady and then I'll sleep") (aw, he's such a tender dad), because she has an inordinately huge collection of cosmetics; she's seductive with men (not their fault that they succumb! two minutes in the presence of Eva in a flimsy nightgown that shows her "virginal breasts" and a man can't help but be shamefully "vanquished!"); and most damning, prefers attending parties to staying home on holidays and doing the things mothers should like doing (given the animosity within her family, can't say I blame her!). It's an "inherited thing," Beauty explains, speaking of the reason he had to put his "beautiful" dog Queenie out of her misery with a "quick bullet," but really, transparently referring to Eva. Eva's mother, we were told earlier, also placed more importance on her husband than children, often leaving them so she could gallivant, apparently not "busy with her house, her flowers, her husband and children" in "crisp gingham house dresses" like Jennifer's mother (oh, those tainted genes!). Eva Avery's vanity and infidelity, we are meant to believe, warrant her isolation in the family, her mistreatment and eventually her murder. The lines of the camp for females is drawn clear — good women are unpretentious, unworldly, motherly, wear little makeup; bad women are vain, worldly, use their sexuality for power (never mind it's the only power they're assigned), don't confine themselves to the home, and have far too many lotions.

The irascible (what else?), but "lovable" (what else?) housekeeper Miss George ruefully explains the root problem to Jennifer who has already been putting such pieces of the puzzle together herself: "It's like this, child. It used to be that man was master. And he kept the woman in her place. At home. To keep her there contented he told her she was too delicate, too fine to rastle with common things. Poor fool! He came to believe it himself. 'Nothing too good for my wife' — oh child, I've heard it all my life. And women used it, the very thing he'd taught 'em, to get what they wanted from him. Silk stockings and fur coats and servants and cars. And too good to wash a dish or hang out a tubful of clothes." Little does Miss George know, but that unrest was going to become a nationwide movement.

Jennifer, meanwhile, "comes of age," realizing just in time, no doubt, that such women, of which her own Aunt Eva is a "shining" (pun intended) example, were "akin to the fatal women of mythology…luring men with their beauty and charm, eager to sacrifice them to the avarice which was the mainspring of their lives" while "workers" like poor Jen toiled (Lee's attempt to maintain the bee motif). At one point as her aunt tells her how men value primarily women who are good in bed, the appalled Jennifer now sees before her an expensive "strumpet," beautiful so she could sell herself like merchandise "coldly and with calculation as a strumpet's passion is always cold and calculating beneath its imitation of living warmth." Apparently, Jennifer's "awakening" does not extend to the fact that "strumpets" are indeed living beings so-employed because it's their only mode of survival, a status and state of objectivity created and encouraged by men.

Crawford in some ways doesn't fit the role of Eva Avery, as described in the book, yet at the same time she's the only reason *Queen Bee* is a cult favorite. Sashaying around in her Jean Louis gowns, she has the virile presence, authority and maturity to command the screen and everyone in her orbit, not to mention the "fatal charm." She brings velvety, barbed delight to her lines, my favorite being, "Really, that Dr. Pearson, he's so absurd. He actually trembles when I talk to him. You'd think he'd never seen a beautiful woman before." Her reading brings a humor to the line lacking in the book, since she is also walking backwards — as Jennifer observes — waving her little handkerchief coquettishly, then fluffing her hair in the mirror. It's a hoot. While straddling camp, her performance is charged with the emotional commitment she brings to every role, making her deliciously magnetic. Crawford also bothers to invest Eva with back story and pathos to make her human and seeing how this Eva really loves husband Beauty, it makes his murderous treachery all the more monstrous. John Ireland makes a perfect embittered Beauty and, amusingly, with all the lascivious subterfuge going on onscreen, it was in full swing offscreen, too, with Ireland and Crawford having a hot affair. It began with double entendres unintentionally underlying their dialogue that brought the two stars to giggling fits, much to the director's frustration. (Beauty/Ireland: "Are those real?" [supposedly about Eva's jewels; actually said about Crawford's breasts] Eva/Crawford [understanding]: "Everything I have is real.")

As usual, there are those silly, amusing parallels to Crawford's offscreen life in *Queen Bee* with a mogul in the book having made his fortune from a soft drink just as Crawford is about to marry Pepsi exec Alfred Steele. Like Eva Avery, Crawford has gotten flack from detractors for being allegedly vain, phony, promiscuous, and a diva, although she was also kind, generous, and loyal, too. However, like Eva, her defiance and sauce, offscreen and on, is exactly what makes her resonate so enduringly, thumbing it to the narrow conventions assigned to women even while remaining gracefully and dutifully a lady.

Rain by W. Somerset Maugham (Written 1922) ★★★★

Rain tells the story of a group of people who are temporarily stranded on the South Seas island of Pago-Pago when an epidemic of measles develops on the schooner that is to take them to Apia. Two couples — Dr. and Mrs. Macphail and the Davidsons, who are missionaries — have formed a shipboard bond, and they are put up at half-caste trader Horn's meager rooms, along with a second-class passenger named Sadie Thompson who is coarse, outgoing and plying her trade with the local sailors. Although the reserved Dr. Macphail (who serves as the focal observer and voice of tolerance although the story's viewpoint is third person omniscient) is somewhat awed and intimidated by the spare, forbidding Mr. Davidson's seeming courage, he is also irritated by his harsh self-righteousness. The Davidsons glory in stamping out pleasure under the guise of driving out sin, fining natives for dancing or stealing or not wearing proper clothes, cowing and breaking traders who dare to defy them. When Sadie Thompson unwittingly crosses their path and rebels against Davidson's interference in the gramophone playing and revelry in her room, he goes on a merciless campaign to "save her soul."

Rain is a brilliantly crafted tale of moral frailty and hypocrisy. At the onset, Mrs. Davidson crows to the indifferent Dr. Macphail, "You'll hardly believe me when I tell you it was impossible to find a single good girl in any of the villages." The rain is an obvious metaphor for oppression and relentless torment, for Davidson himself and his persecution of others. ("[The rain] was unmerciful and somehow terrible; you felt in it the malignancy of the primitive powers of nature. It did not pour; it flowed. It was like a deluge from heaven, and it rattled the roof of corrugated iron with a steady persistence that was maddening. It seemed to have a fury of its own. And sometimes you felt that you must scream if it did not stop, and then suddenly you felt powerless, as though your bones had suddenly become soft; and you were miserable and hopeless.")

Some modern interpretations read an indictment against British colonials into this story; however, this tiresome politically correct spin proves simplistic and invalid. For one thing, colonization, mindlessly demonized in current times, brought necessary medical and economic advancements to indigenous societies that were steeped in primitivism and not prospering on their own; without it, many countries would be without rails, roads, piped water and schools. As exploitive and primarily self-serving as it evidently was, it also brought beneficial progress. Most importantly, this was the attitude that W. Somerset Maugham took, who believed that colonialism brought more positive than negative. In *Rain*, Dr. Macphail observes "the yaws from which most of the children seemed to suffer, disfiguring sores like torpid ulcers, and his professional eyes glistened when he saw for the first time in his experience cases of elephantiasis…" Rather, *Rain* incisively looks at moral hypocrisy and intolerance, weakness of the flesh and spirit.

In the novella version, the focus is on Davidson's fall from grace. The natives and Sadie, who enjoy dance and music and sensuality, and the mild Dr. Macphail are a great contrast against the repressed and "cheerless" Davidsons. In the finale, when Horn wakes up Macphail, he is suddenly seen as a primitive, heavily tattooed man — the primitive waking up the reserved man as primitive urges are "awakened" in Davidson by Sadie Thompson.

In the Joan Crawford film, unlike the novella, the chief protagonist is Sadie Thompson, which is one of the reasons I enjoy it more. It has Crawford's riveting, heartbreaking, appealing performance as a huge asset. She projects a ripe vitality, vulnerability and a likeability ("I'm a happy-go-lucky sort of a fellow"), along with the uncouth rawness, that makes Sadie completely sympathetic and her plight all the more affecting. Sadie is also given the chance to triumph which makes the film doubly ahead of its time and satisfying; it allows compassion and even a feeling of closure to the storyline. Both novella and film version(s) of *Rain* are wonderful, timeless indictments of moral hypocrisy and cruelty, far ahead of their times.

The Story of Esther Costello by Nicholas Monsarrat (Written 1953)
★★★

With the occasional deadly seriousness of *Dragnet*, Nicholas Monsarrat's *The Story of Esther Costello* exposes the corruptive nature of charitable institutions and the public's need for collective emotion that feeds such exploitation; it also exposes a gratuitous prurience on the part of the author that makes it all a bit icky and revealing (no pun intended) in more unintentional ways than one. As in the film version, the story begins with an irritating recreation of how Esther Costello became blind, deaf and dumb in her impoverished village of Cloncraig in Ireland and picks up momentum as the attractive figure of wealthy American and benefactress Mrs. Bannister comes on the scene to rescue Esther from appalling neglect. Belle Bannister's motives are originally compassionate and fueled by philanthropy and good faith mixed with uncertainty, although the village, sensing a chance to assuage its collective guilt over Esther's abandonment, also conspires to force her hand to relieve them of responsibility for Esther's care. Soon Mrs. Bannister, doubtful and uncertain over her own decision to take Esther under her wing, finds herself pleasurably championed and idolized by the public for her good deed and her commitment snowballs. Devoting herself to a year of hard work in which she and Esther learn the deaf and dumb language and make inroads towards "civilization," she becomes more isolated from friends and more deified by the media and public. Simultaneously the public, as had the villagers, feeds its ego and charitable need by fevered giving. At first conflicted, Mrs. Bannister eventually accepts these donations as security for Esther, charity for the blind, and to ensure her own financial security and defray her considerable expenses for Esther's care. She still struggles to keep that fine line between good intention and exploitation, but as the thing becomes larger than she ever expected, former husband and no-good scamp Captain Charles Bannister forces his way back into her life to throw all selfless intention to the wind. By a combination of blackmail and his power as a man to weaken her better instincts, he makes her a tool in his amoral ambition regarding Esther, forcing Mrs. Bannister to support him as he had in the past. The dark tide continues as huckster Jack Lett (presented in the book's occasional sledge hammer fashion as veritable carney barker with his card reading "Jack Lett- Novelties") becomes third party in the unholy alliance. Mrs. Bannister, powerless against the tide, tries to protect Esther from harm initially, but she is

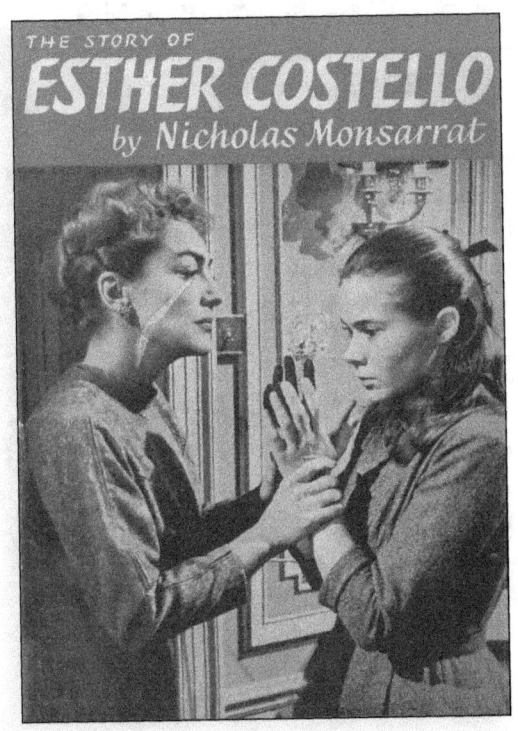

ultimately dictated by fear and increasingly complicit in keeping the monster alive. When a reprehensible deed restores Esther's senses, the truth is hidden and fear of exposure by a young newspaper man leads to an ultimate evil act.

Apart from what author Monsarrat intended, there is something smarmy and loathsome about the novel, beginning with the gratuitous whispers among Cloncraig villagers regarding "handsome" visiting American Mrs. Bannister's lace nightgown "you could see half a mile through," "paint" and "scent." There are numerous references by various male characters to Esther's beautiful body and smug allusions to Mrs. Bannister's affairs. (If her "sleeping with the devil" is a metaphor, it's a heavy-handed one as is the general moralistic tone of the story. How outraged should anyone be by meant-to-shock absurdities like these reflections of a jaded newspaper editor: "In France, a woman took a lover on the kitchen table while her children looked on, and told her twelve-year-old daughter: 'You can watch, but you oughtn't to start till next year.'") The most telling scene of all is when so-intentioned hero, cub reporter Harry Grant, who loves Esther yet loves his job a little more, to my mind, climbs a fire escape to enter Esther's bedroom, peeping into windows en route and observing an illicit, possibly adulterous scene in one. Responsible for initiating media fever for the Esther Costello story and ultimately choosing to expose it as a scam when it tips full throttle in that direction, Grant strikes me as one of the biggest hypocrites in the story. As he later waxes indignant about innocent Esther's exploitation, one can't help remembering his earlier smarminess:

> *When [Esther] sat down, smoothing her dress, [Grant] winked at Charles Bannister, and said:*
> *"She really is a honey, isn't she? Just look at that figure!"*

When Charles Bannister retorts, "You oughtn't to talk like that about her," Grant, angered "to be thus rebuked by this second-rate, drunken hanger-on," counters roughly: "What the hell? She can't hear, can she?" Later, torn between exposing the Esther Costello scam and love for its heroine, "he knew that the story would win, because he was that sort of man, in that sort of job." Evidently all characters are all-too-willing to sacrifice ideals for their own personal advancement and gain. And what if Esther were not such a "glowing beauty?" What if she was plain or homely? Would her story be less sympathetic? The scene when Grant enters Esther's bedroom rankles further as Esther's "innocence" seems to hinge on her purity not only in the Costello machine but as a woman. Are blind people necessarily so naïve, innocent and "untouched?" Isn't this a condescending view of the blind? Are they so less "normal?" Must a girl be a virgin to be a victim?

The fine film does a commendable job in adapting the source story, making it less distasteful, although the distasteful aspect leaks through in some of the ridiculously exploitive outfits chosen for actress Heather

Crawford on the *Esther Costello* set with David Miller. PHOTO COURTESY OF THEO POUROS

Sears who plays Esther Costello, such as a jumpsuit that over-emphasizes her breasts. The dress is as inappropriate as the short dresses child star Erin Moran was forced to wear way past her growth spurt on *My Three Sons*. In most respects, the film improves on the book by making Mrs. Bannister a wholly noble character, unsurprising since Crawford wanted audiences to like and identify with her film roles. As a result, the film's Mrs. Bannister is more in keeping with the way I felt the book should have gone with her rather than turning this three-dimensional, principled woman into primary villainess. However, removing the element of blackmail from the script makes it much less believable in the film that a smart, capable cookie like Belle Bannister would so quickly welcome her errant husband (played by Rosanno Brazzi) back into her bed and invite destruction. The self-sacrificial ending, sanctifying Mrs. Bannister in the extreme, is also a great misstep. In the novel, the "hear no evil, see no evil, speak no evil" theme used to hawk Esther Costello could also apply to Mrs. Bannister's fall from grace.

As Belle Bannister, Joan Crawford gives one of the finest (and most underrated) performances of her career. She is attractive (as befits the character), subtle and poignant. Her scene in which she first becomes

Rosanno Brazzi with Crawford and my least favorite of her husbands, Pepsi honcho Al Steele, and director David Miller on set of *Esther Costello*. Love Joan's coyly crossed ankles. PHOTO COURTESY OF THEO POUROS.

aware of oily hubby's less-than-fatherly interest in Esther is stunning. She had a talent, nurtured in the silents, for expressing everything with her face and particularly eloquent eyes. As is tiresomely par for the course with Crawford, however, her detractors seem hell bent on negative distortion when assessing her, fond, for one, of unfairly painting her as somehow more narcissistic than the average film star, which only underscores that sanctimonious self-righteousness the public has and their need for blood that the story of Esther Costello partially addresses. Truth and balance are always sacrificed for sensation, as they are in this case, when Crawford is faulted for being ridiculously glamorous while walking around the ruins of Ireland at the start of the film as if this had been arranged by her in the script solely out of vanity. In actuality, it is faithful to the story where the worldly woman (as the leering villagers see her) is described as being "in black, with furs: her stockings were of fine mesh, her heels (by Irish village

The co-stars make a cute couple. PHOTO COURTESY OF THEO POUROS

standards) wonderfully high. She looked 'for all the world like a French whore,' said Paddy Finane, who had never seen a whore of any nationality." Furthermore, I am hard pressed to understand why Crawford's desire to present herself as a star would be considered a negative and not the positive it is, since more than most stars, she was committed to her public and often did things solely to give her fans what they wanted. She had also grown up in a star system at MGM that demanded its stable to look and behave a certain way and Louis B. Mayer was one of her respected father figures whose dictates she largely obeyed. Certainly that old-style Hollywood glamour is sorely missed, but her appearance here is in fact faithful to the source story. Her good looks, charm, charisma and sensitive face (and yes, the smart way she dresses) makes her well cast as a public relations ambassadress, the role she was successfully playing for her Pepsi exec husband's company in real life.

In sum, *The Story of Esther Costello* is fairly well written, but it more than errs on the side of stodgy morality and heavy-handedness. While widely distributing its criticism to indict more than the central villains in greed and corruption, it errs by placing the primary blame in Mrs. Bannister's lap ultimately, a woman who began with dimension and sympathy, a sympathy it would have been wise to continue rather than shifting heroism to the ambitious reporter. The film version is reasonably faithful to the original text, tendencies to floridness included, and contains a fine and vastly underrated performance from Joan Crawford as Mrs. Bannister.

Sudden Fear by Edna Sherry (Written 1948) ★★★½

Sudden Fear, adapted into the Joan Crawford noir classic of the same name, is a tightly-plotted novel of suspense with vivid characters and page-turning twists, ultimately somewhat marred by a lack of moral ambiguity. The film with its nifty expressionist visuals and quirky inspiration is a lot more fun, but both are clever nail-biters.

Like the film, the story begins with famous playwright Myra Hudson observing with dissatisfaction rehearsals for her new play (ironically titled *Immoral Courage*) from the orchestra of the theater. She finally decides that what's wrong is the young supporting actor Lester Blaine. This is where direct parallels to the film end. In exact opposition to being not the sort of charm boy "that would make every woman in the audience sit right up and go, 'Mmph!,'" as her film counterpart Crawford observes, Lester in the book is so blindingly handsome that he outshines the leads and thus must be canned.

Myra Hudson is drawn with fascinating detail, much less sympathetically than Crawford's version, although they are both accomplished and wealthy powerhouses susceptible to the right flatterer. Possessing "practically everything but youth and beauty," she is feared for her "mordant wit and biting tongue," "arrogant, high-bred [and] clever-ugly." (Clever-ugly?) But behind her steely, accomplished exterior lies a vulnerability — her slavish devotion to youth and beauty. When Lester worms his way into her life, initially questioning her about his rejection and then turning romantic, she weakens against her better instincts, although she still holds the purse strings and refuses to cast him or allow him to use her influence to get parts. Lester drives home his advantage and succeeds in marrying her and contents himself playing a devoted role that affords him ease and luxury. Myra's friends and inner circle — who include physician Edgar Van Roon (in love with Myra since childhood); financial advisor Miles Street (who appreciates Myra's masculine brain but has no illusions about her character); and Steve Thatcher, brilliant criminal attorney whose "fruity slang" and "breezy personality" Myra enjoys — are skeptical at first, but ultimately decide their fears are unjustified as the marriage appears to be a success. Things indeed go swimmingly until gorgeous blonde gold digger Irma Neves surfaces (literally in the water) and Myra saves her from drowning.

Film and book follow an essential thru-line with Myra discovering the nefarious treachery of two schemers via her Dictaphone which is built into a soundproof study and activated by sound so she can dictate without the need to press buttons. But Myra of the novel doesn't shatter the evidence accidentally as she does in the film; it is her egotism and pride that stand in the way of going to the police. As a high profile celebrity, she can't bear the idea of public humiliation.

The details at variance from the film version, Myra plots her elaborate revenge with the zeal she would one of her plays. However, will she be too clever for her own good?

Sudden Fear is enjoyable and tight, but ultimately not in the league of the greatest Golden Age writers' work in this genre — i.e., Agatha Christie and Sir Arthur Conan Doyle. While clever, it contains what I consider to be a cardinal no-no of mysteries: a fate or ending I don't like. Even Christie alienated me, the reader, a few times this way. At this point I want to dictate an alternative version into my own machine. It sort of thrills me that Joan Crawford herself read and chose this property, appreciating its potential — astute woman that she was — and I'm sure she enjoyed the Clark Gable mention in it.

In any case, although the book is a fine read, the film *Sudden Fear* completely satisfies and I never tire of the milk, the metal dog, Crawford's silent screen eye acting in the closet and the sight of her racing down the steep hills of San Francisco in mink and stilettos with only a few beads of sweat to stain her glamorous brow.

Turn About by William Faulkner (Written 1932) ★★★★★
Filmed as *Today We Live*

William Faulkner's "Turn About" (which first appeared in *The Saturday Evening Post*) was turned into one of my favorite Joan Crawford films, *Today We Live*, a film that has a strange and yet hauntingly beautiful and romantic Haiku quality and certainly captures Crawford at one of her exquisite peaks, although her character, Diana Boyce Smith, does not appear in the original story and the film generally baffles viewers. Set during World War I, "Turn About" is masterfully written and ultimately chilling. It has Faulkner's trademark lack of pronouns (in this case, obviously to denote "Britishness" — i.e., "Not in bed yet. Insomnia. Knew so. Told them. Trucks go that way. See now?") mixed with superb turns of phrase that are like brush strokes. The story begins with a British teenaged sailor, Claude Hope, found asleep in the road and blocking traffic, being brought before contemptuous soldiers who are quickly shocked by his seemingly naïve and cavalier attitude toward war.

When Claude discovers that the men fly:

"Find it jolly, eh?"
"Yes," somebody said. "Jolly."
"But dangerous, what?"
"A little faster than tennis," another said.

Claude particularly arouses the ire of Captain Bogard who observes his "raked cap and his awry-buttoned pea-jacket and a soiled silk muffler embroidered with a club insignia which Bogard recognized to have come from a famous preparatory school, twisted about his throat." The captain determines to show the kid "some war," resentful of his attitude "like a sophomore in town for the big game," although he insists that other soldiers leave the kid alone and stop razzing him. He wants to teach the boy a lesson himself. "Confound it," he reasons, "it would be a shame for his country to be in this mess for four years and him not even to see a gun pointed in his direction." The "lesson" comes when the obliviously cheerful Claude is taken into a bomber plane with Bogard, commenting to their fury, "Lark. But dangerous, isn't it?" and given, as Bogard intends, a first-hand experience with battle. Amazingly, however, Claude appears delighted and almost gleeful, unaffected, looking over the side of the plane frequently with the fascination of a child. One aviator, McGinnis, observes the enemy in the air ("They look like mosquitoes in September") and advises Claude not to "spew it overside" when the boy is given a bottle of liquor for motion sickness: "It'll blow back in Bogy's and my face. Can't see. Bingo. Finished. See?" To their shock, the boy handles a machine gun surprisingly well and reacts with enthusiasm to all around him. He emerges from the flight unruffled, prattling on with seeming naiveté about his friend Ronnie. ("Oh, good gad! What a chap! What a judge of distance! If Ronnie could only have seen!") In a great touch of wit, the aviators discover that the bomb's tip is just touching the sand which is what had preoccupied Claude during their landing.

("Frightened myself. Tried to tell you. But realized you knew your business better than I.")

The "turn about" of the story (and pivotal character reversal) comes when Bogard cheekily decides to sail with Claude and Ronnie. Ronnie is arresting from first sight when Bogard catches something in his initial glance, "a flicker; a kind of covert and curious respect, something like a boy of fifteen looking at a circus trapezist." He has "something stolid about the very shape of his shoulders, his slightly down-looking face It was the face of a man of twenty who has been for a year trying, even while asleep, to look twenty-one." Clamped upside down between his teeth is a short brier pipe. Interestingly, this upside down pipe which many viewers took to be a faux pas when depicted on film is not only no mistake, but an intrinsic part of the story, a symbol or metaphor for civilization turned upside down, a world gone mad. Then Bogard observes the machine gun in the boat, thinking quietly and soberly that it is made of steel.

The scene builds beautifully as Bogard slowly realizes the danger of his own situation and how naively he had underestimated this boy. It is a torpedo that lies beneath them, poised to be fired.

> *"I thought you knew," the boy said.*
> *"No," Bogard said. "I didn't know." His voice seemed to reach him from a distance, dry, cricket-like[.]"*

The voyage is even rockier than their earlier flight, but the boy rejects Bogard's offer of the bottle. ("Never touch it on duty…Not like you chaps. Tame here.") Slowly and inexorably, the boy's own chilling nerves of steel become apparent, as his head turns "with listening delicate and deliberate as a watchmaker" and it is clear that the torpedo will be fired against an enemy, something that must be done with lightning precision or they could be blown to bits. They head for a freighter at "terrific speed" and "[Bogard] crouched, not sitting, watching with a kind of quiet horror the painted flag increase like a moving picture of a locomotive taken from between the rails." Ronnie and Claude allow the freighter to shoot first ("Sporting," as the boy puts it) and Bogard's face becomes "the color of dirty paper." Faulkner crafts this picture with breathtaking details, no phrase empty, as in his description of Claude: "The pea-coat was too small for him; shrunken, perhaps. Below the cuffs his long, slender, girl's wrists were blue with cold." And, even more powerful: "[Claude] paused, diabolical — Machiavelli with the face of a strayed angel." Bogard observes "Ronnie's hand on the wheel and the granite-like jut of his profiled jaw and the dead upside-down pipe." Bogard is now trapped within a nightmare.

"Turn About" is an incredibly powerful and seamless story, a portrait of corrupted innocents, the inhuman bloodlessness created in those caught up in war. The film version uses only elements of the story and eliminates the essential character reversal, instead adding Crawford's Diana Boyce Smith and placing her at the heart of a love triangle. Personally I love the addition of a beautiful woman and think it is a necessary element for the film, enriching it with romance while still preserving the key portrait of lives rocked and torn apart by war. Her warm and sensual presence also creates a war within a war as the men compete for her sexually, adding to testosterone-laden battle. Robert Young as Claude, however, fails to convey the powerful and deceptive character of his fictional counterpart, coming off as near-idiotic with no later revelation of layers. No matter, though. Crawford's absolute poetry onscreen — her phenomenal beauty and eloquence — makes the film magnetic and all its idiosyncrasies add an arresting haiku. Interestingly, Faulkner never flew in combat, the war having ended before he completed his flight training for the Royal Air Force in Canada, although he apparently enjoyed playing the role of a disaffected war veteran by donning the uniform.

Whatever Happened to Baby Jane? by Henry Farrell (Written 1960)
★★★½

> *"A boisterous Hollywood party, a searing family quarrel, the inevitable 'one for the road' — and then the too-late screech of brakes and the heart-stopping, deafening explosion of metal against stone.*
>
> *When the dust had finally settled on the crumpled Rolls, two glamorous careers were ended: Blanche Hudson, the beautiful, smoky-eyed young star of those early talkies, a permanent cripple, and her sister Jane — the same Baby Jane who once danced her dimpled way into the hearts of millions — retired forever to devote herself to Blanche's care.*
>
> *…Who lives in the shadowy palace today? Why does an aura of evil surround it? And when the tuneless keys of the once magnificent Grand are depressed, what funeral dirge do they play — and for whom?"*
>
> the back jacket of Henry Farrell's
Whatever Happened to Baby Jane?

Although this macabre tale of a former movie star Blanche Hudson — crippled and trapped within the faded Hollywood mansion she shares with her increasingly unhinged and sociopathic sister, former vaudeville child star Baby Jane — is masterfully written, it is too relentlessly grim to be much fun. The mild, likeable Blanche, still beautiful, is at the mercy of Baby Jane who is "getting worse" and her suffering is agonizing to read about, her attempts at escape cruelly thwarted. (Even the "heavy exterior grillwork" over Blanche's bedroom window which she had failed to have removed reinforces her mausoleum-like imprisonment.) Both sisters are prisoners of the past. Blanche watches her former self — svelte with lovely sooty eyes, clad in glamorous gossamer gowns — in old movies, clinging to the studio-created illusion as defense against her invalid's grim life. Jane has taken over Blanche's old rehearsal room, sitting on the center of the floor at dusk and losing herself in the reflections of the mirror as if she is at the beach with her beloved Daddy. This is definitely the dark side of Hollywood and familial relationships. We do learn — unfortunately — what happened to Baby Jane and it isn't pretty.

If ever roles were a match made in heaven for two actresses, Jane and Blanche Hudson seem letter perfect for infamous alleged rivals Bette Davis and Joan Crawford. Passages eerily sum up what has become popular belief, if not truth, about each diva's image or certainly their combustive relationship. It might be Davis herself speaking to Crawford as Jane rebukes Blanche: "Oh yes…you got the looks all right. But that's all you got! I got the talent! Even if nobody cared…And I've still got it…So don't go trying to act so — so big with me you — you — nothing — nothing-at-all!"

As in the film, the story opens with Baby Jane in her heyday where it is shortly established that she is a monstrous brat and poor Blanche languishes in her shadow. Baby Jane is the family breadwinner, so Daddy caters to her every whim, cruelly isolating Blanche further. These roles reverse in the 1930s when Baby Jane (and vaudeville) become passé and Blanche's star ascends. While Baby Jane's fame is in the dustbin, Blanche is in the limelight, bringing into play the twisted dynamics and resentments that will prove tragic. Blanche is crippled in a terrible car accident, which may have been caused by Jane. Now the two are holed up in Blanche's once-glorious mansion which has become a veritable Venus fly trap for Blanche. The psychosis of the sisterly relationship continues to ferment, increasingly frightening and dangerous, ultimately murderous.

(Spoilers!) Basically the novel is about Blanche's horrific predicament. Baby Jane, getting bolder in her delusion, decides to make a comeback, reviving her old act. Her ad for an accompanist which infers that she is an "established star" is answered by Edwin Flagg. Shiftless, surly and obese, he is also living out a quiet hell with his common, too-doting mother

Del, two more of Hollywood's disillusioned outcasts. Initially sizing Baby Jane up as a "silly, drunken old woman, got up like a Main Street harlot," he notes the faded, but fine furnishings in the house, recognizing wealth, and decides to play along with her. He doesn't fit her romantic imaginings either, but she shortly clings to him as her one potential friend. Baby Jane is the personal ad from hell that applicants fear. Self-centered rat that he is, however, Edwin does nothing to get help for Blanche when he makes the horrifying discovery of her — starved and strung-up — in her bedroom. He is concerned only with his own narrow escape. In fact, to the reader's frustration and anguish, the only humane character regarding Blanche's plight — one who seemed to have a heart and some guts — is the housekeeper, Mrs. Stitt, who has long abhorred Baby Jane and only stayed on for Blanche's sake. She meets a ghastly end.

Obviously we're meant to see Blanche as somewhat responsible for the nightmarish turn her life with Jane has taken when we learn the "truth" about the accident (and it is indeed a much scarier revelation than the tepid one the film provides), but this reviewer was gunning for Blanche all the way. Even if she had been complicit in her own hell for hanging onto a foreboding situation out of spite and against the better advice of her friends, she was still a smart and sympathetic woman who had been wronged in her childhood whereas Baby Jane seems a born sociopath. Perhaps she did have an evil intention initially, which backfired. It doesn't justify the torture she endures or make it any easier to bear. She is helpless and vulnerable and one longs to see her triumph. How much of her pain and suffering can a reader take:

> *Blanche looked up, tears of fright streaming down her face. "Please — Jane — I'm not trying to do anything! It's just — " A third time the hand shot out, hitting her, this time, glancingly across the cheek and the nose. A stabbing pain shot through her head, driving the words from her mind. "Don't, Jane don't — !"*

There are also some discrepancies that irritate, the author stretching believability to force his grim conclusion. How is it that Mrs. Bates, nosy neighbor of Blanche and Baby Jane — a woman who speculates endlessly about Blanche Hudson and clamors to meet her as Blanche's films enjoy a renaissance on television — fails to read a note that is dropped out of the same's window? This note is Blanche's attempt to get help and engage the neighbor that she watches daily from her prison. It rings absolutely false that the note would not be read immediately by Mrs. Bates and her gossipy friend. Curiosity alone would surely drive them, plus she is the very celebrity they have been speculating about! Why wouldn't they immediately want to see what was written on this paper? And how is it that not one person out of a crowded beach, fog or no fog, would help an older woman who was obviously dying? Someone surely would discover and approach her when she was so clearly ill and emaciated and the beach is full of people!

A much preferable solution would've been to have Blanche rescued in the denouement at the beach. It would not preclude the splashy, powerful scene of Baby Jane in full delusion facing her crowd, but it would've been at least more satisfying and humane. We find out what happened to Baby Jane, but remain never quite certain about Blanche's fate (although it doesn't look hopeful).

In any case, great writing but in spite of suspenseful pacing, tough going. The film, although superb and impeccably cast, is also, to my mind, more horrifying than campy (as some perceive it), and was apparently genuinely a torturous experience for Joan Crawford, on and offscreen. Give Blanche some water, will ya??!!

Why Should I Cry? by I.A.R. Wylie (Written 1949) ★★★★★
Filmed as *Torch Song*

> *"I'm tough. I got to the top of show business the hard way. Why should I be sorry for a man just because he's blind?"*
>
> I.A.R. Wylie, *Why Should I Cry?*

I was writhing with delicious anticipation to read the short story that inspired the colossally camp howler *Torch Song* starring Joan Crawford in her emotional, Technicolor return to MGM as a Broadway star/hellion and a torpid Michael Wilding as her blind accompanist. The above excerpt promised to deliver a comparable dose of deliriously fun, overheated trash. However, as the story moved on, it became something much deeper altogether, conveying the emotional vacuum behind two lonely and bitter souls, one of whom had been injured in the war by a "Jap," the other a "Hester Street gutter brat" whose only "family" — her all-male business associates of the theater — are milking her talent dry and will presumably put her to pasture when they'd "chew[ed] the flesh off [her] bones," as Tye Bannister "sees" it. The World War II significance made all the difference in setting the "stage," forgive the pun, this ravaged veteran undoubtedly a powerful and timely element when this story debuted.

As in the film *Torch Song*, the protagonist is a hellion redhead of the stage who makes life miserable for all around her, admittedly tough in spite of having feminine appeal physically. The story's heroine, however, is named Jenny Breeze, not Jenny Stewart, and is considerably younger, although her vocal abilities with its "husky imperfections" are well represented by India Adams' dubbing in the film version. "If there's anybody going to get kicked around this dump," Jenny tells her manager (as I assume him to be) Mart Denner, "it's not going to be me." The story opens with her confronting the new blind accompanist after her original guy quit because, as replacement Tye tells Jenny: "He told me you threw a prop at him and that you aim straight. He says he's grown too old to dodge." So far, it keeps in line and tone with the film, but shortly parallels break away. For one, Tye is no milquetoast and it is Jenny who quickly becomes subordinate to him, wanting to break through his "ivory tower." He holds his own against her, not afraid to call it as he sees it. The connection between them is a little forced and rushed, but then Wylie has to accomplish it in abbreviated time and space.

Half of the lavish illustration by Coby Whitman that spanned two pages.

As in the film, Jenny fires Tye for his insubordination and quickly rehires him after they dine together in a restaurant. Their banter keeps them on an even level, both self-protective and blunt. There is no preposterous backstory, like the film's, where Tye had reviewed Jenny's first performance when she was a sweet, young thing and secretly carries a "torch." Instead Tye sees something worthwhile in Jenny, in spite of his jaded soul, the excerpt below revealing elements that would be adapted in different ways in the film:

> *"It's none of my business. But I hate good things to be misused and broken. Besides, I've liked working with you. You've never been sorry for me. You've never said, 'Poor devil.'"* He turned towards her, as though he were trying hard to see her. *"You didn't, did you?"*

"Never. I've never been sorry for anyone — not even me." She boasted, "No one's ever seen me cry."

"I never shall." His fleeting embittered grin just missed her face like an ill-aimed blow.

The ending is a magnificent revelation of character as one learns that Tye's seeing-eye dog, Trigger (not Duchess, as in the film), his faithful friend, is going blind and he fears that Trigger might be put down if found out. Basically, it's about people who are scarred and fear their own uselessness, who have given everything "and then…get a bullet for thanks." Jenny, moved by this proud man, takes the initiative to save all three of them by offering her love. The last line is terrific in which she says, "Sure [I'm sorry]. For me, for you, for the whole cockeyed world. But I love you. And I'm not a nice girl. I'm tough. I'll never tire."

Since I read the story in its original home, the 1949 issue of *The Saturday Evening Post*, I also have to comment on the beauty and richness of the magazine itself, representative of the way magazines once *valued* literature and featured not one, but several (in this case, four) stories in one issue, lovingly and lavishly illustrated, not to mention the wonderful spot cartoons. It almost makes me want to cry, since few magazines carry short stories and offer the quality articles that this particular issue had. This is why it was once possible for writers to make a living from short stories, my own favorite form. For all our progress, we've regressed on some levels, sacrificing quality for quickness.

In any case, a wonderful story superior to the film adaptation, yet *Torch Song* has its own merit as a brassy, bawdy camp musical that allows my gal another chance to sing and dance on screen; appear in full-blown Technicolor; pull off production numbers with moxie (Joan sells it!); and represents an emotional return to the studio in which she had literally grown up. (The image of her dressing room filled with flowers from old pals alone is touching.) For all of that and that pointed leg ("And spoil that line?"), the film *Torch Song* remains a sentimental favorite for me as well.

Within the Law by Marvin Dana, from the play by Bayard Veiller (Written 1913) ★★★½
Filmed as *Paid*

Within the Law by Marvin Dana from the play by Bayard Veiller, was the basis for *Paid* starring Joan Crawford as unjustly imprisoned Mary Turner. The role was a longed-for and much-deserved meaty one at that juncture in her career. Although the writing has a tendency to be stilted and, to use one of the author's own words, plethoric ("'Can you beat that!' he rumbled with a raucously sonorous vehemence"), the appealing female heroine and sensitivity to the plight of exploited workers provides a compelling and fascinating read. The rich detail, which now would be considered "overwriting" is far preferable, in my opinion, to the staccato, dialogue-heavy and narrative-barren writing that has sadly come into favor in the digital, short-attention-span age. Also welcome is the correct use of English and sharp vocabulary, again with classical references that were familiar apparently to the average reader and now have sadly become obscure (even Tennyson's "Lady Vere de Vere" — once applied to Crawford –gets a mention). But the prose isn't particularly beautiful or fluid; the strength is in a solid, impassioned story. Mary Turner, a beautiful girl forced by circumstance to toil in a low-paying shopgirl position, is falsely accused of theft and sent to prison for three years, largely on the callous testimony of her rich employer, Edward Gilder. While in prison, the bright girl determines to seek her revenge when she is released and with the aid of an unscrupulous lawyer and her own brilliance, she leads a band of petty criminals who file and win breach of promise suits, all "within the law." In short, she is beating an unscrupulous system that favors the rich at its own game. Refreshing is the moral struggle Mary experiences; a life fueled by anger and vengeance is never truly satisfying. The central theme is of a young woman's journey to self respect and justice, an indictment against exploitation.

Since Mary is only sixteen-years-old when she comes to work at the Emporium at $6 a week, the horrors of "sweat shops" and child labor at the turn of the 20th century is illuminated; people forget that our European forefathers toiled for what they achieved. Crawford certainly is a good fit for Mary on many levels. She, too, was forced into child labor and remained hard-working and honest on many levels. Like Mary, she also had beauty, strength, and self-control, a fitting symbol of the underdog fighting with dignity. Like Mary, she kept herself "supple and svelte by many exercises." Mary, violet-eyed with lustrous dark hair, has, like Crawford, "the straight line of the nose…fine enough for the rapture of a Praxiteles" and "a generous mouth…desirable for kisses…more desirable for strength." Crawford obviously gave this part her all, willing (and perhaps glad) to look at times unglamorous after being utilized so often for glamour in formula pictures. But the film is much creakier than the novel, particularly since the existing prints of it have not been restored. Much of the acting is florid. The book is at times extremely heavy-handed and obviously stage-bound (most strikingly, the "stenographer behind the curtain") and none-too-subtle. (In an interrogation, one character says, "[I]f it's anything about Mary Turner, I don't know a thing — not a thing!") Characters in both book and film have tendencies towards stage hamminess.

The book paints store owner Gilder and son Dick in more depth and, although Dick ultimately grows and proves himself loyal and laudable, father Edward fails to redeem himself in my eyes as he is meant to; he is essentially self-serving and cruelly exploitive of the underclass. Forger Joe Garson who saves Mary from drowning does not strike me as an "evil" man at heart, but rather more sympathetic and "moral" than Gilder and the police. I also fail to see why "squealing" on a "pal" is any worse than robbery, blackmail or murder. But the story moves well, in spite of awkward lines and occasional stiltedness. Comic relief is provided by Mary's cohort Aggie, a colorful, stock, baby-faced blonde with typical '30s "moll" lingo. ("Ain't that fierce?" and this classic: "Say, what are you trying to hand me, anyway?") There are also some great lines: "No man is a hero to his valet, or to his secretary"; "Any one with brains can get rich in this country if he will engage the right lawyer"; "The girl's plight was like a shuttlecock driven hither and yon by the battledores of many tongues"; and this fabulous show-stopping speech by Mary when she finally confronts her tormenter after marrying his son: "Four years ago, you took away my name — and gave me a number…Now, I've given up the number — and I've got your name."

In all, an enjoyable page turner, quaintly stilted and formal but emotionally powerful. One really cares about the plight of Mary Turner as she plots her revenge, since she's a fundamentally decent and kind person who is fighting on behalf of impoverished, exploited workers like herself for true justice. This was the kind of role hard-working, once-impoverished Crawford understood and imbued with passion.

Plays Made Into Film

A scene from *The Women* where two ladies meet with jungle red claws extended. PHOTO COURTESY OF JERRY MURBACH

The following are reviews of miscellaneous plays that were made into Joan Crawford films. Any novelization of a play only available in a foreign language will not be reviewed. Any play made into a film that I haven't seen will also not be reviewed. This is the case for a number of the silents not yet available to the public. This list only represents works located at time of printing; the quest to retrieve them all remains a work in progress. All quoted text follows the format of the original play. Dates of plays courtesy of Internet Broadway Database.

The Besieged Heart by Robert Hill (194?) ★★★½
Filmed as *Female on the Beach*

Robert Hill's play *The Besieged Heart* was adapted into the film *Female on the Beach* and, although as flippant, tawdry and amusingly steamy as its cinematic spawn, it is also far more literary replete with character

reversals, twists and metaphors. The action builds admirably with sharp left curves propelling the momentum, aided by often fascinating interplay between characters. Teresa "Tess" Braggiotti, the "female on the beach" who became Lynn Markham in the film, is a great "lead" — intriguing, smart, and deeply sympathetic. Ultimately, despite these strengths, the impact and credibility of the play is weakened by a too clever ending and preposterous premise. Still, both play and film are entertaining in unique ways, each with its own subtext.

The Besieged Heart opens "in salon of the Villa Capri on the Florida coast" with two men, Jowett and Moore, evidently in law enforcement, discussing a recent murder. They are both cynical and callous. The victim, Mrs. Teresa Braggiotti, was choked and smothered and found on a small cabin type motor boat that had been set in flames. Her new husband, Drummond, was discovered unconscious aboard and is the prime suspect. Jowett and Moore assume he planned to destroy both body and boat and swim away, but these "best laid plans" were snagged. Carruthers, the man who married the couple, peculiarly (to my mind) expresses sympathy for "Drummy" because of his youth as if Tess, probably all of forty, has had her chance. Drummy, we learn, has recovered and confessed.

The action then goes back to the day Tess is shown the house on the beach by a young real estate woman with "odd-shaped glasses," Alice "Rawly" Rawlinson. The scene is set insinuatingly: "The sun porch is in disarray. An empty soiled glass rests on the cocktail table, a pillow lies crumbled on the long low bamboo chaise lounge by the shuttered balcony. At the back the shuttered double doors leading to the bedroom and the kitchen stand carelessly ajar, one of them swinging lightly in some wayward breeze." The "transient quality of the building" is metaphorically noted and with prose descriptiveness, the "sun-white open door." Writer Tess is accompanied by her publisher and dear friend, Tim Hurley ("50, well-dressed, tanned, alcoholic, a gentleman"). She is described as a "slight, red-headed woman with a light, creamy skin; rather frail, rather older than the realty agent." The cottage is on pilings and, as in the film, a boat is in the harbor and Tess says, "I think they'd better moor someplace else." A man's tweed jacket is found in the closet and wryly noted by Tess.

Tim (of Mrs. Crandall, the former tenant): I bet she was happy.
Tess: There are enough gin bottles in the kitchen hall to assure that.

The play, however, has a twist not found in the film. Tess is dying, which is why she wants to be left alone. As a Catholic, she fears suicide, thinking she'd burn in hell, although she longs to end it all before the pain gets worse. Married Tim offers to stay with her, to which Tess responds, "Do you think your pure white body could replace the millions of lovers and mink coats I could buy with my own money?" She also adds this line indicative of the intriguing philosophical touches that lace the play, "With your eyesight and night driving, you may beat me there. There? Where…I wonder?"

Soon Tess meets her neighbors, a prissy and eccentric mother and son, Queenie Berliner and Osbert Rollins, and the disarmingly "obvious" hustler, Drummy. Tess is clearly no easy fool or mark for Drummy. He "waits, like a pretty child, for more admiration. When it is not forthcoming, he is not displeased, only puzzled." Queenie and Osbert set themselves up pretty quickly as smarmy. They reveal that they adopted Drummy, having discovered him in a "sordid environment," but when Tess is alone with the beautiful stud, she discovers he has no particular affection for them or anyone else. Tess was a San Franciscan whose husband Mario died on a cable car (another idiosyncratic tidbit) and Queenie tactlessly observes, "I'm glad you don't look your best. It means you can always surprise us when you want to. So many pretty women can never get any prettier."

All the characters have secrets. Tess is dying. Queenie and Osbert are cold-hearted pimps, exploiting Drummy (and vulnerable older women) to enable parasitic idleness and Drummy is prepared to seduce and kill to ensure his own ease. In one amusing scene, Osbert sits on a railing, barking, and "an answering bark from some furious Pomeranian can be heard in the distance." The conversations between Tess and Drummy are unexpectedly philosophical and deep in flashes, their interplay intriguing. He is forthright about what and who he is, and, as in the film, when he describes the life of idle nothingness he aspires to, Tess responds, "That sounds like rather an expensive nothing." Drummy describes Mrs. Crandall, who was romantically entangled with him, callously, "She had the soul and the appetite of a 16-year-old hash-slinger" and when he asks Tess what she is thinking, she responds, "I was thinking…I didn't like you particularly" but adds, "And then, I was thinking I haven't felt even that much negative reaction to anyone in a long time. So I suppose, by one means or another, you make your impression."

As in the film, the realtor has the hots for Drummy, although he spurns her, and is jealous of his pursuit of Tess. However, Tess overhears Drummy tell Rawly he'd marry and strangle Tess to get her dough and sees it as a way out of her dark fate. She then decides to play into his hand. Wonderful touches of foreshadowing occur, such as when Drummy mentions that it's a shock to see yourself as others see you as in a mirror and "then to think that's only a reflection — and only part of you. And that you can never see..." Tess dresses in an evening gown and walks with him on the beach. The best line occurs when Rawly watches anxiously for the pair to return, thinking she sees them although it's only driftwood. Queenie: "Perhaps it's a seal. They run ashore here sometimes. I remember finding a baby seal on the rocks down the coast. The sweetest thing! And so frightened, poor angel. He would have made a lovely muff."

Bizarrely, after he discovers why she is suddenly willing to marry Drummy, Tess' ally, Tim, censures her for her masochistic motives. He actually blames her for enabling Drummy to murder her by playing into his insidious game as if she is the evil one, not Drummy. "You will die...feeling dirty," he accuses. But another plot twist occurs when it is revealed that Drummy actually loves Tess and sees her as his own chance at salvation.

A saucy, yet interesting play with strong female lead is upended by an absurd premise and weird ending that tries to absolve the unsavory Drummy of his earlier murderous intentions through a suicide pact. Ultimately, however, film version bests because of dynamics Joan Crawford brought to the table. At the height of her 1950s persona, she is somewhat steely yet vulnerable, a woman who thirsts for love and isn't easily vanquished. Her triumph is my happy ending of choice for the female on the beach.

Craig's Wife by George Kelly (1925) ★★★¾
Filmed as *Harriet Craig*

In all versions of George Kelly's Pulitzer Prize-winning *Craig's Wife* (filmed three times, once with Rosalind Russell in 1936 and most notably with Joan Crawford as "Harriet Craig" in 1950), the agenda is clear — this is a cautionary tale about a woman daring to dominate, however covertly, and "wear the pants." (That very phrase speaks volumes.) Allegedly we are to perceive Harriet as more attached to her palatial home than any human being, but her subtle control of husband Walter is transparently most at censure. When one thinks of the images ad nauseam — culturally sanctioned worldwide — of women subordinate to men, particularly the sex/violence pairing which offensively insists our sexuality is inherently masochistic (more on that later), it rankles greatly that a "controlling" woman is viewed as "shrewish," selfish and even evil. The man, allegedly, has the right to rule, not she. In no way does Harriet strike me as unsympathetic. Rather she comes off, particularly in the original play, as perhaps the most level-headed character in the household. Her concerns over emotional

In this publicity still from *Harriet Craig,* Crawford is wearing a dress from her own wardrobe. The Hollywood Newsreel scooped that it is "white organdy with over all eyelet embroidery worn over a pale aqua taffeta slip. The blue-flowered organdy is also from her own wardrobe." Oh, behave! It's these kind of details the Joan fan lives for! ACME ROTO SERVICE

and financial stability strike me as sound, given her position and history, and her advice to her niece on marriage downright sane. I wonder why wanting a neat home or valuing aesthetics is considered so diabolical? Is disorder really preferable? And did this man who was clearly attached to his late mother, living in his mother's house and favored by his boyhood, matronly housekeeper (still in his employ) not *deliberately* choose another capable woman like Harriet to look after him? Ironically, in a play allegedly lambasting attachments to "possessions," the title *Craig's Wife* treats Harriet as one.

Harriet Craig is considered a signature role for Joan Crawford, due to much-hyped parallels to her own fastidiousness (her house, according to gossipy director/lover Vincent Sherman, was fanatically up to "Emily Post" standards) and she is riveting, sexy and impeccable in the role, but the Roz Russell version is closer to the source. The play takes place entirely in the Craig living room which "reflects very excellent taste and fanatical orderliness of its mistress," a "frozen grandeur." The housekeepers, wryly contemptuous of their mistress, are somewhat relaxed when Harriet returns unexpectedly from visiting her ill sister, Estelle, with niece Ethel (Estelle's daughter) in tow. She is chagrined to find Mrs. Frazier, widow next door and rose-grower, in her home, the bouquet of roses a dead giveaway, and the skittish maid using the front stairs. ("No matter how many times they have to go up or down stairs, they must go tramping up and down this front way. And you know what stairs look like after they've been tramped up and down a few times.") The staff has also been gossiping about the Passemores, a local couple both found dead in their home — a scandal yet unknown to Harriet. The notoriously jealous husband killed his wife (who we later learn was having an affair) and then himself.

Ethel, engaged to a Gene Fredericks, tells Harriet how anxious her mother is to see her marry. Harriet (to my mind, sagely) responds, "I don't know why your mother should be so panicky about your future, Ethel; you're only twenty-one… I think you're a very foolish girl…if you allow your mother's apprehensions to rush you into marriage." ["Ethel. She didn't want me to rush into it — she simply said she thought it would be better for me to be settled. Mrs. Craig (*bringing her hat back to the table, and taking a powder puff from her bag*) Well, naturally, I can understand that, of course. But, after all, simply being settled isn't everything, Ethel — a girl can be a great deal worse off being settled than when she was unsettled."] Ethel tells her that Gene is a Professor of Romance Languages, to which Harriet remarks, "And I suppose he's told you he loves you in all of them." Then Harriet confides her own philosophy/strategy:

> *I saw to it that my marriage should be a way of emancipation for me. I had no private fortune like you, Ethel; and no special equipment, outside of a few college theories. So the only road to independence for me, that I could see, was through the man I married. I know that must sound extremely materialistic to you, after listening to the Professor of Romance Languages; — but it isn't really; because it isn't financial independence that I speak of particularly. I knew that would come — as the result of another kind of independence; and that is the independence of authority — over the man I married...I have a full appreciation of Mr. Craig — he's a very good man; but he's a husband — a lord and master — my master. And I married to be independent.*

Harriet embellishes further that she's exacting her share of a bargain — a wife and home for Mr. Craig in exchange for security and protection for her, but she remains insecure about her share of the pact, "because I know that, to a very great extent, they are at the mercy of the *mood* of a *man*." She ensures it by securing the control. Realizing her niece is shocked, Harriet adds, "It's very much safer, dear — for everybody. Because, as I say, if a woman is the right kind of a woman, it's better that the destiny of her home should be in *her* hands — than in any man's." Interestingly, Julia Lesage in *The Hegemonic Female Fantasy*, astutely observes that "Kelly's pejorative use of the word *independence*, repeated various times, indicates that his dialogue stands as an ideological reaction to women's gaining the right to vote in the U.S. in 1920." She believes that he deliberately used feminist rhetoric to make Harriet seem *unnatural*, that "[she] should self-consciously and from the start oppose a husband's authority." (So it's not just me who sees through all this?)

Walter is surprised but delighted to find his wife returned early. His erotic attachment to her is inferred (note also that irritating sex/violence pairing, however understated it may be; — and I wonder at its significance here — only to convey his "passion" for Harriet?):

> *Craig (drawing her back into his arms):* I'm glad to have you back again.
> *Mrs. Craig (laughing lightly):* Stop it, Walter.
> *Craig:* Seems you've been away a month instead of a week. (*He kisses the side of her head*)
> *Mrs. Craig:* Don't break my bones, Walter.
> *Craig:* That's what I think I'd like to do sometimes.

He then releases her and she straightens up, touching her hair. He seems amused by her distrust of Mrs. Frazier whom he finds perfectly innocuous. A great line is when Harriet retorts, "Mrs. Frazier is very likely one of those housekeepers that hides the dirt in the corners with a bunch of roses." She feels the widow deliberately insinuated herself into the house to see it ("It's a form of curiosity that women have about other women's houses that men can't appreciate") and him. (And is that so hard to believe?) Soon Walter learns of the Passemores' deaths through his friend Billy Birkmire, but doesn't want to upset Harriet with the news. He had been at their home the night of the murder for a game of cards while Harriet was away. Learning someone from that number called Walter, Harriet had dialed it to find out who which alerts the police to investigate the Craigs. Meanwhile, the rest of the household is getting annoyed with Harriet, amazingly all sympathizing with Walter (author intrusion?), and Miss Austen, Walter's aunt who lives with them (yet another maternal figure), advises him to impress on his wife that there is a "man" of the house "and that *you* are that man." (Never did enjoy these interfering old busybodies who betray their own sex.)

Walter is at first reluctant to accept his aunt's words, but when Harriet proves more worried about scandal than his involvement in the Passemores affair, he "sees the light" or his aunt's version of it. Suddenly everyone is coming down on Harriet for every infraction imaginable and abandoning her, one by one, Miss Austen even accusing, "It's a great wonder to me you haven't asked us to take off our shoes, when we walk across the carpet." (Hilarious since Crawford was famous for having people remove their shoes before walking across her white carpets and I do the same). Walter is angry he can't smoke throughout the house and must do so in the den *with the door closed*, as if this is somehow unreasonable. Symbolically he smashes Harriet's beloved vase. Here comes the full frontal revelation of Kelly's agenda: "I saw your entire plan of life, Harriet, and its relationship to me," Walter says. "And my instinct of self-preservation suggested the need of immediate action — the inauguration of a *new regime here*...And I was going to smash all the other little ornaments — and Gods you had set up in the temple here, and *been worshipping before me*. I was going to put my house in order, including my wife; and rule it with a rod of iron." (emphasis added) Er — didn't Harriet already have the home in order until *he* made it disorderly? Harriet returns that he hasn't "lost anything by it, have you?" He benefited from the set-up as well. Almost crying, she tells him of her "I will follow thee, my husband" mother who was betrayed by her father and died of a broken heart, losing her home, and how their new stepmother got rid of her and her sister as soon as Esther was marriageable. Ironically, he makes no attempt to explore this key issue with her, but only says, "I guess I'm a bit old-fashioned — I must be trusted — and you never trusted me." He walks out, leaving her the house and all the things.

As if it's not enough punishment, Harriet gets a telegram that her sister is dead, which causes her to burst into remorseful tears that she didn't remain longer at her side. Doubtless, we're meant to see her lonely misery among her possessions as a fitting comeuppance (not!) but since Mrs. Frazier drops over with more roses and promises to come again, there's hope that Harriet will develop a rewarding friendship with the lonely widow.

Forsaking All Others by Edward Roberts and Frank Morgan Cavett (1933) ★★★★★

Not since James Warner Bellah's *Dancing Lady* have I enjoyed a Joan-Crawford-film source this much! *Forsaking All Others*, a smashing joint creation of Edward Roberts and Frank Morgan Cavett, opened on Broadway in 1933 with Crawford's friend Tallulah Bankhead in the lead. It's smart, fast-paced, witty as all hell, and not a bit dated with lively banter that rivals the most divine of the era and soufflé lightness. The arch, wise acre familiarity among the character/friends rings true and timeless. Sophisticated delights like this were why they called it the Golden Age.

(As an interesting note, Henry Fonda played a bit part in the Broadway production).

The play opens at Mary Clay's drawing room in the East 30s in New York, her fashionable digs filled with flowers, where some of Mary's friends are awaiting her return from her bridal shower. "Arthur Smith is sitting at the piano playing rather well," we're told (bring back the word "rather!") and Pamela LaSalle, who had been a Gibson girl with Mary's mother, is ordering the butler Dent about, trying to straighten the room. Jefferson Tingle ("around thirty years, old world weary, clothes good, conservative and he's slick and well brushed") arrives and rescues his favorite chair which Pamela had ordered removed. Best man Shep Perry of Wisconsin also returns from the party for Mary and fiancée Dillon Todd. Jeff and Dill went to Yale together. Dent mixes them a "ripsnorter" as Dottie, reading the society pages, notes that Constance Barnes is back in town. When Shep asks who she is, Jeff says, "Nobody. Take my word for it" and Smith responds, "Quite somebody" and Dottie adds, "Take my word for it." Apparently Connie Barnes is an old flame of Dill's, known for stealing other women's husbands.

Mary (to Jeff of Paula): Before I creep into my little white bed, I'm to slip into her room with my hair down my back and learn what a young girl should know.
Jeff: God I'd like to be there! I'll bet the stories she can tell will send you back with your hair in ringlets.
Mary: Put on a nightgown and go with me.
Jeff: A nightgown's no protection.

Mary receives more flowers and is especially delighted by the box of cornflowers ("How sweet of Dill to remember"). When Mary asks Shep, "How come some nice girl hasn't snapped you up?," Jeff responds, "The trouble with Shep is, he hasn't found a girl he thinks he's good enough for." When tall, slender and "very assured" Dill arrives, Jeff drops a heavy hint to Shep to leave the pair alone. Dill has known Mary since they were kids. Mary thanks Dill for the cornflowers after they kiss. He says he never sent any, but she thinks he's kidding. Connie Barnes makes a surprise appearance ("tall and slenderer than any woman present"). "Her walk is a cultivated glide," her appearance appealing, "bordering on alluring." She tells Mary she's a clever girl for putting Dill through his paces, noting that Dill always said he hated big weddings. Mary greets her with friendliness and invites her to the wedding. Everyone eventually leaves, so Connie is alone with Dill.

At the day of the wedding, Paula, Matron of Honor, and Dottie are waiting anxiously for Mary. Everyone is nervous. Mary arrives late, looking marvelous and carrying lilies. They are all ready to go down the aisle when Jeff stops the "Wedding March" and announces to Mary that Dill has married Connie Barnes.

The next day the friends are sitting in Mary's rooms, waiting for her to come down. Jeff tells Shep to take Mary to Michigan to get her mind off things, but Mary suddenly enters, looking ravishing. Everybody is constrained. She is in a good humor, says it was her "best sleep in years, thank you," wants to know the details of Dill's wedding. When they suggest she should sue Dill for alienation of affection, she pooh-poohs it. Shep, uncomfortable, leaves and when alone, Mary breaks down. Jeff interrupts her to announce that Dill is there and Dill rushes in, lamenting that he made a terrible mistake. Mary sends him packing finally and asks Jeff to take her out to get plastered. She also discovers Jeff sent her the cornflowers.

The scene with Mary, Shep and Jeff at a new speakeasy is hilarious. Shep kisses Mary unexpectedly, then proposes as Jeff makes light of it. Shep, hot under the collar when he is sincere, says, "You won't be sorry, Mary...You don't know the satisfaction of tilling the soil, of knowing the wise and simple things of life — you don't know the kick of having two thousand dumb animals dependent on you. I want you to be dependent on me, too, Mary." Jeff, "still bland," quips, "I gather, Mary, that you're to be the favorite wife among two thousand concubines." Mary refuses Shep's proposal, however. Just as they're all swilling drinks, Connie Barnes arrives, looking for Dill. "I know what you all must be thinking," she says and Jeff responds, "You're good--" Lots of rapid-fire, wise acre dialogue as Connie awkwardly tries to cover with Mary ("It was really unfortunate — I mean that our marriage should have to be at such a time"). A great line is when Connie says, "Someone always gets hurt" and Mary responds, "Is Dill all right?" It transpires, however, that Connie has also been kept waiting, because Jeff knows she hasn't seen Dill since the wedding. Dill is staying with Jeff and is utterly miserable, in fact. Connie, embarrassed, leaves. Jeff has actually asked Dill to come. The man in question, sure enough, runs in. He pleads with Mary, explaining how he met Connie a year ago in a whirlwind romance, and how she called him before wedding, hysterical, begged to see him. They met and drove up the Hudson, she told him she loved him over and over, crying a little, and he lost his head. To Jeff's chagrin, Mary takes Dill back, seeing that he is genuinely sorry.

A month later the friends are again planning the wedding for Mary and Dill. (Dottie: "This is positively the last time I'll be a bridesmaid — at their wedding.") Dill and Jeff went to Mexico and Mary hadn't heard from Jeff since, aside from a postcard. When Jeff arrives, looking very slick, bathed and brushed, Mary runs to him: "Jefferson! Well, it's time — the kid himself!" There is lots of fun banter between the characters when Jeff finally announces that he won't be going to Mary's wedding because of work obligations. Mary, joking still, says she won't feel her wedding is the same without him and insists that he come to live with them then. When Mary is finally alone with Jeff, she confesses that she's been feeling life is far from satisfactory and is conflicted about marrying Dill. Jeff flies off the handle. "Are you one of those women who worry themselves into a fever trying to decide between pink and green? Haven't you got strength of character enough to know what it is you want and ask for it in a loud clear voice?"

The banter, never missing a beat throughout, now rises to breathtaking heights.

> *Mary:* I know the truly wise ones are simple. That's what I meant about you a minute ago. But it still doesn't necessarily follow that the truly simple are wise.
> *Jeff:* Shep, for instance.
> *Mary (smiling):* Shep. I expect him any minute to bring me his kite to fix.
> *Jeff:* Most people's kites need fixing.

Jeff proposes, Mary accepts and only minutes before the wedding, they both tell Dill. The same preacher as before arrives to marry Mary and Dill and Mary says, "Mr. Tingle for Mr. Todd."

Forsaking All Others is a treat with warm, believable friendships and wonderful sophistication, smart in a way literature has forgotten to be. Although padded and at variance from the play, the film with Crawford as Mary Clay and Clark Gable aptly as Jeff is a commendable adaptation, maintaining the lively spirit.

Goodbye, My Fancy by Fay Kanin (1948) ★★½

Originally I assumed the play *Goodbye, My Fancy*, adapted into one of Joan Crawford's least notable films, would supply the substance and purpose missing from said film which concerns Congresswoman Agatha Reed (Crawford onscreen) returning to her old alma mater, Good Hope College for Women in Massachusetts, for an honorary degree and confronting two romantic rivals. Allegedly the film had "watered down" the freedom-of-speech-on-campus issues at the plot's heart. The film, however, proves far preferable to its source which reeks of smarmy double entendres; a colossal and ironic disrespect for women; and an insulting, heavy-handed, general ickiness symbolized by the character of *Life* photographer Matt Cole. The import of the documentary Agatha wants to run for Good Hope's students only becomes clear in the final act which is a strong suit, but unintended ironies still abound. It boggles my mind that author Fay Kanin was herself a successful industry and social leader who became president of the Academy of Motion Arts and Sciences for a period. I wonder if she, like her character Agatha Reed, had all the men wondering what she would be like in bed (and one of them actually telling this — as gauche Cole does — to someone in her employ - way to go! — when not discussing if she puts her shoes on before her girdle) while she was so "respectfully" appointed. Are we to believe a man who treats her so smarmily and contemptuously is more "principled" than the elegant president of the college and former flame, Jim Merrill, whose supposedly unforgivable crime is his reluctance to show her anti-war documentary to the students? Pick your poison. Actually, Jim (embodied by elegant and charming Robert Young on film) comes across as the far worthier candidate, pun intended, in both versions. He ultimately proves himself a man — if less crass and aggressive than Cole — willing to go the mile for love.

The play, requiring a cast of eight males and twelve females, opened on Broadway with Madeleine Carroll in 1948. Nearly from the get-go, it is forced and vaguely discomforting. Even the brownies hidden in a secret dorm drawer, just as they'd been in Agatha's girlhood, are too — er, overbaked. Musing on what Agatha Reed is like as they prepare their room for her visit, improbably attempting to recreate the room exactly as Agatha remembered it (this requiring the faculty to unearth a musty couch with a broken spring from the basement), student Mary Nell hedges this guess: "Busty probably. Most women with brains, I notice it goes right to their bust." There is a staginess to the whole thing like *Bye, Bye Birdie*, which I can't believe it didn't influence, although it has little of the latter's charm. At one point Mary Nell enacts how she'd talk to a boy on the phone while lying down. Elsewhere she rhapsodizes over the honor of giving her room to this VIP: "Like people who slept in Napoleon's bed. (*Hastily*) I mean after he was dead, of course." Innocent as that remark may be, it tallies with the gratuitous and continuous leering undercurrent, particularly attached to blonde Agatha who evokes images of Tippi Hedren in *The Birds* — so feminine as she "fixes her face" and fixates on former love affairs as to appear completely disinterested in Washington. She is introduced tellingly as "undoubtedly the best thing that's happened to the United States Congress in a long time" as if her chief contribution to the Senate is that she's a fox. That remark sums up the tone of the entire play and the reason it is so problematic.

It's a pity these unsavory factors are at war, pun intended, with the heart of the play because the basic idea is good and Agatha — if not so trivialized and degraded by Cole and even by her own secretary Grace "Woody" Wood — is an attractive, potentially intriguing character, although scarcely credible as a D.C. bigwig. Ostensibly, Kanin made the co-eds naïve and Agatha's old school chum, Ellen Griswold, hen-pecked and dithery ("If there's anything I want to know I just ask Claude") to underscore (in red) how non-progressive or sheltered the students are. Like the broad stereotypes of the athlete and drama student, however, it's hokey. Referring to a girlhood pact made with Agatha to send each other a telegram when they lost their respective virginities: "Ellen. (*With a touch of embarrassment*) You know, Ag, I never did send you that telegram — like we promised. I guess I figured the wedding invitation would-- (*A vague gesture*)." Fortunately, Agatha rescues this humiliating scene when explaining her own excuse for not sending one: "Must have slipped my mind at the moment."

The premise has it that our gal was actually expelled from Good Hope twenty years ago for being caught climbing in the window at six a.m. after an all night tryst with a man. The man, whose name she never revealed to the faculty, was Jim Merrill and her disappearance allowed him to go on to the presidency at the school, free of scandal. Doesn't this very detail conflict with the play's theme of suppression of truth? Jim's own daughter, Ginny, who impresses Agatha with her thoughtful dignity, is ashamed of her father for his cowardice, for allegedly "selling out" and going along with what trustees — Claude Griswold being one — want. Given that money is indeed a factor in running a college, it doesn't seem so diabolical. Although Agatha never answered Jim's letters, she apparently carried the torch all twenty years unabated and, in fact, plans to be engaged to Jim over commencement weekend, her key motivation for attending. As if that isn't peculiar enough, the engagement occurs, Jim evidently similarly unchanged in ardor. All parties in the central love triangle carry on, in fact, as if five, even twenty years, is of no consequence.

A conflict occurs when Cole, another former flame from wartime, arrives to record the momentous occasion. From the get-go, he is less than chivalrous, to put it mildly. Contemptuously — calling the school dated — he says he'd like to print side by side the shot he got of Good Hope kids rolling hoops down the lawn with a picture he'd taken in Rome of fourteen-year-old girls soliciting in the streets ("Higher education — 1948"). Soon he's referring smarmily (what else?) to an allegedly compromising photo he took of Agatha in France and which she *actually offers to buy back*. Whatta guy! (And what is so scandalous about a photo of someone sleeping?) His rough kiss ("here's another memento since you've gone in for collecting them") contrasts with the tender, reassuring one given to her by Jim later.

"Revolting," as Agatha calls Cole in one lucid moment, also describes the inappropriate gossip that transpires between Agatha's "confidential" secretary and Cole. Upon discovering Agatha is not in for his photo session, he says, "Too bad. Thought I might pick up a little cheesecake for the piece." Woody actually supplies the picturesque detail that Agatha "doesn't wear a girdle," then ludicrously snaps, "That's not for publication." It gets worse:

> *Cole:* The first time I saw [Agatha] she was up to her hips in mud in a shell hole. I thought she was a native, and got a shot of her. That night the siege broke and she took a bath — came out a blonde from the *Detroit Free Press*.
> *Woody (sits hassock):* Was she a good reporter then?
> *Cole:* The only reporter I ever knew who could sit in a poker game, win the biggest pot and still have every guy wondering what she'd be like in bed.
> *Woody:* How long did it take you to find out?

If this is a woman who worked for Senators and cabinet members where one would imagine discretion was paramount, then I'm Mahatma Ghandi.

Was this supposed to be a happy ending — Agatha improbably abandoning the debonair, distinguished, virile, kind Jim, her heart throb of twenty years, for a man who comes off as a pig, pure and simple? Her attraction to him is as far-fetched as her friendship with Ellen who is under the thumb of blowhard Claude ("Claude won't let me diet") and can never get "anything straight." (On the Spanish Civil War: "That is the one where the Russians were fighting it out with the Nazis or something." — guess she wasn't in Jim Merrill's history class!)

In any case, Agatha's ultimate choice, if symbolic of letting go of a memory (you can't go home again), is more upsetting than satisfying. It's the reason neither play nor film ring "true," and the chemistry between Crawford and Young underscores which pair really belonged together. The most tender and "real" moment, in fact, occurs when Agatha/Joan recites the theme poem to ex-love Jim:

> *Goodbye, My Fancy,*
> *Farewell, dear mate, dear love.*
> *I'm going away, I know not where*
> *or to what fortune, or*
> *whether I may ever see you again.*
> *So goodbye, my fancy.*

If only the play sustained this beauty! Fay Kanin, alas, is no Walt Whitman.

The Last of Mrs. Cheyney by Frederick Lonsdale (1925; revised and rewritten 1929) ★★★★★

The play, which premiered at the St. James Theater in 1925, opens at Mrs. Cheyney's house at Goring where a charity concert is apparently under swing and the "servants" are gossiping inside (and thereby "introducing" the cast of characters, a rather obvious device), "servants" who evidently aren't quite what they seem to be. In true British tradition, they drolly poke fun at themselves.

> *George:* I never believed I would see a garden so full of swells as I have today. I've called everybody "my lord" and I ain't been contradicted once!
> *Charles:* The English middle-classes are much too well-bred to argue!

Clearly butler Charles is the "leader" of this group and possesses suave charm and savoir-faire, a quality he isn't afraid to share with his "betters." He intrigues the family in the household, striking them as a gentleman, his wicked humor delighting them. (Joan. "I suppose clothes do make the man, Charles?" Charles. "Many a bride has been disappointed when they have taken them off, my lady!") Of Lord Arthur Dilling, Charles remarks, "He has a reputation with women that is extremely bad; consequently, as hope is a quality possessed of all women, women ask him everywhere!" Lord Dilling apparently has "two eyes" for their mistress, Mrs. Cheyney. Lord Elton and

Lord Dilling apparently both have their sights set on Fay Cheyney who bills herself as "widow of a rich Australian; meaning to stay in England only a little." She liked the group so much, she decided to settle amongst them, we learn. The sophisticates are arch and cutting as they coolly take tea; predictably civil but somewhat amoral. ("If a man is prepared to give the woman he married such divine pearls, what would he be prepared to give the woman he loves?") Lord Dilling, a dishonorable man with thirty thousand pounds a year, meanwhile, feels sure he's seen Charles before.

The entire party clearly adores Mrs. Cheyney, vying for her attention when she makes her entrance with parasol. They extend invitations to her, one by Mrs. Ebley of the pearls who is hosting a party on an upcoming Tuesday. Mrs. Cheyney is aloof enough to get under playboy Arthur Dilling's skin, but charming: "You know, you're all too kind to me. I don't know why you are; I'm not the least amusing or modern; I don't drink; I don't smoke, and I don't swear — I'm really terribly dull." Arthur and Elton are civil rivals, but their dislike of one another is discernible. More exasperating is the fact that Mrs. Cheyney actually tolerates prig Elton while unimpressed by woman-magnet Arthur. There is the same great line as in the film:

> *Arthur:* When you were in London staying at the Ritz last week, I rang you up five times, and each time I was told you were out!
> *Mrs. Cheyney:* What a shame!
> *Arthur:* Were you out?
> *Mrs. Cheyney:* No! Each time I was in…Twice I answered myself and told you I was out!

Her banter keeps Lord Arthur Dilling interested and more determined than ever to win her over. After he leaves, she says, "Damn!" This is the cue that she is not who she appears to be. She begins to play the piano and, as the servants relax around her, the whole scenario is exposed. They are a gang of jewel thieves with Charles their ringleader and Mrs. Cheyney their operative, hired to ingratiate herself to this family and steal Mrs. Ebley's pearls. However, she is feeling resistant to going through with the plan, given how much she likes her "marks." Charles is sympathetic, tolerant, and charming about her misgivings. Subtly but surely, he talks her back into it.

At Mrs. Ebley's country home ten days later when the sting is set to take place, the party is playing bridge and drinking tea, very British. Arranging to be alone with her, Arthur tells Fay Cheyney he'd marry her if it's the only way he can have her, but she protests, "I know too much about you, and you know too little about me." She is forbidden fruit for him and when he asks if she is "all the things that a man demands from a woman he is going to marry," she says, "I'm every one of the things you mean," a requirement I find cryptic, wondering what "demands" exactly he would make.

The tables turn, however, when Arthur at last remembers Charles as a charming crook he'd encountered in Monte Carlo. He intercepts an empty cigarette box that Charles is having delivered to Mrs. Cheyney which says, "Courage, my sweet!" Now enlightened, he determines to trick the tricksters — namely, the delectable Mrs. Cheyney — and sets his trap (literally), waiting for her like a cat with a mouse. But things don't go quite as expected when his mouse is trapped. In a twist of irony (perfect for Crawford whose films often parallel details in her own bio), Fay Cheyney had been a shopgirl in stockings and began a life of crime under Charles' tutelage to improve her social position.

The denouement has many twists and a delicious interplay that actually brought tears to my eyes. The relationship between Fay (her real name was Jane, we learn) and Arthur, in fact, is delectable. He makes an appointment with a bishop: "I said we would be there at five minutes to eleven." Mrs. Cheyney: "Oh! Does he think I'll come?" Arthur: "He's more certain of it than I am."

Ultimately "the last of Mrs. Cheyney" is very charmingly assured. It is a sublimely sophisticated and sexy parlor drama with a wonderful heroine and a butler more suave than the alleged playboy (true also of his screen counterpart as embodied by the divine William Powell).

The film does justice to the urbane script and Joan Crawford and William Powell are superb choices in the leads. They make a wonderful team, both being favorites of mine, and have a fascinating chemistry, although, sadly, they were paired only this once.

The Shining Hour by Keith Winter (1935) ★ ★ ★ ½

I'm tempted to give Keith Winter's play *The Shining Hour* more stars on the strength of his refreshingly compassionate portrait of a beautiful, "misunderstood" woman, a female character of spirit and intelligence, but I'll restrain myself from overrating it. The film with Joan Crawford as the femme fatale in question who upsets the happy homestead follows the original play quite nicely, but with significant, loopy MGM alterations that are so goofy, they are priceless. (Henry to Judy in film: "You've become lovely to look at." Judy: "What do you mean 'become?' I don't like that word. So gradual." This favorite MGM moment was not in the original play.)

Set in Yorkshire at an Elizabethan farmhouse, Windsend, the play has an amusing and telling set notation for a baby grand piano: [it] "wears an air of mild surprise," as if symbolic of its owner David Linden who never fit into the country. Through expositional conversation as the table is being set, the relationships of the characters become understood. Boyish, sensible Judy is married just over a year to David who owns the house, but is overshadowed by David's grey-haired, "capable," no-nonsense, spinsterly sister Hannah. Continually acerbic and domineering, Hannah infers she told David to marry Judy. "'She looks willing enough,' I said, 'and you can't expect more than that, these days.'" Judy is shocked and wants to know if David really asked Hannah's advice on his marriage, which Hannah then rebukes, typical of the devilment Hannah dishes out. Apparently brother Henry, 48, newly remarried and in early retirement, will now be living with them at the farmhouse as his own home across the valley is completed. Hannah already dislikes Henry's new wife, Mariella.

> *Judy:* For heaven's sake, Hannah, she's only been in the house for a few hours.
> *Hannah:* Well, you wait and see…Too pretty for this part of the countryside.

Judy shows magnanimity: "I think she's attractive…There's something rather elusive about her." Henry is besotted with Mariella, Hannah acidly observes, and infers that her name is "sheer affectation." When Henry, "the most polished of the Lindens," enters, the slight bitterness about his mouth indicates that he has some of his sister's stick-in-the-mud, judgmental personality. We learn that Henry made the farm over to David and is "happier now" with flashy, young wife. Fittingly Hannah is carrying pickles. Henry worries Hannah won't be nice to Mariella.

> *Hannah:* What do you think I'm going to do? Eat her?
> *Henry:* I wouldn't put it past you.

Youngest Linden Micky arrives — "20, extremely handsome with an easy assurance that seems somehow misplaced." Both Micky and David race horses, David a frequent champion. "Tall, fair and unusually beautiful" Mariella finally appears and Micky is "agreeably startled" by her. (Stage description: "In a curious way she seems to combine the nervousness of a child with the assurance of a woman. There is something wild about her, but there is also something very still…She is probably about thirty.")

Mariella is clearly unused to the country and has already encountered small-mindedness on her walk: "The whole population turned out to see me as though I were the bearded woman, or something. Then they just stood about and stared at me with dull loathing." Judy expects Mariella's bare legs startled them, too, to which Mariella responds, "But I always have bare legs. Haven't they seen them before?"

Clearly Hannah is going to give Mariella a hard time similar to the reception by the villagers. Mariella dares to have a drink in the afternoon, although Henry tells her none of the Linden women drink, and accepts whisky when Henry can't find gin. She is an outcast of sorts, not a neat fit into household. She is also not English; it's her first time in England (although author uses British colloquialisms frequently in her dialogue). After Mariella leaves the room, Hannah makes digs about her drinking, even suggesting that Henry has "gone and married another drunk." David, age 25, meanwhile, has come in, his face a mixture of the weak and strong, and even without having met Mariella yet, he says, "Come off it!"

When David first encounters Mariella on the stairs as the family is about to have dinner, they stare at each other in slight embarrassment. David is so distracted by this beauty at the table that when Hannah asks him to pass the mustard, he passes the salt. It's also learned that Mariella is an extremely good rider, something she has in common with David. Henry, by contrast, is clearly out of their league.

David: Can you still sit on a horse, Henry?
Henry: If it's very old and not too healthy.

By the second act, it is clear Judy is preoccupied while playing bezique, a card game, with Henry. We learn David is out riding with Mariella and this is why. Henry observes "some nasty looking clouds rolling up," obvious foreshadowing. It starts to rain and Mariella comes in, wearing David's tweed coat over her riding-clothes. Henry observes that Mariella has come back "in a very playful mood." Meanwhile, Micky is also transparently sexually attracted to Mariella and reacts in a huff when she has forgotten her promise to ride with him.

Tensions escalate between the characters. Mariella feels she should live somewhere else while her house is being worked on, indicating it's because of Hannah, but Judy bluntly asks her why she ever married Henry. Mariella supplies the rest: "you mean…when I wasn't in love with him?" Both women, as it turns out, married for less than love. David was never in love with Judy yet she persuaded him to marry her. Mariella never told

Henry she loved him. Judy *told* David he loved *her*. David, interrupting them, senses the gaiety Mariella had during their ride is gone. The scene grows tense and ends with David stopping her from leaving and kissing her. She's upset and crying, and runs to her room. He calls after her. Judy, meanwhile, has the agony of trying to pretend she doesn't know what is going on.

Mariella begs Henry to take her away and he shows a disagreeable side of himself by shaking her when she screams she won't stay in this house any longer. He says, "You'll stay exactly where I tell you, see!" He is an oblivious prig. Again a storm is brewing. Mariella is evidently trying hard to snub David and distance herself for Judy's sake, while Micky reveals David doesn't belong on a farm either, too sensitive and arty. It seems Hannah's earlier accusation that Mariella "was a disturbing influence on the household" has come true. Judy, however, can no longer deny the truth, urges Mariella to run away with David, and frees the way with tragedy.

The Shining Hour has many truly laudable qualities, a very grown up and sophisticated perspective, especially in its indictment of small-mindedness. Mariella is a wonderful heroine, refreshingly not painted as the villain even when odd girl out, and eventually comes into her own, asserts her needs and triumphs. Her courage in flying in the face of disapproval is wonderful and, although MGM put a silly spin on things, Joan Crawford remains an apt choice for this role.

Susan and God by Rachel Crothers (1937) ★★★★★

> *Susan (calling from outside at right):* You darlings — you darlings — you <u>darlings!</u>
>
> *Susan and God*, Rachel Crothers

The two scripts available to me of *Susan and God* were a "pre-Philadelphia" one and an "after Philadelphia" version when presumably it had had its tryout and opened at the St. James Theater in New York City. Naturally, I chose the "after Philadelphia" play, believing (rightly) it would be more polished. The script was superb, full of fantastic dialogue with rapid-fire wit (as in the film), far more cohesive and multi-dimensional than the film really conveys, its biting quality and irony more transparent and fresh on paper. However, it was missing the third and final act! Chagrined, I sought out the "pre-Philadelphia" script which was filled with pencil edits. Although one could see how the edits improved the flow, it was still in draft form and unpolished, but at least I was able to finish the play. I'd still love to get my hands on that missing "after Philadelphia" third act!

The relationship between the characters, particularly Susan and Barrie Trexel, is much more clearly defined in the play. It opens at Irene Burroughs' Connecticut home where languid and outwardly superficial society types are at "play," their gossip centered around mercurial

PHOTO COURTESY OF JERRY MURBACH

Susan Trexel of their set who is planning to drop in on them with some important announcement. Irene, not yet divorced, is having an affair with Mike O'Hara, "tall — dark and good-looking — with a slightly indolent manner — great charm and a great attraction for women." She is eager that Susan not find out. As in the film, she says of Susan and Barrie, "I adore them both — but not when they're together." It is quickly established that this "gay" party is not what it appears. Barrie gets tight and has smash-ups and, although Susan was once madly in love with him, she tired of him. Middle-aged Hutchins Stubbs "with a general air of being somebody and rather a slow moving superior manner" has married a beautiful actress, Leonora Stubbs, but is threatened by her friendship with Clyde, an actor from her former career in theatre ("with a laugh and a cheerfulness very irritating to the uncheerful"). When asked what Susan's trouble is, Stubbie says: "Too much charm. Life has never disciplined her at all!" Irene says of Susan and Barrie: "They <u>destroy</u> each other." And: "Sometimes I think that's why Susan's always mad about some new fad trying to fill up her disappointment in Barrie." Charlotte remarks that Susan "gets tired of everything," even daughter Blossom. But their lives clearly center on Susan who blows onto the scene: "35 — a woman with so much charm that it covers most of her faults — most of the time — for most people. She is slender and alert and pretty — with a very individual style and chic."

The action moves at a whip-like pace, the dialogue and wit keeping time, with one great line after another. Susan goes to kiss Leonora, then realizes she doesn't know her. Stubbie introduces her as his wife to which Susan responds: "Your <u>first</u> <u>wife</u>! How wonderful!" She is hyped up about a new experience she wants to share with the group. When Stubbie asks her how the "good old Riviera" was, she says: "Oh, I've <u>forgotten</u> it." Rhapsodizing over new acquaintance Lady Wiggam, she calls her "one of the rarest creatures I have <u>ever</u> known" and, after mentioning how distinguished and well-heeled Wiggam is, she says, "but that isn't it… It's her soul." The whole sequence is hilarious, as are many others. Susan tries to describe this new movement which isn't a religion: "Well, — it <u>is</u> — in a way — but you can keep right on being what you <u>are</u> — an Episcopalian — or Catholic or a Jew — or colored — or anything. It's just love — love — love — <u>love</u> — for <u>other</u> people — not for yourself." Although MGM did not convey the complexity found in Crothers' play or in Susan, Crawford delivered these lines marvelously, using her voice in a new technical way for full comedic potential. It was another vastly underrated role for her. The original script has much brilliance as when Susan waxes on her new enlightenment: "It's <u>thrilling</u> and <u>alive</u> and <u>fun</u> — so people aren't <u>ashamed</u> <u>to</u> <u>be</u> <u>good</u>."

Double entendres abound:

Charlotte of Susan's peonies: They're bloomin' their bloomin' heads off — with nobody to admire them.
Susan: I expect they admire themselves. All beautiful things do.

And one of my favorites:

Armine (butler): I beg pardon, sir — Mrs. Burroughs says she is extremely sorry not to see you — but she's in the bath.
Barrie: Oh — I'm sorry not to see <u>her</u>.

In spite of her delirious conversion, Susan is transparently still interested in gossip and determined to "convert" her friends, pinpointing everyone's faults and problems but her own. Still the couples orbit around her like satellites. They don't take her seriously, but become annoyed and alarmed when she seems to "see" through them to the underlying situations and furtive entanglements. The entrance of Blossom, neglected daughter of Susan and Barrie, has a genuine pathos and is a pivotal point in the action. Seemingly unwanted by her frivolous parents, she worries that her father is bored by her: "We've been together four hours…It's the longest I've ever been with you in my life." Her plight is much more affecting on paper than it ever is in the film. Barrie also delivers a sly, telling line, summing up the whole play when Blossom says she likes him "like this" (not drunk): "Somehow what we mean to be and what we are — are quite different."

The great lines go on and on: When Charlotte says Susan is just being polite for wanting to buy two of her pups, Susan says: "No — you can't accuse me of that. I have millions of faults but at least I'm not polite." Susan's friends conspire to turn the tables on her by inventing "confessions," all the while preventing Barrie from knowing she is there. But this backfires when Barrie stumbles on her professing her belief that people can be "made over" to Mike. He is drunk, yet moved, which humiliates and exposes her. They have a confrontation the next morning while she is in bed where she tells him she isn't in love with him anymore and can't live with him as his wife. He makes an amazing proposition, stricken by Blossom's unhappiness which he is recognizing for the first time. He wants them to live together as a family in their country home and should he stray once with alcohol, he will grant Susan a divorce. This will be an enormous sacrifice for him, since he is still "much in love with" her. ("I'm perfectly on to you. You don't fool me a bit — any more — and still you're the only woman in the world for me.") Interestingly, it becomes clear that Susan has actually "lost faith" in her intimate relationships.

The love-starved Blossom is thrilled with the arrangement. Another fabulous line occurs. Blossom asks Susan what she thinks God is. Susan (after a pause): "I'm sure I haven't the faintest idea." And when Blossom wears Irene's negligee over too-long pajamas, Susan says: "Take it off. You look like a girl scout — gone wrong." (They try to do this in the film, substituting another situation, but the wit doesn't come off, even though Crawford in that white suit is worth the price of admission and delivers the lines perfectly.)

Interestingly, Susan's obvious posturing about God effects everyone around her in spite of its original shallowness. She exposes the lost faith in all, their need to believe in something. Irene wonders if Mike is serious about her or if it is only an affair. Susan realizes how much Blossom has felt unloved. By the third act, we see that the experiment of the "happy family" has not worked quite so seamlessly, however. (When Mike mentions that Susan hasn't talked all summer about "the thing you came back on fire with," Susan replies, "I've been too busy running this amusement park — to think about God.") But the final twist comes where love and faith are restored — happily and hopefully, but not simplistically. As in the film, Susan gives love another chance, praying: "Dear God, don't let me fall down."

An impressive, intelligent, fast-paced tour de force of wit by Rachel Crothers. Although the film conveys little of the play's depth and clarity and its Susan comes off more as an absolute airhead than a multi-dimensional woman, Joan Crawford does a sensational job as the dizzying dame, using her voice delightfully. She is at the peak of her sculptural, goddessy beauty in Adrian's classical Greek gowns. Unfortunately, she and Fredric March (as Barrie) are given scant opportunity to express any depth to make their marriage credible in MGM's version, although the actors try. Part of the problem is that the film script — in typical sexist and MGM fashion — places all the blame for the marriage's failure on Susan, whereas in the play Barrie's alcoholism was the chief issue and reason for Susan's behavior. Without that clear delineation, the central dynamics are weakened. While not realizing the play's potential, the film is still enjoyable, however, and a delicious and unique comic showcase for Crawford.

Torch Song by Kenyon Nicholson (1930) ★★
Filmed as *Laughing Sinners*

Torch Song, which was adapted into the Joan Crawford film *Laughing Sinners*, opened at the Plymouth Theater on Broadway in August, 1930 with Mayo Methot in the lead as Ivy Stevens, the role Crawford played. Like the film, the original play is very dated yet has a saucy grit and a genuinely touching core which "redeems" it (excuse the pun). Set at a variety of cheap roadhouses in the Cincinnati, Ohio area, it follows the plight of appealing, tender-hearted Ivy Stevens, a chorus girl in love with a faithless traveling salesman, Howard Palmer. Ivy is described as "an attractive, vivacious girl of about 20, bubbling over with an infectious enthusiasm. She wears a gray squirrel coat thrown over her shoulders. Under the coat, a scanty stage costume — rhinestone brassiere and shorts." Crawford — young, voluptuous, cuddly and sweet in those early years — embodied this girl with breathtaking sincerity and was certainly stunningly beautiful without any of the hardness she would display in her later career. Howard's friend Fred aptly describes Ivy as "a little dame with bedroom eyes and a pretty voice" — true of 1931 Crawford as well. Nice touches abound with fellow chorus girl, Ruby, clad in a "garish décolleté gown" and suffering from a head cold, opening with, "Hello, Otto. What do you know that's nasty?" As in the film, open-hearted Ivy sings a ballad to her man who is, meanwhile, planning on dropping her to marry the boss' daughter. Unlike the film, however, the play makes much clearer that Howard has a conscience and genuine feelings for Ivy, but is egged on by his no-account friend to leave the girl a note when he can't tell her in person. He runs out on her in the middle of her song. As he admits later, "It was the yellowest thing I ever did in my life."

The '30s lingo and dialogue is a hoot. Ivy describes a drink as "hotter than the hinges of hell" and of her torch song to Howie, it is said: "It'd bring tears to a glass eye." *Torch Song* depicts the tawdry realities of traveling salesmen in honky tonk towns and run-down hotels. It's frank about "easy virtue" yet somehow sympathetic and that "kindness" is what makes it appealing. Meals are a dollar at the flea bit hotel, which is seen as an outrage, and amusingly rooms fall into the same range, going up to $2.50 "and more." The salesmen don't have an easy life with chain stores cutting into their trade, but find passing amusement with "baby dolls" in the towns they blow into. Fred and Howard, in fact, are about to have a good time with one such "doll" named Edna ("about 20 — a product of small-town viciousness") and her teen friend, Betty, a shy country girl. Howard obviously has a way with women as Fred laments: "Edna'll stick to you like a wet bathing suit." (Edna: "Is he so much of a lady's man?" Fred: "Is he! When he says frog, they jump!") Meanwhile, unknown to Howard, Ivy is now a disciple of the Salvation Army, trying to save souls under the protective wing of comrade Carl Loomis ("big and gaunt with the hollowed cheeks and intense eyes of a born religieu. These eyes, dark and sunken, have an almost hypnotic power in their fierce, unwavering glance"). The fetching girl, even under the cloak of piety, has caught the eye of the men, inspiring ribald conjecture. (Fred: "A Salvation Army lassie…Well, she could save me and not half try.") Ivy sees Howard on the street, shaken by his presence, and when she and her Salvation Army associates request rooms at the hotel, not aware that Howard is also staying there, she is put in the room next to his. The man at the desk figures Howard will appreciate the babe, unaware of their former relationship.

Meanwhile, Ivy soon makes the discovery that Howard is her neighbor, inspiring the jealousy of Edna who picks up on the attraction between the two. Her dialogue is almost identical to a line found in the Crawford film *Untamed*. ("Edna — She's got a lotta crust! Who does she think she is anyway!") Ivy, bearing Howard no malice, begs him to give up this party for his own sake and extols what she calls "the surrendered life" (a line which gave me the willies, given the subservient position allotted to women in most religions). Still smitten by her, he reluctantly agrees.

Carl, meanwhile, encountering this man Ivy had told him so much about, is wary and unconsciously jealous as Howard is of him, although he demonstrates a gentle care towards Ivy which impresses Howard. He questions Ivy about her feelings for her ex. "It's funny, but when I saw Howard," she says, "I only felt sorry for him. It was like he was in a dark prison and I was on the outside. Free and in the sunshine."

The party with Ida, Betty, and the boys invades Howard's room because of the downpour and somewhat drunk, the couples begin to get out of hand. Fred begins ravenously kissing Betty who sits on his lap while trying to get her drunk so he can take advantage of her. Another of these phrases so popular in early Joan films crop up: "Can it be he doesn't mean right by our Nell!" Howard, fearful of Ivy's disapproval, chases out the marauding couples, and Ivy comes into his room. She insists she bears Howard no malice for the past, as much as she had been hurt by him. Carl Loomis came to her room nightly and talked with her, introducing her to a greater cause. Leaning out the window, Howard smells lilacs and remarks pointedly, "Funny how a shower brings out their perfume. When I was a kid and used to visit my grandfather's farm, the lilacs after a spring rain would nearly make me dizzy, they smelled so sweet." Unable to convert Howard, Ivy cries in despair, but Howard, obviously still caring deeply for her, quickly comforts her. "Everybody can't think the same way about religion any more than they can about politics. We'd still be friends if you were a Republic and I was a Democrat, wouldn't we?"

However, the night goes astray on many levels. Betty becomes unconscious after being forced to drink too much ale and Fred is in a panic that they can't revive her. Ivy, striving ecstatically to convert Howard ("Yield yourself to Him, do what He desires! Kneel in full surrender — let His love flow into you!"), succumbs herself to her old flame and the next day does an about turn on her newfound commitment in despair and shame. ("From now on I'm going to take my scriptures with a grain of salt. Once bit twice shy.") As in the film, she drinks hooch and dances on a table, shaking her tambourine, throwing all caution to the wind (Crawford was absolutely adorable in this scene). Howard is in an "agony of self-denunciation," realizing he once again did a number on the poor kid ("And the worst of it is, she's really crazy about this plaster saint she's traveling around with…") and is determined to rectify the damage. He also recognizes that Ivy is the one he has always loved, more than he ever has his wife, and does the noble thing by restoring her to Carl's fold, putting her welfare above his own desire. Carl, seeing Ivy in her debauched condition, reacts partly as a jealous man and belts Howard. Then Ivy breaks up the fight with this phenomenal speech that made the whole play for me:

> *Ivy:* You quit fighting over me, do you hear? Get this — both of you. I don't belong to anyone. (Turning fiercely on Howard) You — you think you own my body, don't you? And Carl here, he's staked a claim on my soul. Well, you can both get that idea out of your head! I'm the one that has to carry them about, love with them, hate with them — and suffer with them. And they're not separate like you seem to think; they're all mixed up together. I'm not a bitch and I'm not an angel! I'm a woman.

Wow.

With a fab speech like that cutting timelessly through the cloth of time, *Torch Song* proves to still have guts. Dated as some of it may be, it also has a real kindness, caring and compassion that touches, bringing dimension to its players. Howard puts Ivy's needs above his own and Carl recognizes he loves this girl as a man as well as a preacher. He convinces her he will not censure her for stumbling, teaching a great lesson in self love through self-forgiveness. All is well that ends well.

When Ladies Meet by Rachel Crothers (1932) ★ ★ ¾

It is difficult rating certain works which leave me conflicted. Usually original literature has advantages over film versions, such as greater insight/detail, and although that is true to some extent here, *When Ladies Meet* still works better in the 1941 Joan Crawford/Greer Garson film because the play's humiliating virginity conflict has been excised. In general, this Rachel Crothers' effort is much weaker than her superb *Susan and God*. The concept is intriguing — a writer falls in love with her married publisher and her longtime admirer arranges for her to meet the publisher's wife unknowingly at a country getaway. The character of dithery Bridget Drake (played onstage and onscreen by Spring Byington) is hilarious and often inspired, but publisher Rogers Woodruf's excruciating flowery wooing wouldn't fool even a fool — let alone a thirty-year-old woman as writer Mary Howard (Crawford onscreen) is supposed to be (although, according to the play, it does). There are uncomfortable double standards here reminiscent of "The Women" in which women apparently expect and often tolerate infidelity from men. Only they are judged for sexual transgressions, too, and never do they question the inequity of it. That aside, the two women are fairly complex and both likeable and their meeting generates some interest, if only there wasn't the haggling about grown women's virginity along the way.

The play opens at Mary Howard's New York/West 10th Street apartment where apparently she has a balcony and wonderful garden. (Must be nice!) Mary ("an extremely pretty woman about 32…[h]er Spring clothes are smart and alluring") and ardent suitor Jimme Lee (unorthodox but with a great "likeableness") are "relaxed with Spring laziness, cigarettes and cocktails." Jimmie wants Mary to marry him, but she insists it's never going to happen. He brings up her publisher, Rogers Woodruff, tellingly noting, "Woodruf's married — isn't he?" He feels her latest book is artificial and that she knows nothing about these characters. Mary insists she does, the book transparently based on her own situation — a woman in love with a married man. Love, she attests, "[c]changed them both from just *people* — into something *fine*." She feels Jimmie puts women in pigeon holes, "a *man's* idea of women. There are just as many reasons and conditions for women as there are for men." Jimmie, with typical chauvinism and double standard, retorts, "Nope! If a woman's good — she's good — and if she isn't — she *isn't.*"

> *Mary:* That's the greatest bunk in the world. It's just what the book is *about*. You don't even *get* it — Damn you! [Getting out of her chair and moving to the Right.]

> *Jimmie:* [L]et me tell you what I *do* know. Man is a *very law abiding animal when it comes* to *decent women*. He wants a decent woman to *stay* decent — and if she *doesn't* he cusses her out for doing the *very* thing he told her was the greatest thing a woman *can* do — *giving him all her love*…God — I've persuaded so many women and hated 'em afterwards!

This contemptible speech, cut from the film, made Jimmie (embodied so charmingly by Robert Taylor onscreen) less "likeable." Crothers displays her flair for dizzying dames with the entrance of Mary's friend Bridgie: "She speaks in a quick sputtering sort of way — knowing as well as anyone else she isn't saying anything." Over forty, Bridget has a younger boyfriend, Walter, which evidently is supposed to be shocking. What *is* shocking, actually, is the inference that she isn't sleeping with the young stud. She invites Mary to her new country house for the weekend and casually Mary mentions Rogers as another good guest, claiming they need to work on her book. Mary feels Bridget need not invite other people for appearances sake, either, especially not jealous Jimmie. When Rogers ("42 — a man of the world with the poise of success — and an irresistible charm for women") arrives, he accepts Bridget's invitation to the country home and, after she goes inside, he and Mary look at one another with infatuation. Mary advises him to be careful when he moves towards her, adding, "Jimmie's here," to which Rogers snaps, "Damn him!" He moves closer to her and they carry on incandescently in the way of old films. "You're prettier than ever — this minute. Your throat is — " Mary: "Sh!" Tiresomely and predictably, he rhapsodizes on her *physically* and she over his being "wonderful" and *understanding* her.

Jimmie cagily mentions a hot author he could get Rogers to publish, suggesting *that* Saturday to bring them together. He unsuccessfully attempts to get himself invited to the house. Clearly he's on to them. Meanwhile, Mary tries to break it off with Rogers, not wanting to break up his marriage, and Rogers is as subtle as a sledge hammer: "You don't think I could go on in the old way with her *now* — do you?" She suggests they stay friends so she won't have to give him up, but he feels she's talking hot air: "We're not friends." He plays the usual emotional game, sulking, insisting that now he can't go up to the country if it's all it means to her. Obviously he is trying to break her down. He uses every trick, accusing her of being a coward and not loving him. Mary protests and he counters with this old saw: "If you did you wouldn't hesitate one second." Soon she is in his arms, wondering how anything "so right" can be wrong and he is ramming home his advantage when they are interrupted by Jimmie. Mary and Rogers immediately address each other as "Mr. Woodruf" and "Miss Howard" — once again, completely stiff and phony. Deftly Jimmie succeeds in whisking Rogers away before Mary can be "compromised."

At Bridget's lovely country home that weekend, again Rogers is nagging Mary as to why she kept away from him for two days when she seemed so sure before. She responds she *was* sure but then Jimmie came by. It would have only been emotion that night, had she done it, but now she *knows*. Mary sets up the situation perfectly for Rogers: "I *will not* let you get a divorce till we know our love *is what we think it is*." And this awful line: "Oh, Rogers — you don't know—what it means — for my kind of a woman to do this." He, naturally, is adverse to her confronting his wife and telling her about them. More insipid dialogue ensues: Rogers to Mary: "Oh, dearest you're awfully honest — and awfully sweet — and I love you and you've got the best looking feet in the world — *thoroughbred*." To infer any woman would fall for this or that this badgering is appropriate for anyone out of their teens is downright insulting. In any case, Rogers gets called into town to meet author Bix via Jimmie, saying to Mary as he leaves, "And tomorrow — we'll put in a good day — and finish off the job." Ouch.

Here chalk begins really scraping blackboard, making me squirm, as Bridgie hands down the sort of crippling slush that's been creating problems for girls for years, a bald attempt to *justify* Mary to the audience: "Men mean a great deal more to women than women do to men…Women *have got to be loved*. They're daring to have lovers — good women — because they just *can't stand being alone*."

The real meat of the play occurs when Jimmie shows up unexpectedly, claiming to have gotten lost — with Rogers' wife, Claire ("about 36, very intelligent face"), in tow. He asks Claire to pose as his cousin and flirt openly with him to make Mary — the woman he's nuts about — jealous. Good sport that she is, Claire agrees, calling him "Jimmie Dimmie." Mary and Claire are given bedrooms next to each other, Bridgie having quietly moved Rogers next to Walter. Still not knowing who Mary is and vice versa, Claire tells Mary that Jimmie has the makings of a great husband, to Mary's shock. Her reason is that, unlike most men, it wouldn't occur to him that anybody else would want him, so he wouldn't be looking around. (Oh, yes, ladies, we should be grateful for crumbs.) Later, as it storms conveniently, Mary invites Claire into her room to talk. She is eager for a woman's reaction to her book — "I mean my *own kind* of woman." In Mary's scenario, her character Eileen has an affair with a married man and confronts his wife about it. Eileen wants to live with the man first before he gives up his wife to be sure it's true love. Claire diplomatically offers that the man wouldn't appreciate the sacrifice the "other woman" is making, "apt to wish after a while she hadn't been *quite* so magnificent for his sake." She then lets drop the bomb that her own husband is cheating with this sickening admission, "I can always tell when an affair is waning.

He turns back to the old comfortable institution of marriage as naturally as a baby turns to the warm bottle." (Hey, women like nurturing and sex, too!) She fears, however, he may have met someone who is "the real thing." When Mary lets slip the name "Rog" and then tells Claire he is her publisher, Claire *knows*. At this convenient juncture, Rogers enters the room, shocked to find Claire there. Claire quickly says, "She doesn't know who I am, Roge." To Mary: "I'm Claire Woodruf."

The next day Mary, furious at Jimmie who admits to posing as Bix to lure Rogers away and masterminding the whole thing, plans to leave. She begs Rogers to tell Claire the truth now about their love, but when he hedges, she at last sees the truth about where she stands. She is prepared to give Rogers back to Claire, but Claire feels differently, now that she's met Mary and seen what her husband has done to both of them. She no longer loves or wants Rogers. ("I've *seen* her — and something has happened to *me*. I've seen *all* of her — her whole heart and soul and self. And I know — *so well* how you made her love you like that.") For his part, Rogers at least admits that Mary was special, "not like the others" (how white of him!) and would have married her, if not for Claire (so he could cheat on Mary?). At first wanting to leave immediately, Mary is convinced to stay on at the summer house where one anticipates and hopes that she will eventually get together with Jimmie who, however chauvinistic, seems to genuinely love and care about her.

Although the play has an interesting premise with wife and mistress understanding consequences of an affair for one another, the film improves it considerably by eliminating the silly virginity dilemma. Given barbaric practices like honor killings inflicted on "impure" women worldwide, it is not at all endearing. Mary's moral character is overemphasized, although she is indeed likeable and has integrity, and the sanctimoniousness, especially related to female sexuality, grates. ("Bridget: I can see that I'm going to lie the straight and narrow way for the rest of my life — and be *bored stiff* — but it's an *awfully wholesome feeling*."). Doesn't this make the men who clearly sleep around *unwholesome*? Were we to think less of either Bridget or Mary if they were playing more than bridge? Basically, however, the situation works out well. Rogers loses both women, as he deserves, and Mary is free now to love devoted Jimmie. The film shines with the fascinating pairing of upcoming MGM star Greer Garson with Joan Crawford, both extremely beautiful and glamorous — *thoroughbreds* — and excellent nuanced actresses. It's worthwhile to see these two meet, although Herbert Marshall is severely miscast as the object of lust.

The Women by Clare Boothe Luce (1936) ★★★★★

Second Saleswoman (in Crystal's Booth): What are you most interested in, Miss Allen, evening gowns?
Crystal: Until I-I organize my social life — I won't have much use for evening gowns.

Clare Boothe Luce's *The Women*, the queen bee of catty comedy, always arouses mixed emotions in me. While I appreciate its clever brilliance and biting wit and recognize its perfect pitch and orchestration — indeed, would label it a masterpiece, it is still an agonizingly painful reminder of where women were at (and still are) in a man's world and how they turn on one another and themselves rather than demand respect or accountability from their men. In any case, the cast is, of course, all female and the plot concerns an extramarital affair as observed — deliciously and maliciously — by a group of women. Luce is so good at picking up on tiny nuances, it's as if she had a glass to the wall and was recording private conversations. Wholly dependent on men for "security" and trained to resign themselves to a subordinate lot, indeed often maltreated and desperately unhappy, the women channel their aggression and frustration into petty gossip (and self-loathing). At the hub of the hive is Sylvia Fowler ("glassy, elegant, feline, 34") whose cattiness is an art form. ("You know I go to Michael's for my hair. You ought to go, pet. I despise whoever does yours.") Sylvia sets the wheels of treachery in motion against friend Mary "Mrs. Stephen" Haines ("what most of us want our happily married daughters to be like" [we do?!]) by recommending Mary see a fabulous new manicurist who will paint her nails the latest color - Jungle Red. The new manicurist also happens to know the inside scoop about an affair between shop girl Crystal Allen and Mary's husband, Stephen. Sylvia can hardly wait for Mary to find out.

Sylvia: The whole thing is so disgustingly unfair to Mary. I feel absolutely sick about it, just knowing about it.
Ethel: I adore Mary —
Sylvia: I *worship* her.

Since the play was written in 1937 but revised in 1966, references to Clark Gable, Joan Crawford, and Harpo Marx sit incongruously aside mentions of the Beatles and even Communism. (When cook Maggie remarks that maid Jane is "quite a[n] actress" as she mimics a conversation,

Jane responds, "My boyfriend says I got eyes like Joan Crawford.") Luce notes, "Today, Park Avenue living rooms are decorated with a significant indifference to the fact that ours is still a bi-sexual society," adding that Mary Haines' living room would be comfortable for a man — ironic when actually the confines of the living room and salon are the one outlet for female "power" in an otherwise male-dominated world. Luce is very good at picking up "lower tier" discontent ("Nancy. God, I'd love to do Mrs. Fowler's nails, right down to the wrist, with a nice big buzz saw!"), and the women, rich and poor, all ostensibly occupy this tier by virtue of gender. Little Mary Haines' nanny sums it up when reporting on the child's behavior to mother Mary, "In England, Mrs. Haines, our girls are not so wretchedly spoiled. After all, this *is* a man's world. The sooner our girls are taught to accept the fact *graciously*---" Jane adds, "Them English ones always stand up for the boys. But they say since the War, ma'am, there's six women over there to every man. Competition is something fierce! Over here, men aren't so scarce. You can treat them the way they deserve[.]" Another irony hidden in humor. The women continually advise one another to swallow pride for men and to distrust their own sex. As the ever-pregnant Ethel complains about her suffering in childbirth, there is this achingly piquant retort from her nurse:

> *Nurse:* Oh, no, Mrs. Potter. You had an easy time. (She is suddenly angry) Why, women like you don't know what a terrible time is. Try bearing a baby and scrubbing floors. Try having one in a cold filthy kitchen, without ether, without a change of linen, without decent food, without a cent to bring it up — and try getting up the next day with your insides falling out, to cook your husband's —

All the women abnegate themselves for love. Housekeeper Lucy is married to a man who beats her and almost escaped, only to be stymied by pregnancy. Mary's mother admits to waiting twenty years (upon her husband's death) to order the kind of meal she liked. Dithery Countess De Lage ("Ah! L'amour! L'amour!"), married solely for money, is puzzled by the near-fatal accidents she escapes with each husband. Edith complains, "I wish I were a virgin again. The only fun I ever had was holding out on Phelps." (And of his indigestion: "You should hear that man at night. Like a truck on cobblestones.") A corset model believes all a woman has to offer a man is her body. Never do they challenge the source of their discontent. It is mild Mary Haines, in fact, who initially takes action against hubby's philandering, although she is advised even by her own mother (citing a long history of wives, herself included, accepting infidelities) to grin and bear it. Ultimately, rather than blaming he who errs, Mary blames her girlfriends for *telling* her about the affair and then becomes a militant proponent of self-effacing love. To the Countess upon her latest humiliation: "Flora, let him make a fool of you. Let him do anything he wants, as long as he stays." Tellingly she quotes from a book: "When love beckons to you, follow him, though his ways are hard and steep. And when his wings enfold you, yield to him — Though his voice may *shatter your dreams* as the North Wind lays waste the garden." (emphasis added) The women reinforce this defeating philosophy, yet betray the unnatural model of docility and domesticity. (As Peggy comes to visit Edith who is lying in the hospital bed, nursing her new baby and smoking: "Peggy. (Alarmed) What's that on his nose? Edith. What nose? Oh, that's an ash. (Blows away ash.)")

In play and film, the show down between Crystal and Mary in a dressing room and the equally brilliant tête-à-tête between little Mary and Crystal in the bath are gems. One can't help rooting for Crystal (particularly in the film as embodied by a superb Joan Crawford who aces every line and look with consummate artistry), the one woman (besides little Mary) with any — er — balls. At the very least, she is willing to take a man for a ride who bloody well deserves it and maintain the upper hand on some level. She is also economically strapped. "Oh, can the sob-stuff, Mrs. Haines. You don't think this is the first time Stephen's ever cheated?...I have just as much right as you have to sit in a tub of butter." Obviously, as the earlier speech about competition foreshadowed, these ladies are all trapped on some level, their machinations survival tactics. ("Miss Trimmerback. I'm sick and tired...working like a dog. For what? Independence? A lot of independence you have on a woman's wages. I'd chuck it like that for a decent, or an indecent, home.") And, hilariously, when Sylvia discovers her husband is embroiled in an affair with Miriam: "You just want Howard for his money." Miriam: "And what do you want him for? I made Howard pay for what he wants; you made him pay for what he doesn't want."

With often spot-on, realistic dialogue, Luce holds up a mirror to her female world, capturing the petty meanness which is the domain of the oppressed and bored. It is brilliant and masterful. Building to a final coupe, Mary learns to unleash her own nails of "jungle red."

Sylvia: Just that uplift, Mary, you need. I always said you'd regret nursing. Look at me. I don't think there's another girl our age who

can boast of bazooms like mine. I've taken care of them. Ice water every morning, camphor at night.
Mary: Doesn't it smell rather like an old fur coat?

A timeless comedy tour de force, both laugh-out-loud funny and stinging with social realism about woman's place. The impeccably cast 1939 film — with an outstanding Roz Russell and Joan Crawford (and delicious real-life rivalry between Crystal/Crawford and Mary/Norma Shearer) — fulfills and immortalizes every moment.

Non-Fiction

Bette and Joan: The Divine Feud by Shaun Considine ★★★★★

Hold onto your hats! It's going to be a bumpy night!

Even if some "facts" need to be taken with a grain of salt, *Bette and Joan: The Divine Feud*, which chronicles the alleged rivalry between superstars Joan Crawford and Bette Davis, is divine fun. Just thinking about a passage would send me into spasms of laughter — on the subway, in the office, on the street, by myself. It kept me in book pleasure Nirvana, one of those rare books you want never to end. Shaun Considine is an assured, talented writer on a scale with the best satirists in *The Onion*, the farcical newspaper. Any lapses in biographical veracity are forgiven, yet in spite of stretches in truth, *The Divine Feud* contains a surprising amount of real information about each star and clear affection for both. Along with being a comic masterpiece, it is a moving and intimate portrait of two one-of-a-kind dames — "Sherman tanks," as Robert Aldrich called them.

Delving into the biographies, characters, fabled idiosyncrasies and urban legends surrounding both ladies, Considine follows them from their vastly different childhoods to their alleged first meeting — when Bette was upstaged by the arrival of Joan and Douglas Fairbanks, Jr. at an awards presentation for "stars of tomorrow" — to their deaths (Crawford's lonely end always bring a tear to my eye). Starting with the fact that both stars were born under the sign of Aries, arguably in the same year (Crawford's exact birth date has never been verified), *The Divine Feud* presents the thesis that these two, in spite of oil and water antagonisms, were "sisters under the skin," the parallels stretched to dubious lengths. The roots of both divas, as outlined by Considine, suggest why each developed her distinctive qualities. Davis, being from crusty New England stock, was loved, although her father was not affectionate. When he left, she boasted that she "replaced" him. Her mother was a formidable ally and financial supporter when Bette came to Hollywood. Crawford, born in poverty and possibly illegitimate, was abandoned by all father figures, leaving her, according to Adela Rogers St. Johns (a gossip without bounds), traumatized and seeking daddy figures in other men throughout her life. She was over-worked and beaten at home and more severely at school. Particularly harrowing is the account of Rockingham Academy headmistress grabbing her by the hair and throwing her down a flight of stairs, then beating her with the handle of a broomstick "until" she "was dazed" for the mere trifle of having asked a girl for a dustpan. As a movie star when called upon to cry on cue, she "would only have to think of those early days and tears would come, 'flowing long after the director yelled cut.'" Bette, brought up a "chaste and modest New England maiden," bedeviled lovers parked in cars by shining flashlights in on them. Crawford, on the other hand, with her perfect features and ripe sex appeal was a boy magnet early on, losing her virginity at age thirteen (ouch). According to St. Johns, she had "men stacked up to the left and right of her," while notorious ladies' man and lover Greg Bautzer claimed, "A night with Joan was better than a year with ten others." With marked hyperbole, *The Divine Feud* "asserts," "Her physical conquests, like Catherine the Great's, were said to be in the thousands, not counting repeats." (Who, I ask, was taking this census? Christina? She seemed to be taking notes on everything else!) "Sex was God's joke on human beings," Davis said in her memoirs; Crawford's response: "I think the joke's on her."

Each star's foibles is exaggerated with Crawford depicted as somewhat frivolous and gushy and romantic, often primping (this book made me realize how often she actually *does* primp in her films) and courting crew and press, whereas Davis is repeatedly caustic and above concessions to looks, preferring to be known as an actress, not a star. "I never got lost in a role," she says. "Actresses who do that are just plain silly." (Davis actually comes off as downright mean, which is much as I see her, anyway.) ("Miss Crawford always says good morning when she walks on the set. Miss Davis seldom answers her," observed Lily May Caldwell. "Three hours later she may say 'Hi,' and Miss Crawford looks around to see if she's addressing her or someone else.") The hypothesis posited is that Crawford was the beauty and movie star, her career and life built on looks and glamour (according to her agent who feels she lost her confidence when both began to go), whereas Davis' foundation was her acting talent. (This reviewer feels Crawford's prodigious talent was grossly underrated, her insecurity having everything to do with her childhood and not with deficiency in talent.) But Considine also challenges these assumptions, so portraits are well-rounded and touching, however frequently humorous. Louise Brooks' comment that she liked Davis, "a real star" and not Crawford who was "a washerwoman's daughter," seemed to speak volumes about the snobbism attached to each star's social position.

Allegedly the two women's rivalry extended to their love lives. Davis fancied Franchot Tone and, according to St. Johns, kept "those huge eyes fixed like a bayonet" on him, although he ardently pursued and married Crawford. Both women were rejected as they got older in Hollywood and valiantly fought back and hung on. Both women, sadly, had their fair share of hard knocks from men as well as from Hollywood. Davis professed that all her husbands beat her, while Crawford once exhibited a black eye from tempestuous lover Bautzer as if, according to St. Johns (who else?), it was a "badge of honor." Such things sadden me deeply, the abuse inexcusable, particularly given that both Davis and Crawford were physically tiny women (if large in spirit). Davis comes off generally as a bully of sorts. There is an indication that she was inadvertently responsible for one husband's death (she pushed him) and cruel to her sister, character flaws which receive no fanfare. It's not hard to see these personas, looking intimately at each woman onscreen. Joan, for all her over-hyped hardness, actually appears far more soft and vulnerable, and her learning to do chores to perfection and "ask for more" while at Rockingham and "living" for the occasional words of praise from her sadistic schoolmistress speaks volumes about her need for acceptance.

Refreshingly, Considine also doesn't soft soap Christina or allow her to dominate Crawford's portrait. He shows the flip side of the self-professed martyr. "I was there when Christina would deliberately bait Joan," says author Larry Carr. "She was a willful and devious little monster." Shirley Temple recalls Christopher punching Joan in the thigh for not giving him attention and Christina boldly striding to her closet and gaping at her clothes. Considine seems to have Christina's number. "'Our maid and butler left us, to work in a defense plant,' Joan said. 'Christina was asking everyone to wait on her. 'Please get me this or that,' she would order. I explained to her we had no help and that she had to wait on herself.'" Best is the description of Christina at her mother's funeral where, as reporter Arthur Bell noted, nobody recognized or seemed to care about her. "She held the children's hands when they were on the operating table," said Sheilah Graham, who then criticized Crawford's tough in-house rules. "[But n]o matter how strict you are, kids leave toys behind…bring garden dirt into the kitchen. No one can be perfect all the time, except for Joan."

Vince Sherman, another tireless gossip now immortalized on DVD, claimed Crawford felt Davis was superior to her, while Davis continually bad-mouthed her. Both women had affairs with him. He paints them as pining to marry him and Crawford even threatening suicide — needless to say, these allegations were made after the Sherman tanks (no pun intended) had passed. Allegedly Bautzer, who knew how to court beautiful women, sent Crawford orchids daily; a gold cigarette case encrusted with rubies and engraved with "Forever and Forever," and a matching lighter that said, "Here's my torch and love." (I have to admit that's a good line!) Crawford was equally extravagant with him, notably giving him a black Cadillac convertible.

Hilarious passages leave one gasping for air (or, in my case, causing a lot of stares on the subway). They are far too numerous to mention. Where did he come up with them? There are the "quotes:" Crawford while still Lucille LeSueur: "Harry Rapf had a nose so big it kept his private parts dry in the shower." Or when Crawford has Marilyn Monroe try on one of her dresses and as Monroe slips out her own clothes, "the nubile young beauty sent the semi-intoxicated Joan into a state of cold sobriety." The scene (oh, come now, much of this is fudged) with Bette's husband at the psychiatrist's office had me howling. Or Joan auditioning fathers for her newly adopted children, disappointing their expectation for hot sex. She offers one a drink: "I've got ginger ale, club soda, or RC Cola." Also hysterical is a tale of Crawford being tailed by a private detective to see if she was really ill during the filming of *Hush, Hush, Sweet Charlotte*. "She gave the *fool* the slip," Bette Davis later blared.

Of course, the pièce de résistance is the two stars coming together for *Whatever Happened to Baby Jane?* and it doesn't disappoint. Not one iota.

Davis scorned and rejected Crawford's numerous bids to befriend her — at times shockingly low even for Bette. Crawford told friend Carl Johnes about her ongoing peace efforts, including this attempt in 1943: "[Joan] went to [Bette] one day and said, 'Bette, we are now at the same studio. We have the same boss, the same friends in New York. We've had a similar career.' And Davis listened to all this, then, waving her arms and popping her eyes, she said, 'So *what!*'"—which Crawford mimicked perfectly." To her credit, Crawford remained gracious about Davis (publicly) to the end of her days. Touching is when Considine spoke to Crawford personally, describing her voice as "soft" and "she spoke very slow." She recalled attending a screening of *Baby Jane* in 1962 and said, "Bette Davis was superb as Jane. I sent her flowers and champagne that evening. She never acknowledged the gesture or even bothered to call the next day, when she saw the movie." Bette later finally did admit the picture was good and praised *her own performance*. "That was it," Joan told Considine. "She never said anything about my performance. Not a word."

Crawford spoke of her early self-consciousness to the author: "My nose always seemed to be too big, and I hated my mouth. I seldom smiled, because there was a space between my teeth; it was slight, but on the screen I thought it looked enormous. I was vain and silly, like any young actress who thinks the world is looking only at her." (We are looking, Joan! We're still watching!)

In any event, a wonderful, intimate portrait of two incomparable dames. Thanks, Shaun Considine! Laughter is a great tonic.

The Complete Films of Joan Crawford by Lawrence Quirk ★★★★

The Complete Films of Joan Crawford, which revises an earlier edition (*The Films of Joan Crawford*), is author Lawrence Quirk's attempt to catalogue the Crawford canon, which he does serviceably. After an introduction about Crawford, "The Actress and the Woman" (more on that later), he lists each film in sequence, liberally illustrated with black and white photos, with a brief paragraph of credits, a detailed synopsis, and sample critical reviews. He keeps each synopsis simple and refrains from inserting his own opinions, presenting the book as a resource guide/reference book for Crawford film aficionados.

Quirk also lets us know that he comes from a long line of film journalists, his uncle having been the Editor-Publisher of *Photoplay Magazine* at its apex (1914-1932). A photo taken with Crawford (and dog) in 1956 proves that he met the star firsthand and his respect and admiration for her is clear.

In his introduction, however, he feels tiresomely obliged to acknowledge and address the negative image dogging Crawford in the wake of daughter Christina's book, *Mommie Dearest*, published a mere year after her mother's death, when said malcontent already has a hugely disproportionate and biased part in her mother's image/story/legacy. It's tasteless and unfair, to say the least, that Crawford is too often viewed through the prism and shadow of her daughter. The breadwinner for family, husband, child, and studio most of her life, Crawford rightfully earned her place in Hollywood and deserves respect for her hard-won achievements and positive qualities, such as generosity and loyalty, as real as any character flaws/maternal shortcomings.

In any case, Quirk panders to common stereotypes, then gives the star her due. Tiresomely, as ever, he claims "[h]er ego was too strong for the give-and-take of marriage, and no husband lasted longer than four years." Is four years such a short time? And why assume the breakup of said marriages was due to some fault in her and not in the husband or indeed that it was anyone's fault at all? Many marriages last much more briefly and some last but at considerable expense, so it's not a simple issue. Men have strong egos, too, yet are not faulted for it; additionally, that she remained friends with all her husbands says much. Gender bias also comes into play with his comment on her "manic careerism." However, the tribute is, by and large, compassionate, touching and a fitting acknowledgement of well-earned achievements. He very obviously merges new notes with an older biography apparently written while she was alive without bothering to edit the earlier text; there are, thus, inconsistencies and a few inaccuracies. Controversy remains as to when she was born. Quirk lists her birthdate as 1904 (this reviewer believes 1906), then drops the ball on the math, saying she was fifteen in 1923 and sixteen in 1924 although earlier he has her twenty in 1924. Basically, however, a few inaccuracies and questionable details notwithstanding, he does justice to his subject as a major Hollywood star and force. He distinguishes her as an uniquely American star "in that she projected enterprise, resiliency and drive…[and] that she hung on to her gains despite all odds, and when many of her contemporaries had fallen by the wayside."

It is possible to trace the trajectory of that dazzling career through the reviews and see how quickly her ascension was achieved against all obstacles (and there were plenty, given Crawford's straitened background), remarkable in itself. She made an impression fairly quickly and held audiences enthralled, evolving with the times, and in her youth, a symbol of, role model for, and popular with American youth. It is interesting to read reviews when motion pictures were in their infancy. Photoplay's review of *Across to Singapore* amuses: "Don't try to follow the intricacies of this plot — just keep in mind that the turmoil of villainy and the sea will not overcome either Ramon Novarro or Joan Crawford...Crafty Chinese complicate matters with mutiny, dope dens and attempted seduction. Recommended as a stimulant." Quirk does a good job at summarizing plots, although, as expected, a few details are debatable. It made me wish more of her silents were available particularly *The Taxi Driver, Rosemarie* and *The Understanding Heart*, the latter in which Crawford — very pretty, pert and girlish at the time — is allegedly given a lot to do.

On the cover is a lovely colorized headshot from approximately 1939-1940 in which Crawford's large, expressive, beautiful eyes jump out at one, the broad lip line she adopted, arched brows, manicured hands and expensive baubles, framed with ruffles. Oh, what a star! Three more photos adorn the back, each black and white, one of her in slinky satin dress from the early '30s when she did a stint as a blonde; one from the latter '40s when she had morphed into her signature style of shoulder pads, shoulder-length hair, thicker arched brows, beautiful dress and earrings, and thickly lipsticked lips; and the center one a lovely bust-length pose from the early '50s where she is in a sleeveless, black halter dress and looks regal and divine, chin lifted, leaning with both arms on the edge of a table. Funny how her eyes in the '30s were always notably blue, even in black and white, yet in the noir period in particular, they could appear dark.

From the photos, it is impossible not to see what an incredibly beautiful woman she was, even to the end when older, more harshly lit and a "valiant survivor of life's vicissitudes," as Quirk aptly puts it. From the large, expressive eyes to the delicately sculpted bone structure with perfect profile and chin to even her graceful hands and legs, she was undeniably striking. Naturally this beauty is most overwhelming in her dewy youth, but it is notable and discernible throughout her life even in the mid-'50s when an arguably harsher countenance and severe brows tended to overpower it. To her credit, Crawford maintained her lithe, chic and shapely figure throughout her career and fought valiantly to overcome typecasting and ruts although she often played a version of "odd woman out"/pride and resilience against social disfavor.

In any case, a nice reference book with quick film facts, details about even rare silents, and always welcome photos, a desirable collectible for any fan.

Conversations with Joan Crawford by Roy Newquist ★ ★ ★ ★

Roy Newquist conducted a series of interviews with actress Joan Crawford that were presumably arranged chronologically in book form and he not only has captured vividly this complex, candid, highly astute and fascinating woman — deeply felt, reflective and articulate even when hitting the sauce — but also offers an incredible window into the Golden Age of Hollywood and the star system. It's one of the best books on Hollywood I've ever read from the perspective of one who achieved the "shopgirl-makes-good" dream of thousands of hopefuls and became "the ultimate movie star." This raw and frightened girl from an impoverished background arrived for her MGM contract via freezing train and entered a sunlit paradise with palm trees and no smog. "My treatment [at MGM] — [was] for the most part, divine," she said. "To be cliché about it, they promised me a rose garden and they gave it to me — not just plot by plot but acre by acre. (The roses withered later on, but that's another story.)" Crawford gives a frank account of her life as woman, wife, mother, actress, and one of the rarefied beings given keys to the magical kingdom of movie super stardom which had its share of thorns.

As in all things Crawford, there is controversy. The main controversy lies in whether Newquist actually spoke with the lady in question, since he (incredibly) did not use a tape recorder, allegedly took it all down by hand, and no records of the encounters exist in Crawford's own date books. I happen to believe him. I believe him, in fact, whole-heartedly. Crawford leaks out of every word and, if this is a fake, it's a brilliant uncanny one. But mostly I believe him, because like Crawford, he was a seasoned pro, too much of one to resort to silly trickery and besmirch his own reputation. The conversations began as a result of a formal publicity session when Crawford was signing copies of her sanitized autobiography, *Portrait of Joan*, a book Newquist had reviewed unfavorably. When he accidentally stumbled upon her reclining in a room after the "terrifying" (for her) session ended and began to back out, she said, "For God's sake, Newquist, I'm not going to bite you. Would I be working now if I took criticism seriously?" Their "unexpected rapport" led to twenty-one meetings on "one coast or the other" for a proposed magazine piece. He found her "regal, vulgar, cold, warm, highly sexed, puritanical, egotistical, modest, commanding, insecure, tender, tough, principled, amoral, kind, cruel, generous and selfish" — in fact the very mass of compelling contradictions fans know and embrace.

The book is loaded with great lines when Crawford shoots from the hip ("I just couldn't see myself walking into an AA meeting and getting up and saying, 'Hello, I'm Joan, and I'm an alcoholic'" or "Get John [Wayne] out of the saddle and you've got trouble"), but is also deeply moving and perceptive. Her final years were immensely lonely and she never found the love she so desperately sought. Of stardom she says: "Franchot Tone used to say it was like a Christmas tree — when they turn the lights on you know it's Christmas, the rest of the time you sit and watch the needles drop." Of her mother: "I don't think she really loved me, but when you consider the life she led, what the hell." Crawford takes us through all facets of life under the studio system when MGM had the biggest roster of stars of all, "moral turpitude clauses" in contracts, option periods, tremendous control over its stars ("And because the bread was so well buttered — no margarine at Metro, baby — we followed orders…We really forfeited our own private ability to make decisions"), protected images and mystiques, her adaptability to it, heartbreaks and joys, and why this system died. She also gets in some matter-of-fact digs at old rivals (After talking about her ability to be photographed at any angle: "Pity poor Norma [Shearer]; she was slightly cross-eyed, worse than Karen Black, to be truthful, so everything had to be very carefully arranged, especially her"). Her observations about everything from the huge, arranged parties where no one relaxed to growing old to the change in films and her love affairs are sharp, sometimes witty and often betray an innate, wistful romanticism.

Particularly wrenching is when she tries to reconcile the tremendous loss of her old life — or most likely, her mortality.

> *Out there all I find are ghosts…Say you're driving through Beverly Hills and you spot a house where you've been entertained or where close friends lived — you can't stop there, now, because those friends are dead or they've moved and some rock star lives there now. The studios are virtually deserted — my God, I couldn't go near Metro — it would kill me! All the Roberts, most of them, anyway, are dead, and there's no more*

> Clark, no more Spencer. No more Adrian. Oh, hell. I was going to say, "No more me" because that would be true, in a way. Because a lot of the ghosts would be me — as I was, at one time or another, in one picture or another, with a specific husband, my kids at certain ages...Clark's bounce and grin when he was 25, his sad eyes when he was 45. If I went back to the house — and I never, never will — I'd hear Franchot yelling, the kids laughing, my mother slopping around in those awful mules, and me standing in the door wondering what the hell to do with all the horseshit left from the birthday party for Christina...

It's clear from many sources that, all public protests aside, Clark Gable was perhaps the only man she really loved (an admission she did make privately to a few). Her sentimental accounts of him are very touching (and frequent). ("Yes, Clark and I had an affair, a glorious affair, and it went on a lot longer than anybody knows...If [we] hadn't had each other, at the particular time, we might not have gone on. We simply gave each other courage" and later: "But happiness is fragmented, isn't it?") With characteristic inconsistency or unpredictability, however, she tends to react to some of her own films (and people) with surprising harshness (or in the reverse, affection). She cringed at the rushes of "Humoresque," i.e., which many consider to contain some of her finest work, believing she "overacted" and "should have done better." While dismissing marriage to third husband Phil Terry — my personal favorite (he was good looking and kind, ostensibly the combination of "bull and butler" she liked) — as a mistake, she completely idealizes and soft-soaps fourth husband Alfred Steele, even going so far as to call their relationship "perfect," although even daughter Christina rebukes this sentimental whitewashing in *Mommie Dearest*. Marriage to Steele sounded far from ideal. He hit her on their honeymoon, a honeymoon she was paying for; gave her her "share of black eyes," at least once causing her to miss work (and violate her own pure code of professionalism); and ultimately left her in debt that forced her to take on degrading roles. Sweetheart indeed! Obviously, though, her work for Pepsi, his product, provided her meaningful, exciting work and a sense of worth after Hollywood had abandoned her. She continued to blindly love stepfather Henry Cassin, blaming his abandonment on her mother, possibly so adoring him because he was giving her the attention and encouragement she was not getting anywhere else in her family. However, later accounts (admissions by Crawford to friend Lawrence Quirk) indicate that he molested her as a child, which Crawford insistently claimed was entirely her fault. These things are deeply troubling, indicative of severely (and unsurprisingly) damaged self esteem, but as she puts it herself, "What do you expect? Metro never gave me lessons in consistency." Her resilient spirit, however, touchingly defies defeat. ("We all have regrets — I can't imagine even Hitler without them — but I regret the things I didn't do more than the things I did do.")

A wonderful book capturing an indomitable, plucky, audacious, fragile, wholly vital spirit and a knowing look behind the dream factory that manufactured her star. Essential Hollywood reading.

Crawford: The Last Years by Carl Johnes ★★★★★

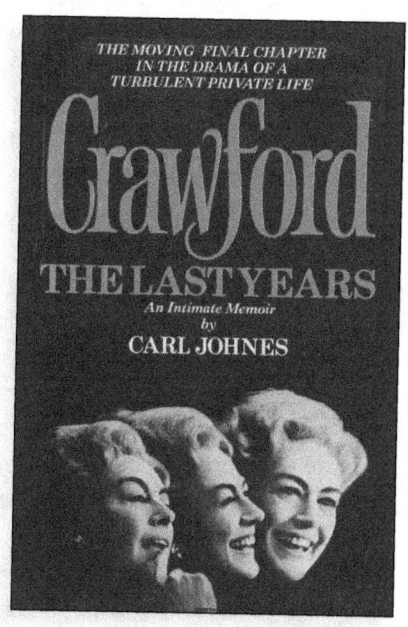

This slim volume recounts the friendship that developed between the author, a young fledgling Columbia Pictures assistant story editor, and film legend Joan Crawford in her later years when Johnes was hired to help her weed out her massive book collection. As Johnes was called back to assist in small projects, he realized that Crawford wanted his company more than anything else and shortly he began playing backgammon with her, which led to a deepening loving friendship and trust. Initially imposing the game on him, she turned out to be a "stern, gentle, impatient, entertaining, obsessive, and ultimately hilarious instructor."

Crawford: The Last Years was one of the best books I've ever read about a star and one of the best nonfiction books, in general, I've read. Unlike many biographies which go largely by hearsay and research, not all of which is accurate, these are memoirs written from his personal experience and they prove to be extremely poignant and even profound. He captures her in all her complexity and discovers that beyond the image, she is also "extremely vulnerable with a heavy dose of shyness," shyness being something she later admits. Crawford in her last years was lonely, but she invited this man into her inner circle which included many of her associates from the businesses in which she was involved (acting and Pepsi) plus her twin daughters and their families with whom she remained close. He has many touching insights into Crawford herself and into the nature of fame, life, happiness and friendship. Along with being a dear friend, he became almost like a son.

Aside from being a warm and deeply moving account, the book is extremely witty. It reveals that all people not only need and want love, but at heart truly want to have fun, too. He shows the childlike side of everyone, whether star struck fledgling, Columbia executive or major film star. Some of the scenes are priceless. One of my favorite among many of his stories was when he was in Crawford's apartment, looking at the view, feeling absolutely heady and almost chilled with excitement that he was living out this childhood fantasy of his own and millions of people, in fact, to be having cocktails in a film star's apartment. He suddenly envisioned Joan Crawford sweeping into the room, looking exactly like Helen Wright in *Humoresque*. Suddenly he hears her cursing mildly and she comes out of the hallway. As he put it, "Joan Crawford in a snit." She tells him that someone left the lid of the toilet up and she almost fell in and drowned! Very funny!

There were also wonderful, incisive parts about the way the media manipulates the image, such as when a magazine did a layout of Joan Crawford's apartment and ignoring her books and the tiny figures she had collected from around the world, they chose to photograph the very rare portrait of herself that was hanging very unobtrusively in her apartment behind a plant plus her Academy Award to make it look as if she was obsessed with her career and image when it actually wasn't the case. She had very few items of memorabilia from her career around. Wonderful was the fun gossip these two shared at the Academy Awards when Crawford was actually not quite in vogue with the times, remaining more of her own time, and when he confesses to her that he no longer thinks of her as Joan Crawford, but as his friend, and she says, "Well, honey, that's what it's all about, isn't it? Good friends are more important than almost anything else in the world."

Anyway, I laughed and cried reading this one. He paints a portrait of a complex, loving, formidable, witty, lonely, warm, proud, generous, pained human being and shows that it's human connection that really matters in the end.

A Wonderful Addendum to This Review: One day Jim Sibal, a man who had been Carl Johnes' spouse, contacted me and said that Carl had died seven years ago and Jim still had some of the silly presents Joan Crawford had given him. Carl respected Joan immensely and, seeing from my site that I did as well, Jim offered to "pass the torch — as it were" to me. Specifically, he had the remains of the beloved crockpot and a Pepsi cooler. Needless to say, I was thrilled, deeply touched, and honored! I remember Carl talking about both items in the book, the crockpot being the most treasured gift Joan gave him and the Pepsi cooler billed as his "Queen of the Stardust Ballroom" Pepsi cooler. What a happy, happy, unexpected blessing!

As luck and providence had it, Jim lives also in New York, so I went to his home to pick up my treasures. It was as wonderful as it could possibly be to meet him. He was a very erudite, warm, interesting, gracious person, much the way I imagined Carl Johnes to be. His apartment was absolutely amazing — just beautiful. Since he is involved in archaeology, he had many great artifacts around from Egypt, etc. and loads of books. I loved the details. I got to see Carl's picture and we had a lovely conversation. He was very well spoken, which is how he perceived me from my site. Anyway, he said that one of the things Carl had gotten from Joan was embracing people from all walks of life. Carl had a wide circle like Joan. He had wonderful things to say about her. Sometimes brief encounters have led to lifetime friendships for me. I told him - it's so strange how things happen, my fascination with Joan led to our meeting and my inheriting these special gifts. I went away with the warmest glow in my soul, feeling so lucky and happy to have these items so personally meaningful with their significant history-- a little piece of Carl Johnes and a little piece of my beloved Joan Crawford. Now Jim has kindly written the wonderful "Epilogue" to this book. Bless you, Jim Sibal!

Carl's "Queen of the Stardust Ballroom" Pepsi cooler.

Crawford's Men by Jane Ellen Wayne ★ ★ ½

As I've said elsewhere, it's very difficult to write a biography. The biographer is doubtless largely dependent upon hearsay and outside sources, some of them dubious. It's an advantage if they've actually met their subject or knew them, but in the case of far too many celebrity bios, the author has only had superficial contact, if that. Thorough and meticulous research is crucial as is a real passion and connection to the subject, the latter also often not the case when authors "specialize" in celebrity bios and spin them out like term papers. The problem with *Crawford's Men* is that author Wayne recreates Joan Crawford's alleged private conversations constantly — meaning they are all completely fudged. She has Al Steele say, "You get your goddamn ass home when you finish work!" — colorful, yes, and in keeping with his obnoxious, domineering personality, but fabricated, not an actual quote. She recreates the banter between Crawford and lifelong pal Billy Haines, intimacies between Crawford and Clark Gable, and even wisecracks during luncheons for the "Wampas Babies" (making Crawford ridiculously saucy), none of which she was privy to in the least. The small percentage of actual conversations she had with the star, originally related to her Robert Taylor bio, although full of fascinating and salty observations, are also "ad-libbed" since she openly admits she doesn't carry a tape recorder. Her opinion of Joan Crawford remains hard to gauge, which lends an indifferent quality to the whole thing. It's as if Wayne was a Taylor devotee who, while using Crawford as a source for that bio, decided to take a stab at the Grand Lady as well, although not quite liking or ever understanding her much. It rankles me when I see my favorite actress used this way — *indifferently* because far too much misunderstanding, slander and misrepresentation exists as it is, and Crawford deserves better. Still, Wayne has ferreted out a few unusual tidbits.

Opening with her first meeting with Crawford, Wayne packs a wallop, a quick punch. Evidently it was an older Crawford she encountered, the post-Steele Crawford who was drinking vodka heavily and terribly lonely, shorter than expected with carrot orange hair. She kept Wayne on her toes and it makes my heart ache when I see her proud excuses to continue the connection, which Wayne easily saw through. She comes across much as her Amanda Farrow in *The Best of Everything*, but again, given that Wayne is recreating dialogue from her head, these are embellishments, not facts. Odd that some of Joan's more famous quotes are found here like, of John Wayne: "without a horse, he's lost." Her meetings with Crawford, however fudged the dialogue, are the highlights of the book. ("She lit a cigarette with so much finesse that I almost decided never to smoke again.") The author, meanwhile, comes off as cheeky and arrogant in these encounters and gives herself the best lines, while Crawford is kept one-note. But I do love:

"I'll be going." *(Wayne)*
"Am I boring you?" *(Crawford)*
"You said you were tired."
"Do I look tired?"

Cherry picking juicy details out of sequence, Wayne boldly reassembles the moment when Crawford catches second hubby Franchot Tone in his dressing room with another starlet. The invented conversation is heavy on exposition. (Crawford: "Maybe that's why I'm making three hundred thousand dollars a year and you only make fifty thousand dollars. Everything, sex included, should be kept in proper perspective. I might add that your excessive drinking hasn't helped." Tone: "How else can I face you at the front door each night?" Crawford: "Perhaps you blame my ambition, but I put the blame on your lack of it!" Then there is an alleged loud clatter which causes the guard to move closer to the door. Crawford to Tone: "Go ahead. I've become quite adept at covering black eyes and bruises with clever makeup.") Was Wayne there in the dressing room at the time? No. And if she was, she didn't have a tape recorder. Ain't it nice when nonfiction allows writers to create fiction?!

These bogus recreations reach foul and downright loathsome heights — or rather, depths — such as the imagined encounter between L.B. Mayer and Crawford at MGM. Mayer suggests he has something special lined up for Crawford (which is the role in *Grand Hotel*) and Wayne depicts Crawford crossing her legs seductively and responding, "So the time has come at last…but [I] thought you were above trading sex for a good part." As if this isn't bad enough, she has Mayer smirking and saying, "Why don't you discuss it with your girlfriend, Billy Haines?" The entire exchange which goes on forever is repellant — and manufactured. Most offensive is the insinuation that Crawford — in her last days of sickness — somehow coerced a female attendant to sleep with her. Evidently Wayne's primary resource was *Mommie Dearest*, which besides having self-indulgent rants by Christina also eludes to Joan's "lesbian prolictivities." These inferences were doubtless meant to be slanderous and scandalous — that is, until Christina decided how profitable and press-savvy it was to pose with stigmatized homosexuals for photo ops, waving wire hangers, at which point she suddenly became gay-friendly. In any case, anyone who has ever had cancer knows how cruel and outrageous it is to suggest sex would be at the forefront of Crawford's mind when she was bedridden and emaciated. The cruelty in unfounded slander never ends, does it?

Amazingly, too, after recounting abuse and horror stories from Crawford's childhood, Wayne claims the star's "hunger for sympathy and publicity" is "common knowledge." Next her source will be the ubiquitous "they." Wayne says of the abuse suffered by Crawford at Rockingham Academy, "How severe the beatings were isn't known…Her [Joan's] stories changed from year to year." Then adds that Crawford's autobiography differs from "well-researched" biographies and her daughter's *Mommie Dearest*. (Geez Louise — hope she isn't counting the latter in the former category and what kind of comment is this, coming from an author who doesn't let reality stand in her way?!) Disgustingly, although it was known that mother Anna's boyfriend Harry Hough made the young Lucille LeSueur's life miserable (Crawford was born Lucille LeSueur) and came on to her, Wayne makes up a conversation in which Lucille calls Hough a "filthy bastard" and he threatens to throw her out, "looking at her deep cleavage." Thanks for sharing these "phantoms," Ms. Wayne (not)!

The portrait is somewhat schizophrenic (as most Portraits of Joan are). Most laughable is when Wayne claims that, according to Christina, it was Joan who chased first husband Douglas Fairbanks, Jr. "relentlessly," although he claimed she avoided him, arousing his curiosity (and how would Christina know, the whole thing having taken place before she was even a twinkle in anyone's eye? Another author who makes things up liberally in support of her trash-bound thesis!) Wayne rivals the adopted saint in her quest to write a juicy "tell-all" and, like the film *Mommie Dearest*, she adapts details from Crawford's films to embellish blatant fabrications: in a bogus conversation between Crawford and Haines, she has Crawford lighting a cigarette and blowing smoke in his ear, mimicking an actual movie scene between Crawford and Gable in *Dance, Fools, Dance*; elsewhere she has Gable calling Crawford "babe" as he does in *Strange Cargo*. She claims Crawford "danced nude for train fare" pre-Hollywood in a risqué vignette at age nineteen, not fifteen as she [Crawford] claimed, when actually neither the nude dancing nor Crawford's birth date has ever been confirmed — least of all by Crawford. Details, details. Why let them stand in the way of good scandal? Truth and fiction are blurred without integrity.

Wayne does, however, bring up some good points and interesting quotes (the great majority without identifiable sources — footnotes, like tape recorders, are apparently dispensable). For one, she reminds us that Crawford was a woman's woman. "Even at her most glamorous," Wayne says, "Joan never talked down to her fans." She does a good job of illustrating Crawford's choice of Phil Terry as third husband during a low point in her life, at which time she (Crawford) became a devoted housewife and threw herself into the war effort. "Joan didn't care whether Phillip was ambitious. She craved love, companionship, and a warm body lying next to her at night. Her life empty and uncertain, Joan prepared herself for the worst at M-G-M, and she could not bear going it alone." She also, thankfully, says of Tone "no man [has] the right to beat his wife," mentions Joan's gift-giving generosity with cast and crew on film sets, and makes hypotheses about Crawford's abuse of alcohol, beginning approximately in the 1950s when her career was shaky and bills were falling behind. Of *Torch Song*, Wayne nicely observes: "Technicolor removed the veil from Joan Crawford's famous cheekbones, strong jawline, and lavish eyes. Moviegoers felt they were seeing her for the first time."

Much ground is covered, known stories mixed with possible urban legends and colorful, invented scenarios. Captured is fourth husband Alfred Steele's dominating personality and heavy hand with Crawford, including verbal and physical battles on their honeymoon voyage - what a guy! ("She [Crawford] said Alfred wanted her to know right from the start who was boss…She wondered if his first two wives had been put through the same introduction.") (I wonder why such men don't get the same brickbats as faulty mothers!) There is a copious recollection from one of Crawford's paramours, identified as William W., a former real estate broker, who talks about his one night stand with her. He was thrilled to be chosen to drive her home, during and after which time she completely bewitched and "almost hypnotized" him. "I had never been with any woman like Crawford," he recalled. "I'd been around, but never met anyone who thoroughly enjoyed making love as much as she did." (Are women who actually enjoy sex so unprecedented?) While focusing tiresomely overmuch on Crawford's alleged maternal shortcomings, Wayne also relays parallels to America's sweetheart Betty Grable, of all people. Apparently Grable, having been psychologically abused by her parents, victimized her children (but one never hears about this as with Crawford, does one?). However, since Grable was beaten by husband Harry James, one wonders why no correlation or connection is ever made between these two forms of domestic abuse!

Among the interesting quotes, I especially like Crawford's from *Modern Screen* (and how reliable are they?): "This is a man's world, and a girl has to fight for everything she wants. Men taught me how to fight. They taught me how to live." Sadly, as Crawford says during *Mildred Pierce* and true of her in real life, men also taught her how to drink hard liquor. (In early years, she barely touched alcohol). There is also a great passage from one of Crawford's favorite directors ("and a lover") "who requests anonymity": "Joan was an alcoholic. She had a lifetime to drown in alcohol. She was wrong, I admit, but how can anyone possibly understand her tortured life? There was a saying around M-G-M - Shearer got the productions, Garbo supplied the art, and Joan Crawford made the money to pay for both. Joan was forever struggling... If it hadn't been for her fan mail, Joan would have had nothing to look forward to." While assessing these alleged maternal shortcomings which have had such disproportionate fanfare, he notes, "Her only solution was to send the oldest kids away to school, but long-distance problems made it more aggravating for Joan — running back and forth, trying to make a living, and always, always, always reaching out to be liked and admired. *Through it all*, I sympathized with Joan." (Me, too!)

In sum, one of the lesser biographies on Joan Crawford with scant cited sources and not a single bibliography, the golden nuggets or gems (which are there!) buried among pages of fabricated conversation. Still, worthwhile reading for discerning fans.

Jazz Baby by **David Houston** ★ ★ ★ ½

Jazz Baby chronicles the early life of film legend Joan Crawford from her hardscrabble childhood in Lawton, Oklahoma and Kansas City, Missouri where she nursed a dream to dance (a dream cruelly thwarted by an accident and yet amazingly — due to Crawford's seemingly unvanquishable spirit and will — ultimately realized) through her Dickensian years as an abused work drudge at St. Agnes and Rockford Academies up to her timely landing of a contract at MGM in its infancy. Since this was the first biography I read on Crawford, much of this information was new to me, but even if it weren't, the story remains extraordinary.

Although initially I was startled and put off by the author's credibility issues in recreating scenes and conversations that he obviously wasn't privy to, I eventually made grudging allowances because, embellished or not, the details provide a solid biographical framework. Houston interviewed a variety of people from Crawford's early years, including nuns from St. Agnes, ballroom admirers, neighbors, and classmates, whose opinions of the young girl were mixed (and, I suspect, sometimes prejudicial, given that she was ostracized in her community). Born Lucille LeSueur in San Antonio, Texas, she was raised by a struggling, overworked and therefore indifferent mother and a shady stepfather, Henry Cassin, who ran a vaudeville house and whom she adored, going by his name "Billie Cassin." Her real father had abandoned the family, as Daddy Cassin later would, and she got along poorly with favored brother Hal. Attired in odd costumes from Cassin's theater (her "wonderful gypsy dress"), part scrappy tomboy, she was often isolated and ridiculed, neighborhood children forbidden to play with her. She and her brother were also forced into labor and suffered aborted educations. Her lot in exchange for classes included scrubbing floors on hands and knees, washing dishes and making beds from dawn to dusk (which led to a lifelong obsession with cleanliness) and being beaten "almost daily" for any signs of resentment. Lacking love, the fact that she was canoodling with boys in the park in the third grade seemed less a sign of precociousness to me than pitiful desperation. Her aces in a bad hand included good looks, a hard work ethic, boundless vitality and, as she put it in the 1931 film *Possessed*, "whatever it is about me that fellows like." When she finally escaped one dire situation only to end up with no food or money in the office of a producer who, sensing her hunger, figured "there was nothing she would refuse to do," it was heartrending as when I read the relentless hardships of Scarlett O'Hara in *Gone with the Wind*. Shopgirl indeed!

Thankfully, however, fate provided guardian angels along the way for Crawford, those who championed her dreams, and they included her first love, Ray Sterling, with whom she had a chaste relationship and friendship, and James "Daddy" Wood, president of St. Stephens College who encouraged her not to quit school and with whom she corresponded until his death in 1963. He also gave her three inspirational maxims that she embraced, involving never stopping a job until it was finished; making laughter merriest when problems were deepest; and attempting impossible jobs that promised growth as opposed to those easily accomplished. To these advocates, she remained grateful for life, as she would to her fans and various technicians and others in the film community. A vaudeville act, the Cook Sisters (Nellie and Lucille), also took her in when they discovered her sobbing in the bathroom at a high school fraternity dance, having been locked out of her own home. However, when Crawford ultimately left the Cook house for promising chorus work (which fizzled), she took all their new costumes with her. The sisters, however, bore her no ill will, Nellie explaining, "We forgave her...she did what she felt she had to do."

Throughout the formative years covered in *Jazz Baby*, Crawford was neglected, kicked, drug by the hair, beaten with canes, abandoned, overworked, scared and promiscuous, yet she also made a stab at college, won numerous Charleston trophies and admirers, posed for Walt Disney's camera, danced on Broadway and in reviews, radiated charm, developed important alliances, and found a career and home with what would be one of the most celebrated and powerful studios in film history. It's astonishing, whichever way you look at it.

What struck me most about her story, besides its unbearable pathos, is the Hegelian karma. Dickens' opening to *A Tale of Two Cities* — "It was the best of times, it was the worst of times, it was the age of wisdom, it was the age of foolishness,...it was the season of Light, it was the season of Darkness, it was the spring of hope, it was the winter of despair" — could be applied to her life, which was both destitute and rich. While going through unseemly strife and setbacks, whether seriously injuring her foot when dreaming of a dancing career and then having to walk miles on the bum foot because the family can't afford trolley fare or running away from school after a severe beating to find life at home even less tolerable — Crawford also seemed to be at the right place at the right time and a true player and participant in the most exciting innovations of her time with key movers and shakers. Hers is the moving, complex story of the pursuit and realization of the American Dream, part dream, part nightmare, self-actuated.

And this backstory, warts and all, does much to illuminate with compassion the actress' future problems and enigma, her willingness to escape into and maintain a studio-manufactured identity of glamorous fantasy and remain slavishly devoted both on and offscreen to the fans who made it possible. It explains her chutzpah and intensity and the wistful vulnerability beneath it all, those huge and rueful eyes.

Joan Crawford, A Biography by Bob Thomas ★★★★★

Back cover of the Thomas biography.

Bob Thomas' book was one of the first Joan Crawford biographies I read and still is one of my favorites. One reason it succeeds is that Thomas genuinely cares for Crawford, willing to portray her with fairness and compassion, and another, equally important, is that he's a damn good writer. As I've said elsewhere, writing a biography is difficult, since the author is dependent on secondary sources, for the most part; sometimes falsehoods and urban legends get passed on down the line unknowingly. Thomas has done a commendable job, highly professional and solid, but even he picked up a few misleading tidbits in his research (i.e., Crawford did *not* dress in a car on the moors in *Trog*, her final film, and Douglas Fairbanks never put his footprints in Grauman's Chinese Theater, to name two). It detracts not a whit from a skilled and moving work. Opening with Crawford winning her Oscar for *Mildred Pierce*, he encapsulates the strength, neurosis, kindnesses, discipline and insecurities that made up her complex character. He also paints an incisive portrait of Hollywood and should know, having reported on the Hollywood scene for thirty years. The depth of his experience bleeds through.

Thomas is such a good writer that he makes it look easy. Conveying the hardships and pathos of Crawford's childhood when she was known as Billie Cassin, he speaks volumes with one line: "At the age of eleven Billie Cassin started supporting herself, beginning a lifetime of almost unremitting work." He shows an understanding of what that childhood meant and the spirit and courage Crawford possessed in spades to overcome repeated crushing defeats throughout her life, often replacing them with triumphs, but always dogged by class snobbery and rejection. There was rejection and abuse at school where she had to work as a drudge; rejection by a sorority at college; film studios never giving her scripts based on bestsellers as it did its favored daughters; rejection by Pepsi after she had worked tirelessly on its behalf; ridicule in later years by the press she had once faithfully cooperated with as if "young reporters wanted to make a name for themselves by pulling down monuments." (They're still at it.) All was doubly overwhelming and damaging to a woman who had been neglected, unloved and abandoned in childhood. Like point counterpoint in music, themes echoing repeatedly, every individual and group has its "through-line." Seeking paternal figures throughout her life, including Louis B. Mayer, the mogul of MGM, she found herself "second best." Although she worked hard to please and gain acceptance, she found only temporary security. MGM edged out its "daughters" when they were in their thirties (outrageous) and when its worker bee and huge moneymaker Crawford was no longer the Golden Goose, she departed with no one there to say goodbye to her but the gateman.

She remained a romantic. Of an early love Ray Sterling who championed her dreams, she rhapsodized, "He believed I was going to amount to something. He believed I had a beautiful *soul* as well as a dancing body." She found mentors along the way, often men, and was an apt pupil; later she attempted to mentor others. While in the Broadway show *Innocent Eyes*, she also finally found female camaraderie. "I was a girl, at last, being understood by other girls who wanted to be understood. I imagine people think chorus girls are just a gaudy crew bent upon being Wall Street's collective mistress. I thought so myself until I became one of them. Hard? Yes, they're hard. They can't be serious and successful. It just isn't in the Broadway racket."

The way Crawford uses words always intrigues me. From examining letters, it's certain the idiosyncratic style is hers, but sometimes one wonders whether at any times a magazine writer's artistic license came into play or altered the language. Still, she appeared to use words and phrases uniquely with a certain rhythm.

Although mother Anna demonstrated little love, my contention is that an effervescent, charismatic, though very shy, girl existed in her similar to her famous daughter, which had been allowed no expression and became buried under hardship and disappointment.

Thomas covers the bases, including his own firsthand interviews — her allegiance to Christian Science, popular among stars at some points, her "gardenia" phrase when she carried one incessantly and pressed them in books, her growing eccentricities, her publicity and business acumen. She was also high-spirited and had a sense of humor or spunk, enjoying surprising people. At one point, she sent friends on a wild goose chase down the freeway, but my favorite anecdote from Thomas is when Crawford plays studio mogul Harry Cohn at his own game. According to Thomas,

Cohn "operated on a divide-and-conquer policy, distrusting too close an association between his producers and stars." When he telephoned Crawford with this ploy, saying he doesn't understand why Bill Dozier doesn't like her, she answered sweetly, "But he *does* like me. In fact, he's here with me now. Why don't you ask him?" Cohn began sputtering. Go, Joan!

Some of Thomas' phrases are terrific: "New York City was the heartland of the Joan Crawford cult in the 1930s." Crawford reveled in her fans, as it is well known, writing a monthly column for the fan club, welcoming them into her world and keeping them abreast of her schedule. "Listen, honey, those fans put me where I am," she said. "If they want to know my whereabouts at any given time, they damn well better be told. If it wasn't for them, I'd be back in Kansas City." Her correspondence was prodigious, in itself lending pathos. She sent over 6,000 Christmas greetings each year, the majority with personal messages. Her closest friends received notes written entirely in longhand. She answered every fan letter, including repeats, sent thank you notes for thank you notes and bought expensive gifts for all cast and crew members.

She was always trying to live up to expectations, to win approval. Although without doubt she loved her adopted children (her adoration of Christina was certainly clear in the private home movies I observed, movies not for the public), she had only her own insufficient upbringing in which to make decisions, at some points having to be both mother and father, and subjected them to the same standards and discipline she did herself along with much extravagance. She believed it would make them self-sufficient and strong, as it had her. Her relationship with Christina deteriorated in a battle of wills and neither could forgive the other. Obviously Crawford really wanted love, but her own turbulent childhood had left its scars and huge pressures and mixed messages from the studios and husbands exacerbated her problems. She repeated some of the harshness she had known, permanently estranging her older children. Her relationship with her two younger daughters remained close.

Crawford was navigating in a world of men, in what was considered a male domain (and, in many ways, still is), and often castigated for "masculinity." Magazines, even in early years, posed questions as to whether her career was affecting her femininity and marriages. The attitude towards aging actresses, even those approaching middle age, was and remains appalling. After losing husband Alfred Steele who left her in debt, she consoled herself by immersion into work on the Pepsi Cola board where she was one of the first female board members, but found herself in an antagonistic relationship with a new mogul, Kendall (nicknamed by

Crawford "Fang") who resented the attention she generated as a celebrity and the letters insistently addressing her, not him, as President of Pepsi-Cola. He ultimately removed her from the board and much of her financial subsistence was lost. With movie offers drying up until Crawford valiantly told her agent to stop sending them, no work for Pepsi (and, once again, a lack of appreciation for her dedication), Crawford began enjoying the company of fewer friends and leaving her apartment less. A woman of enormous vitality and resourcefulness, she was ultimately and sadly isolated, as the elderly often are, although Thomas maintains she found inner peace after a lifetime of pleasing the public.

His eulogy after her death by cancer remains one of my favorite pieces ever written about the actress:

> *If she had appeared in no movies, the photographs would have made her famous. The broad patrician brow that belied her beginnings, the pencil-line eyebrows, lifted with an air of hauteur, the bones almost visible beneath the sculptured cheeks, the firm, determined chin, and the sensuous painted mouth. Most of all, the eyes. Those huge, luminous, omniscient eyes that had known so much agony, not all of it self-inflicted, and the endless, unrealized pursuit of love.*

Joan Crawford (A Pyramid Illustrated History of the Movies) by Stephen Harvey ★★★★

The Pyramid Illustrated movie history books bring back many great childhood memories when these compact, photo-filled tributes to a favorite star were a must-have. They still are, being a basically positive, critical assessment of the body of work of a particular movie star, heavily illustrated, as the title suggests, with photos (one of the great drawing cards of the series).

The *Joan Crawford* edition of Pyramid follows the usual formula of fitting respect for its subject, honest criticism of her films, and a generous array of photos, many of them never seen before. For the latter alone, the book is highly desirable.

But the analysis of each film is enjoyable, too, even though I disagreed with his take on a number of them, as would be expected in something of this scope. For instance, where I agreed with him that the Burt Hanson character played by Cliff Robertson in *Autumn Leaves* "is so blatantly peculiar that even the most desolate of old maids would keep company with such a crackpot only attended by a few white-jacketed keepers," I took issue with his dismissal of *This Woman is Dangerous* as "irredeemably shoddy and clichéd" (although he acknowledges Crawford's "immutably regal presence" as a highlight) and *Rain* as "pretentious kitsch" with Crawford's performance "the most problematic." Time has proven Crawford and the critics wrong on the latter, in particular. These dissenting viewpoints, however, don't detract from my enjoyment in the least. He considers Crawford's most reliable virtue to be "the sense of absolute conviction she brought to everything she attempted," which few would deny.

Another great plus about this *Joan Crawford* edition is that she was actually alive when the book was published, so, touchingly, hope is expressed that "some movie role will come along calling for that unique alchemy of style and skill which Crawford has been conjuring up through the decades." How wonderful to read a book B.C. (before Christina), as well, when Crawford received the respect for her achievements and contributions that she was due without undue and unjust focus on her alleged maternal shortcomings. Sadly and ironically, *Trog* would be her last film and that "unique alchemy of style and skill" would see no more incarnations onscreen.

In any case, a fun collectible which acquaints fans with a star's body of work and gives them plenty of eye candy. A must for the Joan library.

Joan Crawford: Her Life in Letters by Michelle Vogel
★★★ *(four stars for the letters)*

With *Joan Crawford: Her Life in Letters*, Michelle Vogel gathered together representative or available correspondence of the actress from her early years to her final decade with a potpourri of miscellanea ranging from films she almost made to comments from people who knew her and even her meatloaf recipe(!) as filler. Crawford was an avid letter writer, something that endears her yet further to me, and in addition to avidly answering fan mail and remembering tidbits about each fan's life, she also sent countless "thank you" notes and greetings for all occasions, often sending a "thank you" for a "thank you." This civilized expression of manners is indeed a lost art. Vogel includes an introduction from Crawford's grandson Casey LaLonda and makes an attempt at biography, but, unfortunately, she was not diligent about typos (including the misspelling of Joan's original last name "LeSueur" in LaLonda's section) or reigning in the focus. Having read many Crawford biographies at this point (although not all), I find few that don't contain inaccuracies and hyperbolic opinions that might go along with the author's slant but have little to do with the truth. There are also typos, misidentified films or photos, and general evidence of sloppy editing in most ranging from mere nuisance (such as the wrongly named dog) to gratuitous slander. Vogel, while obviously making an effort by obtaining a handwriting analyst for Crawford's signature and a psychic to offer commentary, was not successful in placing the letters into proper biographical context or keeping the format consistent. Jibes by Bette Davis and comments by Marilyn Monroe open chapters and have little to do with them and the text, in general, tends to range wildly, however heartfelt the author's intentions were.

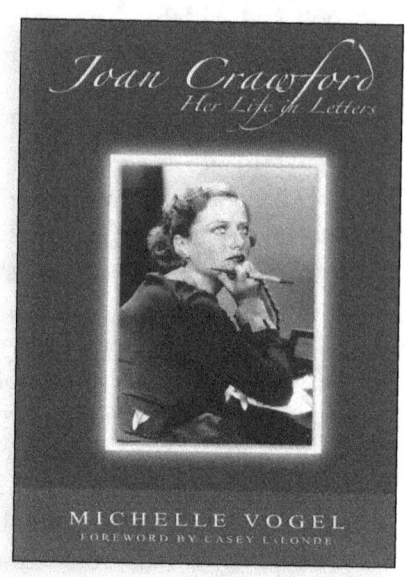

But the meat of the book is the letters themselves and it is a welcome and wonderful thing to have them assembled in book form. They offer the rare window, even when merely gracious and polite notes, into Crawford herself, the sort of thing any fan can eat up. Evidently the actress was deeply scarred by a harsh and loveless childhood, adopting an organized, outwardly perfect movie star identity that supplied the deficient love and adulation. Her youth (and yearning) shows in the rhapsodic letters to early boyfriends ("My sweetheart, please forgive everything I've done and love me. And I'll do all I can to live up to your expectations and you to mine and write me later when you're home and lots when you go and lots when you come back. I know not where you keep my picture but I would gladly give a year of my life to be in its place right now.") and fans ("Perhaps, Dan, someday I may do something equally as beautiful as The Three Musketeers, make an audience sit in their seats, spell bound, want more, love me, and all that"). Her early personality, in fact, tallies closely with the one onscreen and supports her unsurprising reputation for being easy with boys. It is unsurprising that anyone growing up in the loveless atmosphere Crawford did would look for love everywhere and in any form as voraciously as she evidently did. Of course in those early years, she is still an innocent, raw and insecure ("My hobby is collecting dolls," she tells one fan). She often admits to being "scared to death," particularly in relation to the studio, and confides openly via correspondence in at least one loyal fan, Dan Mahoney, as if to a genuine friend. (At one point, her first husband Douglas Fairbanks, Jr. even adds a postscript, asking if he might be Dan's friend, too, noting: "Joan's friends are dear to her, she speaks of you incessantly.")

Disturbingly, there is an indication that she was forced into having an abortion by the studio (although she never alludes to it specifically). ("Am rather depressed today. I just came home from the doctor and he made up his mind for me to go to the hospital the day the picture is completed. In a way I'm glad, so as to get the darn thing over with, and too I'm scared to death...I'll write again before I go under ether. Pray for me in the meantime.") Abortion seems a possible explanation when her next letter to Mahoney begins, "Some things are awfully hard to destroy aren't they???" Amazingly, she seems concerned that this fan may be mad at her for not writing sooner, reassuring him that he was the first person she contacted after her surgery. ("You knew I went back to work, therefore you thought I should write. You did not know this, that I went to work three days after my operation and had to practically be carried, did you? You thought I went to work two weeks later, didn't you? Well, my one day at work too soon put me back exactly three weeks. I was so weak, I couldn't think of telegrams, letters or anything...And, too, you were the first person I did wire," ending with, "Am still so nervous I can hardly hold a pen in my hand. However, I tried to write this so you can read it. Do write me and say all is forgiven, won't you please?") In a later letter, she tells "Dear Tired Dan" that she counts him as "my bestest, truest most devout friend."

The early letters, needless to say, are much more unguarded and sincere although she remains a warm and gracious correspondent, particularly with fans, through the years. There are two later letters, in particular, that astonished and touched me. One was the injured, but polite remonstration to a disapproving fan written at the height of her career, addressing this person's criticisms and doubts one by one and capping with "I have no desire to be suspended, taken off salary, and let my children suffer merely because I refuse to do a picture such as WHEN LADIES MEET.

I had no choice. So please in the future do not be so ready and willing to criticize us in the motion picture business." I can't imagine any star today who would take such stock of his or her public or give so much to them and be so fearful and mindful of their disapproval. Another letter is the one to her devoted secretary Betty Barker, addressed "Bettina Darling," that shows Crawford's wit and generosity of spirit:

> ...I happened to pick up that exquisitely beautiful mirror and looked into it without lipstick — or anything — I happened to look into the good part...I turned it over, saying, "Isn't it beautiful?" and I got a magnified view of me that scared the B'Jesus out of me! When I'm made up, it won't scare me as much — It'll scare me a little, but not quite so much.
>
> And you, of course, with that eagle-eye of yours, Bettina, knew that my little hand mirror in my make-up kit was broken — cracked beyond repair on one side. Darling, let's hope that this will bring me luck. Not for an Oscar — I don't mean that. But let's hope this mirror will bring me luck. I want you to carve something on the handle of it, or around the rim, so that I'll always have your signature in front of me. I'll always know that you gave it to me — that's very easy to remember, but thank you, thank you, thank you. Now — if I can only remember <u>not</u> to look in the wrong side. And unless I put lipstick on, any side could be the wrong side.

In any case, the letters in Vogel's *Joan Crawford: Her Life in Letters* are real treasures and worthwhile reading. My only regret is that there weren't more of them. The book also includes delightful photos which show the joy on Crawford's face when interacting with fans, my favorite being a 1940s shot of the star with pen in hand and feet up contemplating what to write.

Joan Crawford: The Enduring Star by Peter Cowie ★★★★★

Peter Cowie's stunning, coffee-table-sized book, *Joan Crawford: The Enduring Star* proves why Crawford continues to seduce, fascinate and resonate, illustrated with large, gorgeous quality photos, some rare, some never-before-seen, some spanning two pages and many from her heyday at MGM. There are representations from some of my favorite Crawford sittings, including one of her from the '40s in strapless black gown, flawless jewelry, and choker, her hair softly waved and shoulder length as in *Daisy Kenyon*, where you feel you can reach out and touch her. Also love the relaxed pose from the '30s and the never-before-seen photo of Joan sharing a meal with the crew of *Strange Cargo*, a photo that speaks volumes about her professional work ethic and camaraderie. These high quality photos are meticulously chosen and Cowie's accompanying text gives attention to the sensuality, glamour and power of Crawford's image, complimenting them well. *Enduring Star* is a classy and desirable addition to any film library and definitely a must for Crawford fans. As Mick La Salle puts it in his introduction, "Certainly, the photos make a better case than I can that this is one of the sexiest women who ever stepped in front of a camera."

Cowie endeavors to highlight Crawford's MGM years, so that audiences may examine her in that fresh light rather than the perspective of her later years when she was reduced and sometimes humiliated onscreen. He opines that if Crawford had retired from the movies, like Garbo, at the age of 36, "her reputation might be greater than it is today." Perish the thought! Thank all the stars in heaven that Crawford didn't retire at thirty-six (such a ridiculously dismal age for retirement, inferring that women should be put to pasture when allegedly no longer at the peak of their sexual allure or cuddly and cute). If she had, we would've been deprived of some of her greatest and most memorable roles — Mildred Pierce, Helen Wright, Myra Hudson, and yes, Lucy Harbin and Monica Rivers! Her chutzpah in staying in the running against all opposition is part of what makes her resonate as the bold, pioneering, vital spirit she was; her full career — even its camp extremes — was fascinating. But his point is well taken that to see Crawford in the '20s, '30s and '40s is to understand the "vast range of personality and emotions" of the characters she played and recognize her "carnal magnetism and…radiant lust for life." In that heyday, as he rightly observes, she was able to "flit from comedy to melodrama, from musical to gangster movie" and play opposite the cream of leading men. Citing *Dance, Fools, Dance*, he also praises an acting range that would be "denied her by critics and journalists not even born when *Dance, Fools, Dance* was made." (So people are finally cottoning on to how underrated Crawford has been as an actress?) He also brilliantly notes how the end of the '30s encapsulate her changing looks and fortunes.

Cowie attests that "independence was [Joan's] primary bliss" and later calls her "competitive to her fingertips," this quality of ambition and drive allegedly interfering with her private life. (Women still get the guilt trip.) She "was usually attracted to fresh-faced types (especially those who danced well), and indeed all four of her husbands could be described as 'gentlemen.'" Clark Gable's "rough male demeanor," in contrast, fascinated her, he opines. Her first three husbands, he feels, were "softer than she," but not so with Clark Gable who would be her equal "and more" in a domestic arrangement. (More below on this obsession with — er, dominance.) He believes she felt more at home on the studio stage than she did in many rooms of her own mansion. Appreciably he gives attention to Crawford's grace. She rarely badmouthed people (in public), even those who clearly hurt her. This quality in her personality is often given short shrift in bios. "I *want* to be liked," she told John Kobal. "I want so *desperately* to be liked."

Many of his astute and enjoyable observations bear testament to the sheer physical magnetism of Crawford. Of *The Last of Mrs. Cheyney*: "With each passing film, Joan appears more relaxed, more assured. Accustomed to receiving compliments, she radiates the self-confidence of a woman widely and intimately desired by the men around her. Her acting technique accommodates the subtle touch, be it a sidelong glance of derision as she plays the piano, or a sly lowering of her false eyelashes, like sun-blinds closing. She sweeps into a salon, shoulders at full stretch, hair drawn back to reveal as much as possible of that gorgeous face and neck. She enunciates and articulates well, giving breath to her diphthongs and stress to her consonants. Joan is containment personified." Of *Possessed* (1931) and her pre-code years, he amusingly observes that at a certain juncture in all these films, she radiated sex appeal, but didn't "ooze" it like Jean Harlow. Of *Humoresque*: "Dressed once again by Adrian, she seemed ageless, no longer a young heroine yet still erotically charged, commanding, and ravishing to regard. Clearly, she yearns for her admirers to be stronger than she is, and when they fall short, she must fill the power vacuum. No longer the sparkling innocent, she seemed to acknowledge instinctively the need to assert her authority." Of *This Woman is Dangerous:* "As in *The Damned Don't Cry*, she flaunted her furs and jewelry as men would their guns and muscles." And perhaps my favorite is his passage on *Mildred Pierce*, which concludes, "The role inspired Crawford to find new resources, fresh subtleties of technique that make of Mildred one of the greatest of all Hollywood screen characters." Hear! Hear!

Cowie rightfully credits designer Adrian and photographer Hurrell as major forces responsible for shaping Crawford's dazzling image. Publicity stills were so much a part of the Hollywood dream machine. For Adrian, Joan possessed "the closest face to Garbo's, to perfect proportions." She was Hurrell's favorite subject. He took more photos of her than any other star, even Garbo and Shearer, calling her "the most decorative subject I have ever photographed." "There is a strength and vitality about her that prevails even in the finished print. If I were a sculptor, I would be satisfied with just doing Joan Crawford all the time." The smoldering photos from *Grand Hotel* featured in the book certainly display that breathtaking beauty and charisma.

With each passing film, Cowie notes, there's more resolve in Joan's features, adding an intriguing quote from *The Shining Hour*, "I look like a lady — sometimes." Actually I think Crawford's fluidity — her ability to be conflicting polar opposites at once disconcerts people, as does her promiscuity (sexual freedom another privilege still deemed a male province — and punishable by death for women in some barbaric cultures). Amusingly, Bob Thomas is quoted as saying that from *Mildred Pierce* onwards, Crawford's portrayals "could no longer be complimentary to men, they were competitive with men. She sought to destroy them, not entice them." It's not that I'd argue that Crawford was meant to be seen as "shrewish" in some of her post-*Mildred* films, but let's get serious. All the outrageous misogyny and flagrant abuse of women in film noir and she gets singled out as some kind of menace to men for "competing" with them or, to my mind, displaying well-earned cynicism? Competing in what? The arena of the world? Frankly, it was during the 1940s at Warner Brothers when Crawford crystallized into the full thrust of her sexuality and persona — less cute and cuddly maybe, but a real glamorous force, thoroughly intriguing, savvy, smart, complex.

I adore the goddessy photo (another of my favorite Joan sittings) heading the chapter "A Woman of Discipline," where Crawford was at a peak of classical beauty, perfectly showcased, but what's with the dominatrix theme? (The next chapter is "The Reluctant Domino.") Cowie notes that she "appeared to grow taller and taller with each passing decade" and adds the howler, "This, too, strengthened the impression of a dominant female surrounded by spavined males." (Isn't feeling subordinate fun, guys? Wonder what men would say if they were forced to wear the burka? New words beyond dominatrix would be added to the dictionary.) There is a silly reference to Joan "emasculating" a man in *Johnny Guitar* because she asks for his gun. Of *Queen Bee*, Cowie says: "Crawford takes vanity to a fresh extreme with shoulders, bosoms, and back displayed to full if never vulgar advantage." Contrast this with his commentary on her in *Possessed* 1931 or *No More Ladies* (1935). (Referring to after the Production Code: "Joan's back could be revealed in all its breadth and beauty… while her bosom — adequate if never ample — had to be concealed.") Apparently, women should disappear after age 50, not call attention to sexuality. Of *The Story of Esther Costello*, he says, however, "[i]n moments of joy, Crawford can still smile like a goddess." Cowie sees the mid-1930s as perhaps the "prime of her life."

There are a few misidentified photos which detract not a whit from the overall beauty of the presentation, such as a photo on page 23 that is identified as Anita Page when it is actually Josephine Dunn. Cowie also claims David Brian had an affair with Crawford (is this true?) Who was his source? David Bret? (Bret's *Hollywood Martyr*, surprisingly, is included in his sources.)

Other great quotes about Crawford include Hedda Hopper's ("She labors 24 hours a day to keep her name in the pupil of the public eye") and among those by Mick La Salle: "In many of [Joan's] films, there's a moment in which her manner falls away, and she suddenly reveals a core of scalding bitterness. In those moments, she never rings false." Or this by Alexander Walker: "A scared Crawford is an awesome sight: her stretched face holds fear the way a sponge holds water."

Joan Crawford: The Enduring Star is a spectacular, grade A book with fabulous photos and delicious, thought-provoking text as a worthy compliment. It gives special attention to Crawford's heyday at MGM when she was in all her youthful glory. A class act and a must for Crawford, film and photography fans.

Joan Crawford: The Essential Biography by Lawrence J. Quirk and William Schoell ★★★

Joan Crawford: the Essential Biography is one of the Crawford biographies eager to "set the record straight," which usually means addressing some of the allegations in eldest daughter Christina's *Mommie Dearest.* This is always particularly vexing and sad to me, Christina already having a disproportionate and distorted prominence in her mother's legend (as Crawford's twins who dispute Christina's allegations are made nonexistent). Unfortunately, biographers continue to misplace the spotlight and thus Christina's "career" as a victim, welding herself like a Doppelganger to her mother's image, gets renewed life.

Not having yet read Quirk's other book *The Films of Joan Crawford*, I enjoyed the dissection of the films here, even if flawed, and information not covered in other bios. One particularly disheartening and startling bit was the allegation that Crawford admitted in her later years that stepfather Henry Cassin (who the authors incorrectly refer to as "Harry"), the man she called "the center of my child's world" and clearly adored, had molested her since age eleven and, worse yet, that she considered herself completely responsible for it. "It wasn't incest," she reportedly said. "We weren't even related. He was gentle and kind and I led him to it." If true (and I have no idea why Quirk, who had a thirty-year association with Crawford, would make such a thing up), was there no end to the suffering in her childhood? Yet it does seem to offer another perspective on what many consider to be her rampant promiscuity or "nymphomania," aside from a mere strong sex drive. As in all things Crawford, this remains controversial and up for speculation.

They also allege that longtime lover, attorney Greg Bautzer, never hit Crawford, as did second husband Franchot Tone (who also revered her and functioned as a cultural Svengali), while other biographies document their highly dramatic, occasionally theatrical and volatile rows that were often loud enough for the neighbors to hear. The publicly dazzling couple's private pattern was fighting and reconciling with the stormy relationship ending, as this bio concedes, when Crawford, secretly miffed by Bautzer's flirtations, asked him to check a tire on her car and then sped off when he got out to look, leaving him stranded on a dark, deserted road. Quirk adds, however — so characteristic of this book's tone: "…but mostly… Joan didn't like taking orders from anyone — why should she have?" They leave out other flamboyant Bautzer/Crawford legends: Bautzer throwing back at Crawford a $10,000 pair of diamond cufflinks she bought him and she, in turn, furiously flushing them down the toilet, then calling in a plumber to dismantle the pipes and retrieve them. Crawford showing up at Bautzer's office for a hoped reconciliation and searching it when told he wasn't in, shocked that he was nowhere to be found. (He had actually climbed onto a narrow window ledge twelve stories above Hollywood Boulevard to avoid her.) Crawford leaving with four trunks and children in tow, after one fight, and returning with eleven trunks, all of them filled with presents from Bautzer. Other bios also report that, after their final break up, Crawford saw Bautzer dancing with Ginger Rogers at a nightclub and left in tears, later sending her own concerned companion — who came to her house to console her and whom she wouldn't see — a bouquet that said "Please forgive a poor frightened little girl. Love Joan."

These intriguing details, and others, are not in the "essential" biography. (But is it ever possible to cover everything? Absolutely not.)

Another "spin" at variance with other bios is their take on Crawford's relationships with certain co-stars — notably, that she and Margaret Sullavan were "cordial but not warm," while others (like biographer Bob Thomas) say Sullavan became a close friend. They also soft-soap hard-edged fourth husband Alfred Steele, the Pepsi magnate, as did Crawford herself, and relay that Crawford admitted to Adela Rogers St. John that Clark Gable (with whom she reputedly had a 30-year on/off affair and friendship) was actually the only man she ever really loved. They touch on Crawford's longstanding friendships with Myrna Loy, Billy Haines and Cesar Romero, her feuds with Mercedes McCambridge and Bette Davis and, sadly, note a tear-filled conversation with Quirk because Christina was writing "a terrible book" about her. Of note are her rare comments on her affair with married director Vincent Sherman, who also was violent and less the gentleman with her while later sanctifying his own image: "Sherman was a user. I knew it. He knew it. We used each other. He would holler at me that he didn't like the way I tried to control him, but he never gave me back any of my gifts, did he? He made it clear that I was only a diversion, but he didn't understand that that was all he was to me. At times he could really be a prick."

The second half of the book holds up less well than the first as Quirk descends into downright bitchery, sniping at anyone who ever made a critical remark about "Joan" (as she is continually and chummily referred to while last names are used for everyone else). ("Joan Crawford was the woman [Hedda] Hopper, failed actress turned gossip hen, always wanted to be.") Although at times obnoxious, I didn't mind it overmuch, since it gave the book a bit of idiosyncratic humor. Meanwhile, fond as he is of dishing about his revered subject, he makes lame excuses for other "gossips." ("When [Jerry] Asher told these stories about Joan, he wasn't trying to be nasty... Rather, he found her various sexual entanglements too fascinating to withhold from people he knew were sophisticated enough to deal with them." Like — uh — the general public?) and throws in the occasional dubious detail ("Besides being handsome, well-endowed and charming, Michael [Cudahy] represented an upwardly mobile catch...").

For the most part, the book concerns itself with discussing Crawford's films at each stage in her career with a side of gossip. While the authors don't hide her troubled side, however defensive they are, they also capture her essential decency, her consummate professionalism, loyalty and frequent generosity (which gets forgotten). Known for constantly showering co-stars, film technicians, lovers and even children with gifts, she was obviously desperate for love and never quite found it.

Not the most professional or comprehensive of Crawford bios, caught up as it is in author Quirk's — er, quirks, but still worthwhile reading with new information and opinionated analysis of her films. There's a generous array of nice photos, too.

Joan Crawford: The Last Word by Fred Lawrence Guiles ★★¾

Fred Lawrence Guiles' *Joan Crawford: The Last Word* attempts to address Christina Crawford's malicious tome, *Mommie Dearest*, stating rightfully, "There is no earthly reason why Joan Crawford's life should be so tarnished by her daughter's writings that we should view her story only through the latter's eyes." And, again, rightly: "Perhaps it is time that the scales were balanced, and that the voices of the many who saw Joan Crawford from a different perspective, as their lives touched, were finally heard… It would be grossly unfair if we allowed a prejudiced account of this great film star's life to obscure the human being within." Unfortunately, *The Last Word* thwarts its own objective by disproportionately oiling the squeaky wheel.

A noted Marilyn Monroe biographer, Guiles conducted extensive research, his sources including Crawford's dear friends Cesar Romero and William Haines. Ultimately the perspective becomes a bit twisted and, as in all things Crawford, contradictory, but he does offer a fresh spin on various points. While recounting the star's familiar childhood story, he places it into the context of the times, stating that "there is more space in Texas, Oklahoma and Missouri for the individual spirit." Since the area retained vestiges of pioneer days, "ambition in even the poorest child was often limitless." Appreciably, he observes that "like many gifted but undiscovered children, she [Crawford] was bored by rote teaching and blackboard exercises." He notes that her childhood, although it began respectably, was far more straitened than even Monroe's. He contends that, although she was overworked and treated harshly at times, Crawford enjoyed much of her childhood, which I seriously dispute. Crawford notoriously romanticized and made the best of even the most painful experiences, following mentor Daddy Wood's maxim of always making a smile merriest in bad times, but quite evidently, her past was the cornerstone of all her future problems.

Overmuch is made, as usual, of Crawford's voracious sexuality, the term "oversexed" applied to her as it would never be to a man, as if such appetite in a woman is abnormal. Infuriatingly, he contends of Crawford's early forays into chorus work when she was still known as Lucille LeSueur: "It is an American tradition that girls brought into a convention as entertainment are invariably available after the performance, but *this could not have distressed Lucille very greatly, promiscuous as she had been as recently as her stay at Stephens College the previous autumn.*" (emphasis added) Because a female chooses to be sexually active does not mean that she is sexually indiscriminate or enjoys being farmed out for sex (she did not; Myrna Loy recalls her in tears because of sexual harassment at the studio). (In fact, Crawford, greatly exploited by men, learned to play men at their own game in later life). He also notes that no work permits were required for girls as for boys in laundries.

As always, details vary from bio to bio, from account to account. Guiles lists her salary from Pepsi as $40,000 a year (Bob Thomas listed it as $60,000 in his Crawford biography). He disputes that MGM never said goodbye to Crawford when she left the security of its womb, which is interesting, that perhaps Crawford *left* without saying goodbye. He cites inaccuracies and inconsistencies in Christina's account of things, which have been confirmed, and mentions Joan Crawford's generosities that are rarely heralded like her involvement with the League of Crippled Children. A boy, Clover Kerr, lost both legs and arms in a traffic accident and wanted to ride in the motion-picture polo tournament and when Crawford learned of it, she had a special saddle made for him within two days. He also recounts the gay-bashing assault on William Haines and his lover Jimmy Shields, which was hushed up by Hollywood. Although much is made of Crawford's lean times following her departure from MGM, Guiles points out that she quickly had an offer from Warner Brothers and, in fact, her greatest movie triumphs came after she left and, also, that she maintained a lifetime friendship with Louis B. Mayer.

Contradictions include when he says that Gable and Crawford had no other resources, such as love of literature or good conversation, "to consider any alternative to sex as the most satisfactory pleasure in life… [B]oth were self-obsessed takers (except with the less fortunate in Joan's case)." Yet, clearly, Crawford wanted to be culturally cultivated and valued books highly. She read many of the novels that were made into her films and brought them to the attention of producers as potential properties. We're told some considered Alfred Steele and Crawford wonderful together and Guiles believes Crawford gives "an honest statement" by calling her days as Steele's wife "the most blissful years of my life." Later he concedes that Crawford romanticized her relationship with Steele, "forgetting the black eyes that he had given her on occasion and the debts he had piled up." There are also, as is so bafflingly common with Crawford biographies, details to films that are dead wrong, including misidentified actors. Why none of these details were fact-checked when so much research was being done is beyond me; she is a *movie* star, after all, so the movies aren't incidental. He also claims Crawford appeared on *The Twilight Zone* (not so — but, puh-leez, don't tease Joan fans that way!). The "first Christopher" Crawford adopted who was later, traumatically, taken back by his birth mother is listed as blond, but home videos identify him as black-haired.

After trying to give Crawford "her due," Guiles suddenly backtracks sheepishly by saying that she was not "loveable" (hello? what of her lifelong friendships and all those who loved her?) and that if she "had not been a studio creation, one might assume that she suffered from schizophrenic episodes, aggravated by alcohol abuse." But it was a mistake, he adds, because as an actress, she could assume the role of a whole person even if she wasn't one. (Hello?) How about simply that her childhood background of abuse damaged her on some level, even if she was fundamentally a decent human being? Furthermore, he comes to this conclusion because she was unable to forgive certain family members, even though she supported all of them. Why is it so incomprehensible that she would want to disinherit a son and daughter she had no relationship with, especially a daughter who was writing a scathing book about her? Why was it so hard to accept that she wouldn't attend her brother Hal's funeral when he was allegedly "monstrously cruel" to her and sponging off her when she made good? Guiles contends that she was ashamed of her mother and brother, but I'm not so sure I buy that, given that she never made any attempt to deny her own meager background. How about that she felt her mother and brother had gotten more from her than they had ever given?

Finally, it irritates the B'Jesus (to use Joan's own expression, spelled as she spelled it) out of me that he concedes Crawford was attracted to abusive men, since a few of her romances were abusive. Actually, the media has shamelessly promoted masochism as an inherent part of female sexuality, romanticizing abusive men, as wrong and damaging as anti-Semitic propaganda. Because a culture condones maltreatment of women (true worldwide, sadly) does not make it "natural."

In conclusion, *The Last Word*, although containing admirable research, leaves me ambivalent. His original strong ending is thwarted by yet another addendum about *Mommie Dearest*. "If undue emphasis has been placed on putting her role as a mother in proper perspective, it was forced upon her biographer," Guiles states. Who is doing the forcing? Christina? Whose life is it anyway? Stick with the Bob Thomas bio for a fairer treatment of its subject.

Joan Crawford: The Raging Star by Charles Castle ★★½

Raging Star is the so-called authorized biography of Joan Crawford, although since author Charles Castle covered Crawford's life up to and including her death, suffice to say some material did not (and would not) have received the star's blessing. Evidently, she was generous enough to acquiesce to his proposed book and documentary about her life, but like so many who knew Crawford, particularly those who knew her only cursorily, he ultimately betrayed that trust by imbalanced "dishing" and inaccuracy at times. (Author Carl Johnes, who became close with Crawford in her last years, said of *Raging Star* in his book *Crawford: The Last Years*: "Authorized by whom? I can vouch for the fact that it wasn't Joan Crawford, although I have a sneaking suspicion that she might be somewhat amused by all the inaccuracies within its pages," citing even her misidentified dog!) To his credit, Castle included interviews with numerous people who knew the star, even if not particularly well, from co-workers to chauffeurs and even Pepsi personnel, many of her closest friends presumably having passed on, and begins the book promisingly. The first few chapters, in fact, which include interviews with first husband Douglas Fairbanks, Jr. and others from Crawford's earliest years, are quite illuminating with rich insight into Fairbanks as well as the subject. They move with dramatic momentum and have the quality of good prose, although given the glaring errors throughout, even these chapters ultimately get called into doubt.

The young Crawford emerges as a beautiful, but insecure and somewhat gauche girl from an abused, impoverished past who was terrified of making a misstep in society yet took her place in that rarefied world with amazing assurance, much the same sort of character she would play repeatedly onscreen. Those interviewed, including Hollywood insiders Jesse Lasky Jr. and Howard Dietz, mention her striking beauty and a presence that caused heads to turn when she entered a room. This had nothing to do with what she wore or any particular behavior, but rather her own innate magnetism; it was apparently present in her earliest years when she was raw and louder in appearance and continued into her old age. Dedicated to self-improvement, according to Fairbanks, she toiled arduously on everything from dance to carriage and speech, even working on the set through illness, cultivating friends from all walks of life. She was both housewifely domestic and glamorous. The fairytale Fairbanks marriage eventually broke apart, due to career and social pressures, no doubt aided by her intense love affair with Clark Gable. Interestingly, Castle mentions that Crawford met her real father for the first time on the set of *Chained* and then never saw him again, adding this rarely mentioned (if indeed true) tidbit that they continued to correspond.

Assurance in the author's veracity deteriorates when he gives a synopsis of Crawford's films and gets even the details of *Mildred Pierce* wrong, then nose-dives when he does an about turn in his portrait midway through and paints his subject notably and abruptly more harshly, leaving out significant details. In particular, he soft-soaps her men and any co-stars with whom she had conflicts, even suggesting that she alone was at fault in her celebrated "feud" with Bette Davis when most books clearly show that Davis rejected Crawford's numerous bids for friendship. There are a number of glaring falsehoods beyond these distortions. For instance, Castle claims that Crawford had no further contact with daughters Cyndy and Cathy after they grew up or their children, not wishing to be known as a grandmother. While it has been confirmed elsewhere that she preferred being called "JoJo" to grandmother, both twins and grandson Casey LaLonda describe visits and telephone calls to Crawford, and Johnes recalls them as part of the star's social inner circle and frequent callers in those later years. Al Steele, in particular, is white washed entirely, painted as a man with "no aggression" (?) who, according to friend Dorothy Strelsin, "never lost his temper" and married Crawford "on the rebound." All of this, if balanced against other bios, is absolute horse puckey. Steele didn't rise to the top of Pepsi Cola because he was sweet. Author Alexander Walker, in particular, makes strange hyperbolic assertions, saying of Crawford's later films, "If you're no longer able to project a sexually desirable image, what you've got to project is a sexually neurotic image. In each case, you're keeping the focus on attention." This, he fails to mention, is because of Hollywood's attitude towards older women, not the women themselves. And: "She was the perfect example of the flapper-girl on the rebound." (You mean it's a popular category?) He continually and tiresomely makes illusions to her being "the eternal mother" as a way to get love, the fans being her children, even stating, incredibly, "My first impression of her was of the working mother who has sacrificed all for the family and the daughters and who still retains around her the air of having scrambled up the ladder." All this because she was ironing a party frock at the time of their interview. Given that she knitted constantly, perhaps she merely needed to do things with her hands.

Not much explanation is offered as to the hostile shift in Castle towards his subject in the second half where his occasional snide asides are not in her favor. Although it is feasible that Crawford became more difficult and demanding as her power grew, she also was known as kind, loyal and generous, which a number of interviews in this book support (including Van Johnson, Earl Blackwell, Sydney Guilaroff). Castle aligns himself with author Walker in drawing incredible conclusions. In one instance, Walker finds a parallel between Crawford and her masochistic character in *Autumn Leaves* "in that nothing that happens is going to change anything." (Say what?) Pandering to gender stereotype, he further characterizes the actress as "not being a terribly perceptive woman in the sense of being able to judge the rationale behind things that have nothing to do with the emotion." Later Castle also makes this absurd gender-skewed statement regarding Crawford's compulsive cleanliness: "[It is] an upper-class version of the working-class woman's obsession with house cleaning which we recognize as an attempt to wash away guilt or atone for forbidden desires." Outrageously (to my mind), Castle concludes that while Bette Davis (of all people!) "contrived to make her substantial ego likeable," (hello?) due to, among other things, her "genuinely keen brain," "Crawford by contrast remained enigmatic and glacial…solemn, arguably self-pitying, certainly self-regarding…and in the last analysis not an especially agreeable human being." He also incredibly insists that she never had the true star actress capacity to transcend mediocre material. Close friend Johnes paints her differently in her last years. Exploited largely for her looks by Hollywood, even Crawford's lesser films continue to be shown chiefly *because* of her ability to triumph over thin material. Walker also opines that in her last years, she was "breaking up and dissolving," "maybe because she'd already stopped," and that "she had ceased to find out where she was." It seems ridiculous and cruel to suggest that, having lost her looks and career, she saw no further options in light of the fact that she had cancer and was dying. The fact that she was suffering and physically deteriorating better explains her reclusiveness, these health issues ostensibly caused by years of self-abuse (smoking, vodka drinking).

Raging Star does have some rich and unique highlights, not found anywhere else (to my knowledge). Among its assets, obviously, are the many interviews. The impressions are, as in all things Crawford, a mass of contradictions. She was driven and never idle. If she felt comfortable with you, she didn't have to make conversation. She was a very feminine woman; she smoked, drank and played cards like a man. She had impeccable manners and her Christmas cards always arrived first. She "had no area of her life when she [wasn't] a film star, when she [was] just a woman." She was "utterly unpretentious" and devoid of mannerisms; her one flaw was pretentiousness. She was very warm; she was glacial but human. She developed a pathological sense of hygiene and cleanliness. "[She] did everything one thousand per cent," according to Earl Blackwell. "If there was no maid and she did not like the looks of the floor in a hotel bathroom, she would get down on her hands and knees and scrub it." If even only six people came to dinner, there were six placards on the table.

Most fascinating is the uncanny parallel found between British stage director Allan Davis' visit to Crawford's home and a movie star called Julie Forbes described in Gavin Lambert's story "The Closed Set":

> *The first thing I noticed was her dress, deep, deep, flaring crimson. Like everything else about her, it had a bright perfect glitter. The diamond choker round her neck. The silver sandals with jeweled toes. From the smooth legendary face, beautiful luminous cat's eyes flared out...Her skin was golden, her figure trim and pliant as a young girl's. She had been created a moment ago. There was no childhood, no past, nothing... Julie Forbes, I decided, was an instant person. That must be her secret. Every few years she was reduced to ashes, then reconstituted in a new form. Different. Shining. Instant.*

Contrast with Allan Davis noting Crawford's neat dress and the "enormously big, huge orbs, [that] dominated her appearance" and her "slimness…everything was neat…terribly neat and groomed." Lambert's fictional story and Davis' real event echo each other repeatedly, although I'd contest the parallel Castle finds with this assessment of Julie Forbes' skill: "Most of it was galvanic concentration, for she had very little natural talent…Acting was hard labour like coal-mining or road-mending." Davis wittily recalled: "[Crawford]'s got noticeable hands and she had a huge brandy glass. She poured a large brandy into it, and she very seductively warmed it with both hands and handed it across to me, murmuring, 'Mr. Davis, *do* have a brandy.' I always remember that brandy arriving in this huge glass, *at* me, and I must say, I have used that bit of business, and it always gets a laugh in *No Sex, Please, We're British!*"

Another favorite bit was this from critic George Oppenheimer:

> *She gave good parties, pool parties where you dined out, and people kinda made fun of her, which I didn't think was quite justified. She was essentially a nice dame. When she put her feet up on the table with her knitting and started taking verbal swipes at her contemporaries, she was such goddamn fun, but the moment anybody important came in, she suddenly took her legs off and became Lady Vere deVere, full of graces and airs.*

A particularly priceless story by actor Tim Hardy is from the set of *Berserk* where Crawford indeed "mothered" them all. The cast was mulling around the site of Billy Smart's Circus in Blackheath, waiting for her arrival when she pulled up in an elderly Rolls Royce three and a half hours late, the young driver apparently having gotten lost. "…[O]ut stepped this rather small, grayish ginger-haired lady, in tears because she was late…I guess it was only the third time in her entire life that she'd been late for a movie call, and above all on the first day of the movie." Crawford is ushered into her caravan and emerges an hour later, staggeringly transformed: "Reassuming the image, the mask, the stance, she seemed to come out of the caravan taller, younger, tougher, and it was the Joan Crawford one recognized."

In all, after an impressive opening and even with a wonderful array of sources, photos (many, needless to say, misidentified), and some priceless stories, Castle dropped the ball for me in the latter half. Rather than illuminating Crawford, this bio — as so many others — only succeeds in increasing her enigma. Who Joan Crawford really was we may never know. She remains a complex contradiction. Perhaps, as Walker suggests, she had been so subsumed into the roles that not even an Egyptian archaeologist could excavate her (for that matter, we're all wearing masks, few completely of our own invention). Perhaps the real Crawford is no one's business, anyway, and all we have the right to expect is what she gave so whole-heartedly onscreen. As George Cukor said, "The nearer the camera, the more tender and yielding she became — her eyes glistening, her lips avid in ecstatic acceptance. The camera saw, I suspect, a side of her that no flesh-and-blood lover ever saw."

Joan Crawford: The Ultimate Star by Alexander Walker ★★★★★

> "Speaking to Hedda Hopper…[Crawford] added reflectively: 'You know, the great thing about our business is that we're allowed to see ourselves as others see us. Some of the new kids see themselves and say, 'Oh gee, I look pretty good.' They don't know that what they are seeing is the loving photography — all the singing, posture, dancing lessons they have taken. Where else could you get all these? And the publicity? They believe it. They're going to be awful lonely hearts — they're going to be awful lonely with all those goddamn clippings.' Love and loneliness: the two poles of the film world she occupied."
> <div align="right">Alexander Walker, <i>The Ultimate Star</i></div>

Alexander Walker's *The Ultimate Star* is another absolute in any Crawford/film collection, beautifully laid out, masterfully written and densely illustrated with a wealth of photos (over 250) from every facet of Crawford's life and career, some rare, some extraordinarily beautiful and large, all fascinating. Walker accessed MGM files for his research, looking at the studio as a corporation, and inserted his own opinions and analysis. While I don't always agree with his conclusions, it's a remarkable piece of scholarship, visually delicious with unique material, and one of the grade A, "must haves" of Crawford/Hollywood memorabilia.

Walker opines that Crawford was born in 1904, while I've concluded the correct date is 1906. My own consensus seems borne out when Walker states that Crawford, still Lucille LeSueur, gave her birth date as 1906 when registering at Stephens College. There is no earthly reason she would fudge her age at that point in life; later, after she made it and was more pressured to shave off years to stay competitive, she understandably adjusted this date to 1908. He believes that Crawford's life closely paralleled her screen persona and she took advice to heart. Teacher James Wood's maxims about never quitting were applied to her career; early first love Ray Sterling's prayerful invocations at the end of at least of one letter to Crawford surfaced in her later habit of attaching the same to even the humblest correspondence; and she apparently absorbed Lon Chaney's advice to "concentrate." Walker even finds parallels to Crawford accepting Christian Science as her religion at a time when she was portraying religious conversion in *Rain*. This is interesting speculation, but not conclusive.

When he sticks to facts and not conjecture (although both are fascinating), he explains a lot — why Gable never married Crawford, for one. He gives insight as well into Franchot Tone as a typical liberal — decrying capitalism while living high off its fat and seducing Crawford with radio, theater and "valid" work while she kept her toe firmly in Hollywood. (Interestingly, Walker states that seven was Crawford's lucky number, reflected in her license plate, and in my website, I have seven photos for nearly every film review and 700 in the photo galleries.) There is also cheeky dry wit ("[Mayer] used to invite the stars he loved to come and tell him what they wanted, and then let him talk them out of it"), gorgeous passages and insights, as well as sentences and concepts that I had to chew on like tough meat. He notes that she always deferred to her husbands in the beginning, who were valued as much for education and savoir faire as sex appeal. Franchot Tone got her to do radio, which she feared so much that her script pages were glued onto cardboard, "lest her shaky hand made them rustle. Franchot Tone kept a reassuring hand on her shoulder pad." Steele had her flying — and almost immediately.

Many tidbits are amusing. While married to first husband Douglas Fairbanks, Jr., their home was "furnished for a perpetual honeymoon" with a knocker on the hall door "sculpted in the shape of two heads, male and female, their lips pressed together in a kiss." The sunporch was stacked with hundreds of dolls, "as well as mechanical baby pigs, clucking hens, and Doug's electric railway, which was his wife's Christmas present to him." When MGM signed Colonel McCoy, a stickler for authenticity, to the frontier drama *Winners of the Wilderness* (one of my favorites), he "was not at all pleased when Pete Smith put out some publicity stills showing Crawford teaching Chief Big Tree the Charleston."

There are the occasional errors, though few. A photo of a leaping skater is erroneously identified as Crawford; Fairbanks' footprints are not outside Grauman's Chinese Theatre; a plot point is misconstrued or wrong (as in *I Saw What You Did)*; and most glaringly off is his statement that shortly before her death Crawford knew Christina was writing a book about her, but "it apparently made no impression on her." Was he being facetious? She was not only tearful, as Lawrence Quirk attested, but it was probably the reason Christina was left out of her will — and a valid one. He astutely observes that the American Dream of providing one's children with greater opportunities for success than one had one's self fell to pieces in Crawford's life as it did in Mildred Pierce's (her signature role). In both film and real life, the child was driven to an extreme act of rebellion. Ironically, one learns, the birth of Brooke Hayward (who wrote movingly about her mother Margaret Sullavan in *Haywire*) inspired Crawford to adopt Christina who was to "write so uncompassionate a set of her own family reminiscences in *Mommie Dearest* after Joan's death."

We part ways on some of his assessments of her films (and why wouldn't we?). For instance, he claims that Greta Garbo would've made a better Letty Lynton than Crawford and can even picture her in some of Letty's signature clothes or uttering some of her lines! Perish the thought! Letty Lynton is one of Crawford's ultimate roles, showcasing her at her most enchanting and drop-dead glamorous. In the book, Letty is not an abstract enigma like Garbo, but a vivacious, beautiful, young woman, full of charm, exactly as Crawford embodied her, with an unloving mother (which Crawford clearly felt). I'll take her fresh, exquisite beauty, girlish laugh and feral ferocity in the murder scene over Garbo any day. Similarly, Crawford is my choice over Carole Lombard (whom she replaced) in *They All Kissed the Bride*, much as I am a huge admirer of Lombard. Rather than being an "emasculating harridan," as Walker sees her, for me, Crawford is delectable as Maggie Drew with her "hey hey" flapper background and edge appropriate fits. Her duality and richness of personality fascinate; she is soft, insecure and vulnerable yet hard-edged, aggressive and authoritative all at once. The 40's suited Joan (no pun intended), embodying her best and sexiest qualities. Besides, is it emasculating when a woman gives men directions with authority or commands a board room of her subordinates in a meeting, something male VPs do routinely? Nice how men have stacked the power deck in their favor. Additionally, the very edge he feels makes *The Bride Wore Red* not a success is what I consider one of its greatest strengths.

Of *Rain,* Walker claims Lewis Milestone reveals "the male will that inhabits Sadie's assertively female body. This is precisely the conjunction that fascinates many of Crawford's admirers today, even those who do not find her sexually attractive. She is a woman with a power over men — and part of that power is the disconcerting discovery a male makes that the power is of the same gender as himself." He calls Sadie a bitch (a word I hate), but is standing up for one's self bitchy? Towards the end of Crawford's reign at MGM, Mayer was grooming Greer Garson into that ideal of "self-sacrificing womanhood," Walker says, "on which Crawford held the patent for so long." Although this infusion of new talent undoubtedly made established stars uneasy, it is refreshing and welcome to see the two beautiful women together in *When Ladies Meet*. Too often Crawford was paired with character actors, perhaps not to deflect from her glow as the star, but against another beauty, she lost none of her own. When Mayer worried that she would be upstaged by stage actresses in *The Shining Hour*, she replied, "I'd rather be a supporting player in a good picture than the star of a bad one." Ultimately frustrated by poor scripts, she left MGM and was put on Jack Warner's pay roll two days after coming off MGM's.

Most effectively Walker captures the sheer magnitude of her film stardom which curiously few biographies do. Yes, Joan was a superstar with all the perks and pressures that the title implies. He illuminates surviving inside a "star system." MGM records during the late 30's and early 40's note illness and absences from work in this stickler for self-discipline, indicating "a troubled spirit as well as an ailing body." (Ah — that mystery period where Crawford's melancholy was visible onscreen.) During the 1950's, there are again signs of mounting pressures in her life, broken by an escapist sprint across country she took with her French poodle Cliquot (recorded in carefree letters to Hedda Hopper). A "disconcerting change" was taking place in her, Walker says, as a result of these pressures. "In her films, her talents were hardening into the mould of an emasculating woman. [My note: That old saw again.] This didn't deprive her of sex appeal," he adds, "but it converted what she had of that into such things as 'power' and 'control.' Put together, these are potent parts of her screen appeal; but they are also responses to a Warner Brothers world of male values by a star who had discovered the advantage of exemplifying them." She found herself in "an aggressively masculine stronghold where women's responses had to be strong-willed and unsentimental to survive the latent or overt male chauvinism." Love the photo of a sexy young Crawford in boots sitting confidently atop a table in a room full of men during *Grand Hotel* rehearsals.

Humoresque is pegged as beginning her "menopausal melodramas." (Hello? Ouch!) He cites *Flamingo Road*, *The Damned Don't Cry* and

Harriet Craig as jumpstarting the "neurotic descent" into her "panic period," "in which the roles are fashioned to exploit her emotional dependence, usually on a much younger man who treats her roughly, treacherously and sometimes murderously." The irony is that these are the roles leading ladies of a "certain age" were offered, yet men play against younger women ad nauseum without any comeuppance or degradation provided by script writers. As Crawford aged, Walker believes, she was playing a "maternal instinct" against the increasingly masculine grain of her character and appearance. She imported this "kind of perverted protectiveness as a mother or mother-figure," he says, particularly in her last "cheap" films, but this is true only of perhaps *Strait-Jacket* and *Berzerk* and, stretching it, *Trog* and *Esther Costello*. Many actresses, in fact, played long-suffering mothers, notably Barbara Stanwyck; it is not unique to Crawford. And are we to believe Mildred Pierce, Daisy Kenyon or even Harriet Craig are masculine? Crawford couldn't control Hollywood's attitude towards older women which is to reduce them to has-been "waxworks" by age thirty-five. *Sunset Boulevard*, anyone?

In any case, *The Ultimate Star* is an exceptional, fascinating and valuable piece of work and a must for the film library, presenting the dazzling tapestry of characters Crawford embodied in life and onscreen. Bravo, Alexander Walker!

Legends: Joan Crawford by John Kobal ★★★★★

> *"She remains an electric presence even in some very unsatisfactory movies. Everything about her shone — her hair, her lips, her handsome hands, her graceful strong body and legs, her elegant feet. Everything looked as though it had sprung from nowhere, shining. Perhaps we know too much nowadays about what it takes to make a star and what a price is paid. All I know is that Joan Crawford shone. That's why they called her a star."*
>
> Anna Raeburn, *Legends*

Legends was a series edited by John Kobal and this edition on Joan Crawford with an introduction by Anna Raeburn is one of the best biographies ever on Crawford, a few factual errors notwithstanding, with an outstanding array of photographs that capture the star's magic and sculptural, haunting beauty. Using a simple style devoid of fanfare, Raeburn perceptively, frankly and compassionately nails Crawford's essence, giving due as well to the talent that was tragically gravely underestimated (as it still is). Coming from a turbulent childhood marked by poverty, neglect, abuse, and shiftless father figures that provided her with little comfort or love, Crawford found her "one chance at anything" through the movies which arguably became, at least in Raeburn's estimate, "the only love [she] permitted herself to fully reciprocate." Frightened and inadequate, Crawford devoted herself tirelessly to success and to her public, experi-

menting endlessly, welcoming any chance to observe at the studio or pose for the cameras. (Other bios note that she worked even when ill.) The cameras loved her as much as she loved them. But, as Raeburn noted, the strain of this commitment to a "script" defined by "the times, the available opportunities, the studios and their attitudes towards her" exacted a high price, publicly and privately. After MGM dealt a "low blow" to its "loyal worker" by edging her out after seventeen years of service, in spite of her astute efforts to overcome obstacles and take risks that would enable her growth, she "knew her fans still loved her and she couldn't continue to let them down," so she signed with Warners at a third of the salary she'd previously received and fought for and received "script approval." Just as "the leitmotif of Crawford's life had been the expenditure of energy in order to stay calm" (i.e., the endless knitting, swimming, exercising, dieting, etc.), she continually toiled to maintain hard-won success. Warners eventually handed her potboilers and once again she overcame defeat by going freelance, but it was ever an uphill battle and her life, onscreen and off, was marked by psychodramas that revealed the strain. Still Crawford strove to give the public what they expected in way of a Hollywood star. "She came of a breed who believed that to admit difficulty was to countenance defeat," Raeburn notes. The back jacket sums it up nicely: "Despite being haunted by the public failures of her fifty-year, eighty-one film career, Joan Crawford never gave anything less than tireless effort to her dazzling performances that lifted even the most mediocre scripts."

Also of interest are Raeburn's observations of Crawford's troubled home life which included four marriages and four children. "She had nobody on whom to model herself as a mother and so she tried vainly to give the children the framework she thought would help them, which had been so noticeably missing in her early life," Raeburn notes. The unhappiness and running away and drama that resulted was, as Raeburn puts it, "all too redolent of [Crawford's] far from happy childhood." When hopes of renewing a contract with MGM failed with *Torch Song*, "for the first time, there were reports of her being unpleasant to her colleagues on the set. It is easy to see how, as she knew she had peaked in terms of how she looked and what she could accomplish, so she began to increase her demands that she should be noticed, have attention paid to her, be acceded to — in the manner of somebody who feels they haven't made it but cannot give up. Take away her work and she had nothing," Raeburn concludes. Like a cat with nine lives, however, Crawford did find new expression through her work as an ambassadress of Pepsi for fourth husband Alfred Steele, which gave her a measure of purpose and satisfaction, but after Steele's untimely death, Pepsi ultimately and cruelly dropped her as had her studio. Crawford had tried to mold herself according to the requirements of the times, but she was continually valued more for her looks than her acting, not given opportunity by MGM "to go far enough to discover whether she was more than they thought she was or not," pelted by critics at times in spite of continual whole-heartedness, sometimes with remarkable results, and as illness took over, she withdrew. It would be cancer that killed Crawford and Raeburn notes it was in the perfect Freudian place — the back, an aching back being a side of mourning. Raeburn believes Crawford mourned that her contributions to the industry that had been her life were not acknowledged. "She lives through the movies she made, and even when they were frankly mediocre and inadequate, she gave them the very best her dazzling armoury could offer." Author Carl Johnes reports in his book *Crawford: The Last Years* that Crawford was indeed trying to let go of stardom and finding it difficult, but he also beautifully captures her spirit — almost childlike in its enthusiasm and spunk — which too many other biographers, bereft of the advantage of knowing the star personally as Johnes had, conspicuously neglect.

The book ends with a wonderful essay by Ross Woodman on photographer George Hurrell. The photographs indeed speak for themselves as testaments to the mutual love affair of star and camera. Two of my favorite photos, both by Laszlo Willinger, include a 1938 full-length photo that reveals Crawford's sensuality and womanly beauty like a Greek goddess and a close-up from *Strange Cargo* (1940) that captures her wistful quality and exquisite features — the stunning shape of her face, the finely chiseled and spectacular nose and profile, and those incredibly expressive eyes lushly veiled by long lashes with true Hollywood enigma.

Legends is a stellar and deeply satisfying tribute to the great Joan Crawford that defines in words and images her enduring effervescent star quality.

My Way of Life by Joan Crawford ★ ★ ★ ½

My Way of Life is a rather odd book detailing the lifestyle of Joan Crawford by the lady herself for the benefit presumably of her large female following, although its tips on how to please a man and keep house are probably a little behind the times — not to mention, few of Crawford's audience traveled with as many wardrobe changes, hats and jewels as she did or reams of hygienic tissue paper. A photo of her in full "grand lady" ensemble (hat, jewels, dress and gloves) greeting females in Africa who didn't wear shirts, let alone shoes, may have an amusing irony, but then, what was she supposed to do — wear a grass skirt? Should Al Steele? According to Carl Johnes' *Crawford: The Last Years*, all her "autobiographies" were ghost-written. (As in all things Crawford, this is a matter of controversy, since elsewhere she denies that any of them were.) In any case, basically, the star liked a genteel, organized way of living and *My Way of Life* is designed to show us the way to it — Joan's way. If anyone can get things running and keep them running, she can. Less energetic mortals might be run ragged trying to keep up with her as, like the Red Queen in *Through the Looking-Glass*, she attempts "six impossible things (at least!) before breakfast." "Plan," Crawford exhorts. "And everything will get done!"

Oh, what kind of a sourpuss can't love Joan? "I like to get up early in the morning because I can't wait for the day to begin." Or when she reports that phone call from Cary Grant that made her feel wide awake again. (Personally I'd rather get a letter on blue stationery from her!) Since Crawford is a celebrity, not the average housefrau, it's only natural that her associates are going to include other names like Noel Coward and Grant, but sometimes, as she describes an existence that is clearly privileged, it's hard to know if she has lost sight of her target audience, wants to rub our face in her rarefied world, or — the scenario I believe — convince everyone and herself of how active and in demand she still is. Obviously she missed her late husband and needed to assuage the loss with work and optimism. If your "fella" wants caviar, we females are told, don't say you're not Joan Crawford and can't do it, because she can't either. Skip the hairdresser a couple of times. Give up a hat that you don't need! (Elsewhere in the book we're told about the special shelving in her own large closet just for hats!) Add this to her growing list of other things "no woman should be without" (chiffon, three-way mirrors, etc.). After telling us of juggling film offers, the stray good television show on "the coast," panel shows, talk shows, the fifteen charity boards she's on that demand attendance at meetings and weekly public service announcements, the late and light lunch, Crawford adds this howler, "[I] try to find twenty minutes to relax completely. There'll be a lot more work to finish before dinner." *(Phew!)*

Beyond the amusing side of a book such as this, it's hard not to feel, as Charles Busch put it, "infinitely touched" by this broad who came from the grimmest nothing and all-too-understandably submerged herself in a fantasy world. Anyone who knows anything about her realizes this whirlwind of etiquette and order didn't keep her life on keel or protect her from hard knocks, shoddy treatment by studios and people, or loneliness, but who could make it through without illusions and delusions and denial? Why shouldn't a woman of Crawford's vitality, obvious sharpness and ambition channel that energy into some kind of regimented hullabaloo? She worked hard to overcome numerous obstacles and, as she puts it, "inactivity is one of the great indignities of life!" Although her cheery frankness and warm tone charms, I winced at the '50s mentality of deferring to men that even this sassy star bought into ("if [your husband] gets moody, you get brighter!"), but was moved and impressed by her proud, airbrushed attempts to fly in the face of defeat — yet again! Although she doesn't hide the extravagance that her star's life afforded, this is her attempt to appeal to the average woman with an appreciation of beauty and gracious living. She goes at it full throttle, as always, occasionally throwing her audience a bone. (Country club memberships, she concedes, are only if you can afford them — unlike other pricey niceties that she recommends acquiring at personal sacrifice. After all, she gave up her memberships - "too expensive!") At times she is wistful and perhaps sad as when recalling grand parties where she floated candles and gardenias on her pool and created a fairyland: "Those were the most extravagant days of my life."

One reads *My Way of Life*, propped up on a sofa with a bowl of popcorn, with the same sense of admiration, exhaustion, and amusement that one reads *Martha Stewart Living*. This woman was ahead of her time and an inspiration with her truly American entrepreneurial spirit, deep romanticism and unapologetically anal excess! Are we really going to ensure our jacket is lined in the same fabric as our blouse or not buy a dress unless we can afford the appropriate accessories? Yet the advice on taking care of and valuing clothes and possessions strikes me as sensible, especially from one who worked hard for them as Crawford had. If only she were alive today, she'd give domestic diva Martha Stewart a run for her money! The rest of us are mere turtles in the race to seize the day!

The book is filled with many nice photos of latter day Crawford, including my favorite — her clothing ensembles laid out on the bed (with matching gloves, headware, handbags and shoes). There's also a great recipe for meatloaf involving four hidden hard-boiled eggs, but then, as our gal tells us, she makes these (and pot roast, beef bourguignon, lobster Newburg, and creamed chicken) ahead of time and keeps them frozen for emergencies!

Not the Girl Next Door: Joan Crawford by Charlotte Chandler ★ ★ ★ ★

Charlotte Chandler's Joan Crawford biography *Not The Girl Next Door* attempts to put a kind and refreshing spin on the star's celebrated and dramatic life, notably including interviews with Crawford's daughter Cathy Crawford LaLonde, and eschewing most of the darker aspects of Crawford's relationships. The author has impressive credentials. She is a board member of the Film Society of Lincoln Center with numerous celebrity biographies under her belt (including Bette Davis). She met the grand lady through John Springer, Crawford's friend and publicist, and they had several lunches leading up to Chandler being invited to Crawford's New York Imperial House apartment (the visit detailed). With the majority of the story in "quotes" alleged to be made by Crawford or one of her intimates like Douglas Fairbanks, Jr. (many quotes given their own paragraph), these conversations must have been considerable. Evidently Chandler inspired trust to gain biographical confidences from Crawford such as, "If you were telling the story of my life, you could say that I believe my greatest weakness was I needed love too much. I was love-deprived when I was a child, and my life has been a search for love the way a child craves it" — the exact sort of thing a biographer or fan would surmise about her. Oft-tread details are relayed in Crawford's voice (occasional poetic license here?) and Chandler's interviews with Hollywood notables for other bios are included as relevant. Whatever its flaws, the material is rich. It is a sensitive portrait of a star who was undoubtedly very sensitive herself, and offers some entertaining and surprisingly fresh information. Moreover, Chandler lends it the class and respect her subject deserved and would have approved of. By focusing on those who really loved Crawford, it gives a necessary balance to those hatchet jobs masquerading as biographies that favor scandal and sources who dish negatively and one-sidedly. Always mindful and respectful of her public and never one to dish herself, Crawford is long overdue for such a graceful turn.

As laudable and welcome as this approach is, however, crediting the sweet, tender, loving side of Crawford that was discernible often in her work and netted her lifelong friendships, it is less than honest to exclude the dark side of her various relationships. In the interest of being comprehensive and thorough with the subject, why not give her life its full due? That was my initial reaction, yet ultimately I felt won over by a portrait that captured so much of the human being. It is never mentioned, for instance, that Henry Cassin, whom Crawford clearly adored, sexually molested her at age eleven — in fact, the age she was in the rare photograph where she is holding a doll; yet hearing Crawford's glowing memories of him sheds light on how critical it probably was for her to keep her illusion of him as perfect daddy. Given that he was the only adult showing her love, the only one who acknowledged and celebrated her birthday, it's understandable that it might be too unbearable to believe otherwise. She idealized her relationship with him as she did Al Steele and even Clark Gable (in the latter case, occasionally insisting that she was happy she never married Gable, although the depth of her love for him was transparent). The extensive interviews with Douglas Fairbanks, Jr. are especially a strong suit, alternating with accounts by Crawford of their youthful, passionate marriage and an intriguing contrast to the in-depth interviews with lecherous Vincent Sherman (more on both later). With much to recommend this new biography, particularly the way it sheds light on Crawford's humanity and positive influence on others, plus dispels a few myths, it does have its shortcomings that detract and distract (more on that later also).

Douglas Fairbanks, Jr. gives an extremely revealing and touching account of his early relationship with Crawford when she was still called "Billie" (a practice he never stopped). Their mutual love, passion and naiveté was clear and quite endearing. Beyond the "spontaneous combustion," as Crawford puts it, of two young "beautiful people" coming together, there were a number of things they had in common, one of which — sadly — was lack of parental love and approval. Fairbanks calls Crawford "unforgettable" and "stunningly beautiful." ("Every man who met Joan Crawford fell in love with her. Couldn't help it.") He recalls that first "charmingly handwritten and extravagantly complimentary" note she wrote to him on her trademark blue stationery after his performance in *Young Woodley*, naively asking him for a signed photograph. ("Of course she could have a signed photograph of me. Actually, she could have *me*.") Her house on Roxbury Drive in Beverly Hills, he remembers, was "tiny and overdecorated with a kind of yard-sale elegance, but nicely put together, beautifully kept, and she was so proud of it. I liked the way she felt about her home." Crawford recalls, "Perhaps an intense love like that has to be experienced when you are very, very young…It's something new, you aren't afraid, and you don't hold back."

A story which has long been circulating about Crawford is finally given clarity here. Fairbanks recalls how "absolutely terrified" his young love was of his finding out about a film she made in a "financially desperate moment." She told him about it when they first got deeply involved "in case it makes a difference." He tried to get details, but only got tears; it involved a blackmailer claiming to have a copy of the print. "I've always found a woman's tears a powerful weapon," he says. "I could more easily face a duel in a film or a real-life naval battle in World War II...Billie threw herself on my mercy, which wasn't necessary. She only had to throw herself on *me*." Gallantly Fairbanks took the next blackmailing call and put an end to it. "Billie asked me if there was anything more I wanted to do about the blackmailer. I said, 'Yes. I want to know where we can get a print of the film.'" His humor aside, it is a painful illustration of Crawford's vulnerability and exploitation as a young girl in Hollywood.

Fairbanks also relays when Crawford called him in a happy, giggly mood to tell him she had wonderful news, but wouldn't say what. He was away for the week. When he arrived, she had no more news and didn't want to speak about it. He suspects it might have been a pregnancy. This story brings to mind one of her early letters, in which she pours her heart out to a fan about an "operation" her doctor "made up my mind for me" to undergo. She is obviously distraught and sick and says, "Some things are awfully hard to destroy, aren't they???" Since it was written during the same period as her marriage to Fairbanks, could it possibly refer to that incident? Fairbanks had his own theory, although he never knew for sure, that it was indeed a baby. "I know I rather missed that baby that never was," he said. He also admits that, although strictly faithful before they married, he began to cheat after their marriage, due to his sexual inexperience, curiosity, and his young wife's long hours at the studio. This is another aspect biographers unfailingly overlook, preferring to frame Crawford as the cheater when obviously his infidelity contributed to their drifting apart. He, again gallantly, admits that he was "so self-centered, I didn't even know I was self-centered." His attempt to salvage their marriage with a honeymoon to Europe — in which he sadly ignored his wife's wishes to go to Italy where they would be alone — failed miserably.

Fairbanks sounds nostalgic and wistful, ruing the dissolution of a couple that "lived happily ever after — for a while." "I'll tell you the way I remember Billie," he says. "Whenever we were in crowds, she would cling to me. It made me feel very good. I suppose it made me feel that she depended on me as her gallant protector. It was the role my father played in films. She was so tiny and clinging to me, she seemed very much in need of my strength. She had this frightened, worshipful look in her eyes, and when I held her tightly, she stopped trembling. That's the way I remember her, clinging to me."

Vincent Sherman, Crawford's director in three films, sums up his relationship with her as a "black silk panty affair." That pretty much sums *him* up. According to his account, she was an impressive professional and he was resolved not to get personally involved until she put his hand over her breast during a screening of *Humoresque*. Naturally he was powerless in the face of this full frontal (no pun intended) seduction. Hilariously, he admits that he was having "marital difficulties" that "weakened any reluctance" (can't think why!), but his "remarkable" wife didn't blame him for sleeping with Crawford. Without a trace of irony, he even has the gall to suggest that Hedda, his wife, "embodied the new liberated woman" as opposed to Crawford who "remained a slave to convention" as if women's liberation was designed to allow men to cheat on their wives without guilt! Surmising that Crawford seduced him in order to control him and the film, he resolved to get the upper hand; he also didn't relish being compared to "all those other men" who had been in Crawford's life. He felt she went after what she wanted with a "masculine approach to sex." Nonetheless, he alleges that Crawford told him she loved him repeatedly and wanted him to leave his wife for her. He was chagrined that she tried to make their affair more open while he wanted it confined to the shadows. He found it convenient that the studio was close to his home and she remained there in her dressing room during the week so he could see her. He also accepted the expensive gifts she gave him as helplessly as he accepted these sexual favors. Crawford tried to make him jealous by walking on the beach with another cast member. "It was not possible for me to refrain from being amused at such an outlandish situation," he concludes. "On one hand, we have a wife who can accept sharing her husband with another woman, but on the other hand, this woman resents having to share the husband with his wife." Then he adds the kicker: "I believe it was the difference between true love and possession." (One understands why Crawford later called him a "prick.") Seems gentle Fairbanks' self-admonition that he was so "self-centered, I didn't even know I was self-centered" more aptly applies to Sherman.

Some of the other recollections are priceless such as this one by producer Joseph Mankiewicz on his first visit to Crawford's home:

> *She was sitting at her writing desk like a lady of the nineteenth century. She had been writing notes on thin, monogrammed blue paper. She looked like the true movie star, and I complimented her on her lovely dress.*

> She said, "It's one of my dresses for writing letters," and she wasn't joking. She hadn't known I would be coming by to leave some material. I had expected to leave it for her with the maid, so she hadn't dressed up so beautifully for me. She had dressed like that for herself.
>
> She invited me for lunch. She took off her sleeve guards and said she was going to change for lunch. I said, "It's not necessary. The dress you're wearing is beautiful."
>
> She said, "I know, but it's one of the dresses I wear for doing my correspondence. I'm going to change to one of my eating-lunch-at-home afternoon dresses."

Interspersed throughout are synopses of Crawford's films, which can be slightly intrusive, but certainly are a necessary part of the "big picture" (pun intended). The problem is many of them are wrong. Even details to films available on DVD are bolloxed. This is a grating faux pas. In *The Best of Everything*, for instance, she states "Gregg" found success and happiness ("Gregg" committed suicide); in *I Saw What You Did*, she has "Amy" protecting the girls (hello?); and even the quote in *Rain* is wrong. Any fan, certainly a large part of her readership, is going to notice. There are also head-spinning omissions. For one, she claims Crawford enjoyed making *Johnny Guitar*. Aside from *Baby Jane*, by all available accounts, it seemed to be the production from hell. Much press was given at the time to the "discomfort" level and Crawford's feuds with Mercedes McCambridge and others. Given the care and respect Chandler shows her subject, which is infinitely laudable, why not ensure accuracy in all details? One suspects that she used her ample interviews to construct her bio, but passed over anything that fell outside of this. Fine, but ensure that whatever is included is accurate. Chandler might err too far in minimizing Crawford's failings, but thankfully she does give credit to and remind readers of Crawford's enormous decency and correct distortions in that vein. (Bless you, Charlotte Chandler!)

Thankfully also, Chandler isn't afraid to expose Christina's recalcitrance or to reveal Christopher's combative personality that, according to longtime secretary Betty Barker, "resented women." Myrna Loy recalls Christina's arrogant behavior when they worked in Neil Simon's *Barefoot in the Park*. In a great contrast to her mother, she arrived unfailingly late and wouldn't do anything she was told. Finally Neil Simon fired her. "My own personal theory was that she wasn't just *jealous* of Joan, she wanted to *be* Joan," Loy says. Chandler also includes a very important detail, now misconstrued with pathetic caricature: when Crawford replaced her daughter for five episodes in the daytime serial *The Secret Storm* during Christina's illness, the ratings *soared* with Joan and went down when Christina returned. Needless to say, Christina was furious. Also — at last — a wonderful interview with daughter Cathy is included. Yes, Crawford had two other daughters, both of whom are worthy of inclusion in her memory.

In any case, a welcome and warm addition to the Crawford biographies with several rare photographs as an extra bonus!

A Portrait of Joan by Joan Crawford (with Jane Kesner Ardmore)
★★★★

To my surprise, given the disparaging reviews, *A Portrait of Joan* is perhaps the most revealing of the books available on Joan Crawford, giving a very strong sense of who she was — for one, a dynamo. Some readers accuse the book of being "sanitized" (that tiring sawhorse due to the public's unending thirst for dirt like Romans at the Coliseum), but au contraire! Even the fact that Crawford uses grace and diplomacy when recounting less savory details or relationships is indicative of her personality. My own feeling is that this woman gave her all to the public. She doesn't owe us her skeletons and it is to her credit that she doesn't "dish" overmuch. But a full sense of both her personality and the less happy aspects of her life comes through loud and clear, anyway. Evidently Crawford had to earn everything she achieved and continually strove for self-improvement. Her enormous vitality and demanding work ethic was sure to intimidate, especially in light of the fact that ambition has never been encouraged in women and she had her share of opposition, yet her overwhelming spirit was that of a survivor who wants to thrive. It didn't negate pain or terrible experiences in the least, but it did enable her to achieve on an amazing scale and reflect the astute, bright nature that lie beneath an inadequate formal education.

In spite of the bravado and discipline she showed on the face of things, her sensitivity, vulnerability and insecurity also are apparent and the latter had its own pathos. It's only too clear that her upbringing offered little in the way of love or security, the cornerstone of all her future problems. When she seriously injured her foot as a child, she recalls her mother's rare exhibition of devotion to her, which is unintentionally wrenching. "Mother took tender care of me that year and a half," she says. "Like many mothers she adored her son and favored him, but during that time she felt genuine compassion for her daughter." Genuine compassion. Ouch. Genuine compassion, not love. How very sad and yet mother Anna was clearly too oppressed by hardscrabble struggle for niceties, a victim in her own right. Like many in those times, Crawford and her brother were forced into child labor. Then Crawford suffered the added mental burden of feeling responsible for driving away the only "Daddy" she knew (revealed in another bio as being sexually abusive - does the tragedy of that childhood ever end?) because of a perfectly innocuous "discovery" in the basement. The whole picture shows enough abuse, defeat and tragedy to crush any spirit, yet Crawford's spirit was as defiant and strong as the one she exhibits onscreen. Still, the ongoing volatility in Crawford's life proves it waged an inevitable toll.

Jane Kesner Ardmore does a good job of putting biographical details and Crawford's own commentary into fluid, sequential form and adds some nice, evocative touches. (Of Michael Cudahy, an early Crawford romance: "He was the reckless scion of the F. Scott Fitzgerald era just as I was the flapper of the John Held, Jr. cartoons." And the description of Mrs. Cudahy in the Cudahy mansion in the Hollywood hills is eerily reminiscent of the Walter de la Mare tale *Seaton's Aunt:* "This *belle dame sans merci* lived in the past, dressed unlike other mortals, and the whole atmosphere was strictly Sunset Boulevard. I often wondered if we raised the blinds, flung back the curtains, opened the windows, would the ornate cushions gleam satin as they seemed, or would they be revealed in shreds and tatters." It's safe to say this is Ardmore's contribution in "Crawford's voice.")

In some ways, in spite of being very commanding and self-sufficient, Crawford remained the little girl, trying to do everything she was told to win approval and obviously the love she sought. Whatever notes Stephens College president James "Daddy" Wood gave her in those early lonely years as a teen, she took deeply to heart, as she evidently did her critics. When she talks about refusing to change makeup to differentiate character while playing "twins" (actually a split personality) for *Zane*

Grey Theatre, one can easily assign that as fallout from *Rain* when fans and critics bashed her, taking to task, for one, her makeup. Apparently Crawford blamed herself (unfairly) that the makeup (used to differentiate "tramp" Sadie from "repentant" Sadie) was a cop-out. ("I didn't even know then that you could work from the interior to the exterior," she says. "I was still working from the exterior. My fans wouldn't accept her.") As in all things, she immediately changed the "offending" behavior, just as she changed from lip-biting and hand-wringing in early nervous days to using her hands as little as possible in her later career, rehearsing allegedly with her hands tied. "How can an actor or actress walk on a set not knowing the dialogue, or fail to study the rushes every day?" she asks. "Most professional actors are instinctively prepared *and* punctual. To any job you value, you give value." In an earlier part of the book, she tellingly reveals that she worked so hard because she had nothing to go back to. As she said of first husband Douglas Fairbanks, Jr.: "He hadn't developed the muscles for fighting because he hadn't had to fight."

The demands on her were huge and balancing professional and private life was a strain. Tiresomely, since if she were a man there would be no need for such defense, one can hear her trying to justify her desire to sleep at the studio while shooting a film and, frankly, it sounds reasonable enough, although it is somewhat amusing; it is women who have to strike such "compromises" since they are primary caretakers of children and in Crawford's case at this juncture, the *sole* caretaker. She did, after all, pay her dues for that career and generally love it. ("Better to leave the twins to their busy days at school, their competent nurse at home, and for me to stay right at the studio in my dressing-room — except, of course, at week-ends.") She goes on rapturously, "After my cohorts leave I'm locked in that dressing-room at night with my script, getting ready for the next day, evaluating all that we've discussed. Sometimes I go over to the empty set and walk it, rehearsing. One of the most wondrous places in the world is the night studio, quiet, shadowed, the vast equipment standing idle, the city of a million fantasies and as many combined talents, ready to spring into being at daybreak. Try to sleep!" Perhaps one of the things she shared with fourth husband Al Steele is a love affair and devotion to work. Again, particularly in Crawford's day, men could indulge that virtually guilt-free unlike women. (More about Steele later).

Admirable is the way Crawford navigated her career. *A Portrait of Joan* makes clear the risks taken. To her credit, she was never one to languish in a comfortable zone when she felt she was stagnating or not growing and moving forward. She even went off salary while new at Warners, waiting for the right property. Her instincts were acute and right-on as when she got control enough to acquire and co-produce *Sudden Fear*. Unfortunately, she was often not allowed her pick of choice vehicles. Being this focused perfectionist, she explains her approach to child-rearing, "I believe the most important thing a parent can give children is the ability to stand on their own feet, achieve their own personality, slug it out with the world if necessary, and still not lose dignity, integrity or a sense of humor. You don't try to keep them children. You keep giving them responsibilities, preparing them for an adult world." Tragically, this approach didn't seem to work too well with two of her children, leading to permanent estrangement. I also enjoyed the silly, little details like her reason for wearing ankle straps — even ones made of plastic (for Jerry Wald's sake who disliked them).

In the latter half, Crawford lapses into grandstanding, acknowledging and thanking lists of people. Can't say I fault it, tiresomely political as it may be. Crawford evidently was a pro who believed in "team work," as she attests here, grateful to all who contributed to her success, whatever their station, and felt it was just and due to credit and reward these people; it made sense from a professional as well as personal standpoint and I believe it was genuine enough. Clearly she respected and treasured her fans, keeping life-long correspondence with many of them, even amusingly putting them to her own use [and yet I believe her when she praises them for being givers, not takers — one can only imagine in her high profile position there were plenty of the latter]. For the first time (for me, anyway), Crawford also almost makes understandable her affection for Al Steele (almost, not quite); she certainly does her best to convince us of his devotion and more positive qualities ("For the first time in my life a man was giving me emotional security...He was loving me for what I am"). But anyone who blackens his wife's eyes (as we know he did from other accounts, including Joan's own admission) gets black marks from me. "Before we left [Capri], Alfred bought me a superb diamond plume, the coat of arms of a noble Capri family," she says. "He always said I'd earned those diamonds, they were my service stripes." Ouch. The price sounds high, Joan. Sadly, domestic abuse concerning adults, in contrast to child abuse, is inexplicably and infuriatingly ignored and even dismissed with claims like "She deserves it or likes it." No one wants to be abused. In spite of Crawford's sentimental idealizing of her marriage to Steele, my own take is that it is the "way of life" he offered that was so satisfying and fulfilling for her, a chance to be needed, wanted, learn about big business and even be active in the company, and travel internationally, very exciting and rewarding stuff at a time when her career was winding down and she still had enormous vitality. Transparent, however, is that the men she really loved, including Clark Gable, never came to fruition, a fact even confirmed by Christina in *Mommie Dearest* (and one of the few I'd trust, devoid as the observation was of malice). Not one to stagnate, however ("Tomorrow is my destination"), Crawford was determined to overcome and thrive.

A Portrait of Joan is a remarkably revealing portrait of a woman on her own since age nine who achieved against the odds due largely to her own will, vitality, talent, passion and resilient spirit. In spite of a refusal to revel and languish in dishy details, one sees that it was a hard road that extracted its own toll; Crawford endured enormous suffering, yet really did give of herself, whatever her flaws, in the hopes of earning love in return. One can read between the lines just as anguish, yearning and wistfulness is often rawly exposed on her face and in her eyes beneath the mythologizing key lights.

Fun with Joan Puzzles

Here are puzzles to test your Joan know-how, challenge your brain, and have fun with. They should keep you in the swim, in fact, about all things Joan Crawford! Don't ask what Joan would do — you know. She'd roll up her sleeves and give each a go, as she always did in life! Remember those three maxims James "Daddy" Wood of St. Stephens College gave our gal (and which that apt pupil never forgot): *1. Never stop a job until it's finished; 2. make laughter merriest when problems are deepest;* and *3. attempt impossible jobs that promise growth as opposed to those easily accomplished.* Joan would do six impossible things before breakfast! What time is it? These can be your first!

Crawfordgram I

There is a complete Joan-related message hidden in the square below. It can be found by drawing a continuous line through the correct letters, vertically, horizontally, or diagonally (backwards or forwards). The pencil lines, when done correctly, will give a symmetrical design. No letter may be used more than once. Start at the shaded box with the "V" and finish at the shaded box with the "A". Enjoy! *(Please note: all punctuation has been eliminated! C for Crawford, C for Challenge!)*

B	H	P	R	J	O	L	C	M	D	G	E	K	X
S	K	N	Z	L	U	V	E	D	P	O	G	D	L
W	I	Y	P	V	M	S	R	A	T	Q	E	U	W
A	N	D	S	I	Z	V	M	I	X	M	P	A	O
T	E	I	F	J	E	I	H	T	I	L	B	V	N
M	U	R	Z	R	A	N	O	A	B	T	N	D	F
Y	D	N	J	O	C	K	E	M	T	O	A	Q	Y
M	B	L	A	E	Z	I	M	S	Q	S	U	O	Q
T	I	O	N	K	T	S	U	E	R	P	E	W	U
H	Q	M	A	O	M	V	Y	E	X	I	B	R	C
G	D	U	V	I	V	G	N	I	F	A	D	K	E
D	S	I	C	E	W	Y	C	D	W	E	M	C	B
H	A	R	O	F	D	O	L	Z	H	C	N	L	H
N	K	S	X	A	J	U	F	O	R	T	R	E	P
S	W	E	Z	M	L	P	A	U	L	I	S	A	K
Z	R	L	B	I	R	R	O	H	D	N	A	P	X
V	A	M	E	U	O	L	D	W	Z	Y	K	E	M

Crawfordgram II

There is a complete Joan-related message hidden in the square below. Same instructions as before — it can be found by drawing a continuous line through the correct letters, vertically, horizontally, or diagonally (backwards or forwards). The lines, when done correctly, will give a symmetrical design. No letter may be used more than once and all letters in this case are used. Start at the shaded box with the "E" and finish at the shaded box with the "R". Enjoy! *(Please note: all punctuation has been eliminated! C for Crawford, C for Challenge!)*

E	E	N	B	E	E	R	E	A	L	L	B
U	J	E	C	E	I	A	E	T	Y	A	S
Q	E	P	S	T	N	R	P	H	A	O	U
N	N	I	L	O	R	S	R	D	T	S	R
I	N	I	L	H	E	O	N	H	E	S	D
Y	H	P	A	V	E	U	T	C	A	E	H
R	E	S	A	I	D	A	L	L	Y	T	M
O	W	L	U	F	I	E	H	E	R	I	Y
F	O	E	N	A	T	N	W	M	B	H	O
E	M	E	S	B	U	I	S	E	L	O	U
B	A	E	R	E	A	T	A	L	K	T	D
N	V	E	N	D	E	H	K	N	I	H	T

These "Crawfordgrams" are based on the 1930s Liberty Magazine *"Yardleygrams" by Herbert O. Yardley.*

Let the games begin! PHOTO COURTESY OF JERRY MURBACH

Joan Logic Problem

Bootsie and four of her friends were members of the Joan Crawford Fan Club. They each had a favorite Joan film, a favorite Joan film character, and a favorite male lead in a Joan Crawford film. Surprisingly, everyone's was different. Determine each person's full name, favorite Joan film, favorite Joan character and favorite male lead.

1. Gilda didn't like Crystal Allen and Bootsie didn't like Robert Montgomery. Ms. Rivers liked John Wayne, but didn't like Lane Bellamy.

2. The girl who loved Lane Bellamy also liked *The Bride Wore Red*. Bootsie admitted that *Humoresque* was her favorite and Bette also said that she wasn't fond of *A Woman's Face*.

3. The one who loved *The Bride Wore Red* wasn't Judy Forbes or Lana. Lana's favorite wasn't *A Woman's Face*. The one who loved Clark Gable also liked *Letty Lynton*.

4. Each of the five girls are represented by the following: Bootsie Drew, *The Women*, Sadie Thompson, Jeff Chandler, and Gilda.

5. Lana didn't like *The Damned Don't Cry* or Sadie Thompson. Ms. Whitehead loved Mildred Pierce but neither she nor Judy liked Clark Gable.

6. Ms. Kenyon loved Robert Montgomery. The one who loved Crystal Allen didn't like *A Woman's Face* but the one who liked *A Woman's Face* liked Franchot Tone.

First Name	Last Name	Movie	Role	Leading Man
Bootsie				
Gilda				
Lana				
Judy				
Bette				

Last Names: Forbes, Rivers, Whitehead, Drew, Kenyon

Films: A Woman's Face; Humoresque; The Damned Don't Cry; The Bride Wore Red; The Women

Characters: Mildred Pierce, Sadie Thompson, Crystal Allen, Letty Lynton, Lane Bellamy

Leading Men: Clark Gable, Franchot Tone, John Wayne, Robert Montgomery, Jeff Chandler

Tips for Solving: Make a large grid with all the variables listed except for last names (first names, movie titles, characters, and leading men) on the left and above this vertically have a connecting grid with last names, movie titles, characters and leading men. Have boxes beneath in grid format so you can check off information. For instance, when you learn that one girl doesn't like a certain leading man, she can get a dash in her box under that leading man's name for "no" or if you discover that one girl likes a specific Joan movie, she can have an x in the corresponding box for "yes." Ultimately, by process of elimination and some brain work, you will be able to solve the puzzle and write the information in the box on the previous page. It's tricky, so don't give up easily!

"The freeway is fun!" especially with a front seat driver. (Dig Joan's socks!)
COURTESY OF THE NEAL PETERS COLLECTION

Fun With Joan Trivia

For those people who stand around gossiping about Joan's husbands and cheeses (as one fan put it) and how many films in which she appeared as a blonde (as Rome burns), this trivia test is just your cuppa! And even if you don't gossip, try it on for size! It might put you on the Road to Ruin!

Please note that only those silents reviewed in this book are included in the quiz. Some silents are not currently available and a few, tragically, may be lost. I hope to track down whatever remains eventually for review. As Wally Fay says in *Mildred Pierce*, "We live in hope."

Answers will follow. No cheating!

1. *Where in the World is Pepsi?*

Have you searched for Alfred Hitchcock's cameos in his films, proud that you could pick out that corpulent profile? How adept are you at spotting soda? After marrying fourth husband, Pepsi bigwig Alfred Steele, Joan Crawford gave her usual 2,000 percent by promoting the product everywhere even in the remotest corner of Africa to tribes without shoes! She also was a pioneer in product placement, displaying and featuring the Pepsi logo, discreetly and not, in her films. Prior to becoming loyal ambassadress to Pepsi, Crawford actually endorsed Coke — and every other product under the sun (see her Peter Pan bra ad and wonder no more about that "bullet point breasts" look of the '50s)!

According to a *Vanity Fair* article called "The Lipstick Jungle" about the making of *The Best of Everything*, when producer Jerry Wald asked her to introduce a young actress in a test scene, Crawford insisted on playing the scene holding a bottle of Pepsi. Director Jean Negulesco objected, "to which she said, 'No Pepsi-Cola bottle, and Joan Crawford goes home.' He replied, 'No, Joan. Pepsi-Cola stays, but Negulesco goes home.'" Crawford cried. Guess she never thought of wearing Pepsi earrings!

How many Pepsi placements have you spotted? Name the film and the spot.

2. *Joan in LIVING COLOR!*

How many films featured Joan in color (television excluded, mind)? Name the films.

3. *No Tears in Your Vodka* — *Films in which Joan **didn't** cry.*

We all know Joan could put on the waterworks on and offscreen. Cliff Robertson, her co-star in *Autumn Leaves*, even recalled with amazement that she would ask "which eye" a director wanted the tear to come from. But in which films did she remain dry-eyed?

4. *Which films did Joan swim in?*

5. *In which films was Joan an actual shopgirl?*

6. *Which films did Joan dance in?* (The answer might surprise you!)

7. *In how many films did Joan* — **gasp!** — *die?*

8. *In which films did Joan give her signature "double slap?"* (The technique that could come in very useful in our own lives with some deserving people...) (Yeah, go for it! I know there are plenty of you out there who notice even the way Joan shakes hands, holding the palm up!)

9. *In which films did Joan sing?* Extra points if you can name that tune!

10. *In which films was Joan a blonde?*

11. *In which films did Joan wear a wedding gown?*

12. *Match Joan's profession to the film.*
   a. blackmailer
   b. senator
   c. anthropologist
   d. novelist
   e. playwright
   f. stenographer
   g. illustrator
   h. salesgirl
   i. movie star
   j. typist

   1. *Sudden Fear*
   2. *Grand Hotel*
   3. *Autumn Leaves*
   4. *Ice Follies of 1939*
   5. *The Women*
   6. *Daisy Kenyon*
   7. *Goodbye My Fancy*
   8. *A Woman's Face*
   9. *When Ladies Meet*
   10. *Trog*

Get out your Number 2 pencils and think, think, think before looking at the answers, kids. Don't bite on your erasers either!

Bring back the Fine Art of Lounging!

Oh, Joan, you do languid so damn beautifully! Look at that twist in the hip!

Loungers need fine settings like fireplaces. Joan demonstrates with her dachshund Pupschen and cheerful, coordinated colors.

The ultimate vamp: A boudoir, that va-va-voom black dress, and come hither look — can anyone lounge like our gal? I think not!

Miscellaneous

Joan Crawford Paper Dolls by Marilyn Henry
(Written or Drawn 1996) ★★★★★

Marilyn Henry's *Joan Crawford Paper Dolls (A Celebration of the Great Movie Queens)* is an absolute delight, a fun and lovingly crafted tribute to a woman who not only was a major star, but a major fashion trendsetter, and for this genuine fan of both paper dolls and Joan Crawford, it did not disappoint. These out-of-print paper dolls came to me in a charming fashion as well from an eBay seller who included a little package of life savers taped to the cardboard inside. The dolls follow suit in warm spirit. There are two dolls in beautiful underwear undoubtedly modeled after Crawford's own onscreen lingerie, each a representation of the actress' 1930s self. Inside are six pages of colorful fashions with a real, black and white photo of Crawford on each page, incorporating, as the artist explains in her introduction, what she considers "the ten or twelve most glamorous years in a star's career" and duplicating the costumes from that period. The costumes, thus, are primarily from Crawford's 1930s films, although not exclusively. The films represented are *Forsaking All Others*; *Letty Lynton* (two costumes); *Strange Cargo* (two costumes); *Possessed (1931)* (three costumes); *Mildred Pierce*; *I Live My Life*; *No More Ladies* (three costumes); *Today We Live: When Ladies Meet*; *This Modern Age*; *Sadie McKee* (two costumes); *Our Dancing Daughters*; *Ice

A close up of Henry's detailed cover illustration.

This photo displays the stunning ring that Crawford characteristically wore throughout the early forties, which Henry so beautifully depicted in her detailed drawing (see previous page). PHOTO COURTESY OF JERRY MURBACH

Follies of 1939; The Gorgeous Hussy; Grand Hotel; Humoresque; and *Susan and God*. As always, it is fascinating to see the vibrant choice of colors the paper doll artist chooses to depict an outfit that has only been seen in black-and-white, sometimes the color at odds with what I imagined and other times so spot on that it's hard to believe the piece has never been seen in color. My favorite, in particular, is the "scarlet" dress from *Strange Cargo* — what else would it be but scarlet? — with its slice and bit of seductive leg.

Henry's paper dolls naturally invite comparison with those of Tom Tierney who also took on Joan Crawford as his subject. Although Tierney was much more impressive, richly detailed and textured in his illustrations of the fashions, eerily capturing Crawford in the headless figures, his facial renderings left much to be desired and Henry's dolls are somehow a little more fun. Her renditions of Crawford in full color, particularly the large cover portrait, are not eerily accurate, but close and certainly lovely. In the cover portrait, she not only sought to get the shape of Crawford's lips (the signature shape Crawford herself had adopted which masked her natural, far less exaggerated lip line), but also, thrillingly, captured some choice pieces of the star's own jewelry.

Most winning of all is the simple and charming introductions the artist has written on the back of the front cover with a column about, first, "the star" and aside it "the artist" with a full-length genuine photo of Crawford, clad in glamorous coat, in between. After a well done mini-biography of Crawford where Henry dutifully acknowledges her as "first and foremost, a Hollywood immortal, a great STAR," she sums up herself: "Movies and paper dolls were my twin passions growing up. If I couldn't find a certain paper doll in the dime store, I drew the star doll for myself. I would go to a movie, come home and draw all the costumes for my star paper dolls. I always knew I wanted to be a paper doll artist."

This immediately warmed me, since my sister and I too drew our own line of paper dolls. Henry was amazed that Joan Crawford was not one of the celebrities from Hollywood's golden era that were done by the big paper doll publishers and sought to fill in the "oversight" by creating dolls for these "missing stars."

I'm glad she did! It almost makes me want to play with them and recreate my own fond childhood memories.

Joan Crawford Paper Dolls in Full Color by Tom Tierney (Written or Drawn 1979) ★★★★

Joan Crawford isn't easy to draw. I've tried myself, so I know. But I didn't put out a line of paper dolls and Tom Tierney did. Disappointingly, his dolls — which depict Crawford at three different stages in her career (early, mid and presumably latter day although the differences are infinitesimal) — fail dismally in capturing any facial resemblance to the actress at any period. Rarely do the hairstyles seem quite right either. But the costumes are often fairly well on target and, yes, they're in full, glorious color. Some of the clothed figures — with faces cut out for the doll — eerily capture Crawford's essence in a headless way and they include outfits easily identifiable with specific films (such as the *Letty Lynton* dress).

The costumes begin with an elaborate hot pink gown for *Pretty Ladies* (1925) at which time Crawford was still called Lucille LeSueur. That is for the first doll and it also gets costumes from the following films: *Sally, Irene and Mary; Our Dancing Daughters; Our Blushing Brides; Possessed; Grand Hotel; Rain;* and *Letty Lynton.* The second doll (which arguably looks least like Crawford although they're all poor likenesses) has costumes for *Dancing Lady* (two); *Sadie McKee; I Live My Life; The Gorgeous Hussy; The Bride Wore Red; The Last of Mrs. Cheyney; Mannequin* (an unusual and beautiful costume); *Ice Follies of 1939; The Women; Susan and God;* and *When Ladies Meet.* The last doll has the post-MGM era with *Mildred Pierce; Humoresque; Flamingo Road* (the harem outfit and one of my favorites); *Harriet Craig* (he depicts this dress as pink interestingly; was it really?); *Torch Song; Johnny Guitar; Female on the Beach; I Saw What You Did;* and *Berserk!*

Love this "harem" costume from *Flamingo Road.*

A bio is given on the front and back covers and apparently Tierney met the actress, describing her as "thoughtful, generous, kind and helpful." He mentions that her detractors call her tough, but adds that he is sure she was "tough in the business of films (and probably toughest on herself)..." and that she would have to be to survive for over four decades in Hollywood.

In sum, although the dolls bear little resemblance to Crawford, the illustrator still has presented a positive tribute through them and they're worthwhile for any serious Crawford collector (or for those who love Hollywood costumes).

One of the fabulous Joan cartoons by author Peter Joseph Swanson. Peter is the author of *The Joan Crawford Murders,* a zany novel not-to-be-missed that features not one but several Joans! COURTESY OF PETER JOSEPH SWANSON

Answers

"Look, Beauty, Crawfordgrams — how quaint!"

You better have given this a good shot, the old St. Stephens' "Don't be a quitter" spirit! You know that Joan always packs heat in her mink and she likes fans to apply themselves to a challenge with the same determination she would. No one promised you that life — or puzzles — would be easy. So don't come up for air unless you have tried your Joan-best to work out the solutions! Before your peepers look at this page — show me your papers! And they better have squiggles, designs, and not too many white spaces! Otherwise I might have to get Louise Howell to come over here from the "Joan Quiz" Answers page and get you to move on quietly. Are you sure you've given it your 200 percent and, as Daddy Wood put it to our girl, made your smile merriest when problems were deepest? Okay. But I've got one finger on the buzzer for Louise in case I've been had…

Crawfordgram I

Hidden message (punctuation added): "Veda, I think I'm seeing you for the first time and you're cheap and horrible," said Mildred Pierce to Veda.

(Yep, the pattern was Christmas trees, kids!)

Crawfordgram II

Hidden message (punctuation added): "Really, that Dr. Pearson, he's so absurd. He actually trembles when I talk to him. You'd think he'd never seen a beautiful woman before," said Eva Phillips to her niece Jenny in *Queen Bee*.

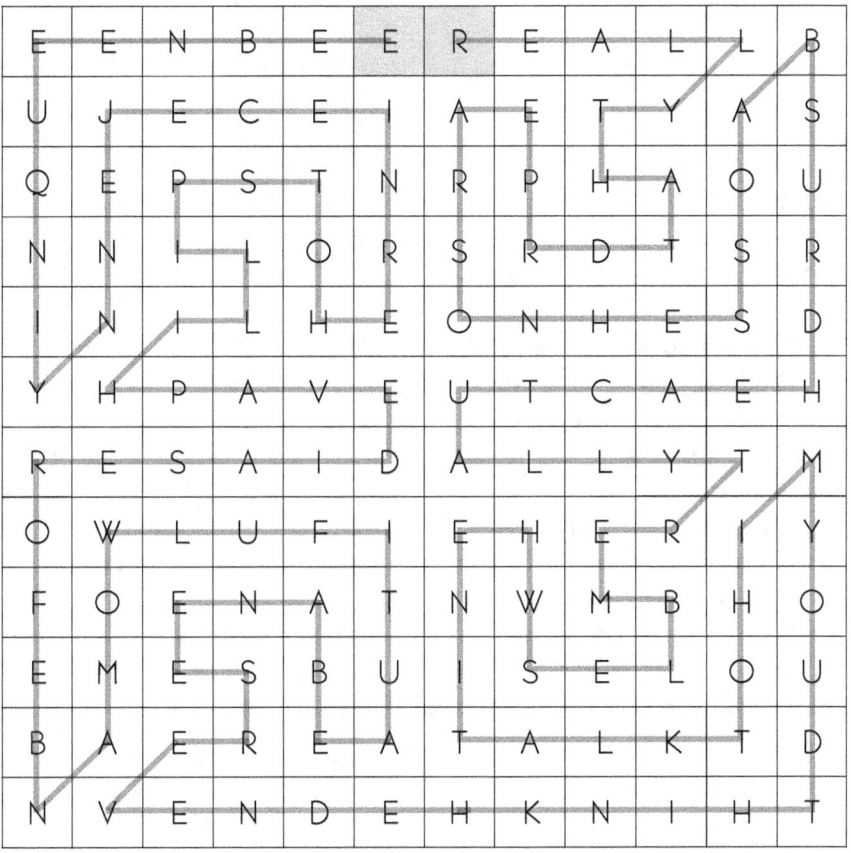

(It was hell — twenty years of sheer hell! — crafting this one!)

Joan Logic Problem

Here are the answers:

First Name	Last Name	Movie	Role	Leading Man
Bootsie	Drew	*Humoresque*	Letty Lynton	Clark Gable
Gilda	Kenyon	*The Bride Wore Red*	Lane Bellamy	Robert Montgomery
Lana	Rivers	*The Women*	Crystal Allen	John Wayne
Judy	Forbes	*A Woman's Face*	Sadie Thompson	Franchot Tone
Bette	Whitehead	*The Damned Don't Cry*	Mildred Pierce	Jeff Chandler

The deductions are made empirically and in layers like unraveling skeins of thread. It's best to start with a chart like the one below. From the clues, you are clearly told that there is Bootsie Drew and Judy Forbes. Therefore, Gilda, Lana, and Bette are either a Kenyon, Rivers or Whitehead. We also learn that Bootsie liked *Humoresque* so you have three of the Bootsie boxes filled in already. The other boxes can be filled in with possibilities based on the clues. You can write all the possibilities in each box and eliminate choices based on clues. For instance, *The Damned Don't Cry* is eliminated as a movie choice for Lana based on clue 5 and *A Woman's Face* is eliminated for Bette, based on clue 2. When you eliminate choices based on clues from the first perusal, your box should look like this:

First Name	Last Name	Movie	Role	Leading Man
Bootsie	DREW	HUMORESQUE	MP, ST, CA, LL, LB	CG, FT, JW, JC
Gilda	KENYON? RIVERS? WHITEHEAD?	AWF, TDDC, TBWR	LB, MP, LL	CG, FT, JW, RM
Lana	KENYON? RIVERS? WHITEHEAD?	TW	MP, CA, LL, LB	CG, FT, JW, RM
Judy	FORBES	AWF, TDDC	MP, ST, CA, LL, LB	FT, JW, RM, JC
Bette	KENYON? RIVERS? WHITEHEAD?	TDDC, TBWR	MP, ST, CA, LL, LB	CG, FT, JW, RM, JC

Narrowing it down further, clue no. 5 tells us Judy doesn't like Clark Gable and since clue no. 3 reveals that the girl who liked Clark Gable also liked Letty Lynton, we know Judy doesn't like Letty Lynton. Letty Lynton is removed from her box under "Movie" as a possibility. We also see from clue no. 3 that she doesn't like *The Bride Wore Red* (another choice removed from "Movie") and if she doesn't like TBWR, she doesn't like Lane Bellamy because clue no. 2 tells us that the girl who liked TBWR also loved Lane Bellamy. Judy doesn't like Mildred Pierce because her name isn't Ms. Whitehead (clue 5). Therefore, Judy's choices for favorite Joan role are narrowed to Sadie Thompson and Crystal Allen. Bootsie doesn't like Sadie Thompson (clue 4), Mildred Pierce (clue 5) or Lane Bellamy (clue 2). We also know Bootsie doesn't like Jeff Chandler (clue 4), John Wayne (clue 1), Robert Montgomery (clue 1) or Franchot Tone (clue 6). Therefore, she likes Clark Gable, therefore she likes Letty Lynton. Bootsie is sorted out now. We remove her choices from the boxes of the other girls. From clue 6, we learn Bette doesn't like AWF and therefore doesn't like Franchot Tone. Lana's favorite movies get narrowed down to TW, so we can eliminate many of her other choices, based on clues. It's a process of elimination, done in stages. This is basically how it is worked out.

First Name	Last Name	Movie	Role	Leading Man
Bootsie	DREW	*HUMORESQUE*	LETTY LYNTON	CLARK GABLE
Gilda	KENYON? RIVERS? WHITEHEAD?	AWF, TDDC, TBWR	LB, MP	FT, JW, RM
Lana	KENYON? RIVERS? WHITEHEAD?	TW	MP, CA, LB	JW, RM
Judy	FORBES	AWF, TDDC	ST, CA	FT, JW, RM, JC
Bette	KENYON? RIVERS? WHITEHEAD?	TDDC, TBWR	MP, ST, CA, LB	JW, RM, JC

The box keeps getting narrowed down. LB is going to be taken out of Lana's box, for instance, because she likes *The Women*. So she is left with MP or CA. Ms. Rivers likes JW, so JW is taken out of Judy's box. If you continue combing over the clues carefully, ultimately the choices will be narrowed down correctly until you arrive at the answers given above.

Answers to Trivia

Not so fast. I asked you not to cheat on me. I explained it to you. Did you try to answer before peeking? You're being square, on the level? Alright, then.

1. Pepsi flowed in the following (and puh-leez if you know of more, don't hesitate to e-mail me; a girl can't have eyes everywhere, can she?):

Autumn Leaves: To be determined.

The Story of Esther Costello: See the Pepsi logo surreally prominent in the airport on a vending machine.

The Best of Everything: To be determined.

Whatever Happened to Baby Jane: At the beach in the finale, in a lightning quick moment (you have to freeze and rerun the film to see the logo properly — but does this matter to Joan? Subliminal product placement works!), a man returns the "empties" of a carton of Pepsi to an ice cream stand!

The Caretakers: At the hospital picnic, described by Lucretia (Joan's character) as "MacLeod's private country club," a stand sports a giant bottle cap with the "Pepsi" logo and bottles of the soft drink are grouped there for sale. Throughout the picnic, people drink

Our gal plugged her product whenever and wherever possible — and she actually drank the stuff!

bottles that are obviously "Pepsi" although the logo is not blatant. Crawford was a great product placement marketer — her placements, though prominent, were still subtle and made sense, not detracting from the motion picture.

Strait-Jacket: A six pack of Pepsi is on the counter in the kitchen. A wooden Pepsi CEO is in the cast. (Don't worry. Joan acts around him.)

I Saw What You Did: To be determined.

Berserk: As detectives are strolling past concession stands on the circus grounds, one booth prominently reads "Come alive with Pepsi."

Trog: As the crowd runs after Trog emerges from his lair, they barrel past a refreshment stand with the Pepsi logo.

2. Joan's first color appearance was in select, three-strip Technicolor sequences of the first all-talkie musical *Hollywood Revue of 1929*. She also appeared in an early Technicolor sequence of *Ice Follies of 1939* and then in full, living color in the following films: *It's a Great Feeling; Torch Song; Johnny Guitar; The Best of Everything; Berserk;* and *Trog*. Joan also, needless to say, appeared in color on television in productions including *Della* and *The Karate Killers*.

3. Yep, even in *The Damned Don't Cry*, Joan cried. You would, too, if you were being slapped around by David Brian. Apparently the damned *do* cry. But Joan got through the following without moisture: *Lady of the Night* (didn't have time; she was the back of Norma Shearer's head); *Pretty Ladies* (again, she was only an extra); *Tramp, Tramp, Tramp; The Boob; West Point; Hollywood Revue of 1929; The Women; Hollywood Canteen; It's a Great Feeling; The Caretakers;* and *I Saw What You Did*. She "tears up" in *Spring Fever; The Last of Mrs. Cheyney;* and *Trog*.

4. Besides her regular dips at Brentwood offscreen, Joan took to the water in: *Our Blushing Brides* (this is uncertain since there is a shot of showgirls diving into a pool, one of whom seems to be Joan, but not sure); *Dance, Fools, Dance; This Modern Age; Dancing Lady; Chained; Forsaking All Others; When Ladies Meet; Mildred Pierce; Humoresque; Possessed* (1947)

(well, they say they were swimming, but we know what that means); *The Damned Don't Cry; Johnny Guitar; Female on the Beach;* and *Autumn Leaves*. This does not include any films where she wears a swimsuit, but never actually is shown swimming.

5. Surprisingly, Joan was an actual shopgirl in only five films: *Our Blushing Brides; Mannequin; The Women; Reunion in France;* and *The Damned Don't Cry*.

6. Joan who started her career as a dancer kept fleet of foot onscreen in: *Spring Fever; Winners of the Wilderness; Our Dancing Daughters; Hollywood Revue of 1929; Our Modern Maidens; Untamed; Montana Moon; Our Blushing Brides; Dance, Fools, Dance; Laughing Sinners; This Modern Age; Grand Hotel; Letty Lynton; Rain; Dancing Lady; Sadie McKee; Chained; No More Ladies; I Live My Life; The Gorgeous Hussy; Love on the Run; The Bride Wore Red; Mannequin; The Shining Hour; A Woman's Face; They All Kissed the Bride; Hollywood Canteen; Possessed* (1947); *Flamingo Road; The Damned Don't Cry; Sudden Fear; Torch Song; Autumn Leaves; The Story of Esther Costello; Strait-Jacket;* and *Berserk*.

7. Joan died in seven films (gulp!), including one of the silents not reviewed on this site (yes, this violates my own rule but I only include it since I know the end) and one television gig that was released in theaters. To reveal the names of any of these films would be the ultimate spoiler for those who haven't seen everything.

8. Joan used her now-infamous "double slap" technique in: *A Woman's Face; Mildred Pierce; Possessed* (1947); *Flamingo Road; It's a Great Feeling* (well, two men got the hand but it was spoofing her double slap); and arguably in *Berserk* (or maybe what she did to the photographers in that could be merely considered "beating them over the head." Should I argue straws?)

9. Joan sang in: *Hollywood Revue of 1929* ("Got a Feelin' For You"; "Singing in the Rain"); *Untamed* ("Chant of the Jungle"; "That Wonderful Something is Love"); *Montana Moon* ("The Moon is Low"; "Let Me Give You Love"); *Laughing Sinners* ("What Can I Do — I Love That Man"; "London Bridge is Falling Down"; "Brighten the Corner Where You Are"); *Possessed* (1931) ("How Long Will It Last"); *Dancing Lady* ("Heigh-Ho, The Gangs All Here"; "Let's Go Bavarian"; "Rhythm of the

Day"); *Forsaking All Others* ("Row Row Row Your Boat"); *I Live My Life* ("Silent Night"); *Love on the Run* ("She'll Be Coming Around the Mountain"); *The Bride Wore Red* ("Who Wants Love"); *Mannequin* ("Always and Always"); *Ice Follies of 1939* (dubbed) ("It's All So New to Me"); *Susan and God* ("Religious Song"); *When Ladies Meet* ("Eternamente [For All Eternity]"); *They All Kissed the Bride* ("You Must Have Been a Beautiful Baby"); *Above Suspicion* ("A Bird in a Gilded Cage"; "My Love is Like a Red, Red Rose"); *Humoresque* ("Embraceable You"); *Flamingo Road* ("If I Could Be With You"); and *Torch Song* ("You Won't Forget Me"; "Follow Me"; "Two-Faced Woman" [all dubbed by India Adams]; "Tenderly" [dubbed by India Adams, but then sang on her own]).

10. Joan was a blonde in: *This Modern Age* and *Laughing Sinners*. She wore a blonde wig in *Our Blushing Brides; Dancing Lady;* and *Ice Follies of 1939*. She was also notably light in *Flamingo Road* and *It's a Great Feeling*.

11. Joan donned a wedding gown in: *Our Modern Maidens; Forsaking All Others; I Live My Life; Love on the Run;* and *Above Suspicion*.

12. a. – 8; b. – 7; c. – 10; d. – 9; e. – 1; f. – 2; g. – 6; h. – 5; i. – 4; j. – 3.

"See, kids, that wasn't so hard, was it?" ARCHIVES OF DETROIT DAILY NEWS

Epilogue
by James Sibal

Crawford in mad hat and mink...So Joan, so very, very Joan.

Crawford Second Hand

How I grew to respect a diva I had never met;
as remembered by someone who knew her well.

If the persona of a famous person is a valid subject of study, then it's transmission at the second or even, third hand, is even more so. After all, we all know that claiming to have been intimate with a famous person is one thing, but claiming to have known them vicariously by their friend, is quite yet another.

Yet Crawford second hand is stronger and, indeed, more significant than many people in flesh and blood, and although I never met her I can readily say that she did, and continues to, influence my life. I was the spouse of Carl Johnes, a late life friend of Crawford and one of her most intimate, if not lyrical, biographers. In our decade together before Carls' death in 2001, seldom did a week go by without him speaking of her, accounting an amusing or timely reminiscence, or perhaps more intriguingly, explaining how she had gone about her life. He had enjoyed being her friend and confidant and from this unlikely teacher, had learned a great deal about life and even himself. In many respects, Joan was an archetypal force in his life.

How Johnes met and became one of Crawford's inner circle is the subject of his 1979 book, *Crawford: The Last Years: An Intimate Memoir*. In brief, Carl, a former actor, by the 70s decided he didn't like acting or actors. With a penchant for books, he had taken a job as a junior storyboard editor at Columbia Pictures. Crawford, equally mad about books, called up Columbia one day and asked them to send someone over to help her organize her library. Her love of books and learning is just one aspect of the "unexpected Joan" and it would serve their friendship well. After meeting, nature and personalities took their course and many years later, Carl would be among the very few invited to her private funeral in NYC.

When Carl met the diva he was a young man who had been around. For high school he had attended the L'Ecole International in Genèva and there he had found a busy life among the children of famous movie industry figures. A 50s haven for the offspring of celebrities reputed to be "pink," among his friends was the son of Yul Brynner, the daughters of Gene Kelly, the producer Melvin Frank and many others. During spring breaks and family visiting days he had dined and shot the breeze with Cocteau, Jean Moreau, Melina Mercouri and her much respected husband producer/writer Jules Dassin and many famous actors; in the course of extended house stays and holidays with fellow students, he had met Paul Robeson, Anita Loos and many of the great in the late 50s and early 60s who gave us some of the iconic images in popular culture of those decades. He had been hit on by Lillian Hellman at a party (she loved young blond boys) and a good raconteur, with a bit of urging, Carl could recount a delightful story of meeting Thelma Ritter quietly sitting in a corner at another party, the two of them spending the entire evening talking about acting techniques. Professionally, Johnes had formally studied acting at RADA, the Royal Academy of Dramatic Arts in London the generation after Anthony Hopkins. His best friend at RADA had been Lynda La Plante, now a dramatist rather famous as a unique personality in the British scene. Carl's address books still make good reading.

Yet amid all this worldly mix Johnes found Crawford unique. Why and how Carl found Crawford would always interest and even, at times, enthrall me. They were a kind of fieldwork for my studies in anthropology and art history. As an academic I had long realized that public relations and the construction of a public persona was an ancient art — already tried and true by the time of Augustus and Cleopatra — but before meeting Carl I knew little about it in my own century. But among all the divas he had met, what made Crawford different?

Most immediately, their friendship was complex and multilayered yet with some careful thought, it doesn't seem all that mysterious or esoteric to me. There was of course the physical. There was an immediate physical attraction; Carl was tall, handsome and fair, with an amazing facility to put people at their ease, especially women. He was traveled and had an easy grace with facts and culture — and a charm which seemed to attract women naturally. Privately, Carl was terribly private and believed in a strict line of separation between public and private worlds.

Crawford was, well, Crawford. She liked, no, rather, loved men. Still quite elegant and always poised, at that point in time in her life she was increasingly a reclusive. The public woman had moved into a private, reflective mode, or perhaps gave this aspect of her personal more room. Officially, she was in retirement which meant much time with old friends, her charities, pontificating on the ruin of her business, but still meeting new people, reading and advancing her intellect. Most of all, I get the sense that they both were curious about the world.

How and why Carl grew to respect Crawford was a combination of her professional qualifications, her personal qualities, and her idiosyncratic but ultimately, archetypal interpretation of femininity. She shared these qualities with other divas of her day, but all summed up, she was in a category by herself. She shared ambition and drive with Bette Davis, was more vulnerable and helpless than Norma Shearer and grander and more ladylike than Olivia de Havilland.

They both certainly had common ground in the Business and had experience in manipulating the boundaries between reality and illusion to varying degrees: Carl as neophyte and Joan as the master. Carl was impressed how almost half a century earlier, she had crafted a public persona which was particularly resilient to the decades. "Every dog has his day," Crawford would say, "and mine was longer than most." He was amused that when motivated, she could be charming and fascinating, or distant and haughty. She could slip into any role demanded by the situation with ease. He was in awe of her skill in that border land between who she was and who she projected. Who she wanted to project.

Professionally, she was disciplined, ambitious and a survivor. And even before her breakthrough role as Diana in the September 1928 release, *Our Dancing Daughters*, Crawford intuited the American zeitgeist although she probably didn't know the word. She knew how to work a famously fickle system and except for a dip every fifteen or so years, had always been on top. She was someone who from the very beginning had dove into life seemingly unconcerned with fear and the consequences of her actions: she had lived on her own terms, defying convention.

Carl felt that Crawford was, most of all, a very real, practical player in a world of make believe. Almost by alchemy she knew when to change techniques to get what she wanted when her former strategies no longer worked. She was flexible, never rigid. As a young dancer touring the US, years before the movies, she had instinctually known when to shift gears and move on to the next level, the next challenge; the change from Buffalo to Broadway was followed by concentrating on the nascent California movie screen: bit parts, tireless self promotion, at this stage by being a flapper and winning dance contests. Cukor, one of the most perceptive men in that world of fantasy, perhaps said it best at her memorial service in Hollywood:

> *...She was the perfect image of the movie star, and, as such, largely the creation of her own indomitable will. She had, of course, very remarkable*

material to work with: a quick native intelligence, tremendous animal vitality, a lovely figure and, above all, her face, that extraordinary sculptural construction of lines and planes, finely chiseled like the mask of some classical divinity from fifth-century Greece. It caught the light superbly, so that you could photograph her from any angle, and the face moved beautifully... The nearer the camera, the more tender and yielding she became — her eyes glistening, her lips avid in ecstatic acceptance. The camera saw, I suspect, a side of her that no flesh-and-blood lover ever saw... I thought Joan Crawford would never die. Come to think of it, as long as celluloid holds together and the word Hollywood *means anything to anyone, she never will.*

Carl knew Crawford in the twilight of her years, at her philosophic best. Quite at odds with a strong element of her official persona, he found her vulnerable and yielding like a retired general, someone who had fought long wars, largely achieved what she intended, and allowed herself a reflective mood. She was not an intellectual, but was quite active about following her interests — she never did anything half heartedly. Crawford, was, like Carl himself, an autodidact. This was a strong bond. When the word "doge" had appeared in something about Venice they were reading she pronounced it dog-y. There was some confusion and Carl explained how it was pronounced and they discussed Venice, which they both knew. It was then decided that Crawford should hire a tutor to help guide her readings and Carl arranged for his former literature teacher from Geneva, John Mowson, now the head master at a private school in New Jersey but living in Manhattan. Mowson, a hard living type himself, had taught all Carl's classmates — the Hollywood Brats as they were known — and had a particular gift with making literature live.

But the personal had a special appeal to Carl; he *liked* her. I think the quality most endearing to Carl was that she was not a snob. Born Lucille Fay LeSueur, her very name had come from a movie contest and although she is reputed not to have liked "Crawford" as sounding too much like "crawfish" — something well known among the poor in the Texas of her birth — she went with the public will. This was unlike many on the top, who in the days when records were scanty, created lofty backgrounds for themselves and acted as they believed was appropriate.

She was a popularist movie icon (unlike Garbo). When just a bit player on the silent set she made it a point to get to know all the publicists, makeup artists, camera men and all the staff who Crawford saw could ultimately make or break a star with their skills. She knew many by first name and always realized that the actor — or more properly the persona projected on the screen — was only as good as the support staff would allow. The wrong makeup line on your face or the wrong lightening on a scene could spoil its magic and make even a Garbo look like Lionel Barrymore — fellow actors she had worked with in one of her early films, the 1932 *Grand Hotel.*

It was a management technique long known in San Antonio, Texas and the American South in general but one seldom understood by those who didn't grow up with servants or a class hierarchy: the staff can make or break the master by making his life paradise or hell. Or more succinctly put: never be rude or haughty to those who have access to what you eat. You don't know where it's been before it's presented to you on fine china at the mahogany table.

In professional terms, after her Oscar for *Mildred Pierce*, she noted:

> *After* Mildred Pierce *I realized what Ernie [Haller, cameraman] was doing. The shadows and half-lights, the way the sets were lit, together with the unusual angles of the camera, added considerably to the psychology of my character and to the mood and psychology of the film.*

Getting along on a first name basis with Ernie and respecting his craft had proven it's worth. Crawford was smart, and amid the make believe pretense world of the Industry — much pretense coming from management which Carl seldom respected from his experiences — Carl found Crawford vital and honest.

Most of all, Carl admired that she toyed with the difference between who she actually was, and the character she created and played in life, Joan Crawford. He saw the care she put into her physical persona. Before going out, more than once she would joke to Carl as he was left waiting in her living room by her housekeeper, "I'll just be a min; I have to prepare Joan Crawford."

Her humor was dry and witty and Carl found her quite funny. When discussing the names in contemporary theater, dance and movies, she would continually quip imperially, "Who ARE these people?" And when they decided to stay in or have people over to play backgammon, she would order snacks from the local deli, identifying herself on the phone in a sonorous tone, "Hello, this is JOAN CRAWFORD" then winking at Carl, "I just LOVE to say that!"

She was one of the best of the early stars at self creation and maintaining a form of that image. Self creation and it's changes over time was a subject of great interest to both of us. Carl and I would endlessly discuss the Great Gatsby element of American society. Carl's view point was that of Hollywood and that cult of fame, mine that of equally intriguing world of antiquity and ivy league academia (THOSE cults of fame). We both believed that self creation had been a primal element of American life from the very beginning and with the creation of Hollywood, largely founded by ethnic minorities from fringe countries and peopled by individuals born out of privilege, it seemed that the techniques of getting ahead had been formalized and a new aristocracy founded. (This new media class is now in its fourth generation.)

Both Johnes and I respected the skill and craft which Crawford used to create professional Crawford persona, the visual clues in particular. She made herself iconic and, more often than not, was instantly recognizable from picture to picture. Crawford made the absolute best out of her assets, and as they changed with age and tastes, so did she. Like her early rival Norma Shearer, she had worked very hard to overcome her initial limitations (which by all accounts were far fewer than Shearer's) and maximize her strengths. To my mind, the mature Crawford image was a sophisticated play on both male and female gender signals. It was much imitated by others in her time and copied even today.

She developed her signature make up early on, by the early 30s, and with the film *Letty Lynton*, in 1932, working with the young designer Adrian, Crawford achieved her visual iconic completion. In this film she ranges from the vulnerable femininity of a white organdy gown with ruffled shoulders (which apparently sold more than a million copies in the midst of the Depression) to power suits with shoulders reminiscent of military and almost in imitation of masculinity. And importantly the visual clues flowed in a continuum and not by rocky disjointed movements — unlike the fragmented clues of our modern age and those of modern divas such as Madonna. Thus, by the early 30s the Crawford look was complete. She would use these elements for decades in various combinations. So secure were these elements that even today they are easily recognized and a satirist can quickly draw her image with very few strokes.

Combined with the visual, the character followed. Although limited in her early MGM contract of what kind of characters she could play, when she had the clout to have a choice of roles, she inevitably focused on the American dream — a woman from great disadvantages making it against all odds.

Johnes, of course, had studied and lived overseas and this gave him a sense of distance to analyze what being American was all about.

Crawford's persona reveled in the rags-to-riches fantasy of American life, most successfully in her 1945 film, *Mildred Pierce*. A lot has been written about *Pierce*, but my own favorite in this genre is the 1950 *The Damned Don't Cry*.

In this *film noire* Crawford plays the Philistine Ethel Whitehead, a weary drudge living in a shack next to the Texas oilfields, who marches up the ladder of success, man by man. She eventually passes through the gum chewing tough gal phase to become the patrician Lorna Hansen Forbes — a society figure consciously created in the film. (Such figures say a great deal about American perceptions of woman and class in this period.) The formula was a standard one and Crawford wallowed in the frumpy, long suffering, rough around the edges, martyred Whitehead as much as reveling in the grandly stylized patrician Forbes. Despite its post-code moral ending — *de rigeur* for the period — it was art imitating life in many respects, and the life of Lucille Fay LeSueur at that.

But in typical Crawford fashion, even the-wicked-must-suffer ending had a twist. Ruined, wounded in bed from a gun battle with gangsters from the numbers racket she facilitated, the coda for much of Crawford's persona can be summed up in the dialogue as two reporters leave the shack where Whitehead has sought refuge after the ruination of her ruse as socialite:

> *Scanning the filthy oilfields:*
> "Well, it must be pretty tough in a place like this."
> "Tougher to get out."
> "Do you think she'll try again?"
> "Wouldn't you?"

If there ever had been a sequel, the *The Dammed Don't Cry II*, without a doubt Ethel would have been transformed back into Lorna, just as Lucille would always be transformed into the triumphant Joan. Joan was persistent, if nothing else.

When Crawford played against the type — since her ambition did entail actually being an actress — her public often didn't follow. The 1932 film *Rain,* and her masterful role as Sadie Thompson, a prostitute, is considered one of her best roles by critics and many scholars today, but was a box office flop.

Carl also admired Joan's personal qualities; in an age of great sexual hypocrisy Crawford was non-judgmental. Aside from her famous quip about Shearer, "It's not hard to get the good roles if you sleep with the boss," she was, to all accounts, matter of fact about sex. Accused of having fucked her way up the ladder (a common accusation at the time and a current one as well. And frankly, probably not wrong) she was well aware of the power of sex for opening doors. And she used it. She had infinite love affairs and a lusty appetite. Carl said she spoke of John Garfield glowingly.

She was a loyal friend. A long time friend of Crawford's from the silent days was fellow actor William Haines. After his 1933 arrest with a sailor at the Los Angeles YMCA she was one of very few stars who stood by him. Under her patronage Haines would go on to be a successful interior designer and in his 30s neo-classical period do much to remove much of the funereal aspect of the interiors of the rich. He was instrumental in mixing antiques and modern design in the 40s and 50s (his modern period) would literally furnish the *film noire*. Spending fifty years in a homosexual relationship with his spouse, Crawford called them the happiest married couple in Hollywood. William Haines Design exists to this day.

Crawford credited Cukor, about as openly homosexual as one could be in those days in Hollywood, as being one of the directors who had influenced her most. She loved intelligence, talent and hard work, and seems to have basically believed that as long as a private decorum was observed, what people did in private should remain so.

Crawford's morality was complex and she believed in standing by old lovers. She spoke to Carl of the difficulties in watching her former husband Franchot Tone die of lung cancer in her home as she cared for him in the late 60s. She sent large checks to children's services anonymously. She was very pleased in using her fame and fortune to help others. She and Carl discussed death and, inevitably, one day she told Carl she was dying and needed to be alone. Carl understood.

But, ultimately, why Carl admired Crawford so profoundly over the more flamboyant Mercouri, Jean Moreau or the other leading ladies he had met, probably lies in her being quintessentially American. Carl saw many American qualities embodied in her, such as optimism, ambition and an independent pride — a pride in being a woman. Studies from both anthropology and sociology have suggest that this was a self feeding expansion of gender created and supported by American cinema moguls of this period who came from traditions of strong women, at odds with the traditional Anglo-Saxon norm of diffidence.

And Crawford had carved her way up from nowhere to the pinnacle of the American popular aristocracy — a movie star. She had taken the cards fate had dealt her — a low birth, little formal education and few connections — and negotiated them into assets. Like many of her heroines, she saw life as a business and recognized this very early on. Carl saw in her a personality of great drive, discipline and purpose, and incidentally one with these elements in far greater proportions than himself.

For Carl, I suspect that Joan was an anima projection of sorts — that mystical completion of the opposite sex speculated to exist by such psychoanalysts as Carl Jung. She was the perfect role model always nourishing and pushing him onwards. For me, Joan is a shadow figure, or what the French call, an *éminence grise*, who called the shots out of sight, beyond what is visible.

Her example certainly encouraged Carl to give up the movie industry and write, to follow his own muse, to further develop his own persona. And Johnes' lyrical account of Crawford, given to me by Carl to read while Johnes and I were courting, certainly encouraged me to take the leap with him. It's nuanced and sensitive portrait of her humanity gave me an insight into Carl. And Crawford's muse had done its job; although Johnes died too young to have achieved great commercial success, or fully develop as a writer, he did make a living and was content with his choice. Crawford's encouragement of lifelong learning, helped cement our bond, since like her, Johnes never went to college. She, more than most academics and certainly more viscerally, realized that knowledge is power.

To the general populace, Crawford no doubt represents many things: mad party girl, martyred wife, mistress, immoral bitch, cartoon mother from hell and distant, unapproachable movie goddess. But to me, as I sit in my study looking at some of the things Crawford gave Carl (and I still use her crock pot, but the plastic flowers are in storage — I guess one day I'll design a plexi-glass shrine), Crawford represents the position and power that many individuals can attain with drive and persistence. (Many, but not all. She realized how lucky she had been.)

Carl nailed her popularity after her death in his 1992 article, *Why Crawford Won't Go Away*. Typically, he does it with an ease of style and fresh wit beyond my skills as someone who labored for their Ph.D in ancient art and archaeology at Columbia, learning to examine and catalogue; analyze and correlate, and yet was taught to abandon the obvious. But for me, Crawford and Carl — or JC and CJ as they styled themselves — will always be associated. Crawford inspired Johnes, and Johnes inspired me.

What does seem obvious to me is that in another age, Rome of the late Renaissance or Venice during the Golden Age, Crawford would have been a famous courtesan. She would have cultivated other Graces and posed for a Mary Magdalena by Caravaggio with the chiaroscuros light raking across those monumental cheekbones (as Carl called them), or with those great eyes downcast as in one of Raphael's Virgins. In shimmering Venice her love of *stoffa* — fine fabrics purchased at great costs — would have seen her as one of Tiepolo's allegorical figures theatrically tumbling downwards from a ballroom ceiling. One easily sees her walking on clouds, clad in watery silk and pearls as Circe, enthralling Ulysses' sailors and turning men into swine. She would have written and received poetry to kings and cardinals, and had an illegitimate son claimed nephew by a powerful ecclesiastic and made a cardinal at sixteen.

Instead, born in the last century, at the beginning of the powerful medium of moving images which could convey the archetypal projections of the masses more effectively than ever before, she made films and inspired countless frumpy Ethel Whiteheads, or Mildred Pierces, to realize what they wanted from life, and get out there and get it.

JHSibal
2009

Crawford with third husband Philip Terry in another mad hat.

About The Author

Donna Marie Nowak is a writer and cartoonist who lives in Brooklyn, New York. She is an active member of the Mystery Writers of America and Sisters in Crime. Her most recent novel is *Dark Horse*, a circus murder mystery. Several of her "Miss Bell" mysteries have been converted into radio plays and broadcast by Shoestring Radio Theatre in San Francisco. *Just Joan: A Joan Crawford Appreciation* is based on her popular website *The Films of Joan Crawford (www.filmsofcrawford.com)*.

Me with Ann Blyth at the Castro Theatre in San Francisco during a *Mildred Pierce* gala.

Bear Manor Media

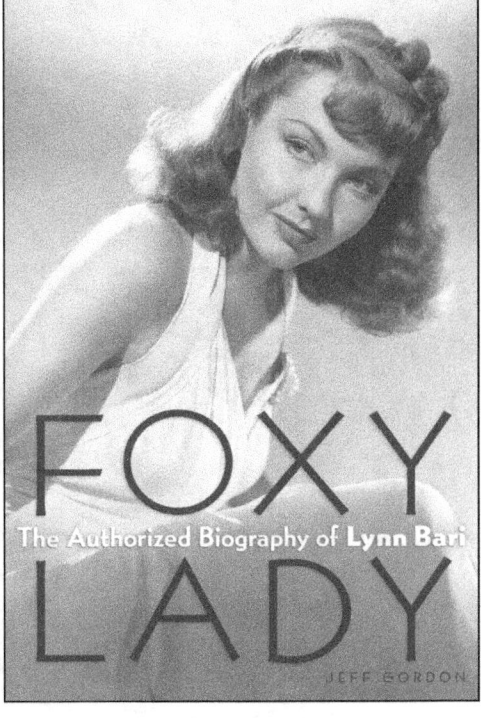

Classic Cinema.
Timeless TV.
Retro Radio.

WWW.BEARMANORMEDIA.COM

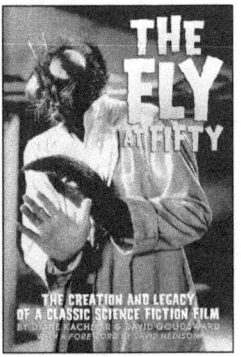

www.ingramcontent.com/pod-product-compliance
Lightning Source LLC
Chambersburg PA
CBHW071932240426
43668CB00038B/1221